Filmography of World History

Deanne Schultz

GREENWOOD PRESS
Westport, Connecticut • London

Library of Congress Cataloging-in-Publication Data

Schultz, Deanne, 1962–
    Filmography of world history / Deanne Schultz.
        p.   cm.
    Includes bibliographical references and index.
    ISBN 0–313–32681–9 (alk. paper)
    1. Historical films—History and criticism.   I. Title.
    PN1995.9.H5S39   2007
    791.43′658—dc22   2006029485

British Library Cataloguing in Publication Data is available.

Library of Congress Catalog Card Number: 2006029485
ISBN: 0–313–32681–9

First published in 2007

Greenwood Press, 88 Post Road West, Westport, CT 06881
An imprint of Greenwood Publishing Group, Inc.
www.greenwood.com

Printed in the United States of America

The paper used in this book complies with the
Permanent Paper Standard issued by the National
Information Standards Organization (Z39.48–1984).

10 9 8 7 6 5 4 3 2 1

For Mom

Contents

Acknowledgments

As a teenager in a small prairie city in 1970s Manitoba, I annually attended the film festival held at Brandon University. Programmed by Professor James M. Skinner, the festival introduced me to foreign, enthralling—and occasionally confusing—cinematic images and stories. I have vivid memories of poring over the festival program, wondering about then unfamiliar titles like *Knife in the Water* and *Diabolique*. Watching movies in the crowded Evans Theatre was one of the most important influences in my longing to experience and understand more of the world. In my adult life as a historian, I have become an unabashed fan of feature films' engagement with the past. I am very grateful for this opportunity to produce my own modest "festival" of world history on screen.

This work would not have been accomplished without the help of many people. While responsibility for the final outcome is mine alone, I acknowledge with gratitude the following players in the production of this filmography: Grants for travel expenses and leave were generously provided by the Malaspina University-College Travel and Conference Funding Committee, and the Malaspina Faculty Association Leave Committee. Arts and Humanities Dean John Lepage and History Department Chair Clarence Karr provided much encouragement, as well as recommendations for my funding and leave. Earlier versions of portions of the work herein appeared in a paper delivered to the 32nd Popular Culture Association/23rd American Culture Association Annual Conference, Toronto, March 13–17, 2002; in "What Is History and Does it Have Anything to Do with Historical Films?: Teaching an Undergraduate Course in Film and History," *Film & History CD-ROM Annual*, 2003; and in "Don't Be Square, *mon cher*': History and Imagination on Screen," Karr Symposium, Malaspina University-College, April 11, 2006. I am grateful to conference participants and *Film & History* editors for their questions and comments. Rob Kirkpatrick of Greenwood Press first presented me with his idea for this book, outlining his ambitions for its content, structure, and purpose. Greenwood's Debra Adams was a steady and genuinely supportive editor and I cannot thank her enough for putting up with me, and for her sound advice about what makes a good reference book. Greenwood editor Nicole Azze and anonymous reviewers and copyeditors helped me greatly improve my prose. Two Malaspina history students, Tegan Evans and Elizabeth Moore, deserve thanks for their cheerful and efficient work as my research assistants. The expertise and generosity of librarians and library staff have been crucial to my research. Malaspina University-College Library Video Service's Jennifer Franklin found me so many films to watch; Interlibrary Loan Service's Joanne Whiting and Mary Wood were equally indefatigable. Many thanks also to Kate Challenger, Rosemary Flem-Ath, Cate Muir, Janice Buie, and Lyn Makepeace of the Malaspina Library. Staff at University of Washington's Odegaard Undergraduate Library Media Center, and University of Toronto's Robarts Library Audio Visual Library were very generous with their time and provision of access to many films in their collections. Roselly A. Torres Rojas of the Latin American Video Archive, filmmaker Solrun Hoaas, and contacts at Ronin Films, Mypheduh Films, Eros Entertainment, and Facets Multimedia were very responsive to my requests. Ros Davies, a member of the Malaspina Arts and Humanities staff, has helped in innumerable ways throughout the process of producing the book. My colleagues in the Department of History have offered valuable insights and encouragement; special thanks are reserved for Helen Brown, Cheryl Warsh, and Gordon Hak. The responses of my students at Malaspina to historical films are always interesting; thank you especially to my students of History 368A, *Popular Film and European History*, for your willingness to engage in the literature about history's interpretation on screen. The support of family and friends as I spent more time with my book than with them is a source of my guilt and gratitude. I owe so much to friends Deborah Torkko, Ruth Kirson, and Warren Baker; my brother Glen and sister Trish; and my parents Edward and Isabel Schultz. To my wonderful children Anna and John: Mom thanks you with all her heart. Their father, my husband Dan Hawthorne, is my partner in every way, and he unquestionably deserves the most thanks of all.

Introduction: Definitions, Parameters, Possibilities

HISTORIANS AND FILMS

> This is how I conceive an ideal piece of filming: the author takes millions of metres of film, on which systematically, second by second, day by day and year by year, a man's life, for instance, from birth to death, is followed and recorded, and out of all that come two and a half thousand metres, or an hour and a half of screen time.
> Andrey Tarkovsky, *Sculpting in Time: Reflections on the Cinema*[1]

The disjunction between Tarkovsky's "ideal piece" of cinema and the more prosaic reality is acutely felt by professional historians as they watch historical feature films. The ability of an hour and a half of screen time to meaningfully synthesize "a man's life" is often painfully compromised by time, budget, and narrative constraints. The end result, even if praised by critics or the public, is often lamented by historians as overly simplistic, error-ridden, or—worse—complete invention.

And yet there is perhaps something of the Tarkovsky idealist in an emerging number of historians who are researching, analyzing, and teaching with these feature films, embracing the multifaceted rewards of history on screen. Writing in 1990, German historian Anton Kaes said, "It is amazing how little research is done on the question of *how* the past is represented, how it is narrativized and visualized, shaped and 'rewritten' by film and television."[2] The intervening years have seen a corrective to Kaes' observation. Many historians, as well as scholars of cinema, critical theory, literature, and anthropology—to name a few—have now produced a sizable body of work on historical feature films, documentaries and telefilms. No longer content to dismiss such films as error-prone, misleading, or ideological, the literature acknowledges the enormous influence popular films have on the public's engagement with the past.[3]

One of the most influential North American scholars of history on film, Robert A. Rosenstone, has argued eloquently for the contribution of feature films to a "revisioning" of the past: "What I want to insist is that the historical film can do 'history'—that is, recount, explain, interpret, and make meaning out of the people and events in the past. Like written history, it utilizes traces of that past, but its rules of engagement with them are structured by the possibilities of the medium and the practices it has evolved. So its claims on us will inevitably be far different from those of written history."[4] While there is yet little in the way of a developed theoretical or methodological approach to historical films, Rosenstone's comments capture well the increasingly accepted premise that history on screen cannot be asked to "do" what written history does and that it contains different potentialities as a source of history.

Before this book considers the potential of historical films to represent world history, the term itself should be defined. "Historical films"—sometimes called historical dramas, historical fiction films, period films, or costume dramas—might simply be described as those feature films that depict events, people, and societies of the past. Often associated with widescreen epics, romantic melodramas, or war films, such films enjoy the freedom to employ a mix of fact and fiction in their desire to reconstruct the past and tell a good story. Placing his emphasis on both elements in the mix, Leger Grindon describes historical films as "fiction films that have a meaningful relationship to historical events."[5]

Sometimes the most "historical" of films are those that least assume the appearance of those spectacles or period pieces that carry the obvious designation as historical. Comedy films, family sagas, experiments with chronology, or those that flaunt their invention might well be films that explore the past, albeit in unconventional ways. Often, the historical consciousness of these films is sharply attuned to any number of methodological or conceptual issues that are familiar to historians.

It is convenient, but insupportable, to ignore the difficulty of defining historical film. Some analysts argue the role of the film's audience in determining the designation. The idea that a historical film is historical because the audience confers that status upon it is perhaps tautological, but importantly acknowledges the palimpsestic quality of our understanding of history—and of our experience in the cinema. As Anton Kaes says, "This, of course, is the aporia of historical representation in film: how to break out of the circular recycling of images that are mere replicas of previous images. Only if the spectator recognizes a film's images as historical ones, as images one has previously seen and knows, only then does the film qualify as a historical film."[6]

WHY A FILMOGRAPHY OF WORLD HISTORY?

This book is intended as an introduction to feature films relevant to the study and teaching of world history. It makes the argument that there are numerous such films, each in its own way a unique and intellectually supportable avenue into discussion of its historical subject, or generic issues of representation and methodology that are so central to the way academics and the public apprehend the past.

Three main goals have conditioned the scope of this book, its organization, the films selected, and the analysis of the films themselves.

First, the book is intended as a practical guide for those who wish to use historical feature films to teach or study aspects of world history. The filmography is designed to help readers discover films that are applicable to their study or teaching, and to provide sufficient description, analysis, and references to assist readers in their choices.

Second, despite factors that limit the filmography's ability to be truly representative of every era and region in world history, the book is intended to critique a Eurocentric and strictly geopolitical approach to world history. Various perspectives on events in world history are provided here, partly through the inclusion of films from a range of national cinemas. Including films that are fundamentally world-historical in approach is a critical aspect of representing world history on screen. To that end, films that consider such aspects of world history as migration, westernization, or cross-cultural exchange have been given a place herein.

Third, the book is intended to show the broad meaning of the term "historical film," and to argue that these films can stimulate understanding of the past—and historiography—in unique ways.

It is a satisfying challenge to consider representations of world history in feature films. If this collection of titles and their discussion in any way stimulates for readers an expanded sense of the past and the creative possibilities inherent in the practice of history, provides tools for a critical investigation of historical films, or facilitates their caring about the past, I have met my aims.

WHY USE FEATURE FILMS IN THE CLASSROOM?

Approaches to teaching history are as varied as the historians in the classroom. Here are some suggestions of the utility of historical feature films in that setting:

1. Historical feature films are "curiosity builders" from which further inquiry can follow. Defenses of fiction film in the study of history often suggest that feature films engage the interest of students and sometimes encourage their desire for further study of the film's subject.
2. Historical feature films offer excellent lessons in historiography. A narrative film that tries to explain an event of the past, for example, can be analyzed for its selection of evidence, emphases, or documentation. Issues of ideological bias or the relative weight of individual and structural agency abound in historical films.
3. Historical feature films teach about the historical period in which they were produced, two examples being Sergei Eisenstein's works of the Stalinist era and Ingrid Sinclair's production of *Flame* in postcolonial Zimbabwe.
4. Historical feature films sometimes provide emotional engagement with the past. This is sometimes a welcome variation on the discourse about history, which in an academic setting often privileges the rational and analytic.

FILM SELECTIONS EXPLAINED

This filmography fashions from the thousands of extant historical films an extensive, but limited, list of films. This has certainly been a most interesting, and painful, challenge. One of the most difficult facets of the selection process was excising films about the history of Europe. Such films are more widely available in home video form in the United States and Canada than those of other national cinemas; an extensive filmography devoted to European history alone is a highly feasible enterprise.[7] But this book, as much as it includes many films about European history, is about world history, and the delete button was (reluctantly) used on numerous films about Europe, whether the subject was the world wars, British monarchs, the Napoleonic era, the Cold War, or social manners.

No doubt the selections herein reveal my preferences. As much as this is a reference book, it is drawn from the subjective experience of watching movies, and I am perhaps more helpful when sharing ideas about the ones I am most interested in. Thus there are herein some limits on military films. (There are many fine works that consider war films comprehensively; see the "Further Reading" section that follows my discussion of "Themes in World History on Screen: Civil, International, and Sectarian Conflict.") Echoing the enthusiasm of Polish filmmakers and audiences, I can't seem to quell my interest in films about Polish history. And special affection is reserved for films that imaginatively revision the past using nonlinear narratives, draw attention to themes of memory and historiography, and that (sometimes) flaunt their blatant disregard for the historical record.[8]

Apologia complete, the selection criteria for the filmography can be described:

1. Films that represent world history were privileged in selection as much as possible, given limitations of availability, subtitling, and extant English-language literature. The "world history" here excludes U.S. domestic history. Films whose subject is the U.S. international presence were also excluded. The splendid forerunner to this book, Grant Tracey's *Filmography of American History*, examines American history on screen.[9]
2. Films that might be considered dated in their interpretive approach, but nevertheless are popular, cannot be ignored. In other words, there are many films here that aren't very good (in either an aesthetic and/or interpretive sense), but they are famous. Even the most objectionable mishandling of history can be very instructive, both about its subject and the nature of historical film.
3. Conversely, critically acclaimed but obscure titles also deserve inclusion, even if not easily found.
4. To a great extent, the geographical emphases, availability, and critical literature of extant historical films discouraged a selection that equitably represents all the time periods encompassed in the book (the Middle Ages through the twentieth century). Certainly filmmakers'—and perhaps audiences'—preoccupation with recent history is evidenced in the weight of films set in the twentieth century. Further, films about the ancient, classical, and biblical eras were excluded with the intent of creating a broader selection within a shorter time frame. (Literature on historical films set in earlier periods is listed in this book's "Further Reading" section.)
5. Demonstrating the reach of historical films into a variety of subjects, themes, and styles has conditioned selections as well. The adoption of five themes for the filmography— History as Biography; Crossing Cultures; Civil, International, and Sectarian Conflict; Society: Modernization and Tradition; and Redefining Historical Narrative—reinforces the argument that historical films have much to say about the diversity of human experience. This book's "Themes in World History on Screen" explores some of the dimensions of those themes in more detail.
6. There are many documentaries and dramas that engage history made expressly for airing on television. This filmography excludes these, concentrating on films produced with the intention of theatrical release.

NOTES

1. Andrey Tarkovsky, *Sculpting in Time: Reflections on the Cinema*, trans. Kitty Hunter-Blair (New York: Alfred A. Knopf, 1987): 64.

2. Anton Kaes, "History and Film: Public Memory in the Age of Electronic Dissemination," *History and Memory* 2(1) (1990): 125.

3. This "veracity test" of historical films is reinforced by some current work in history and film, most notably in Mark C. Carnes, ed., *Past Imperfect: History According to the Movies* (New York: Henry Holt, 1995). Robert Rosenstone has criticized the approach: "The title says it all: *Past Imperfect* . . . As if, somewhere on the page, one can locate a perfect and knowable past. One that cannot make it onto the screen. This theme is underscored by the format. On the top half, History. On the bottom half, Hollywood. Never the twain shall meet?" "Reflections on Reflections on History in Images/History in Words," *Screening the Past* 6 (1999), http://www.latrobe.edu.au/screeningthepast/firstrelease/fr0499/rrfr6c.htm (accessed May 30, 2006).

4. Robert A. Rosenstone, "The Reel Joan of Arc: Reflections on the Theory and Practice of the Historical Film," *The Public Historian* 25(3) (Summer 2003): 61–77.

5. Leger Grindon, "Analyzing the Historical Fiction Film," in *Shadows on the Past: Studies in the Historical Fiction Film* (Philadelphia, PA: Temple University Press, 1994): 2. Vivian Sobchack has described the conventional Hollywood historical epic as "not so much the narrative accounting of *specific historical events* as it is the narrative construction of *general historical eventfulness* [italics in the original]." See "'Surge and Splendor': A Phenomenology of the Hollywood Historical Epic," *Representations* 29 (Winter 1990): 28.

6. Kaes, "History and Film": 117. With respect to the audience's definition of historical films I acknowledge the ideas of Chris Healy, *From the Ruins of Colonialism: History as Social Memory* (Cambridge: Cambridge University Press, 1997).

7. See for example Kevin J. Harty, *The Reel Middle Ages* (Jefferson, NC: McFarland, 1999); Michael Klossner, ed., *The Europe of 1500–1815 on Film and Television: A Worldwide Filmography of over 2550 Works, 1895 through 2000* (Jefferson, NC: McFarland, 2002); Charles P. Mitchell, *The Hitler Filmography* (Jefferson, NC: McFarland, 2002); Caroline Joan (Kay) Picart, ed., *The Holocaust Film Sourcebook* (Westport, CT: Greenwood, 2004); and Nathan E. Richardson, *Postmodern Paletos: Immigration, Democracy, and Globalization in Spanish Narrative and Film, 1950–2000* (Lewisburg, PA: Bucknell University Press, 2002).

8. As John Brewer and Stella Tillyard comment in their discussion of Graham Swift's *Waterland*, a novel (and later, film) about a high school history teacher: "Ruminating on the nature of history is one of the occupational diseases of the historian. Like so many serious complaints, it usually strikes in late middle age." No doubt my own preference for historiographic "ruminations" on film is in no small part symptom of my own "suffering" from this stage of life. See Brewer and Tillyard, "History and Telling Stories: Graham Swift's *Waterland*," *History Today* 35(1) (January 1985): 49–51.

9. Grant Tracey, *Filmography of American History* (Westport, CT: Greenwood Press, 2002).

Themes in World History on Screen

HISTORY AS BIOGRAPHY

Gandhi: "What's the matter with me?"
Wife: "You're human. Only human."
Gandhi

Biopics are as often the subject of critical derision as they are of mass popularity. For some historians, these screen lives suggest the worst qualities of historical films: they laud heroic individuals in predictable narratives, they privilege the role of the "greats" in the public sphere over other forces of historical causation, and they evade well-established interpretations of the figure in order to entertain or inspire audiences.

The ubiquity of biographical films is consistent with the penchant of historical films to produce characters with whom audiences can identify. Biopics, like other historical films, also provide a (usually optimistic) resolution by the film's end. As Robert Rosenstone argues, "both dramatic features and documentaries put individuals in the forefront of the historical process. Which means that the solution of their personal problems tends to substitute itself for the solution of historical problems. More accurately, the personal becomes a way of avoiding the often difficult or insoluble social problems pointed out by the film."[1]

An actor's performance in a film can have such a resonating quality that the viewer is in that film's spell forever. Burt Lancaster as Don Fabrizio in *The Leopard*, Max von Sydow as Lassefar in *Pelle the Conqueror*, Maria Falconetti in the role of Joan of Arc, André Wilms as Albert Schweitzer in *The Great White Man of Lambaréné*, Tabata Ndiaye as Princess Dior in *Ceddo*, and Marlon Brando as William Walker in *Burn!*: all leave an indelible impression.

Two main criteria inform the selection of biographical films for this filmography. First, the inclusion of both conventional and innovative biopics places into relief the weaknesses and potential of the genre. Second, the films' subjects had lives that intersected with political developments of world-historical significance. Notably absent, for example, are the composers, painters, sports figures, or scientists whose exotic or inspiring lives so frequently grace the screen. While regrettable, this omission allows a focus on a narrower field of candidates who were powerful players in ideological movements, revolutions, international conquest, or even national political myths.

There is no sign the biographical treatment of history is on the wane. Moreover, our fascination with interesting people and their stories often provides a compelling introduction to some aspect of the past. As Kathryn Millard says, "biographies inevitably raise questions about our ability to know about the meaning of other lives...." When biopics challenge or ignore some of the genre's conventions they provide an especially dynamic interrogation of their subject and our conception of the relationship of individuals to history.

Further Reading

Anderson, Carolyn. "Biographical Film." In *A Handbook of American Film Genres*, edited by Wes D. Gehring, 331–51. Westport, CT: Greenwood Press, 1988.

Anderson, Carolyn, and John Lupo. "Hollywood Lives: The State of the Biopic at the Turn of the Century." In *Genre and Contemporary Hollywood*, edited by Steve Neale, 91–104. London: BFI, 2002.

Custen, George. *Bio/Pics: How Hollywood Constructed Public History*. New Brunswick, NJ: Rutgers University Press, 1992.

Dening, Greg. "The Theatricality of History Making and the Paradoxes of Acting." In *Performances*, 103–27. Melbourne: Melbourne University Press, 1996.

Gustafson, Richard. "The Vogue of the Screen Biography." *Film & History: An Interdisciplinary Journal of Film and Television Studies* 3(3) (1977): 49–54.

Karsten, Eileen. *From Real Life to Reel Life: A Filmography of Biographical Films*. Metuchen, NJ: Scarecrow Press, 1993.

Man, Glenn. "Editor's Introduction." *Biography: An Interdisciplinary Quarterly* 23(1) (Winter 2000): v–x.

Mason, Laura. "Looking at Life: Biography on Film." *Rethinking History* 1(3) (Winter 1997): 327–42.

Millard, Kathryn. "Projected Lives: A Meditation on Biography and Cinematic Space." In *Screening the Past: Film and the Representation of History*, edited by Tony Barta, 229–37. Westport, CT: Praeger, 1998.

Munslow, Alan. "History and Biography: An Editorial Comment." *Rethinking History* 7(1) (Spring 2003): 1–11.

Thomson, David. "The Invasion of the 'Real' People." *Sight & Sound* 47(1) (Winter 1977/78): 18–22.

CROSSING CULTURES: CONQUEST, EXCHANGE, DIASPORA

"Modernism has its limits, Altmeyer. Our age is dazzled by science. We forget that only the spiritual truly dazzles! Let's not disturb our primitive habits!"
    Albert Schweitzer, *The Great White Man of Lambaréné*

Moviemakers in the West have long been fascinated with other "worlds," and in the process these other lands, peoples, and stories on screen have been exoticized, patronized, vilified, and idealized (as suggested by Schweitzer's "lesson" in Africa). Historical films that treat foreign cultures as their subject have been a popular vehicle for attracting audiences, offering the mysterious "other" veiled in the less threatening and safely scintillating past.

The postcolonial era of the second half of the twentieth century introduced new cinematic perspectives on the interaction of world cultures. In the West, the influence of world-historical political and social liberation movements was felt in films that revisited the notion of the subaltern "other." Less sympathetic— sometimes condemning—portraits of Western imperialism were a notable result.

The growth of indigenous, or national, cinemas in the developing world has in the postcolonial era fostered cross-cultural stories from perspectives other than that of the West. The increasingly high production values of such films make them accessible to world audiences accustomed to Hollywood versions of history. Combined with the globalization of the movie industry, these products of national cinemas enjoy wider distribution and critical attention than ever before. In some cases, these films' interpretations of cross-cultural relations in history challenge interpretations comfortable and familiar to Western audiences.

The historical relationship of peoples of different lands, faiths, languages, cus- toms, and social systems is much more dimensional than the simple equation of the conqueror and the conquered. World historians are increasingly analyzing the reciprocal and interconnected aspects of historical conquest, migration, trade, or the dissemination of ideas and technology. Selections for this filmography show a variety of cross-cultural encounters. It's doubtful that historical films yet render this process of cross-cultural interaction with much sophistication. Many of these films adopt the timeworn approach of the Westerner's "discovery" of the "other," and exemplify the cinematic obsession with cross-cultural conflict. In early and more contemporary historical films that engage non-Western stories, the pres- ence of a Western character acting as guide for audiences is a standard mediating device. Some critical filmic approaches to the historical crossing of cultures have been undertaken, however. They hold up an interesting mirror to the conventional cinema's explanation of historical cross-cultural contact and interaction.

Further Reading

Armes, Roy. *Third World Film Making and the West*. Berkeley, CA: University of Cali- fornia Press, 1987.

Budd, David H. *Culture Meets Culture in the Movies: An Analysis East, West, North and South, with Filmographies*. Jefferson, NC: McFarland, 2002.

Carson, Diane, and Lester D. Friedman, eds. *Shared Differences: Multicultural Media and Practical Pedagogy*. Urbana, IL: University of Illinois Press, 1995.

Chow, Rey. "Film as Ethnography; or, Translation between Cultures in the Postcolonial World." In *Primitive Passions: Visuality, Sexuality, Ethnography, and Contemporary Chinese Cinema*, 173–202. New York: Columbia University Press, 1995.

———. "Seeing Modern China: Toward a Theory of Ethnic Spectatorship." In *Woman and Chinese Modernity: The Politics of Reading between West and East*, 3–33. Minneapolis, MN: University of Minnesota Press, 1991.

Cyr, Helen W. *A Filmography of the Third World, 1976–1983: An Annotated List of 16 mm Films*. Metuchen, NJ: Scarecrow Press, 1985.

———. *The Third World in Film and Video, 1984–1990*. Metuchen, NJ: Scarecrow Press, 1991.

Davis, Natalie Zemon. *Slaves on Screen: Film and Historical Vision*. Toronto: Vintage Canada, 2000.

Dissanayake, Wimal. *Colonialism and Nationalism in Asian Cinema*. Bloomington: Indiana University Press, 1994.

Gugler, Josef. *African Film: Re-imagining a Continent*. Bloomington: Indiana University Press, 2003.

Guneratne, Anthony, and Wimal Dissanayake, eds. *Rethinking Third Cinema*. New York: Routledge, 2003.

Kaplan, E. Ann. *Looking for the Other: Feminism, Film and the Imperial Gaze*. London: Routledge, 1997.

King, John, Ana M. López, and Manuel Alvarado, eds. *Mediating Two Worlds: Cinematic Encounters in the Americas*. London: BFI, 1993.

Murray, Alison. "Teaching Colonial History through Film." *French Historical Studies* 25(1) (2002): 41–52.

Naficy, Hamid, ed. *An Accented Cinema: Exilic and Diasporic Filmmaking*. Princeton, NJ: Princeton University Press, 2001.

Pines, Jim, and Paul Willemen, eds. *Questions of Third Cinema*. London: BFI, 1989.

Sherzer, Dina, ed. *Cinema, Colonialism, Postcolonialism: Perspectives from the French and Francophone World*. Austin: University of Texas Press, 1996.

Shohat, Ella, and Robert Stam. *Unthinking Eurocentrism: Multiculturalism and the Media*. New York: Routledge, 1994.

Sponsler, Claire, and Xiaomei Chen, eds. *East of West: Cross-Cultural Performance and the Staging of Difference*. New York: Palgrave, 2000.

Stam, Robert. *Tropical Multiculturalism: A Comparative History of Race in Brazilian Cinema and Culture*. Durham, NC: Duke University Press, 2004.

Stam, Robert, and Ella Habiba Shohat. "Film Theory and Spectatorship in the Age of the 'Posts.'" In *Reinventing Film Studies*, edited by Christine Gledhill and Linda Williams, 381–402. London: Oxford University Press, 2000.

Williams, Alan, ed. *Film and Nationalism*. New Brunswick, NJ: Rutgers University Press, 2002.

CIVIL, INTERNATIONAL, AND SECTARIAN CONFLICT

"I know what's been happening. First we fought the warlords, then the bandits, then we had peace, then the troubles. And through all of it, it's the people who have suffered."

Mr. Kong, *Crows and Sparrows*

China's early twentieth-century history has been studied carefully by Mr. Kong. A newspaper proofreader "all these years," his job has allowed him to observe the sweep of the post-imperial era in all its turbulent phases. Now it's the winter of 1948–49, and Mr. Kong's tenancy in a building he once owned is threatened by his landlord's flight to Taiwan: a contingent of Kuomintang officials is fleeing Shanghai on the verge of the Communist victory.

Historical films are well practiced in the art of telling the story of grand conflicts through the experience of "ordinary" people like Mr. Kong. It is rare to find a film that does not use the microscopic world of an individual or a family to relate the macroscopic world of nations at war or torn by internal strife. And this conflict, depicted on a grand and intimate scale, is the stuff of the majority of historical films, or at least has defined the form since the beginning of the movies. While this book argues for a flexible conception of "history" and therefore "historical films," films that (often conventionally) treat war, conquest, or revolution as their subject are impossible to ignore. Their numbers are testament to audiences' and filmmakers' fascination with personal drama, winning technology, the gamesmanship of war, and epic-scale events.

The production of so many historical films about political conflict also reflects a very persistent notion about the nature of what might be termed "Big H" History. History is often popularly imagined as the clash of great nations, the story of exploitation by elites, or the uprising of the victimized. Certainly decades of historical revisionism have fashioned history as much more than high politics and mass-scale events. Developments in historical films have reflected these changes in historiography, and more "prosaic" subjects like the refugee experience, female emancipation, or personal memory are now deemed historical. But only to an extent: films about war, political protest, government repression, and revolution still dominate historical film productions.

Films chosen for their representation of civil, international, and sectarian conflict in world history offer a modest sample of films about essentially political conflicts within a nation, or between nations, throughout the world. The selections are dominated by, but not confined to, conflicts of the twentieth century, one reason being that filmmakers like to tell stories about recent history. This interest in the last century recalls the contention of Hayden White that modern events are of a uniquely "traumatic" character that has transformed the mode of narrative representation. These are, White says, "events which not only could not possibly have occurred before the twentieth century but the nature, scope, and implications of which no prior age could even have imagined." World wars, genocide, nuclear destruction, population boom, and extreme economic disparity are developments that "cannot be simply forgotten and put out of mind, but neither can they be adequately remembered."

Conventional and innovative modes of representing the enormity—and in some cases banality—of conflict can be found in this filmography. Some films seek to arouse our guilt or resolve. Others challenge us to question techniques of historical explanation. They also introduce readers to subjects beyond the traditional scope of Western interest.

Further Reading

Anderegg, Michael A. *Inventing Vietnam: The War in Film and Television*. Philadelphia: Temple University Press, 1991.

Basinger, Jeanine. "Translating War: The Combat Film Genre and *Saving Private Ryan*." *AHA Perspectives* 36 (October 1998): 1, 43–47.

Berry, Chris. "If China Can Say No, Can China Make Movies? Or, Do Movies Make China?: Rethinking National Cinema and National Agency." In *Modern Chinese Literary and Cultural Studies in the Age of Theory: Reimagining a Field*, edited by Rey Chow, 159–80. Durham, NC: Duke University Press.

Dawson, Graham, and Bob West. "Our Finest Hour? The Popular Memory of World War II and the Struggle over National Identity." In *National Fictions: World War Two in British Films and Television*, edited by Geoff Hurd, 8–13. London: BFI, 1982.

Devine, Jeremy M. *Vietnam at 24 Frames a Second: A Critical and Thematic Analysis of over 400 Films About the Vietnam War*. Jefferson, NC: McFarland, 1995.

Dine, Philip D. *Images of the Algerian War: French Fiction and Film, 1954–1992*. Oxford: Oxford University Press, 1994.

Dissanayake, Wimal. *Colonialism and Nationalism in Asian Cinema*. Bloomington: Indiana University Press, 1994.

Eley, Geoff. "Finding the People's War: Film, British Collective Memory, and World War II." *American Historical Review* 106(3) (June 2001): 818–837.

Evans, Alun. *Brassey's Guide to War Films*. Dulles, VA: Brassey's, 2000.

Gregg, Robert W. *International Relations on Film*. Boulder, CO: Lynne Rienner, 1998.

Hynes, Samuel. *A War Imagined: The First World War and English Culture*. London: Pimlico, 1990.

Jones, K.D., and A.F. McClure, eds. *Hollywood at War: The American Motion Picture and World War Two*. New York, A.S. Barnes, 1974.

Kuzma, Lynn M., and Patrick J. Haney. "And ... Action! Using Film to Learn About Foreign Policy." *International Studies Perspectives* 2(1) (2001): 33–50.

Lauckner, Nancy Ann, and Miriam Jokiniemi, eds. *Shedding Light on the Darkness: A Guide to Teaching the Holocaust*. New York: Berghahn, 2000.

Lyons, T.J. "Hollywood and World War I 1914–1918." *Journal of Popular Film* 1 (1972): 15–30.

Masters, Patricia Lee. "Warring Bodies: Most Nationalistic Selves." In *Colonialism and Nationalism in Asian Cinema,* edited by Wimal Dissanayake, 1–10. Bloomington: Indiana University Press, 1994.

McMahon, Katherine. "Casualties of War: History, Realism and the Limits of Exclusion." *Journal of Popular Film and Television* 22(1) (Spring 1994): 12–22.

Paris, Michael, ed. *The First World War and the Popular Cinema: 1914 to the Present*. New Brunswick, NJ: Rutgers University Press, 2000.

Virilio, Paul. *War and Cinema: The Logistics of Perception*. London: Verso, 1989.

Waalkes, Scott. "Using Film Clips as Cases to Teach the Rise and 'Decline' of the State." *International Studies Perspectives* 4(2) (2003): 156–74.

White, Hayden. "The Modernist Event." In *The Persistence of History: Cinema, Television, and the Modern Event*, edited by Vivian Sobchack, 17–38. New York: Routledge, 1996.

Whiteclay Chambers II, John, and David Culbert, eds. *World War II: Film and History*. New York: Oxford, 1996.

Williams, Alan, ed. *Film and Nationalism*. New Brunswick, NJ: Rutgers University Press, 2002.

Winter, Jay. "*AHR* Forum: Film and the Matrix of Memory." *American Historical Review* 106(3) (2001): 857–647.

SOCIETY: MODERNIZATION AND TRADITION

"Do you know what's wrong? Peasants do all the work and we live off them."
    Gangacharan Chakravarti, *Distant Thunder*

Takao: "His quaint old shop became a concrete building. And you're not ashamed."
Tatsuo: "You're too much in love with the past."
    The Makioka Sisters

Historical films are easily associated with battle scenes, marching crowds, illustrious leaders, grand romantic passions, and extravagant costumes—characteristics that have propelled the form through much of its history. Films that situate past societies on a less grand scale, that eschew political, military, or romantic conflict as the main narrative force, and that instead train their eye on "ordinary" events and people, sometimes struggle to earn the appellation "historical." Revisionist history has established the validity of studying social structure, material culture, or *Alltagsgeschichte* (the "history of everyday life"). And the cinema has long been recognized for affecting a powerful gaze on social pretensions and relations. But the marriage of social history and the historical film is often a secret elopement: as technically real as the extravagant church affair but often discovered late and with some suspicion.

This filmography includes films that interrogate social history. These films to an extent share a preoccupation with a process that is world-historical in scope: the transition from tradition to modernization. Socio-historical films also have a tendency (with many exceptions) to adopt a different texture, tone, and pace than their cousins that revel in the stories of great power relations or famous people.

Some historical films about past society are innovative. Many are not, adopting conventional narrative and thematic patterns. Judging from films that are as superficially diverse as *Drylanders*, *Raden Ajeng Kartini*, *Newsfront*, *Germinal*, and *Cromwell*, the message seems to be that the best thing about historical change is that it is progressive, meaning it brings with it greater individualism, justice, creative freedom, and material comfort. Films that provide a counter-discourse about the costs of change, or adopt a less judgmental approach to the tension between tradition and modernization, are an intriguing counterpoint.

Further Reading

Burton, C. Emory. "Sociology and the Feature Film." *Teaching Sociology* 16 (3) (July 1988): 263–71.

Dressel, Paula. "Films That Put Social Problems in Global Context." *Teaching Sociology* 18(2) (April 1990): 226–30.

James, David E., and Rick Berg, eds. *The Hidden Foundation: Cinema and the Question of Class*. Minneapolis, MN: University of Minnesota Press, 1996.

Lu, Tonglin, ed. *Confronting Modernity in the Cinemas of Taiwan and Mainland China*. Cambridge: Cambridge University Press, 2002.

Stead, Peter. *Film and the Working Class: The Feature Film in British and American Society*. London: Routledge, 1989.

Virdi, Jyotika. *The Cinematic ImagiNation: Indian Popular Films as Social History*. Piscataway, NJ: Rutgers University Press, 2003.

Xavier, Ismail. *Allegories of Underdevelopment: Aesthetics and Politics in Modern Brazilian Cinema*. Minneapolis, MN: University of Minnesota Press, 1997.

Zaniello, Tom. *Working Stiffs, Union Maids, Reds, and Riffraff: An Expanded Guide to Films About Labor*. Ithaca, NY: ILR Press, 2003.

REDEFINING HISTORICAL NARRATIVE: REFLEXIVITY, MYTH, MEMORY, SATIRE

> Louis XVI (Mel Brooks): "How'd you get all the way here from the Roman Empire?"
> Josephus (Gregory Hines): "Don't be square, mon cher; movies is magic!"
>   *History of the World Part* 1

A legendary film director/writer/comedian and an up-and-coming dancer/actor are perhaps an unlikely pair of commentators on time–space contingencies in historical periodization. But their silly take on the history of the "world" (actually, of prehistory, Moses, the Roman Empire, the Spanish Inquisition, and the French

Revolution) uses historical anachronism as its main gag. Hawkers of modern plumbing in an imperial Roman marketplace shout, "Get on the bandwagon; wipe the shit right out of your house!"; others pitch unemployment insurance for gladiators. The incongruities in *History of the World Part I* are intended to produce laughs, but they also reveal—and subvert—a sophisticated sense of historical chronology.

The "magic" of historical films to which we are accustomed is its recreation of past worlds by using conventional dramatic arcs, a linear narrative, and identifiable characters amid mass spectacle. But movie magic can be conjured to challenge those very assumptions we hold about the way the past "unfolds." Movie magic can make characters from the classical and revolutionary eras converse; project medieval villagers into a modern New Zealand city; recreate (and thus validate the historicity of) traditional myths and individual memory; use satire and other forms of humor to interrogate past actions; and expose the film as a production, rather than a mirror of reality. (As a woman playing a social worker in 1970's Quebec suddenly says to an off-camera interviewer in *Les Ordres*: "My name is Louise Forestier and in this film I play the role of Claudette Dusseault.")

Films that revision the past by admitting to history-telling's constructed and contingent nature are as historical as epics or biopics. Rather than describing history as a fixed reality that audiences enter in their viewing, they challenge us to reconsider our ideas about the way the past is understood and explained.

The selections for this filmography ask readers—as hip Josephus exhorted Louis XVI—to stop "being square" in their conception of historical films. Just as romances, meditative social histories, and family dramas attempt to tell about the past (or as likely use the past to talk about the present), films that employ humor, time travel, fracture linear narratives, or invent "everything" sharpen our historical sense.

Further Reading

Klein, Kerwin Lee. "On the Emergence of Memory in Historical Discourse." *Representations* 69 (2000): 127–50.

Skoller, Jeffrey. *Shadows, Specters, Shards: Making History in Avant-Garde Film*. Minneapolis, MN: University of Minnesota Press, 2005.

Sobchack, Vivian, ed. *The Persistence of History: Cinema, Television, and the Modern Event*. New York: Routledge, 1996.

Rosenstone, Robert A. "The Future of the Past: Film and the Beginnings of Postmodern History." In *The Persistence of History: Cinema, Television, and the Modern Event*, edited by Vivian Sobchack, 201–18. New York: Routledge, 1996.

———. "Revisioning History: Contemporary Filmmakers and the Construction of the Past." *Comparative Studies in Society and History* 32(1) (1990): 822–37.

Turim, Maureen. *Flashbacks in Film: Memory and History*. London: Routledge, 1989.

Wallerstein, Immanuel. "The Inventions of TimeSpace Realities: Towards an Understanding of Our Historical Systems." In *Unthinking Social Science: The Limits of Nineteenth-Century Paradigms*, 135–48. Cambridge, United Kingdom: Polity Press, 1991.

White, Hayden. "Historical Emplotment and the Problem of Truth." In *Probing the Limits of Representation: Nazism and the Final Solution*, edited by Saul Friedlander, 37–53. Cambridge, MA: Harvard University Press, 1992.

———. "The Historical Text as Literary Artifact." In *Tropics of Discourse: Essays in Cultural Criticism*, 81–100. Baltimore: The Johns Hopkins University Press, 1985.

NOTE

1. Robert A. Rosenstone, *Visions of the Past: The Challenge of Film to Our Idea of History* (Cambridge, MA: Harvard University Press, 1995): 57.

Filmography

FILM ENTRIES: SOME TECHNICAL POINTS

Basic production information is provided in the film's entry: *Title/Original Title* (Year); Director; Country; Language; Color; Runtime; Distributor; Setting. In most cases, films are listed alphabetically according to their English-language titles in the North American market. I have judged in some instances, however, that the foreign-language title of the film is the more familiar and cited one. No uniform transliteration of foreign titles has been adopted. The form of transliteration used follows that which is most common in the extant English-language literature about the film. In cases where more than one transliteration is commonly found, both appear in the title heading. Sources of information on production and release dates of films are often inconsistent; the release date, for example, will often vary by one year, reflecting the difference between records of theatrical release and a film's premiere. For this filmography, the year cited in production information is, unless otherwise stated, the year of the film's release. The distributor cited for each film is more precisely a reference to its distributor, subdistributor, or reseller. While every effort has been made to provide accurate information about distributors, these conditions change when for example licensing rights expire, or films go out of print. In other cases, where no current distributor exists for a title, it is possible the film will become available with revised or new licensing and distribution agreements, such as for the production of a DVD version.

The comparative viewing of films can be worthwhile. Observing different approaches and emphases in *Stalingrad* and *Enemy at the Gates*, for example, can foreground aspects of each film that go unnoticed otherwise. To this end, some of the film entries include a "see also" mention of related titles found in the filmography. Some of these comparative titles will treat similar events and time periods. Other comparisons suggested are less self-evident in their rationale, and perhaps even a bit capricious on my part. These invite analysis of the cinematic interpretation of historical subjects that span quite different spaces and time, but which might share thematic, aesthetic, or other qualities worth considering. An example is the pairing of *A King and His Movie* with *Ararat*; on the surface, these films engage very different historical eras, but they are also both about filmmakers making historical films.

Finally, a word about the quotation of dialogue, voiceovers, and intertitles in the films. English subtitling of foreign-language film is by no means an exact transcription of the original dialogue. Subtitles are conditioned by practical as well as interpretive constraints, not the least of which are restrictions on length. For English-language audiences, for better or worse, subtitles convey the film's words, and the quotations that appear in film analyses transcribe those subtitles.[1]

FILMS ALPHABETICAL BY TITLE

55 Days at Peking (1963) Nicholas Ray; United States; English; Color; 150 m; Buena Vista Home Entertainment (DVD, VHS); China, 1900.

Often played on television and ubiquitous in the "classics" section of home video stores, *55 Days at Peking* is a major reference point for popular knowledge of the 1900 Boxer Rebellion. The siege of the foreign legations of Peking by members of a Chinese antiforeign sect, and the subsequent suppression of the Boxers by a multinational force, is a dramatic episode in history. The film is easy to dismiss as an ethnocentric and commercially driven representation of events. The Chinese aggressors are generally unindividuated and terrifying, and the socioeconomic and political context of the rebellion is treated minimally here. But the film also invites analysis because of its popularity, its Cold War provenance, and its discourse on race, nation, and gender.

See also: *Khartoum*; *Red River Valley*; *Zulu*

Andrew, Geoff. *The Films of Nicholas Ray: The Poet of Nightfall*. London: BFI, 2004.
Hevia, James L. "The Return of the Repressed, Recirculations, and Chinese Patriotism." In *English Lessons: The Pedagogy of Imperialism in Nineteenth-Century China*, 314–45. Durham, NC: Duke University Press, 2004.

1492: Conquest of Paradise (1992) Ridley Scott; United Kingdom/United States/France/Spain; English; Color; 154 m; Paramount Home Entertainment (VHS); Spain and the Caribbean, 1492–1501.

In this biographical treatment of mariner Christopher Columbus, scenes of the 1492 voyage to chart a western route to Asia provide an almost tactile experience: the sound of ships' masts filling with wind, close-ups of Columbus' log and navigational instruments, and sailors disembarking onto a completely foreign shore are beautifully composed. Despite its often gorgeous imagery, this is ultimately a silly film, its narrative clichéd and its messages contradictory. *1492* offers a very productive lesson in the tendency of historical films to sacrifice history for myth, and to reflect the sensibilities of their production era more than the historical era being recreated.

1492: Conquest of Paradise was released in 1992, the occasion of the five hundredth anniversary of the first transatlantic voyage of the Italian mariner. The film, and events of the quincentenary, evinced the polarized state of the Columbus debate. While scholarly conferences reconsidered historical evidence of the Columbian era and its legacy, commemorations in the United States celebrated a heroic, rational, and modern founding father. Elsewhere, protests on behalf of and by the world's indigenous peoples decried Columbus as the original victimizer of the Amerindians. Director Scott and scenarist Roselyne Bosch try to reconcile opposing ideas about Columbus by portraying him as a heroic figure, and at the same time acknowledging the devastation of native society. This is accomplished in the film by absolving Columbus of any direct or intentional role in the destructive aspects of colonization. Instead, greedy, cruel, and elitist Spaniards—especially embodied in the character of colonist Adrián Moxica—obstruct Columbus' benevolent and progressive goals of establishing a modern colony. Scenes of Columbus' early interactions with natives, and voiceover excerpts from his diary, even convey the impression that Columbus shares in common the "innocence" of the untainted Eden and its inhabitants: mutual curiosity, laughter, and joyous discovery attend the first meeting of Europeans and natives. *1492*, uncharacteristically for a popular film about Columbus, shows locals speaking their native language and their cruel treatment at a gold mine. But this does not go a very long way in creating a nuanced portrait of Columbus' character and motives. As *Stam* argues, "With the upgrading of the native image goes a parallel upgrading of Columbus."

Even Spanish society is caricatured when *1492* resorts to trite juxtapositions of the modern and primitive to explain Columbus and his legacy. Fifteenth-century Spain seems preoccupied with publicly executing heretics, massacring Moors, and obstructing science. Irritatingly, the film perpetuates the myth that intellectuals at the University of Salamanca arrogantly refused to accept Columbus' claims about the westward distance to Asia: here, Columbus' passionate, modern rationality confronts premodern superstition. In a scene of our hero and his son Hernando by the sea, Columbus provocatively peels an orange against the horizon, buttressing our image of the mariner as singularly challenging the prevailing beliefs of the time. Were it not for the long-established fact that fifteenth-century Europeans imagined the earth a sphere, and that views of their belief in a "flat earth" were a concoction of the nineteenth century, this might be an effective introduction to Columbus. Alas, pure invention here serves mythologizing, rather than the creative engagement of the past.

The film's concluding intertitle says of Columbus: "The biography that Hernando wrote about his Father restored the name of Columbus to its place in history." Ridley Scott establishes the authenticity of the record and thereby his interpretation of Columbus by referencing Hernando's biography of his father. Despite weak condescension to the counter discourse, the film argues that Columbus deserves restoration to a legacy of greatness.

See also: *Aguirre*; *Cabeza de Vaca*; *How Tasty Was My Little Frenchman*; *Jericho*; *The Mission*

Alvaray, Luisela. "Filming the 'Discovery' of America: How and Whose History Is Being Told?" *Film-Historia* 5(1) (1995): 35–44.

Le Beau, Bryan F. "Review of *Christopher Columbus: The Discovery* and *1492: Conquest of Paradise*." *American Studies* 34 (Spring 1993): 151–57.

Lipsett-Rivera, Sonya, and Sergio Rivera Ayala. "Columbus Takes on the Forces of Darkness, or Film and Historical Myth in *1492: The Conquest of Paradise*." In *Based on a True Story: Latin American History at the Movies*, edited by Donald F. Stevens, 13–28. Wilmington, DE: Scholarly Resources, 1997.

Phillips, Carla Rahn, and William D. Phillips Jr. "Christopher Columbus: Two Films." In *Past Imperfect: History According to the Movies*, edited by Mark C. Carnes, 60–65. New York: Henry Holt, 1995.

Stam, Robert. "Rewriting 1492: Cinema and the Columbus Debate." *Cineaste* 19(4) (1993): 66–71.

Stevens, Donald Fithian. "Never Read History Again? The Possibilities and Perils of Cinema as Historical Depiction." In *Based on a True Story: Latin American History at the Movies*, edited by Donald Fithian Stevens, 1–11. Wilmington, DE: SR Books, 1997.

Stone, Cynthia Leigh. "The Filming of Colonial Spanish America." *Colonial Latin American Historical Review* 5(2) (December 1996): 315–20.

1900 / Novecento (1976) Bernardo Bertolucci; France/Italy/West Germany; English and dubbed English; Color; 255 m; Paramount Home Entertainment (VHS); Italy, 1900–1945.

Families are everywhere in the movies. Ettore Scola's *Family*, Hou Hsiao-Hsien's *A Time to Live, A Time to Die*, and Kon Ichikawa's *The Makioka Sisters*, to name a few, suggest some of the distinctly "historic" but private quality of family experience, often played out in quiet, everyday acts.

Other family sagas on screen, especially those that command a sweep of several generations, intertwine the private and public spheres more overtly. In Bertolucci's *1900*, the story of members of the landowning Berlinghieri clan and the Dalcos, peasants who work on their estate, is the vehicle for an ambitious study of Italian national history from 1900 to 1945.

Set in the northern Italian region of Emilia-Romagna, the story begins with the birth of two boys on the same day in 1900. Alfredo Berlinghieri will by the 1920s be head (*padrone*) of the family estate, offer little resistance to the fascists (including the brutal Attila, who oversees the farm), and survive the temporary seizure of his estate and a "people's trial" in the 1945 liberation. He will become estranged from his boyhood friend and tenant on the estate, Olmo Dalco, who becomes a leader of peasant strikes in 1908, and after World War I leads the local Communist resistance to the fascists. The gulf between Alfredo and Olmo is profound, rooted in differences in social class and ideology, and in their active and passive responses to the political regimes of the day.

1900 is a passionate and exuberant film whose use of juxtaposition and archetypal characterization leaves little doubt about its leftist interpretation of Italian society and politics in the first half of the twentieth century. But while the portrayal of the landowning class is highly differentiated, Olmo—and perhaps his wife, Anita—is the film's only distinctive representative of the underclass peasantry.

See also: *The Family; The Tree of Wooden Clogs*

Burgoyne, Robert. "Bernardo Bertolucci, or Nostalgia for the Present." *Massachusetts Review* 15(4) (Fall 1975): 807–28.

———. *Bertolucci's 1900: A Narrative and Historical Analysis.* Detroit: Wayne State University Press, 1991.

———. "The Somatization of History in Bertolucci's *1900*." *Film Quarterly* 40(1) (Fall 1986): 7–14.

Horton, Andrew. "History as Myth and Myth as History in Bertolucci's *1900*." *Film & History: An Interdisciplinary Journal of Film and Television Studies* 10(1) (1980): 9–15.

The Adalen Riots / Ådalen '31 (1969) Bo Widerberg; Sweden; Swedish with English subtitles; Color; 110 m; Paramount Pictures (theatrical); Sweden, 1931.

The Swedish army's intervention in the 1931 strike at a Swedish sawmill resulted in the death of five workers. Public reaction to the event is sometimes interpreted as contributing to the defeat of the conservatives and election of the social democrats in the Swedish election of 1932. Bo Widerberg's film focuses on the love story of Kjell, the son of a labor leader, and Anna, whose father is the mill manager. The romance is compromised when the lovers' class differences are amplified by the events of the strike.

Björkman, Stig. *Film in Sweden: The New Directors*. London: Tantivy Press, 1977.
Zaniello, Tom. "*Adalen 31.*" In *Working Stiffs, Union Maids, Reds, and Riffraff: An Organized Guide to Films about Labor*, 14–16. Ithaca, NY: ILR Press/Cornell University Press, 1996.

Adanggaman (2000) Roger Gnoan M'Bala; France/Switzerland/Ivory Coast/Burkina Faso/Italy; More, Gouro, Senoufo, and Dioulo with English subtitles; Color; 90 m; New Yorker Films (theatrical); West Africa, 17th century.

This is a fictional story depicting slave trading and warfare among rival tribes in seventeenth-century West Africa. Young Ossei escapes an attack on his village, and tries to rescue his mother, captured by the native slave trader, King Adanggaman.

Bakyono, Jean Servais. "*Adanggaman*, a Film on History." *Écrans d'Afrique* 7(23) (1998): 33–43.

Adieu Bonaparte / Wadaan ya Bonaparte / Al-Wada' ya Bonaparte (1985) Youssef Chahine; Egypt/France; French and Arabic with French subtitles; Color; 114 m; Francevision (VHS); Egypt, 1798–1799.

Adieu Bonaparte is a structurally complex film that examines an Egyptian family's relationship to the 1798 Napoleonic invasion. Eschewing the traditional epic mode of invasion and conquest, director Chahine considers the interaction of two cultures resulting from the French presence in Alexandria. Young Ali, the film's protagonist, denounces his brother Bakr's participation in the Egyptian resistance to Napoleon. But Ali does not consider his desire to study French language and culture as compromising his patriotism. Portraying French General Cafarelli as having a humane side, director Chahine seems to acknowledge the negative and positive effects of invasion, thus revisioning the significance of the period of French occupation.

Fawal, Ibrahim. "*Al-Wada' ya Bonaparte (Adieu Bonaparte*, 1985)." In *Youssef Chahine: The Many Worlds of an Egyptian Director*, 163–69. London: BFI, 2001.
Shafik, Viola. *Arab Cinema: History and Cultural Identity*. Cairo: American University in Cairo Press, 1998.

Aguirre, the Wrath of God / Aguirre, der Zorn Göttes (1972) Werner Herzog; West Germany; Spanish and German with English subtitles; Color; 94 min; Facets (DVD, VHS); Amazon River, 1560–1561.

"... there is no one who knew Aguirre who ever wrote a good word about him," says historian Stephen Minta. The Spanish soldier who led a rebellion against Pedro Ursúa's leadership of a sixteenth-century Amazonian expedition seeking the mythic "El Dorado" is reconsidered in Werner Herzog's memorable film. Critically acclaimed and unconventional, *Aguirre, the Wrath of God* combines invention and documentary record in a provocative blend. In the words of Dana Benelli, the film manages to "reverse civilizations' judgment of Aguirre and grant him, instead, the fame he anticipates from his actions."

Aguirre begins with the following message: "Late in 1560 a large expedition of adventurers, under Gonzalo Pizarro, set off from the Peruvian Sierras. The only document to survive from this lost expedition is the diary of the monk Gaspar de Carvajal." Director Herzog does not mention that the historical record says Pizarro died in 1548. (Extant written accounts of participants from this expedition are ignored as sources.) Carvajal, the film's diarist and narrator, was not a member of the 1560 expedition; he was present in Pizarro's earlier expedition in search of El Dorado, in 1541–42. These intentional contrivances of *Aguirre* challenge the authority of the documentary record, asking audiences to consider the historicity of experiences left largely unrecorded, such as that of Spanish women on the expedition, the black slave on board, or the Amerindians. This is a film where forged documents "make" history and subvert our ideas about what authenticates the past.

Even the cinematic Aguirre "writes" his own story, delivering a counter-perspective on the official history. Producing a piece of paper that announces his expedition's secession from the authority of Spanish King Philip II, he says, "We must make our position official." And while Spanish records describe Aguirre's capture and killing by forces of Philip II in Venezuela in 1561, the film instead leads Aguirre to a different end, marooned on a raft in the middle of the river, raving about his power.

See also: *1492: Conquest of Paradise*; *Cabeza de Vaca*; *How Tasty Was My Little Frenchman*; *Jericho*; *The Mission*

Alvaray, Luisela. "Filming the 'Discovery' of America: How and Whose History Is Being Told?" *Film-Historia* 5(1) (1995): 35–44.

Benelli, Dana. "The Cosmos and Its Discontents." In *The Films of Werner Herzog: Between Mirage and History*, edited by Timothy Corrigan, 89–103. New York: Methuen, 1986.

Holloway, Thomas H. "Whose Conquest Is This, Anyway? *Aguirre, the Wrath of God*." In *Based on a True Story: Latin American History at the Movies*, edited by Donald F. Stevens, 29–46. Wilmington, DE: Scholarly Resources, 1997.

Minta, Stephen. "*Aguirre the Wrath of God*." In *Past Imperfect: History According to the Movies*, edited by Mark C. Carnes, 74–77. New York: Henry Holt, 1995.

———. *Aguirre: The Re-Creation of a Sixteenth-Century Journey across South America*. New York: Henry Holt, 1994.

Stone, Cynthia Leigh. "The Filming of Colonial Spanish America." *Colonial Latin American Historical Review* 5(2) (December 1996): 315–20.

Waller, Gregory A. "*Aguirre, the Wrath of God*: History, Theater, and the Camera." *South Atlantic Review* 46(2) (May 1980): 55–69.

Alexander Nevsky / Aleksandr Nevsky (1938) Sergei M. Eisenstein and Dmitri Vasilyev; Soviet Union; Russian with English subtitles; Black and White; 112 m; Criterion Collection (DVD), Home Vision Entertainment (VHS); Russia, 13th century.

Alexander Nevsky, Eisenstein's first sound film, depicts the Russian prince's leadership of the anti-German cause in the area of Novgorod. Remarkable not the least for its extended scene depicting the battle of Russians and German Teutons on ice-covered Lake Peipus, and its Prokofiev score, the film's interpretation of

Nevsky's heroism is also fascinating. Eisenstein's Nevsky is a gentle man of the people, who would be happy fishing if his Russian patriotism didn't demand he agree to the request of nobles that he lead them against the Germans. His insistence on the necessity of peasants joining the cause, and his strategic genius, make Nevsky a "great man" of Russian history. This cinematic Nevsky met the approval of the Stalinist regime on the eve of World War II—at least prior to the forging of the Nazi-Soviet Pact, and after the German invasion of the Soviet Union. That the Germans are portrayed as cruel, inhuman, and ultimately vanquished was also a fitting message for late-1930s Soviet audiences.

Goodwin, James. "*Alexander Nevsky*: The Great Man in History." In *Eisenstein, Cinema, and History*, 157–78. Urbana: University of Illinois Press, 1993.

Scherr, Barry P. "*Alexander Nevsky*: Film without a Hero." In *Eisenstein at 100: A Reconsideration*, edited by Al La Valley and Barry P. Scherr, 207–26. New Brunswick, NJ: Rutgers University Press, 2001.

Alsino and the Condor / Alsino y el cóndor (1982) Miguel Littín; Nicaragua/Cuba/Mexico/Costa Rica; Spanish with English subtitles; Color; 89 m; Facets (VHS); Nicaragua, late 1970s.

Based on a novel by Chilean Pedro prado, *Alsino and the Condor* was the first feature film produced in Nicaragua. The conflict between the U.S.-supported Somoza regime and Sandinista rebels in late 1970s Nicaragua is depicted through the fictional story of Alsino, a young peasant boy. His dreams of learning to fly are literally enacted when he leaps off a tree. His injuries lead to his status as a social outsider, and he is soon drawn to the guerillas.

Buchsbaum, Jonathan. "The Debate About *Alsino y el Condór*." In *Cinema and the Sandinistas: Filmmaking in Revolutionary Nicaragua*, 117–22. Austin: University of Texas Press, 2003.

Schwartz, Ronald. "*Alsino y El Condor (Alsino and the Condor)*." In *Latin American Films, 1932–1994: A Critical Filmography*, 31–32. Jefferson, NC: McFarland, 1997.

. . . And Give My Love to the Swallows /. . . a pozdravuji vlastovky (1972) Jaromil Jires; Czechoslovakia; Czech with English subtitles; Color; 86 m; Facets (DVD); Czechoslovakia, World War II.

Maruska Kuderikova was a young Moravian woman arrested by the Nazis for her work with the Czech resistance. . . . *And Give My Love to the Swallows* dwells on Kuderikova's prison experience, as recorded in her diary. With flashbacks intercutting prison scenes, Kuderikova's participation in the anti-Nazi movement is enacted. Her estrangement from her family (devout Christians who are devastated by her dangerous activities and her atheism), her relationships with contacts in the resistance, and her gradual loss of hope in escaping execution are all examined sensitively but without histrionics. The film also offers modest insight into the grassroots impact on the region victimized by the Munich Agreement of 1938. This is an affecting account of a woman who was executed shortly after her twenty-second birthday. Short on explanation of her motives for resisting, save for her patriotic determination to "drive out" the Germans from her homeland, Jaromil Jires' film is nevertheless a moving and instructive introduction to Kuderikova.

See also: *The White Rose*

Anna Göldin, the Last Witch / Anna Göldin, letzte Hexe (1991) Gertrud Pinkus; Germany/Switzerland; German; Color; 105 m; Head-Film AG, Switzerland (VHS); Switzerland, 18th century.

Reputedly the last woman executed for witchcraft in Europe, Anna Göldin's story is recounted here in an adaptation of Eveline Hasler's 1982 novel that drew from extant 1782 trial records. Göldin, a servant in a bourgeois household in the Swiss canton of Glarus comes under suspicion when a child in the family falls ill. The film offers some sense of the milieu wherein Göldin's gender and social position make her vulnerable to condemnation.

See also: *Day of Wrath*

Fainaru, Dan. "*Anna Goldin, Letzte Hexe (Anna Goldin, the Last Witch)*." *Variety* 344 (September 2, 1991): 67.

Flitner, Christine. " 'Searching for the Cultivators of the Stony Soil': Eveline Hasler." In *Post-War Women's Writing in German: Feminist Critical Approaches*, edited by Chris Weedon, 313–15. Providence, RI: Berghahn, 1997.

Rash, Felicity. "Metaphors of Darkness and Light in Eveline Hasler's *Anna Göldin, Letzte Hexe* and *Der Riese im Baum*." In *German Contemporary Writers: Their Aesthetics and Their Language*, edited by A. Williams, S. Parkes, and J. Preece, 181–200. Bern: Peter Lang, 1996.

Anne of the Thousand Days (1969) Charles Jarrott; United Kingdom; English; Color; 145 m; Universal Studios Home Entertainment (VHS); England, 1527–1536.

Based on the play by Maxwell Anderson, this film is about Anne Boleyn—second wife of Tudor King Henry VIII and mother of future queen Elizabeth I—who was executed on the charge of adultery. The film is constructed as a historical romance. The requisite teasing is supplied in Henry's infatuation with Anne, her original disinterest in the man, the development of her love for him, and eventual agreement to marry the King. Anne's downfall provides the dramatic interest: Henry loses sexual interest, has no male heir, and is caught in the power plays of the Reformation.

With a number of outright inventions in the film that are served up for dramatic effect (an example being the scene of Anne begging for the execution of Thomas More), the ill-fated Queen is interpreted as an innocent victim whose efforts to defend herself never operate outside the frame of her gendered submission to biology, patriarchy, and politics. Antonia Fraser offers a counter-reading of Anne as much less the victim of her innocent love for Henry, than as a practical and aware woman of the sixteenth century, who made the calculated choice to marry the King—not for love, but as a means to achieve status and support.

See also: *Elizabeth; A Man for All Seasons; The Private Life of Henry VIII*

Fraser, Antonia. "*Anne of the Thousand Days*." In *Past Imperfect: History According to the Movies*, edited by Mark C. Carnes, 66–69. New York: Henry Holt, 1995.

Warnicke, Retha M. "Anne Boleyn in History, Drama and Film." In *High and Mighty Queens of Early Modern England: Realities and Representations*, edited by Carole Levin, Debra Barrett-Graves, and Jo Eldridge Carney, 239–55. New York: Palgrave Macmillan, 2003.

Ararat (2002) Atom Egoyan; Canada/France; English, Armenian, French, and German with English subtitles; Color; 115 m; Buena Vista Home Entertainment (DVD, VHS); Canada, present day, and Armenia, 1915–1918.

Ararat explores a theme visited often by Canadian director Egoyan: the often devastating emotional effects of the past—especially past relationships and the layers of denial and distortion that accumulate around these over time. Here, the Armenian genocide sanctioned by the Turkish Ottoman Empire in 1915 links characters in the present day, drawing them into personal confrontation with the past and the territory of collective cultural memory and national history. Ani is an art history professor who has published a book about Armenian painter Arshile Gorky, who survived the genocide but not his anguish from the experience. Ani's son Raffi visits Turkey to understand the death of his terrorist/freedom-fighter father. A Canada Customs agent has a gay son whose partner plays a major Turkish character in a historical film about the massacre. That film's famous director, Saroyan, and his screenwriter Rouben are recreating the story of 1915 partly based on the memories passed on by Saroyan's mother.

The pretext for *Ararat*'s exploration of these characters and relationships is the production of the historical film in Toronto, where indoor sets recreate the historical American mission in the Anatolian city of Van. One of the primary delights of this film is its affectionate play with the genre of historical film. A scene of historic Anatolia appears, with the authoritative intertitle "Outside the City of Van, Eastern Turkey, 1915." But Egoyan never allows the viewer to believe they've been transported to a historical era for more than seconds; soon, Saroyan's voice directs actors, a movie camera comes into view, and there is no doubt the setting is a movie's production. Glimpses of Saroyan's film also suggest its conformity to epic melodrama: there is an overwrought film score, evil Turkish soldiers are contrasted with innocent Armenian artists, women, and children and the plot is anchored by the figure of the heroic American missionary.

Without exception, every character in *Ararat* has a story—a history—they are trying to piece together and trying to tell. At once researchers and teachers, they face the problems of source interpretation common to professional historians. Even the contention that Rouben's screenplay for Saroyan's film is based closely on published eyewitness accounts of the events of 1915 is not made without counter-evidence. The experienced customs officer must daily decide which stories are let in, which are left in a pile of untruths over the border. But even on the day of his retirement, this seasoned judge interrogates Raffi about the contents of film canisters brought from Turkey and asks, "What am I going to do? There's no one I can contact. There's no way I can confirm what you're saying is true." Raffi protests; he is telling "exactly what happened." *Ararat* exposes the fragile nature of our links to the past, and its vulnerability to the loss of memory: Raffi realizes during his travels in Anatolia that what is perhaps most terrible is "for the people, the loss of any way of remembering what was." Raffi eventually admits his basis for believing the canisters contain film: "That's what he [a Turkish guide] told me. That's what I need to believe." The contents are eventually revealed to the audience, and we are reassured by the customs officer, echoing the hope of any historian: "The more he told it [the story] the closer he got to the truth."

Another message in this film—with its pronounced use of photographs, paintings, Christian iconography, and film within a film—is that images form our historical memory. Ani apologizes for her lack of enthusiasm for Rouben's script:

"Maybe I'll get more excited when I actually see it [the film]—it's difficult for me to imagine these things." So conscious is Egoyan of this relationship of visual images to our understanding of the past, that his own cinematic representation of the Armenian Genocide is a discussion of the power, fragility, and impenetrability of images.

See also: *A King and His Movie; Ulysses' Gaze*

Egoyan, Atom. "In Other Words: Poetic License and the Incarnation of History." *University of Toronto Quarterly* 73(3) (Summer 2004): 886–905.
Erbal, Ayda. "Review of *Ararat*." *American Historical Review* 108(3) (June 2003): 957–58.
Romney, Jonathan. "*Ararat*." In *Atom Egoyan*, 171–87. London: BFI, 2003.

Ashes and Diamonds / Popiol i diament (1958) Andrzej Wajda; Poland; Polish with English subtitles; Black and White; 105 m; Criterion (DVD); Poland, 1945.

The last of Wajda's "war trilogy" (*A Generation, Canal*), *Ashes and Diamonds* is set in a small Eastern Polish town, where citizens are celebrating the end of World War II on the night of May 8/9, 1945. The invented storyline of *Ashes and Diamonds*, based on the novel by Jerzy Andrzejewski, creates a sense of the possibilities latent in this watershed moment in history. Maciek, a member of the Polish resistance, has been ordered to kill local Communist Party Secretary Sczuska, but his serious misgivings delay the event and create the narrative tension in the story. He is urged by his cell leader to realize that the anti-Nazi resistance was about freedom, but despite German surrender, the only option "in a Poland such as this is to fight." But Maciek is exhausted, is falling in love with the barmaid at the Monopol Hotel, and is surrounded by revelers and those who are already reaping the benefits of toadying to the Party ministers. This collision of romantic sensibility, longing for normalcy, and sense of duty to the future of Poland is a powerful element of *Ashes and Diamonds'* depiction of the country on the verge of the postwar era.

Kalinowska, Izabela. "Changing Meanings of Home and Exile: From *Ashes and Diamonds* to *Pan Tadeusz*." In *The Cinema of Andrzej Wajda: The Art of Irony and Defiance*, edited by John Orr and Elzbieta Ostrowska, 64–75. London: Wallflower Press, 2003.
Krzyzanowski, Jerzy R. "On the History of *Ashes and Diamond* [sic]." *Slavic and East European Journal* 15(3) (Autumn 1971): 324–31.
Young, Colin. "*Ashes and Diamonds (Popiol I   Diament)* by Andrzej Wajda." *Film Quarterly* 13(4) (Summer 1960): 34–37.

At Play in the Fields of the Lord (1991) Hector Babenco; United States; English; Color; 189 m; Universal Studios Home Entertainment (VHS); Brazil, contemporary.

In her 1995 article "Filming the 'Discovery' of America: How and Whose History Is Being Told?" Luisela Alvaray says of *At Play in the Fields of the Lord*: "This film—although it is a non-historical fiction film—calls perhaps for more reflection on this particular episode of history than many other representations set in the centuries of conquest and colonization." Indeed, this fictional story of two late twentieth-century American Christian (Quaker) missionary couples in the Brazilian Amazon, based on the novel by Peter Matthiessen, is a rich study of the collision of cultures. Their attitudes to the Niaruna natives they are trying to convert range from fascination to terror, and are complicated by their relationship to a Native American pilot. His own spiritual quest highlights the history of conquest in the Americas.

Alvaray, Luisela. "Filming the 'Discovery' of America: How and Whose History Is Being Told?" *Film-Historia* 5(1) (1995): 35–44.

Okrent, Neil. "At Play in the Fields of the Lord (Hector Babenco Interview)." *Cineaste* 19(1) (1992): 44–47.

Rendleman, Tood. "'Evil' Images in *At Play in the Fields of the Lord*: Evangelicals and Representations of Sexuality in Contemporary Film." *Velvet Light Trap: A Critical Journal of Film & Television* 46 (Fall 2000): 26–39.

Romney, Jonathan. "*At Play in the Fields of the Lord.*" *Sight & Sound* 1 (April 1992): 43–44.

Schwartz, Ronald. "*At Play in the Fields of the Lord.*" In *Latin American Films, 1932–1994: A Critical Filmography*, 39–40. Jefferson, NC: McFarland, 1997.

Atanarjuat: The Fast Runner (2001) Zacharias Kunuk; Canada; Inuktitut with English subtitles; Color; 172 m; Columbia/Tristar (DVD, VHS); (Canadian) Arctic, unspecified legendary times.

Atanarjuat is a marker in the early twenty-first-century trend toward the popularity of anthropological feature films. The first Inuit-language feature, the film combines modern cinematography with engaging storytelling. *Atanarjuat* relates an Inuit legend: sometime at the beginning of the first millennium, a shaman's curse on a small nomadic community leads to murder and rivalries and these bleed into the affairs of the next generation. Receiving critical kudos and sizable audiences, the film reminded viewers that oral mythic-history traditions beyond the oft-retold classics of the Western canon (*Troy* and *King Arthur* come to mind) are worthy cinema subjects.

The significance of *Atanarjuat* as a "historical film" lies in its validation, for audiences unfamiliar with the culture and society of the Inuit of the Arctic Circle, of the historicity of myth and legend. Apart from universally recognizable themes of brotherhood and betrayal, its very lack of familiarity makes *Atanarjuat* a particularly exotic—and appealing—spectacle.

The authenticity or cinematic realism of the world created in *Atanarjuat* is carefully, and reflexively, constructed by director Zacharias Kunuk and his production team. The result places intriguing demands on the viewer's sense of history: legend is established in the Western mode of realism as "historical," yet *Atanarjuat* is also positioned as the work of imagination. The film seems to take place out of historical time, and at its end the camera pulls back to reveal the trappings of a production crew. Cinematic, historical, and legendary worlds collide in *Atanarjuat*.

See also: *Chac the Rain God*; *God' Gift*; *Keïta! The Heritage of the Griot*; *Yeelen*

Bessire, Lucas. "Talking Back to Primitivism: Divided Audiences, Collective Desires." *American Anthropologist* 105(4) (December 2003): 832–38.

Huhndorf, Shari. "*Atanarjuat, the Fast Runner*: Culture, History and Politics in Inuit Media." *American Anthropologist* 105(4) (2003): 822–26.

Powell, Richard. "Northern Cultures: Myths, Geographies and Representational Practices." *Cultural Geographies* 12(3) (July 2005): 371–78.

Sadashige, Jacqui. "Review of *Atanarjuat the Fast Runner*." *American Historical Review* 107(3) (June 2002): 989–90.

Aya (1990) Solrun Hoaas; Australia; English and Japanese with English subtitles; Color; 95 m; Ronin Films, Australia (VHS); Australia, 1950s–1970s.

Aya and Frank are a biracial couple in Australia, married after meeting in Japan when Frank served with the Australian army after the war. Their fictional story, based on the experiences of the hundreds of Japanese war brides in that country, begins in Melbourne in 1950. The plot of *Aya* elapses over 20 years, relating the eventual dissolution of their marriage, and Aya's move to Hobart. While conforming to a predictable narrative structure that creates dramatic tension and then resolution, the film is unique in refusing to descend into stereotypes of Asian/Japanese women. Aya is undoubtedly confronted by the challenges of adapting to Australian life and conflicts in her marriage, but the film constructs her as an ordinary, not exotic, woman.

See also: *Floating Life*; *Gaijin: A Brazilian Odyssey*

Bowman, Lisa. "*Aya*." *Cinema Papers* 83 (May 1991): 52–53.

Chua, Siew Keng. "A Half Opened Door: Australian Perspectives on Asia." *Cinemaya: The Asian Film Quarterly* 17/18 (Autumn/Winter 1992): 28–31.

Singh, Michael G., and Charlotte Henry. "Rereading Australia-Asia Relations." In *Literacy Matters: Issues for New Times*, edited by Mary Kalantzis and Ambigapathy Pandian, 173–92. Australia: Common Ground, 2001.

The Ball / Le bal (1982) Ettore Scola; Algeria/France/Italy; no dialogue; Color; 109 m; Warner Home Video (VHS); France, 1930s–1980s.

Based on a French stage play, *The Ball* has no character development or dialogue. But a 50-year history of French popular culture, social mores, and politics is told in its setting of a Parisian ballroom, where a succession of dances and musical styles mark the passage of time.

Dalle Vacche, Angela. "Nouvelle Histoire, Italian Style." In *The Body in the Mirror: Shapes of History in Italian Cinema*, 251–84. Princeton, NJ: Princeton University Press, 1992.

Gagne, Cole, and Francis Defalco. "Ettore Scola's *Le Bal* Blends Ballroom Dancing and History." *The Film Journal* 87 (May 1984): 10–11.

Ballad of a Soldier / Ballada o soldate (1959) Grigori Chukhrai; Soviet Union; Russian with English subtitles; Black and White; 89 m; Criterion Collection (DVD), Connoisseur/Meridian (VHS); Soviet Union, World War II.

This is a modest and poetic look at everyday life in wartime Russia. A young Russian soldier's chosen reward for an act of bravery during World War II is a brief leave to visit his mother and repair her roof. Much of the leave is spent in transit, and the film focuses on his encounters with a variety of Russians en route.

Barta, Peter I., and Stephen Hutchings. "The Train as Word-Image Intertext in the Films *Ballad of a Soldier* and *Thief*." *Intertexts* 6(2) (Fall 2002): 127–44.

Chukhrai, Grigori. "A Soldier's Tale from Khrushchev's USSR." *History Today* 45(11) (November 1995): 48–51.

Dunlop, John B. "Grigorii Chukhrai's *Ballad of a Soldier*." *Stanford Slavic Studies* 1 (1987): 349–60.

Levin, Julia. "*Ballad of a Soldier*." *Senses of Cinema: An Online Film Journal Devoted to the Serious and Eclectic Discussion of Cinema* 23 (November/December 2002): http://www.sensesofcinema.com/contents/cteq/02/23/ballad_soldier.html (accessed May 30, 2006).

Youngblood, Denise J. "A War Remembered: Soviet Films of the Great Patriotic War." *American Historical Review* 106(3) (June 2001): 838–56.

Barren Lives / *Vidas secas* (1963) Nelson Pereira dos Santos; Brazil; Portuguese with English subtitles; Black and White; 103 m; Facets (DVD); Brazil, 1940–1942.

Neorealist in style, *Barren Lives* is about a migrant worker family in early 1940s Brazil. Adapted from Graciliano Ramos' 1938 novel, the film follows Fabiano, Vitória, and their two sons as they seek work in drought-stricken northeast Brazil. Finding work tending cattle, Fabiano is the victim of a landlord's extortion, and is jailed following a fight. *Barren Lives* captures the hunger and poverty of peasants of the *sertão* (semi-arid "backland") with sympathy, but without sentiment. As Stam and Johnson say, "*Vidas Secas* elicits no pastoral nostalgia for a simpler time and place . . . entertains no mystical attitude toward 'the land.'"

See also: *Drylanders*; *Earth* (Dovzhenko); *Harvest 3000 Years*; *The Land*; *The Tree of Wooden Clogs*

Barnard, Timothy, and Peter Rist. "*Vidas Secas.*" In *South American Cinema: A Critical Filmography, 1915–1994*, edited by Timothy Barnard and Peter Rist, 134–36. New York: Garland, 1999.

Johnson, Randal, and Robert Stam. "The Cinema of Hunger: Nelson Pereira Dos Santos's *Vida Secas.*" In *Brazilian Cinema*, 120–27. Rutherford, NJ: Associated University Press, 1982.

Sadlier, Darlene J. "A Cinema of the People." In *Nelson Pereira dos Santos*, 1–121. Urbana, IL: University of Illinois Press, 2003.

The Battle of Algiers / *La bataille d'Alger* (1966) Gillo Pontecorvo; France/Algeria/Italy; French and Arabic with English subtitles; Black and White; 125 m; Criterion (DVD); Algeria, 1954–1957.

Pontecorvo's documentary–realist style and interest in both French and Algerian antagonists in the Algerian war of independence (1954–1962) has greatly influenced the style and structure of subsequent political historical films. While it does employ flashbacks, *Battle of Algiers* mostly places audiences in the streets and neighborhoods of the city in 1957. Much of the story is told through the experience of the character of Ali la Pointe, a petty thief who has been radicalized during a prison stint and becomes a member of the FLN (National Liberation Front). The FLN recruits new members, enacts bombing campaigns (including those launched by women from their shopping bags), and leads a general strike. When Colonel Mathieu becomes commander of French military operations in Algiers, FLN members—or those suspected of association with them—try to escape capture, interrogation, and torture by French paratroopers. This is a dense, violent, and harrowing film that suggests Pontecorvo's leftist commitment to colonial independence, but which shows that both sides adopt the excesses they decry in the other.

See also: *Chronicle of the Years of Embers*

Bignardi, Irene. "The Making of *The Battle of Algiers.*" *Cineaste* 25(2) (2000): 14–22.

Dowd, N.E. "*The Battle of Algiers.*" *Film Quarterly* 22(3) (Spring 1969): 26–28.

Morton, Stephen. "The Unhappy Marriage of 'Third World' Women's Movements and Orientalism." In *After Orientalism: Critical Entanglements, Productive Looks*, edited by Inge E. Boer, 165–81. Amsterdam: Rodopi, 2003.

Moruzzi, Norma Claire. "Agents: Feminine Agency and Masquerade in *The Battle of Algiers.*" In *Negotiating at the Margins: The Gendered Discourse of Power and Resistance*, edited by Sue Fisher and Kathy Davis, 255–77. New Brunswick, NJ: Rutgers University Press, 1993.

Orlando, Valerie. "Historiographic Metafiction in Gillo Pontecorvo's *La bataille d'Alger*: Remembering the 'Forgotten War.'" *Quarterly Review of Film and Video* 17(3) (2000): 261–71.

Smith, Murray. "*The Battle of Algiers*: Colonial Struggle and Collective Allegiance." In *Terrorism, Media, Liberation*, edited by J. David Slocum, 94–110. Piscataway, NJ: Rutgers University Press, 2005.

Vann, Michael G. "The Colonial Casbah on the Silver Screen: Using *Pépé Le Moko* and *The Battle of Algiers* to Teach Colonialism, Race, and Globalization in French History." *Radical History Review* 83 (2002): 186–92.

The Battle of Canudos / Guerra de Canudos (1997) Sergio Rezende; Brazil; Portuguese with English subtitles; Color; 165 m; DVDBrazil (DVD); Brazil, 1890s.

Attracting large audiences at the Brazilian cinema, and again when serialized for television, *The Battle of Canudos* is a big-budget recreation of the history of a breakaway northeastern community of Brazil in the 1890s. A messianic priest known as Antonio Conselheiro leads a group opposed to the newly established Republic, and the fictional character of a young peasant girl, Luiza, is caught between opposing factions within her own family. Canudos eventually faces the army's orders to dissolve, resulting in thousands of civilian deaths. The film is based on Euclides da Cunha's 1902 account, *Os Sertões* (*Rebellion in the Backlands*), and as such tends to emphasize the (perhaps overstated) religious impetus for Canudos' organization, rather than the socioeconomic roots of the community founders.

Davis, Darien J. "Review of *Guerra De Canudos* and *Passion and War in the Backlands of Canudos*." *American Historical Review* 104(5) (1999): 1807–09.

Dennison, Stephanie, and Lisa Shaw. "The *Sertão* on Screen." In *Popular Cinema in Brazil, 1930–2001*, 206–15. Manchester: Manchester University Press, 2004.

The Battleship Potemkin / Bronenosets 'Potyomkin' (1925) Sergei M. Eisenstein; Soviet Union; Silent with Russian intertitles and English subtitles; Black and White; 74 m; Facets (DVD); Russia, 1905.

It is impossible to overestimate the value of studying the historical films of Sergei Eisenstein. The confluence of their artistic brilliance, their production and reception histories, and the histories they "write" on screen produces an exceptionally rich arena in which to consider the interrelationship of art and ideology in historical films. *Battleship Potemkin* takes as its subject the 1905 sailors' riot on board the *Potemkin*, and the following uprising in the port of Odessa. Eisenstein's portrayal of the revolt on ship suggests the catalyst for revolution is material want, exploitation, and decisive leadership. In this case, sailors' refusal to eat maggot-infested meat and their superior's blatant disregard for their welfare is met with sailor Vakulinchuk's heroic leadership of a revolt—the starting point for Russia's gradual mobilization and ideological education. The power of the masses, galvanized by their inequality and desperation, is also suggested in the plotting of the Odessa scenes, and in the memorable spectacle of the shooting of the masses on the Odessa steps.

See also: *Earth* (Dovzhenko)

Corney, Frederick C. *Telling October: Memory and the Making of the Bolshevik Revolution*. Ithaca, NY: Cornell University Press, 2004.

Gerould, D. "Historical Simulation and Popular Entertainment: The *Potemkin* Mutiny from Reconstructed Newsreel to Black Sea Stunt Men." *Tulane Drama Review* 33(2) (Summer 1989): 161–84.

Goodwin, James. "*Battleship Potemkin*: Pathos and Politics." In *Eisenstein, Cinema, and History*, 79–97. Urbana, IL: University of Illinois Press, 1993.

Taylor, Richard. *The Battleship Potemkin: The Film Companion*. London: I.B. Tauris, 2000.

Wenden, D.J. "*Battleship Potemkin*: Film and Reality." In *Feature Films as History*, edited by K.R.M. Short, 37–61. London: Croom Helm, 1981.

Before the Rain / Pred dozhdot (1994) Milcho Manchevski; United Kingdom/France/Macedonia; Macedonian, English and Albanian with English subtitles; Color; 113 m; Polygram Video (VHS); Macedonia and London, early 1990s.

Before the Rain is a sustained look at intractable nationalist and religious conflicts in the Balkans. Using the microcosm of relationships in a small Macedonian village as its focal point, the film interconnects the stories of three characters in a challenging nonlinear narrative set in London and Macedonia in the era of the Yugoslav wars of the early 1990s.

See also: *Ulysses' Gaze*; *Underground*

Burgoyne, Robert. "*Before the Rain*: Ethnic Nationalism and Globalization." *Rethinking History* 4(2) (Summer 2000): 157–64.

Christie, Ian. "Landscape and Location: Reading Filmic Space Historically." *Rethinking History* 4(2) (Summer 2000): 165–74.

Friedman, Victor A. "Fable as History: The Macedonian Context." *Rethinking History* 4(2) (Summer 2000): 135–46.

Iordanova, Dina. "*Before the Rain* in a Balkan Context." *Rethinking History* 4(2) (Summer 2000): 147–56.

Rosenstone, Robert A. "A History of What Has Not Yet Happened." *Rethinking History* 4(2) (Summer 2000): 183–92.

Berlin Jerusalem / Berlin-Yerushalaim (1989) Amos Gitai; France/Israel/United Kingdom/Netherlands/Italy; Hebrew, German, and English with English subtitles; Color; 89 m; Facets (DVD); Berlin and Palestine, 1904–1945.

Else Lasker-Schüler was a poet who fled her native Germany in the 1930s to escape the Nazi persecution of German Jews. Mania Shohat, a Russian-born Zionist-socialist, was a pioneer of the Israeli kibbutz movement who first visited Israel in 1904. Based on the lives of these women, *Berlin Jerusalem* adopts a structure of intercutting their stories. Mania leaves Berlin (where she has come to know Else) for Palestine in the first decade of the twentieth century. With her brother and a few other Zionists, she works to establish an agricultural collective. The portrait of the collective's members is a highlight of the film. *Berlin Jerusalem* vividly depicts their ideological commitment, their physical hardship, their arguments over the gendered division of labor, and the increasingly militant views of the male members toward competition with Arab Palestinians for land. Else remains in Berlin until the 1930s, living the life of an acclaimed but impoverished artist, part of the city's café life and observing the increasingly hostile activities of the Nationalist Socialists in the 1920s. Voiceover readings of Else's poetry describe her increasing alienation and feelings of suffocation, and her longing for the sea and the balm of Palestine.

Near the end of *Berlin Jerusalem*, friends Else and Mania reunite in a café in Jerusalem, the city which they've spent years aspiring to reach. But both Else and Mania discover that the mythical stature of symbolic Jerusalem is compromised by poverty, violence, and Arab settlement. Thus *Berlin Jerusalem* punctures some of the myth of Israeli nation-building held by the women in their quest for safety and peace.

See also: *Exodus; Hill 24 Doesn't Answer; The House on Chelouche Street; Kedma*

Garrel, Philippe. "*Berlin-Jerusalem*." In *The Films of Amos Gitai: A Montage*, edited by Paul Willemen. London: BFI, 1993.

Iampolski, Mikhail. "The Road to Jerusalem: A Montage." In *The Films of Amos Gitai*, edited by Paul Willemen. London: BFI, 1993.

Rajadhyaksha, Asish. "Broken Dreams—Three Gitai Films: *Pineapple, Esther* and *Berlin-Jerusalem*." In *The Films of Amos Gitai: A Montage*, edited by Paul Willemen. London: BFI, 1993.

Rosen, Miriam. "The Architecture of Documentary Filmmaking: An Interview with Amos Gitai." *Cineaste* 17(3) (1990): 48–50.

Willemen, Paul. "Bangkok-Bahrain to Berlin-Jerusalem: Amos Gitai's Editing." *Screen* 33 (Spring 1992): 14–26.

Bethune: The Making of a Hero / Dr. Bethune (1990) Phillip Borsos; Canada/China/France; English; Color; 116 m; Fox Lorber (VHS); Canada, Spain, and China, 1920s and 1930s.

Not to be confused with a 1977 made-for-television drama (also starring Donald Sutherland in the title role), or a serialized television "reissue" of this 1990 production, *Bethune: The Making of a Hero* is a feature film about the Canadian doctor who served as a physician during the Spanish Civil War, and with the Red Army in China in the late 1930s. Bethune is as much myth as man in the People's Republic of China—he died of blood poisoning in 1939 while attending Chinese soldiers wounded by the Japanese—and Canadians know much less about him. This placed an interesting burden on those involved in the film's production, including Bethune's friend, screenwriter and (oft-criticized) biographer Ted Allan, and Sutherland, whose admiration for the doctor wasn't dimmed by his appreciation of Bethune's character flaws.

The result is a competent biopic. A flashback structure introduces Bethune's upbringing and medical training in Ontario, the development of his humanitarian and political convictions, his work in Spain, and his sojourn—and death—in China with Mao's Eighth Route Army. But the film is inconsistent in tone, plotting, and interpretation. Portraying Bethune as both dedicated and irascible, Sutherland cannot overcome a script that offers little dimension to this historical, and legendary, figure.

See also: The *Great White Man of Lambaréné*

Hannant, Larry. "A Note on Sources." In *The Politics of Passion: Norman Bethune's Writing and Art*, 369–72. Toronto: University of Toronto Press, 1998.

Sutherland, Donald. "Editorial for 'Two Stormy Petrels': To Dr. Larry W. Stephenson." *Journal of Cardiac Surgery* 18(1) (January 2003): 78–79.

Wise, Wyndham. "The Bethune Myth: Man and Movie." *Cinema Canada* 166 (Sept 1989): 11–16.

Beyond Rangoon (1995) John Boorman; United Kingdom/United States; English and Burmese; Color; 100 m; Warner Home Video (VHS); Burma, 1988.

Beyond Rangoon professes to be "inspired by actual events." The film is about the fictional Laura Gorman, an American physician traveling in Burma in the late 1980s. Flashbacks describe the murder of her son and husband during a burglary attempt at their home in the United States. Laura's voiceover says that she is looking for answers; maybe the "East" will provide them.

Laura's quest for personal peace is paralleled with her increasing awareness of the illegal democracy movement in Burma led by Aung San Suu Kyi. Detained in Burma because of a lost passport, Laura is invited by U Aung Ko, a professor-turned-tour guide, to learn about Burmese politics from an insider's perspective, in the countryside "beyond" the Rangoon to which foreigners are confined. The film is served up as a thriller in plotting and style, and its tension produced as Laura, the professor, and some of his former students—now democracy activists—must try to reach the border with Thailand to escape the clutches of loyalists of Burmese General Ne Win.

Beyond Rangoon suggests that the Burmese—described by one of the activist students as "too polite to resist"—are reliant upon foreigners for the success of their democracy movement. Burma is a closed society; its situation can only be known to the West if Westerners make the effort to expose the story. The character of a photographer, for example, must get his pictures "out" so the world will have knowledge of the regime's brutality. The simplistic equation of foreign knowledge and resulting positive foreign intervention is central to the liberal humanist vision of Boorman, who provides his audience no detailed explanation of Burmese society, culture, and history. Historical explanation largely resides in the unexamined claim of the superiority of democratic systems, and the juxtaposition of idealistic, brave, and youthful Burmese with stone-faced and villainous Burmese soldiers who do the bidding of a faceless dictator.

See also: *The Killing Fields*; *The Year of Living Dangerously*

Crowdus, Gary. "*Beyond Rangoon.*" *Cineaste* 22(3) (September 1996): 48.
Goldberg, Elizabeth Swanson. "Splitting Difference: Global Identity Politics and the Representation of Torture in the Counterhistorical Dramatic Film." In *Violence and American Cinema*, edited by David Slocum, 245–70. London: Routledge, 2000.
Smith, Gavin. "Beyond Images (Interview with John Boorman)." *Film Comment* 31(4) (July-August 1995): 44–47.

Bitter Sea / Amargo mar (1984) Antonio Eguino; Bolivia; Spanish; Color; 90 m; Cinema Guild (theatrical); Bolivia, 1879.

This is a grand-scale reconstruction of the Pacific War of 1879–1884, when Chile invaded and took control of the southwest coast of Bolivia. The film uses fictional and real-life characters to represent the variety of economic, military, and political interests operational in the origins and conduct of the war, including a sympathetic Chilean engineer. *Bitter Sea* has a polemical tone, indicting not just Chile but corrupt Bolivian interests.

Schwartz, Ronald. "*Amargo Mar (Bitter Sea).*" In *Latin American Films, 1932–1994: A Critical Filmography*, 32–33. Jefferson, NC: McFarland, 1997.

Black and White in Color / Noirs et blancs en couleur / La Victoire en chantant (1976) Jean-Jacques Annaud; Ivory Coast/France/West Germany/ Switzerland; French with English subtitles; Color; 90 m; Home Vision Entertainment (DVD), Warner Home Video (VHS); fictional French African colony, World War I.

Black and White in Color illustrates the power of satirical film to engage the past in a reflective and entertaining way. The film is at once an antiwar statement, and a metaphoric interpretation of the origins of the First World War. It also provocatively asserts the folly of colonial race and gender relations. *Black and White in Color* has a rousing musical score (reminiscent of an overly enthusiastic group of marching buffoons), vivid characters, and effective pacing. It also combines humor and pathos to create a very memorable message about human conduct in the past, and its portents for the future.

The film is set in a fictional colony of French West Africa. In the opening scene, relations between the few French inhabitants of the dusty entrepôt of Fort Coulais and their German neighbors seem positive: the obsequious Rechampot brothers, who run the Fort's store, are only too happy to provide wares to German Lieutenant Kraft. Even Marinette, the wife of Paul Rechampot, good-naturedly accepts Kraft's refusal of her offer of sexual services. Marinette's female subjugation—despite her superiority as a white colonist—is contrasted with that of an African woman whose empowerment comes from her status as the consort of Hubert Fresnoy. Fresnoy, a visiting French geographer, experiences the film's most important and troubling transformation. From an admiring observer of African pastoral life and local culture, he becomes a powerful and controlling commander of the local army, who even sanctions the capture of natives from other tribes as indentured soldiers.

The catalyst for the film's action is the much-delayed arrival of newspapers from home. These alert the French colonists—at the time somewhat moribundly celebrating the arrival of 1915—to their country's declaration of war against Germany. In a beautifully charged scene of the pathetic nationalism of this sorry band of colonists, they are roused to patriotism, vowing their duty to defeat their German neighbors: "Vive le France!" they chant, bolstering their courage. Militarist and male pride finally overcomes local Sergeant Bossulet, who until finally convinced to train an army of locals, is bored, dissolute, and disillusioned. Bossulet's service in Africa has provided him a refuge for his past military failures and, like most of his fellow colonists, a place to exercise power over the African inhabitants that is out of all proportion to his abilities. During the New Year's scene, Fresnoy is maddeningly noncommittal, cautioning about the colonists' impetuous strategy and the military strength of the Germans. His cohorts will have none of it. Matters aren't helped by the giddy and aroused passions of the women, who exhort their husbands to fulfill their national duty.

Soon locals are recruited for the invasionary force, and the film reaches its dénouement in a fittingly absurd scene that continues the theme of the myth of white superiority: the British successfully capture the German territory, led by an Indian commander of a Scottish regiment. The witless Frenchmen seem unable to have learned much from these events. As Paul Rechampot muses, "German niggers now British niggers ... serves them right!" Meanwhile, Fresnoy is happy to resume his intellectual friendship with Kraft. The seductive power of war can be dispensed with as a regrettable but necessary duty.

Biggs, Melissa E. "*La Victoire En Chantant* (*Black and White in Color* or *Black Victory*)." In *French Films, 1945–1993: A Critical Filmography of the 400 Most Important Releases*, 279–80. Jefferson, NC: McFarland, 1996.

Bolus-Reichert, Christine. "Imaginary Geographies: The Colonial Subject in Contemporary French Cinema." In *Postmodernism in the Cinema*, edited by Cristina Degli-Esposti, 167–86. New York: Berghahn, 1998.

Cudmore, Pierre Etienne. "From *Banania* to *Chocolat*: The French Colonization of Africa and Contemporary Cinema." *Atenea* 15(1)–2 (1995): 95–103.

Gallagher, Michael. "*Black and White in Color*." *Cineaste* 8(2) (1977): 42–44.

Black Cannon Incident / Heipao shijian

Black Cannon Incident / Heipao shijian (1986) Huang Jianxin; China; Mandarin and German with English subtitles; Color; 99 m; no current; China, 1980s.

At turns satirical, funny, and foreboding, *Black Cannon Incident* is about a modest Chinese engineer who is unfairly investigated as a spy for foreign interests after he telegrams a friend about a missing chess piece. A series of events elapse from the moment of his visit to the post office, including his removal from the role of translator for his firm's German business associate, and the subsequent breakdown of German-made equipment whose technical manuals are beyond the interpretive skills of the tour guide hired to replace him.

One of the most enjoyable features of the film is its use of music, lighting, and settings to create the image of a modern urban and industrial China. This image is somewhat discordant with *Black Cannon Incident*'s portrait of a bureaucratic, oppressive, and paranoid State in this period of China's opening to the West.

Berry, Chris, and Mary Ann Farquhar. "Post-Socialist Strategies: An Analysis of *Yellow Earth* and *Black Cannon Incident*." In *Cinematic Landscape: Observations on the Visual Arts and Cinema of China and Japan*, edited by Linda C. Ehrlich and David Desser, 81–116. Austin: University of Texas Press, 1994.

Pickowicz, Paul G. "Huang Jianxin and the Notion of Postsocialism." In *New Chinese Cinemas: Forms, Identities, Politics*, edited by Nick Browne, Paul Pickowicz, Vivian Sobchack and Esther Yau, 57–87. New York: Cambridge University Press, 1994.

Silbergeld, Jerome. "The Children of Melodrama: No-Drama, Pseudo-Drama, Melodramatic Masquerade, and Deconstruction Drama." In *China into Film: Frames of Reference in Contemporary Chinese Cinema*, 234–304. London: Reaktion Books, 1999.

Black Rain / Kuroi Ame

Black Rain / Kuroi Ame (1989) Shohei Imamura; Japan; Japanese with English subtitles; Black and White; 123 m; Image Entertainment (DVD); Wellspring (VHS); Japan, 1945 and 1950.

Black Rain is a moving story of the prolonged suffering of an ordinary Japanese family in the aftermath of the atomic bombing of Hiroshima in 1945. Almost lyrical in its quiet evocation of the marred beauty of Japan and its people, the film sets up a disturbing juxtaposition of image and reality: beneath the calm and prosaic beauty of the small rural village to which the family moves from Hiroshima is an invisible disease caused by radiation. Most symbolic is niece Yasuko's inability to find a suitor; rumors of her infertility destroy her prospects, despite a certificate of good health obtained in Fukuyama in 1950. Her uncle, Shigematsu, protests that it was the black rain, not the bomb, that hit Yasuko. But prospective suitors and suspicious villagers rightly suspect that the bomb's devastation did not end in 1945. Their fears are confirmed over time: as the film progresses, illness and death slowly but seemingly inevitably claim many, including Yasuko, whose tumor progresses, and Shigematsu's wife, who dies.

Shohei Imamura's meditative pace and respectful honoring of the fate of these people does not disguise a kind of bewilderment at events. A village neighbor who suffers radiation effects wonders why the Americans did not drop the bomb on Tokyo. "How can I die without knowing the truth?" he pleads. The senselessness of ruined lives and families is foregrounded against any rational explanation of events.

See also: *Hiroshima, mon amour*

Cavanaugh, Carole. "A Working Ideology for Hiroshima: Imamura Shohei's *Black Rain*." In *Word and Image in Japanese Cinema*, edited by Carole Cavanaugh and Dennis Washburn, 250–70. Cambridge: Cambridge University Press, 1993.

Dorsey, John T., and Naomi Matsuoka. "Narrative Strategies of Understatement in *Black Rain* as a Novel and a Film." In *Hibakusha Cinema: Hiroshima, Nagasaki and the Nuclear Image in Japanese Film*, edited by Mick Broderick, 203–21. New York: Columbia University Press, 1996.

Dower, J. "Japanese Artists and the Atomic Bomb." In *Japan in War and Peace: Selected Essays*, 242–56. New York: New Press, 1993.

Keirstead, Thomas, and Deidre Lynch. "Review of *Black Rain*." *American Historical Review* 96(4) (October 1991): 1116–18.

Tachibana, Reiko. "Seeing Between the Lines: Imamura Shohei's *Kuroi Ame* (*Black Rain*)." *Literature/Film Quarterly* 26(4) (1998): 304–12.

Todeschini, Maya Morioka. " 'Death and the Maiden': Female *Hibakusha* as Cultural Heroines, and the Politics of A-Bomb Memory." In *Hibakusha Cinema: Hiroshima, Nagasaki and the Nuclear Image in Japanese Film*, edited by Mick Broderick, 222–52. New York: Columbia University Press, 1996.

Black Robe (1991) Bruce Beresford; Canada/Australia; English; Color; 101 m; Facets (DVD), Lion's Gate Home Entertainment (VHS); New France (Canada), 1634.

Black Robe is adapted from a 1985 novel of the same name. Its author, Brian Moore, drew from the historical document known as the *Relations*, reports by missionaries of the Jesuit order in New France sent to superiors in France. The film is about a young priest, Father Laforgue—based on the real-life Noël Chabanel, canonized in 1930—who has been assigned to reach and convert the Huron Indians. His mission is complicated by the love affair of his lay translator, Daniel, with an Algonquin woman, the danger of the journey to the isolated mission of Huronia presented by the hostility of the natives, and his own fears and misgivings.

Black Robe has a very naturalistic aesthetic, accomplished in the attention to period detail as well as its lighting, dialogue, and editing. Naturalism has the potential to create for modern audiences a strong "sense" that they are visiting a close approximation to the "real" past, and *Black Robe* is arguably successful (or, in another view, misleading) in this regard. The representation of natives in the film was clearly designed to be sensitive to differences in languages and cultures; the inadequacies of such attempts have been amply noted by some critics of the film.

The film's seventeenth-century New France is a closed world, admitting virtually nothing of its relationship to a modern movie production or its documentary provenance. The potential to highlight, and even subvert, the record of the Jesuit

Relations as source, for example, is unrealized here. The lack of reflexivity in the film—consistent with other works of director Beresford—undermines its potential to say something nuanced and meaningful about European–native contact in this period. This cinematic writing of history, while cloaked in good intentions, seems little more than an apologia for European conquest, founded on the falsely reassuring characterization of Laforgue's essential humanness and dignity.

See also: *Cabeza de Vaca; How Tasty Was My Little Frenchman; Jericho; The Mission*

Appleford, Robert. "Coming out from behind the Rocks: Constructs of the Indian in Recent U.S. and Canadian Cinema." *American Indian Culture and Research Journal* 19(1) (Winter 1995): 97–118.

Axtell, James. "*Black Robe*." In *Past Imperfect: History According to the Movies*, edited by Mark C. Carnes, 78–81. New York: Henry Holt, 1995.

Churchill, Ward. "And They Did It Like Dogs in the Dirt . . .: An American Indian Analysis of *Black Robe*." In *Indians Are Us? Culture and Genocide in Native America*, 115–37. Monroe, ME: Common Courage Press, 1994.

Freebury, Jane. "*Black Robe*: Ideological Cloak and Dagger?" *Australian-Canadian Studies* 10(1) (1992): 119–26.

Gittings, Christopher E. "*Black Robe*." In *Canadian National Cinema: Ideology, Difference and Representation*, 199–202. London: Routledge, 2002.

Mota Santos, Paula. "Good Indians and Bad Indians: The European Perspective of Native Americans as Depicted in *The Mission* and *Black Robe*." In *Native American Women in Literature and Culture*, edited by Susan Castillo and Victor M.P. Da Rosa, 185–90. Porto, Portugal: Fernando Pessoa University Press, 1997.

Blood of the Condor / Yawar Mallku

Blood of the Condor / Yawar Mallku (1969) Jorge Sanjinés; Bolivia; Spanish, and Quechua/Aymara with English subtitles; Black and White; 72 m; Tricontinental Film Center (theatrical); Bolivia, 1960s.

Jorge Sanjinés created the foreign "Progress Corps" of this film after reading a newspaper account of the practice of the U.S. Peace Corps to force the sterilization of rural indigenous women of Bolivia. Filmed in the indigenous Aymara community of Kaata, *Blood of the Condor* is set in the late 1960s. When locals attack members of the Corps, the Bolivian army intervenes and the *Mallku*—Aymaran leader—must receive treatment for his wounds in La Paz. The racism experienced in their own rural community, and in the city, reinforces the inferior status of Bolivia's indigenous people in the face of imperialism and a militarist state.

See also: *The Courage of the People/The Night of San Juan; The Principal Enemy*

Blade, Gibril. "*Blood of the Condor*." *Cineaste* 4 (Winter 1970–71): 11.

Leonardo García-Pabón, trans. Maura Furfey. "*The Clandestine Nation*: Indigenism and National Subjects of Bolivia in the Films of Jorge Sanjinés." *Jump Cut: A Review of Contemporary Media* 44 (Fall 2001), http://www.ejumpcut.org/archive/jc44.2001/garcia/garciatextonly.html (accessed May 30, 2006).

Hess, John. "Neo-Realism and New Latin American Cinema: *Bicycle Thieves* and *Blood of the Condor*." In *Mediating Two Worlds: Cinematic Encounters in the Americas*, edited by John King, Ana M. López, and Manuel Alvarado, 104–18. London: BFI, 1993.

n/a. "*Ukamau* and *Yawar Mallku*: An Interview with Jorge Sanjinés." *Afterimage* 3 (Summer 1971): 40–53.

Ross, Eric. "*Blood of the Condor* (*Yawar Mallku*) by Jorge Sanjinés." *American Anthropologist* 80(1) (March 1978): 203–04.

Bloody Sunday (2002) Peter Greengrass; United Kingdom/Ireland; English; Color; 107 m; Paramount Home Entertainment (DVD, VHS); Northern Ireland, January 1972.

The intransigency of the civil conflict in Northern Ireland has bred decades of academic and popular interpretation, often reflecting those political, ideological, and social divisions found in the conflict itself. *Bloody Sunday* revisits one of the most contentious events—the 1972 massacre of civilians by the British troops at Derry—and marks the event's thirtieth anniversary with another controversial interpretation. Point-of-view in conventional narrative historical film will give an audience its interpretive markers, assuring them of who is victim and who is villain. In *Bloody Sunday* the perspectives of two "opposing" sets of characters are dramatized: Parliamentarian Ivan Cooper and those citizens of Derry who plan a nonviolent civil rights march, and members of the British military force that plan and execute the response to the march, including Major-General Ford, Brigadier MacLellan, and Derry police chief Lagan. But while director Greengrass puts a human face on members of the British military, its actions of January 30, 1972, are clearly condemned. The British government's investigation that followed events, known as the Widgery Tribunal, generally concurred with the military's claim that force became necessary against armed IRA gunmen. *Bloody Sunday* interprets events as admittedly somewhat confused in their sequence, but with marchers as peaceful in intent.

A minority among critics of *Bloody Sunday* have argued that its documentary–realist style creates a distancing effect, rather than close identification with the characters and their fate: the film has the appearance of grainy news footage from long ago that might appear as just another television news update—footage to which modern audiences are perhaps inured. The naturalistic style achieved through the film's dialogue and performances, soundtrack, editing, and staging might counter any such distance from events. Close shots, a hand-held camera work, and action unfolding in "confused" fashion place the audience in experiential relation to events.

Alcobia-Murphy, Shane. "Unfinished Narratives: Artistic Representations of Bloody Sunday." In *Governing the Tongue in Northern Ireland: The Place of Art/the Art of Place*, 88–98. Newcastle, United Kingdom: Cambridge Scholars Press, 2005.

Barton, Ruth. "Northern Ireland." In *Irish National Cinema*, 157–78. London: Routledge, 2004.

Kelly, Richard. "It Won't Go Away, You Know—*Bloody Sunday* and *Sunday*." *Critical Quarterly* 44(2) (July 2002): 73–83.

McLoone, Martin. "Review of *Bloody Sunday*." *Cineaste* 27(4) (Fall 2002): 42–3.

The Blue Eyes of Yonta / Udju azul di Yonta (1992) Flora Gomes; Guinea-Bissau; Criolo with English subtitles; Color; 90 m; California Newsreel (VHS); Guinea-Bissau, 1980s.

The Blue Eyes of Yonta is about citizens of postcolonial Guinea-Bissau who struggle to adapt to the end of the independence revolution and the advent of urbanization, bureaucratization, and free market capitalism. The tension between the past and the future is symbolized in three main characters, whose romances are thwarted by their continuing idealism.

See also: *Hyenas; Identity Pieces; Utopia; Those Whom Death Refused*

Gugler, Josef. "*The Blue Eyes of Yonta* (1992): Was the Struggle in Vain?" In *African Film: Re-Imagining a Continent*, 147–56. Bloomington: Indiana University Press, 2003.

Racevskis, Maija. "Applications of African Cinema in the High School Curriculum: A Secondary Teacher's Views of *Three Tales from Senegal, Ca Twiste À Poponguine, Udju Azul Di Yonta, Hyenas,* and *Keïta.*" *Research in African Literatures* 27(3) (1996): 98–109.

Ukadike, N. Frank. "In Guinea-Bissau, Cinema Trickles Down: An Interview with Flora Gomes." *Research in African Literatures* 26(3) (1995): 179–85.

The Blue Kite / Lan feng zheng (1993) Tian Zhuangzhuang; China/Hong Kong; Mandarin with English subtitles; Color; 138 m; Kino (DVD, VHS); China, 1953 to 1967.

The Blue Kite has an unassuming, even charming, beginning: using voiceover, a boy narrates the story of his parents' 1953 wedding in Dry Well Lane in Beijing. (A bow to Mao Zedong's portrait precedes the signing of the marriage license.) The boy, Tietou, soon enters the story, and scenes common to coming-of-age films—play with neighboring children in the courtyards and lanes, family meals at his grandmother's home, and kite-flying with his father—reiterate the film's commitment to telling about the private spaces of family life.

As the film progresses, however, family life is the space of almost relentless tragedy. Tietou's father is sent to a concentration camp in 1957, accused of being a rightist. An uncle's girlfriend, an actress, is imprisoned after refusing to perform at an event for Communist Party leaders. By the film's end, set in November 1968, Tietou's second stepfather has died of a heart attack, the result of a beating from Maoist Red Guards. Tietou adds, "Mom was sent to labor reform as a counter-revolutionary."

This is a hopeless ending to a family story that had such a hopeful beginning. Personal life could only afford increasingly thin protection from ideological and Party politics in this era of the People's Republic of China. The strains of successive mass campaigns—collectivization, the Hundred Flowers and Anti-Rightist campaigns, the Great Leap Forward, and the Cultural Revolution—exact a toll on Tietou and adult family members. As Tietou's grandmother says, "They've been carrying out revolution all of their lives. There's no end to it."

While the context of Tietou's family history is the national history of China over two decades, *The Blue Kite* validates personal history as a locus of the meaningful reconstruction of the past. Tietou's memories are viewers' only source here, and they construct a moving history of love, belonging, separation, and trauma.

See also: *Farewell My Concubine; In the Heat of the Sun; King of the Children*

Cornelius, Sheila. "Case Study: *The Blue Kite.*" In *New Chinese Cinema: Challenging Representations*, 49–52. London: Wallflower, 2002.

Nielsen, H.B. "The Three Father Figures in Tian Zhuangzhuang's Film *The Blue Kite*: The Emasculation of Males by the Communist Party." *China Information* 13(4) (Spring 1999): 83–96.

Wang, Ban. "Trauma and History in Chinese Film: Reading *The Blue Kite* against Melodrama." *Modern Chinese Literature and Culture* 11(1) (1999): 125–234.

Xiao, Zhiwei. "Review of *The Wooden Man's Bride, Farewell My Concubine, The Blue Kite,* and *To Live.*" *American Historical Review* 100(4) (October 1995): 1212–14.

Zhang, Xudong. "National Trauma, Global Allegory: Reconstruction of Collective Memory in Tian Zhuangzhuang's *The Blue Kite*." *Journal of Contemporary China* 12(37) (November 2003): 623–38.

The Boat / Das Boot (1981) Wolfgang Petersen; West Germany; German with English subtitles; Color; 149 m (Theatrical), 209 m (Director's Cut); Columbia/TriStar (DVD, VHS); North Atlantic Ocean, 1942.

This drama about a German submarine crew patrolling the North Atlantic in World War II shows the human side of the war experience. The film has been variously interpreted as a rare sympathetic treatment of the German military in World War II, or as generically patriotic and heroic.

Gartenberg, J. "*Das Boot*." *Films in Review* 33 (April 1982): 241–2.

Reimer, Robert C., and Carol J. Reimer. "*The Boat*." In *Nazi-Retro Film: How German Narrative Cinema Remembers the Past*, 72–78. New York: Twayne, 1992.

Rubenstein, L. "*Das Boot*." *Cineaste* 12(1) (1982): 60.

Thompson, David G. "Villains, Victims, and Veterans: Buchheim's *Das Boot* and the Problem of the Hybrid Novel-Memoir as History." *Twentieth Century Literature* 39(1) (Spring 1993): 59–78.

The Boat Is Full / Das Boot ist voll (1981) Markus Imhoof; Switzerland/West Germany/Austria; German with English subtitles; Color; 104 m; Home Vision Entertainment (DVD), First Run Features (VHS); Switzerland, WWII.

This is the story of a small group of Germans who seek asylum in Switzerland during the Second World War. Brought together by necessity, they have disparate stories. Soon, upon the advice of a Swiss priest, they masquerade as a family, hoping that the Swiss government will—despite official policy that states the "boat is full" and refugees must be returned to the country from which they came—exempt their deportation on the grounds that their "son" is under age six. Jews fleeing racial persecution were exempt from the asylum Switzerland allowed political refugees; this "family's" father figure will be the group's only non-Jewish member, a deserted German soldier. The others are an elderly man and his granddaughter, a young woman whose Gentile husband had fled a German work camp for Switzerland two years earlier and was incarcerated in a Swiss prison, the woman's (wounded) brother, and a little boy who speaks French but who will pretend he is mute. The reception of this refugee family is captured in the ambivalence of many of the villagers: torn between fear and morality, they vacillate between the options of denunciation and rescue. *The Boat Is Full* clearly criticizes Swiss wartime policy and its enforcement, but it is a measured portrait of ordinary people's confrontation with the condemned in their midst.

See also: *Boat People; The Dupes; Journey of Hope; Kedma; Welcome to Canada*

Insdorf, Annette. "In Hiding/Onstage." In *Indelible Shadows: Film and the Holocaust*, 3rd ed., 93–110. New York: Cambridge University Press, 2003.

Mahoney, Dennis F. "Personalizing the Holocaust: *Das Boot ist voll*." *Modern Language Studies* 19(1) (Winter 1989): 3–11.

Reimer, Robert C., and Carol J. Reimer. "*The Boat Is Full*." In *Nazi-Retro Film: How German Narrative Cinema Remembers the Past*, 157–59. New York: Twayne, 1992.

Boat People / Tou bun no hoi (1982) Ann Hui; Hong Kong; Cantonese, Japanese, and Vietnamese with English subtitles; Color; 111 m; International Spectrafilm (theatrical); South Vietnam, late 1970s.

The fictional character of Akutagawa is a Japanese photo-journalist who covered the end of the Vietnam War in 1975 and has returned three years later, expecting the new Communist era to have brought positive change. *Boat People* follows his passage from outsider to participant in the historical events of the period. Befriending a young girl and her brother, he attempts to secure their passage out of the country. Like many other Vietnamese of Chinese descent, the children are about to travel the South China Sea as refugees. Despite its title, *Boat People* focuses little on the refugee experience, instead considering—through Akutagawa's eyes—the oppression, corruption, and devastating economic policies that in the film's view explain the advent of the refugee movement.

See also: *The Boat Is Full*; *The Dupes*; *Journey of Hope*; *Kedma*; *Welcome to Canada*

Erens, Patricia Brett. "The Film Work of Ann Hui." In *The Cinema of Hong Kong: History, Arts, Identity*, edited by Poshek Fu and David Desser, 176–93. New York: Cambridge University Press, 2000.

Ho, Elaine Yee-lin. "Women on the Edges of Modernity: The Films of Ann Hui." In *At Full Speed: Hong Kong Cinema in a Borderless World*, edited by Esther C. Yau, 177–207. Minneapolis, MN: University of Minnesota Press, 2001.

Williams, Tony. "Hong Kong Cinema, *The Boat People*, and *To Liv(e)*." *Asian Cinema: a Publication of the Asian Cinema Studies Society* 11(1) (Spring/Summer 2000): 131–42.

Border Street / Ulica graniczna (1949) Aleksander Ford; Poland; Polish and German with English subtitles; Black and White; 110 m; Facets (DVD, VHS); Warsaw, Poland, 1939–1943.

Also known as *That Others May Live*, *Border Street* is one of the first feature films to address the history of the Nazi persecution of European Jews. Its story is about several Polish families—some Jewish, some not—who are affected by the establishment of the Warsaw Ghetto and the later uprising there.

See also: *Canal*; *A Generation*; *Korczak*; *The Pianist*

Insdorf, Annette. "Rediscoveries." In *Indelible Shadows: Film and the Holocaust*, 3rd ed., 250–57. New York: Cambridge University Press, 2003.

Konigsberg, Ira. "Our Children and the Limits of Cinema: Early Jewish Responses to the Holocaust." *Film Quarterly* 52(1) (Autumn 1998): 7–19.

Boycott / Baycot (1985) Mohsen Makhmalbaf; Iran; Farsi with English subtitles; Color; 85 m; Facets (VHS); Iran, 1970s.

Based on the experiences of director Makhmalbaf, *Boycott* is about Valeh, an anti-Shah activist in prerevolutionary Iran. The stresses of participating in the leftist-Islamic movement—trying to evade the *Savak* (secret police), enduring torture in jail, the cost to family life—are suggested in Valeh's growing fatigue and disillusionment.

Dabashi, Hamid. "Once Upon a Filmmaker: A Conversation with Mohsen Makhmalbaf." In *Close Up: Iranian Cinema, Past, Present and Future*, 156–212. London: Verso, 2001.

Hamid, Rahul. "Films by and about Mohsen Makhmalbaf." *Cineaste* 27(1) (Winter 2001): 40–41.

Braveheart (1995) Mel Gibson; United States; English; Color; 177 m; Paramount Home Entertainment (DVD, VHS); Scotland, 1280–1314.

Braveheart was a film sensation upon its release, capturing huge audiences, multiple Academy Awards, and fuelling contemporary Scottish nationalism. While critics were definitely mixed about the film—some calling it overblown and others admitting its success as a rousing epic—*Braveheart* is a film that historians must reckon with. This historical film teaches scores of viewers about William Wallace, who beginning in 1297 led a resistance against Edward I's English occupation of Scotland, whether experts like the lesson or not.

Reviewing *Braveheart* and *Rob Roy*, released the same year, historian Elizabeth Ewan says, "It is difficult to assess the 'historical' nature of these films. Both deal with figures who are as much legends as historical individuals." *Braveheart* has away out of its morass of truth, invention, and national legend. An opening voiceover says: "I shall tell you of William Wallace. English historians will tell you I'm a liar. But history is written by those who have hanged heroes." Adopting the authorial voice of a revisionist, *Braveheart* hopes to silence any complaints about its history, and to even win adherents to its interpretation. But the "lies" in the film go much beyond the conflation of events, contrived meetings of protagonist and villain, or innocent anachronisms that commonly populate historical films. In *Braveheart*, little resembles the known record. Dates, events, costuming, and characterization are all wildly imaginative. For example, the film assigns Scottish King Alexander III's death to 1280, six years before the fact, and English King Edward I's claim of the throne of Scotland the same year. It was not until 1296 that he claimed to rule directly, when with the abdication of King John Balliol, Edward's overlordship turned into his possession of the crown. The only conclusion one can derive from this massaging of dates is that the film must present the period of oppression of the Scots by the English as prolonged and in conformity with Wallace's own life course. The narrator's early description of Wallace's father as a farmer—he was a knight—is a warning that fabricated and simplistic oppositions of "commoner" and "oppressor" will reign here, informing the exploitative manner in which the past is used in the film. What remains is a rousing story set in an imaginary past, one that serves—as the legend of William Wallace always has—a very real function in the construction of the Scottish popular imagination.

Ewan, Elizabeth. "Review of *Braveheart* and *Rob Roy*." *American Historical Review* 100(4) (October 1995): 1219–21.

MacArthur, Colin. "*Braveheart* and the Scottish Aesthetic Dementia." In *Screening the Past: Film and the Representation of History*, edited by Tony Barta, 167–87. Westport, CT: Praeger, 1998.

McArthur, Colin. *Brigadoon, Braveheart and the Scots: Distortions of Scotland in Hollywood Cinema*. London: I.B. Tauris, 2003.

Ray, Sid. "Hunks, History, and Homophobia: Masculine Politics in *Braveheart* and *Edward II*." *Film & History: An Interdisciplinary Journal of Film and Television Studies* 29(3–4) (1999): 22–31.

'Breaker' Morant (1979) Bruce Beresford; Australia; English; Color; 106 m; Fox Lorber (DVD, VHS); South Africa, 1901.

Historical trials and tribunals are a very popular subject for the big screen. Pitting as they often do the individual of conscience against the impersonal forces of the state, these situations are inherently dramatic, and use the resolution of personal problems as a kind of panacea or diversion for the less easily resolved historical issues at work. Opportunity for soliloquies from both the prosecution and defense abound in trial films, giving very concrete expression to some of the political and ethical dimensions of the case. Some trial films, among them *'Breaker' Morant*, situate the courtroom as a place where competing memories and perspectives of an event reside, thus foregrounding issues of interpretation.

Set in the Boer War, *'Breaker' Morant* is about the court martial of three Australian members of the Bushveldt Carbineers, Lieutenants Harry Morant, Peter Handcock, and George Witton. The men are charged with the murder of prisoners of war, having executed Boer captives in what appears to have been revenge for the brutal death of a British captain and a fulfillment of unwritten new orders from Field General Lord Kitchener (the commander-in-chief of British and colonial forces) that no mercy would be offered to prisoners of war. *'Breaker' Morant* excels at delivering through its interplay of tribunal scenes and flashbacks the recreation of witnesses' testimony of events. The film is an engrossing discussion of many aspects of the history of the Boer War itself. Relations of power among the British Empire, the Australian colonial forces, the Boers, and the African natives of the region are explored. The experience of "ordinary" men far from home in a war whose purpose is increasingly alien to them is considered. The potential disjunction between the documented record—in this case that of the court martial—and the "truth" behind the event is a major theme of the film. Ultimately, *'Breaker' Morant* offers a critical discourse on colonialism, and makes Morant and Handcock martyrs to the cause of Australian nationalism.

See also: *José Rizal; Zulu*

Asimow, Michael, and Paul Bergman, eds. "Breaker Morant." In *Reel Justice: The Courtroom Goes to the Movies*, 58–63. Kansas City, MI: Andrews McMeel, 1996.

Clover, Carol J. "Judging Audiences: The Case of the Trial Movie." In *Reinventing Film Studies*, edited by Christine Gledhill and Linda Williams, 244–64. London: Arnold, 2000.

Crafts, Stephen. "*Breaker Morant*: Quibbling over Imperialism." *Jump Cut: A Review of Contemporary Media* 27 (July 1982): 13–14.

Jolly, Roslyn. "'Frontier Behaviour' and Imperial Power in 'Breaker' Morant." *Journal of Commonwealth Literature* 32(2) (1997): 125–39.

Mortimer, Lorraine. "The Soldier, the Shearer and the Mad Man: Horizons of Community in Some Australian Films." *Literature/Film Quarterly* 21(2) (1993): 139–57.

The Burmese Harp / Biruma no tategoto

The Burmese Harp / Biruma no tategoto (1956) Kon Ichikawa; Japan; Japanese with English subtitles; Black and White; 115 m; Facets (VHS); Burma, end of WWII.

A Japanese soldier in Burma is to be repatriated during the process of Japanese surrender to the British at the end of World War II. But his experiences of the war have so disillusioned him that he takes on the garb of a Buddhist monk and remains to bury each of his dead comrades. *Burmese Harp* is often credited as one of postwar Japan's first pacifist films.

See also: *Fires on the Plain; The Human Condition*

McDonald, Keiko I. "Character Types and Psychological Revelation in Ichikawa's *The Harp of Burma*." In *Cinema East: A Critical Study of Major Japanese Films*, 88–100. Rutherford, NJ: Farleigh Dickenson University Press, 1983.

Burn! / Queimada! (1969) Gillo Pontecorvo; Italy/France; English; Color; 112 m; Facets (DVD, VHS); fictional Caribbean island, mid-19th century.

It has been 10 years since William Walker first arrived at Queimada in the early 1840s, a fictional island of the Portuguese Antilles. Covertly acting with the approval of the British Admiralty and British Royal Antilles Sugar Company, Walker had during that first visit successfully engineered a slave uprising, the assassination of the Portuguese governor and the proclamation (by white plantation owners) of the independence of Queimada. Now Walker has returned, this time to quell a revolt of plantation workers under leader José Delores that has compromised the profits of the sugar company.

One of *Burn!*'s main achievements is to create a polemical anticolonial film that effectively considers the growing self-doubt among colonialists about the morality and justice (or at least sustainability) of the colonial enterprise. The charismatic, enigmatic, and successful Walker is less self-assured than a decade before. "Not sure" what he's doing in Queimada this time, he nevertheless does "know that whenever I try to do it well, I achieve it thoroughly and through to the end." Walker's character escapes stereotypes, even if the guileless and ignorant plantation owners who seek his leadership are unredeeming.

Director Pontecorvo has made the character of Dolores—played by a local discovered on location in Colombia—the nemesis of Walker and representative of black oppression and resistance. Contrary to Walker's arc Dolores' doubts appear early on, when he is recruited by Walker to foment an uprising. By the end of the film, Dolores confidently refuses Walker's help in escaping execution. Dolores knows well Walker's claim that "you can't kill a myth," and would rather be a martyr than a "free" man in an unfree society.

Burn! provides a textbook lesson in 1960's Marxist anticolonialism. The film is visually and aurally vivid, capturing songs, dances, and military actions of the slaves with an authentic—and 1960s—sensibility. But it's the highly rhetorical nature of the film—and especially of Walker—that makes confronting positions clear. The instructional value in the film comes, for example, in a luncheon among plantation owners. Here Walker methodically "calculates" the comparative economics of having a wife versus a mulatto prostitute. Walker's later summary of events over 10 years concludes with the observation: ". . . very often between one historical period and another ten years suddenly might be enough to reveal the contradictions of a whole century. And so often our judgments and interpretations and even our hopes may have been wrong."

See also: *The Last Supper*; *Quilombo*

Davis, Natalie Zemon. "Ceremony and Revolt: *Burn!* And *The Last Supper*." In *Slaves on Screen: Film and Historical Vision*, 41–68. Toronto: Vintage Canada, 2000.

Schwartz, Ronald. "*Quemada! (Burn!)*." In *Latin American Films, 1932–1994: A Critical Filmography*, 206–07. Jefferson, NC: McFarland, 1997.

Cabeza de Vaca (1991) Nicolás Echevarría; Mexico/Spain/United States/United Kingdom; Spanish with English subtitles; Color; 111 m; New Concorde Home Entertainment (DVD, VHS); Colonial Mexico, 1520s and 30s.

"I have a world, even though I'm lost," screams Spanish conquistador Álvar Núñez Cabeza de Vaca to his native captor. The dislocation, vulnerability, and loss that Cabeza de Vaca and a small group of stranded sailors experience in a strange culture is utterly foreign to their normal experience as dominant Spaniards in early colonial Mexico. The film *Cabeza de Vaca* disorients Western viewers as well, asking them to revisit their notions of captor and captive, abuser and abused, in the early colonial era. As a result, this highly imaginative and provocative interpretation of Cabeza de Vaca's travels in the New World, based on his 1542 account called *La Relacion*, successfully adopts alternative perspectives. Director Nicholás Echevarría's film challenges the comfortable relationship of empirical fact to history, and instead introduces the dimension of psychological perspective and its conditioning of historical accounts of witnesses.

See also: *Aguirre*; *Jericho*; *The Mission*

Alvaray, Luisela. "Imagi(ni)ng Indigenous Spaces: Self and Other Converge in Latin America." *Film & History: An Interdisciplinary Journal of Film and Television Studies* 34(2) (2004): 58–64.

Gordon, Richard. "Exoticism and National Identity in *Cabeza De Vaca* and *Como era gostoso o meu francês* [*How Tasty Was My Little Frenchman*]." *Torre de Papel* 10(1) (2000): 77–119.

Hershfield, Joanne. "Assimilation and Identification in Nicolás Echevarría's *Cabeza De Vaca*." *Wide Angle* 16 (1995): 7–24.

Kraniauskas, John. "*Cabeza De Vaca*." *Travesia (Journal of Latin American Cultural Studies)* 1(2) (1992): 113–22.

Restrepo, Luis Fernando. "Primitive Bodies in Latin American Cinema: Nicolás Echevarría's *Cabeza De Vaca*." In *Primitivism and Identity in Latin America*, edited by Erik Camayd-Freixas and José Eduardo González, 189–208. Tucson: University of Arizona Press, 2000.

Schwartz, Ronald. "*Cabeza De Vaca*." In *Latin American Films, 1932–1994: A Critical Filmography*, 51–52. Jefferson, NC: McFarland, 1997.

Walter, Krista. "Filming the Conquest: *Cabeza De Vaca* and the Spectacle of History." *Literature/Film Quarterly* 30(2) (2002): 140–45.

Camila (1995) María Luisa Bemberg; Argentina/Spain; Spanish with English subtitles; Color; 107 m; Facets (DVD), Connoisseur/Meridian (VHS); Argentina, 1840s.

In *Camila*'s precredit scene, we are introduced to an aristocratic Catholic family of Buenos Aires, the O'Gormans, when a coach accompanied by soldiers travels down a tree-lined, sun-dappled lane and arrives at the family estate. Juxtaposed with the image of family reunion in a rural idyll is the fact that Grandmother has returned on the occasion from her release from jail, and will be under house arrest. Grandmother meets little Camila, born during her absence, and asks, "Tell me, do you like stories?" Camila answers, "I don't know."

Camila's wisdom belies her age; most of the film—which ostensibly begins in 1847 when she is a young woman—unravels a story that viewers discover is "unlikable" in its final outcome. Filmmaker María Luisa Bemberg here revisits a true story, that of Camila O'Gorman and her love affair with a Jesuit priest, Ladislao Gutiérrez. Viewers with a taste for romantic melodrama will likely enjoy the suspense of the fate of this forbidden affair between the independent, intelligent, and beautiful Camila and the dashing and sensitive Ladislao.

Camila is more multi-layered than appearances suggest, however. The lovers' story is adroitly set in the context of the dictatorship of Juan Manuel de Rosas, the Governor of Buenos Aires province (and later head of the Argentine

Confederation). Rosas inspired populist nationalism and cemented his rule in the support from the conservative Church and Argentine aristocracy for a "law and order" regime. He also used his paramilitary to repress dissent. The execution of (the pregnant) O'Gorman and Gutiérrez remains a potent symbol of the tyranny of the Rosas era. There is little doubt that *Camila* also uses history to make veiled commentary on the present, in this case the military rule in Bemberg's native Argentina that ended just prior to the film's production.

The feminist dimensions of the film must also be emphasized. Consistent with Bemberg's record as a filmmaker whose subjects are historical women, *Camila* interprets the past through the lens of O'Gorman's aspirations. Modern audiences will likely agree with the perspective of Camila—as Bemberg assigns it—that her traditional and privileged social class should be able to bear her enjoyment of personal, sexual, and intellectual freedom. Perhaps Camila has failed to heed her own childhood understanding that stories don't always end as likeably as one hopes.

See also: *I, the Worst of All*

Pauls, Alan. "On *Camila*: The Red, the Black, and the White." In *An Argentine Passion: María Luisa Bemberg and Her Films*, edited by John King, Sheila Whitaker and Rosa Bosch, 110–21. London: Verso, 2000.

Schwartz, Ronald. "*Camila*." In *Latin American Films, 1932–1994: A Critical Filmography*, 53–55. Jefferson, NC: McFarland, 1997.

Stevens, Donald F. "Passion and Patriarchy in Nineteenth-Century Argentina: María Luisa Bemberg's *Camila*." In *Based on a True Story: Latin American History at the Movies*, edited by Donald F. Stevens, 85–102. Wilmington, DE: Scholarly Resources, 1997.

Taylor, Claire. "María Luisa Bemberg Winks at the Audience: Performativity and Citation in *Camila* and *Yo La Peor De Todas*." In *Latin American Cinema: Essays on Modernity, Gender and National Identity*, edited by Lisa Shaw and Stephanie Dennison, 110–24. Jefferson, NC: McFarland, 2005.

The Camp at Thiaroye / Camp de Thiaroye (1987) Ousmane Sembène and Thierno Faty Sow; Algeria/Senegal/Tunisia; French and Wolof with English subtitles; Color; 147 m; Facets (VHS); Senegal, end of WWII.

The Camp at Thiaroye is essential viewing for the study of World War II in film. Its challenging interpretation of the colonial African experience of that conflict offers an important counterpoint to Western master narratives. Directors Ousmane Sembène and Thierno Faty Sow tell the story of a regiment of African soldiers in a Senegalese transit camp on the eve of their demobilization. Returning from their duties in Europe, these infantrymen arrive at port to a crowd of jubilant women and children—many of whom are French colonists—and are soon transported to Camp Thiaroye. At first observed as an isolated compound in a barren landscape, viewers will soon discern that the Camp is entirely "too close" to the city of Dakar for the tastes of Captain Labrousse and Major August. Their command is challenged by a variety of problems, not the least being the soldiers' desire to resume civilian life as free men in their native Senegal, Nigeria, Sudan, and Ivory Coast.

Freedom is a relative term for colonial subjects, however, and *The Camp at Thiaroye* shows the men's realization that their highly praised participation in the Allied/French war effort—which for many included imprisonment at Buchenwald—has not conferred equality with the colonizers. Captain Labrousse tells the men, "We are proud of you.... You have been true to the reputation of your fathers in 1914–1918." But paralleling this generational continuity is the continuation of colonial rule: racism, paternalism, manipulation, deceit, and, ultimately, violence govern the relations of these white military officers with their soldiers. The vulnerability of the infantrymen mirrors the status of the African colonial subject, and the filmmakers have masterfully succeeded in providing a detailed, microscopic look at the particular experience of these soldiers, while at the same time signaling the degrading character of colonial experience in general. "In Africa, there are Negroes, and in the army, discipline," argues Labrousse.

One of the most telling and powerful scenes of the film considers the costs to their identity that these men have suffered as a result of their colonial and military status. The soldiers finally receive French uniforms to replace those charitably given by the U.S. army when the regiment was liberated from Buchenwald. In barracks, some of the men are visibly despondent about the exchange, and are chastised by others that such mourning is misplaced: "We're men! We're Africans!" says one. Another exclaims, "We spent four years of suffering in Europe: cold, snow, bombings. And we're home! Why cry about American uniforms!" But African identity, some of these men know, cannot be so easily recovered, and the wearing of French uniforms only concretizes the reality of their subjugation. Interestingly in this confusing scenario of heroism and victimization, national and colonial identity, one of the main characters, Sergeant-Major Aloys Diatta, is taken for an American soldier in a Dakar brothel; the fact that he is black and American is not a problem until it's realized he isn't American after all. Suddenly he is a "negro" and the French madame insists he leave. To make matters worse, Diatta then encounters U.S. Military Police, who beat and detain him because they don't believe he is with French forces.

Such humiliations escalate in *The Camp at Thiaroye*, until a prolonged dispute over the soldiers' pay leads to the film's violent conclusion, when the men's organized resistance at the camp meets the more powerful force of French tanks and bombs.

See also: *Emitai*

Diawara, Manthia. "*Camp De Thiaroye.*" *Black Film Review* 6(3) (1992): 14–15.

Gugler, Josef. "Fiction, Fact and the Critic's Responsibility: *Camp De Thiaroye, Yaaba*, and *The Gods Must Be Crazy.*" In *Focus on African Films*, edited by Françoise Pfaff, 69–88. Bloomington: Indiana University Press, 2004.

Landy, Marcia. "Folklore, Memory, and Postcoloniality in Ousmane Sembène's Films." In *Cinematic Uses of the Past*, edited by Marcia Landy, 30–66. Minneapolis, MN: University of Minnesota Press, 1996.

Little, Roger, and Nicola Macdonald. "The Thiaroye Massacre in Word and Image." *AS-CALF Bulletin* 8 (Spring/Summer 1994): 18–37.

Murphy, David. "Dis-Membering Empire, Re-Membering Resistance: The Memory of Colonialism in *Emitai, Ceddo* and *Camp De Thiaroye.*" In *Sembene: Imagining Alternatives in Film and Fiction*, edited by David Murphy, 151–85. Oxford: James Currey, 2000.

———. "Mothers, Daughters and Prostitutes: The Representation of Women in Sembene's Work." In *Sembene: Imagining Alternatives in Film and Fiction*, edited by David Murphy, 124–50. Oxford: James Currey, 2000.

Shaka, Femi Okiremuete. "Vichy Dakar and the Other Story of French Colonial Stewardship: A Critical Reading of Ousmane Sembène and Thierno Faty Sow's *Camp De Thiaroye.*" *Research in African Literatures* 26(3) (Fall 1995): 67–77.

Canal / Kanal (1957) Andrzej Wajda; Poland; Polish and German with English subtitles; Black and White; 96 m; Facets (DVD; VHS); Poland, 1944.

From the outset, *Canal* does not harbor any illusions on behalf of its audience about the fate of its characters. Director Andrzej Wajda begins his story of participants in the 1944 Warsaw Uprising with a narrator's claim: "These are the heroes of the tragedy. Watch them closely, for these are the last hours of their lives." Adapted from the memoirs of Jerzy Stawínski, the film's "tragedy" is experienced by a company of the Underground Home Army—men and women under his command. Much of the film takes place in the sewer canals of the city, as the company tries to move from one section of the city to its downtown.

Bukoski, Anthony. "Wajda's *Kanal* and Mrozek's *Tango.*" *Literature/Film Quarterly* 20(2) (1992): 133–37.
Insdorf, Annette. "Styles of Tension." In *Indelible Shadows: Film and the Holocaust*, 3rd ed., 43–58. New York: Cambridge University Press, 2003.

Canoa (1976) Felipe Cazals; Mexico; Spanish; Color; 115 m; Facets (DVD); Mexico, 1968.

Canoa visits the tensions produced by the student movement in 1968—as well as by disparities between rural and urban Mexicans—in this fact-based story set in that year. A small group of hikers employed at the University of Puebla is stranded by inclement weather in the small village of San Miguel Canoa. Two of the hikers are killed in a machete attack and the rest are rescued by the intervention of the Mexican police.

See also: *Red Dawn*; *Night of the Pencils*

Berg, Charles. "*Canoa* by Felipe Cazals." *Film Quarterly* 32(3) (Spring 1979): 50–52.
Schwartz, Ronald. "*Canoa.*" In *Latin American Films, 1932–1994: A Critical Filmography*, 55–56. Jefferson, NC: McFarland, 1997.

The Captivating Star of Happiness / Zvezda plenitelnogo schastya (1975) Vladimir Motyl; Soviet Union; Russian with English subtitles; Color; 168 m; Image Entertainment (DVD); Russia, 1820s.

After the failed Decembrist uprising of imperial Russian army officers, the conspirators are exiled to Siberia. The film focuses on the decisions of their wives to leave their families and social stations in order to reunite with their husbands.

Ceddo / The People (1977) Ousmane Sembène; Senegal; French and Wolof with English subtitles; Color; 120 m; Facets (VHS); West Africa, conflating the 17th–19th centuries.

"The Princess has been captured!" Thus begins the drama of the fate of Princess Dior, daughter of Wolof King Demba. Dior has been kidnapped by one of the *ceddo*, or "people," a commoner subject of the king who is trying to prevent the further incursion of Islam and end the trade in slaves. But the complications of sectarian and internecine strife abound when the king orders two aristocratic rivals (one Muslim, one not) to find and rescue Dior. By film's end, the growing influence of the Imam leads to the killing of a Catholic missionary, and the king, as well as the abolition of idolatry and fetishism. Upon her release, in a reversal of her opposition to her *ceddo* captor, Dior murders the Imam.

Ceddo is set in West Africa in an amalgam of contexts that span the seventeenth through nineteenth centuries; the film compresses the European slave trade, Catholic missions, and Islamization into one period, and even deliberately plays with anachronisms like a scene of a Catholic mass in modern Dakar. *Ceddo* indicts the incursion of Christianity and Islam—and the failure of traditional authorities like the king—as the ruin of precolonial Africa: the village's traditional system of matrilineal inheritance, its economic practices, and its politics are being eroded over the course of the film. Dior's assertion of authority on behalf of the *ceddo* by film's end, however, suggests the possibility of purification and renewal. With this "hopeful" message director Sembène encourages his contemporary audience to realize their potential to reclaim their Africa.

See also: *Adanggaman; Sarraounia*

Cham, Mbye. "Official History, Popular Memory: Reconfiguration of the African Past in the Films of Ousmane Sembène." In *The Historical Film: History and Memory in Media,* edited by Marcia Landy, 261–66. Piscataway, NJ: Rutgers University Press, 2001.

Gupta, U. "Review of *Ceddo*." *Cineaste* 8(4) (Summer 1978): 37–38.

Iyam, David Uru. "The Silent Revolutionaries: Ousmane Sembene's *Emitai, Xala,* and *Ceddo*." *African Studies Review* 29(4) (December 1986): 79–87.

Kindem, G., and M. Steele. "*Emitai* and *Ceddo*: Women in Sembene's Films." *Jump Cut: A Review of Contemporary Media* 36 (May 1991): 52–60.

Murphy, David. "Dis-Membering Empire, Re-Membering Resistance: The Memory of Colonialism in *Emitai, Ceddo* and *Camp De Thiaroye*." In *Sembene: Imagining Alternatives in Film and Fiction,* edited by David Murphy, 151–85. Oxford: James Currey, 2000.

———. "Mothers, Daughters and Prostitutes: The Representation of Women in Sembene's Work." In *Sembene: Imagining Alternatives in Film and Fiction,* edited by David Murphy, 124–50. Oxford: James Currey, 2000.

Rosen, Philip. "Making a Nation in Sembene's *Ceddo*." *Quarterly Review of Film and Video* 13(1–3) (May 1991): 147–72.

Turkanian, Kate. "*Ceddo*: A Review." *Critical Arts Journal* 7(1) (1993): 122–26.

Chac the Rain God / Chac: Dios de la lluvia (1974) Rolando Klein; Mexico/Panama; Tzeltal and Spanish with English subtitles; Color; 95 m; Milestone (DVD, VHS); Mexico, unspecified/mythic.

Chac is about a small group of men from a drought-stricken Tzeltal village in Mexico who follow a diviner on a journey in search of water. *Chac* has been lauded for its visually arresting exploration of a Mayan legend. It has also been criticized. The exchange between director Klein and anthropologist Shelton H. Davis in the pages of *Jump Cut* clearly delineates the argument over whether the film exploited present-day Mayan Indians and misconstrues their culture, or whether art and commerce have combined here to create awareness and focus attention, in the words of Klein, "on a dying culture, ruthlessly crushed by our ever-growing technological society."

See also: *Atanarjaut; God' Gift; Keïta! The Heritage of the Griot; Yeelen*

Childs, James. "An Interview with Rolando Klein." *Literature/Film Quarterly* 5(3) (1977): 235–41.

Klein, Rolando. "The Filming of *Chac (God of Rain)*." *American Cinematographer* 57 (January 1976): 66–68.

Klein, Rolando, and Shelton H. Davis. "Debate on *Chac*." *Jump Cut: A Review of Contemporary Media* 15 (1977): 31.

Schwartz, Ronald. "*Chac (Chac: A Mayan Tale of Ritual and Magical Power)*." In *Latin American Films, 1932–1994: A Critical Filmography*, 60–61. Jefferson, NC: McFarland, 1997.

The Chant of Jimmie Blacksmith (1978) Fred Schepisi; Australia; English; Color; 114 m; New Yorker Films (theatrical); Australia, turn of the 20th century.

Jimmie Blacksmith is the son of a white father and aboriginal mother. As a half-caste adopted into the home of an English parson in an early twentieth-century Australian town, he has achieved the dubious status of conditional acceptance by the white community. Says the local officer who has admitted Jimmie into training for the local constabulary: "You show a lot of talent. You know your place."

Fred Schepisi's film, based on the novel by Thomas Keneally that was itself based on true events, studies Jimmie's eventually violent rejection of this uneasy "place" he has been allowed in white society. The film's bleak portrait of racism, segregation, and oppression is unremitting. A sympathetic liberal white schoolteacher (taken hostage by Jimmie) tries to explain to his captor some aboriginal history, but these paternalistic efforts only reinforce, rather than undermine, the extent of white hegemony. The impossibility of aboriginal assimilation, or autonomy, is also registered in the cinematographic and narrative framing of Jimmie as almost completely isolated from society.

See also: *Utu*

Griffiths, Gareth. "The Myth of Authenticity." In *The Post-Colonial Studies Reader*, edited by Bill Ashcroft, Gareth Griffiths, and Helen Tiffin, 237–41. London: Routledge, 1995.

McFarlane, Brian. *Words and Images: Australian Novels into Film*. Melbourne: Heinemann, 1984.

Mishra, Vijay. "Aboriginal Representations in Australian Texts." *Continuum: The Australian Journal of Media & Culture* 2(1) (1987): 165–88.

Rayner, Jonathan. "Fred Schepisi's Period Films." In *Contemporary Australian Cinema: An Introduction*, 78–84. Manchester: Manchester University Press, 2000.

Van den Bosch, Annette. "Australian History and Its Reconstruction in Australian Film." In *The First Australian History and Film Conference Papers*, edited by Anne Hutton, 244–65. New South Wales, Australia: Australia Film and Television School, 1982.

Wynne-Davies, Marion. "The Rhythm of Difference: Language and Silence in *The Chant of Jimmie Blacksmith* and *The Piano*." In *Postcolonial Literatures: Expanding the Canon*, edited by Deborah L. Madsen, 58–71. London: Pluto, 1999.

The Chekist (1992) Alexandr Rogozhkin; Russia; Russian with English subtitles; Color; 93 m; Cinema Parallel (VHS); Soviet Union, c. 1918–1922.

It is not an overstatement to describe *The Chekist* as an unrelenting and graphic portrayal of the execution of Russians at a Provincial headquarters of the Cheka (secret police, or VChK: "Extraordinary Commission for Combating Counterrevolution and Sabotage"). The film provides little direct explanation of its specific time period, although this is the era of "Red Terror," the Bolshevik campaign against counterrevolutionaries of 1918–1922. Instead of overt attention to the historical context of the Russian Civil War, viewers inhabit the world of the Cheka headquarters and rarely venture into the streets and homes of town or its surrounding countryside, unless to follow the main character, Comrade Srubov, in his interrogation activities as the Cheka chief and his brief respites at his (increasingly tension-filled) family home. At headquarters, a lavish but decaying remnant of the grand homes of the imperial era, a tribunal of three officers spends little time deliberating over the sentence for prisoners crammed into basement rooms: "Invectives against Cheka: firing squad . . . Anti-Soviet activity: firing squad. . . ." The list of offenders and offenses—subversive aristocrats, journalists, members of outlawed organizations, priests, merchants, "colonialists"—is considered with earnest but efficient attention to a thin protocol of hearings and motions. When a senior officer arrives, she exhorts the *troika* to "Pay no attention to details. All you need to know to pronounce a sentence is to know what class the accused belongs to, his education, his job. . . . We don't kill individuals. We destroy the bourgeois class. . . ."

Executions are performed in the same rigorous and mechanical manner. Scenes of naked women and men herded to the room where they are lined up and shot, carted away on an interior rail system, and mechanically hoisted to ground level outside for transport to mass graves are repeated many, many times throughout the film. Each of these scenes is unflinching in its execution, and despite the regularity and repetitiveness of the murders, director Rogozhkin introduces highly individual stories to each: women offer sexual favors in exchange for reprieve, some men cower and weep, some defiantly face the shooters instead of facing the wall of wooden doors, and others pray.

The Chekist's cast of Cheka characters are similarly differentiated. Young men assigned as executioners exhibit different reactions to their job. Some Cheka officers affect resignation while others insist on closer scrutiny of the accused in interrogations. Srubov is at once protagonist, symbol, and observer in the film. Arguably a weak point of the film, director Rogozhkin insists on tracing Srubov's character arc, following his cold complicity in the staggering number of executions, his increasing dislocation from "normal" life outside headquarter walls, his developing public reputation as an "ogre," and his descent into madness.

See also: *Le Coup de Grâce*; *The Red and the White*

Hoberman, J. "Murder Incorporated." *The Village Voice* 42 (25 February 1997): 63.

The Chess Players / Shatranj ke Khilari (1977) Satyajit Ray; India; Urdu and English with English subtitles; Color; 129 m; Kino (DVD, VHS); India, 1850s.

The Chess Players, an adaptation of a short story by Munshi Premchand, begins with a scene of two men facing each other in a chess game. A narrator's voiceover is heard: "If the King is lost, the game is lost."

In the context of Satyajit Ray's magnificent and carefully researched film about the British takeover of the Indian province of Oudh in 1856, the (Muslim) king is Wajid Ali Shah, a man more interested in poetry and other aspects of Lucknow's vibrant culture than the day-to-day challenges of governing. General Outram, the British head at Lucknow, describes the *nawab* as a "frivolous, effeminate, irresponsible, worthless king" who has "no business to rule."

The game at stake is nothing less than Indian national sovereignty, which, the film argues in an extended and satirical prologue that precedes the live-action narrative, has been eroded piece by piece as weak *nawabs* made deals with the British to retain their titles, and little more, in return for British protection. The narrator intones: "Lord Dalhousie was inordinately fond of cherries. How many had he eaten in the last ten years! Punjab, Burma, Nagpur, Satara, Jhansi ... the only cherry left is the cherry of Oudh...." (A still portrait of Dalhousie is animated; he topples crowns off cherries and pops the fruit into his mouth.)

The two chess players are Mir and Mirza, rich hereditary landlords in Lucknow whose passion for the game results in their indifference to their wives and apathy about the British threat. After all, agree Mir and Mirza during a conversation about the differences between Indian and British chess rules, the British have virtually ruled for a hundred years; if the king "pays up" and supports the British campaigns in Nepal or Afghanistan, then he keeps the throne.

Mir and Mirza are wonderfully drawn characters, and their sometimes comic exploits are followed in parallel to the negotiations between Outram and Wajid. The interplay of the two plots—Mir and Mirza looking to play chess in peace, and Outram and Wajid trying to avoid war in the process of Wajid giving up his crown—assumes the back and forth rhythm of a chess game. Arguably, the analogous plots also provide audiences with the opportunity to understand the process of colonization through two vehicles: identification with vivid characters like the Mir and Mirza, and the verbal explanation provided in the dialogue of Outram and Wajid, much of it framed in the form of speeches and pronouncements.

The structure of *The Chess Players* also reinforces the themes of the film. For Satyajit Ray, the apathy, cowardice, and collusion of the Indian elite in the face of the British takeover is a central feature of this period of Indian history. It is a young Hindu boy, Kaloo, who upon encountering Mir and Mirza in his abandoned village (to where they have fled in order to play chess undisturbed by the arrival in Lucknow of British troops) asks, "Why is nobody fighting the British?" The only answer of our two players is resumption of their beloved chess—this time adopting the British rules of the game.

See also: *Junoon*

Chakravarty, Sumita S. "The Recuperation of History and Memory." In *National Identity in Indian Popular Cinema 1947–1987*, 157–95. Austin: University of Texas Press, 1993.

Cooper, Darius. "Satyajit Ray's Political Vision of the Doubly Colonized." In *The Cinema of Satyajit Ray: Between Tradition and Modernity*, 177–212. Cambridge: Cambridge University Press, 2000.

———. "The Representation of Colonialism in Satyajit Ray's *The Chess Players*." In *Colonialism and Nationalism in Asian Cinema*, edited by Wimal Dissanayake, 174–89. Bloomington: Indiana University Press, 1994.

Dirks, Nicolas B. "The Sovereignty of History: Culture and Modernity in the Cinema of Satyajit Ray." In *Questions of Modernity*, edited by Timothy Mitchell, 148–65. Minneapolis, MN: University of Minnesota Press, 2000.

Ganguly, Suranjan. "Poetry into Prose: The Rewriting of Oudh in Satyajit Ray's *The Chess Players*." *Journal of Commonwealth Literature* 30(2) (1995): 17–24.

Robinson, Andrew. *Satyajit Ray: The Inner Eye*. London: A. Deutsch, 1989.

Chronicle of the Years of Embers / Chronique des années de braise/ Waqaii Sanawat Al-Jamr (1975) Mohammed Lakhdar-Hamina; Algeria; Arabic with English subtitles; Color; 177 m; Arab Film Distribution (VHS); Algeria, 1939–1954.

Chronicle of the Years of Embers considers the Algerian experience of French colonial rule and the struggle for independence. The film manages to feel epic or truly "historical" in scale, while traversing two decades of history through the microcosmic story of Ahmad, a poor peasant who becomes a revolutionary. The episodically structured chronological narrative begins with "The Years of Ashes." The desperation and tensions caused by drought in Ahmad's village—including a local war over a dike at a water source—cause Ahmad and his family to leave for the city. The film then follows Ahmad as he works at a salt mine, and then a threshing-gang, and returns to his village after the death of his wife and one of his two children from a typhoid epidemic. Intervening in yet another dispute at the water canal, Ahmad cries, "Aren't poverty, war, hunger, colonisation enough for you? Must blood flow for the drop of filthy water the settlers leave us? Aren't you ashamed?" Ahmad exhorts the villagers to "turn your guns" against the conquerors, and departs with several other armed men. After bombing the dam that redirects water to French settlers, he is captured and conscripted into service in Europe during World War II. Ahmad's return to Algeria is marked by the May 1945 French massacre of thousands of Algerians in retaliation for their killing of French settlers. In "The Years of Embers" the movement for Algerian independence is building. Working as a blacksmith in town, Ahmad meets Larbi, a political exile who is mobilizing locals for armed revolt. This section of the film examines Ahmad's early covert revolutionary activities, and the divisions caused by French-designed elections. After a remarkable scene of a political rally that turns into a bloodbath, Ahmad is imprisoned, and later retreats into the mountains. The final episode of the film, "The Years of Fire," shows Ahmad's surviving son discovering the story of his father's death, and his own flight to join the guerillas.

Ahmad's story is that of an ordinary Algerian man who is seeking a way to support his family. His radicalization is derived from necessity, not ideology: the French colonial authorities and settlers are his obstacle to a better life. Ahmad's friend Koider says, "I'm sick of hunger and poverty...." *Chronicle of the Years of Embers* roots the anticolonial struggle in Algeria in that refrain.

See also: *The Battle of Algiers*

Armes, Roy. "History as Myth: *Chronicle of the Years of Embers* (1975)." In *Postcolonial Images: Studies in North African Film*, 96–104. Bloomington: Indiana University Press, 2005.

Nassar, Issam. "Review of *Chronicle of the Years of Embers* and *The Mill*." *American Historical Review* 99(4) (October 1994): 1256–59.

Shafik, Viola. *Arab Cinema: History and Cultural Identity*. Cairo: American University in Cairo Press, 1998.

Circle of Deceit / Die Fälschung (1981) Volker Schlöndorff; West Germany; German with English subtitles; Color; 108 m; Kino (DVD; VHS); Lebanon, late 1970s.

Placing Western journalists at war-torn foreign sites is a very popular plot device in films about modern civil war. Audiences have in the reporter a character that will engage their empathy and be the conduit for understanding the conflict. The observations and personal dramas of the journalist are often the true subject of the films—rather than the conflicts themselves. Vicarious journeys to deadly climes have commercial appeal; the "history lessons" in these films are a thin veneer for romance and adventure.

Circle of Deceit's reporter is a German newspaperman, Georg. Georg has a disintegrating marriage back in Hamburg, a complicated love affair with a German widow in Beirut, and a cameraman buddy with whom he ventures into the streets to observe the Lebanese Civil War. This is a good film; in the expert hands of Volker Schlöndorff it is suspenseful, poses ethical dilemmas forcefully, is a memorable study of the milieu of foreign reporters, and suggests some of the political, social, and religious dimensions of the conflict. But for all its pretensions of having been filmed "on the still smoldering streets of Beirut" (as stated in Kino's home video promotional material), *Circle of Deceit* could almost be as easily set in any other city where foreign journalists are found around the hotel bar in between their intermittent forays into the real world outside.

See also: *Boat People*; *The Killing Fields*; *The Year of Living Dangerously*

Green, Norma Fay. "Press Dress: The Beige Brigade of Movie Journalists Outdoors." In *Beyond the Stars*, edited by Paul Loukides and Linda K. Fuller. Bowling Green, OH: Bowling Green State University Popular Press, 1990.

Moeller, Hans-Bernhard, and George Lellis. "*Circle of Deceit.*" In *Volker Schlöndorff's Cinema: Adaptation, Politics, and the "Movie-Appropriate,"* 194–205. Carbondale: Southern Illinois University, 2002.

City of Sadness / Beiqing chengshi (1989) Hou Hsiao-hsien; Taiwan; Taiwanese, Cantonese, Mandarin and Japanese; Color; 157 m; Artificial Eye, United Kingdom (VHS); Taiwan, 1945–1949.

City of Sadness revolves around the story of the Lin family of Taiwan, particularly three of four brothers in this extended family. The lives of two sisters, friends of the family, are woven into, and affect, the Lins' experiences as well. With the surrender of Japan in 1945, and the end of almost 50 years of Japanese colonial rule in Taiwan, Chinese Nationalists attempted to establish political control. Each character's story is affected by the February 28 (1947) "incident," when popular protest in Taipei spread into a rebellion against Nationalist rule and the death of thousands of citizens. The aftermath of the quelled rebellion included a wave of arrests and executions. The depiction of the event is largely off screen; the historical meaning of February 28 is defined in its effects on the film's characters, rather than its material actuality as an event.

City of Sadness has a highly complex storyline and a very rigorous cinematic style that supports the thematic structure. It is also a beautiful and poignant film that effectively marries ideas, aesthetic, and narrative. Its elliptical approach suggests, rather than tells, and its distant camerawork creates a relationship between the viewer and the subject/history that is observational rather than experiential or didactic. Ultimately, the film makes marginal people the voice of this period of Taiwan's history, and the conduit to present-day constructions of Taiwan's national history and memory. For the Lin family, and by extension the Taiwanese, the period of 1945–1949 was exceptionally turbulent, conditioned by violence, vulnerability, voicelessness, dislocation, subjugation, and loss.

See also: *Good Men, Good Women*; *The Puppetmaster*; *A Time to Live and a Time to Die*

Li, Tuo. "Narratives of History in the Cinematography of Hou Xiaoxian." *Positions* 1(3) (Winter 1993): 805–15.

Lu, Tonglin. "From a Voiceless Father to a Father's Voice: Hou Xiaoxian: *A Time to Live and a Time to Die*; *City of Sadness*; *The Puppetmaster*." In *Confronting Modernity in the*

Cinemas of Taiwan and Mainland China, 95–115. Cambridge: Cambridge University Press, 2002.

Reynaud, Bérénice. *A City of Sadness*. London: BFI, 2002.

Yip, June Chun. "Remembering and Forgetting Part II: Hou Hsiao-hsien's Taiwan Trilogy." In *Envisioning Taiwan: Fiction, Cinema, and the Nation in the Cultural Imaginary*, 85–130. Durham, NC: Duke University Press, 2004.

The Cloud-Capped Star / *Meghe dhaka tara* (1960) Ritwik Ghatak; India; Bengali with English subtitles; Black and White; 122 m; Facets (DVD); Calcutta, late 1950s.

Nita is a young woman in Calcutta, East Pakistan in the 1950s. Her father's income as a teacher is meager, and her older brother Shankar contributes little as he dreams of success as a classical singer. Nita sacrifices her university studies, her marriage plans, and her health for the sake of the family's welfare. This is a bleak story, critical of the Bengali family, gender roles in this society, and the effect of the 1947 partition of India on the refugees it created.

See also: *Hot Winds*

Bellour, Raymond. "The Film We Accompany." *Rouge* 3 (2004), http://www.rouge.com.au/3/film.html (accessed May 30, 2006).

Bhaskar, Ira. "Myth and Ritual: Ghatak's *Meghe Dhaka Tara*." *Journal of Arts and Ideas* 3 (April–June 1983): 43–50.

Biswas, Moinak. "Her Mother's Son: Kinship and History in Ritwik Ghatak." *Rouge* 3 (2004), http://www.rouge.com.au/3/ghatak.html (accessed May 30, 2006).

Cooper, Pravina. "Ritwik Ghatak between the Messianic and the Material." *Asian Cinema: a Publication of the Asian Cinema Studies Society* 10(2) (1999): 96–106.

Kemp, Philip. "*Cloud-Capped Star/Meghe Dhaka Tara*." *Sight & Sound* 7 (September 1997): 39.

Levich, Jacob. "Subcontinental Divide." *Film Comment* 33 (March/April 1997): 30–37.

Colonel Chabert / *Le Colonel Chabert* (1994) Yves Angelo; France; French with English subtitles; Color; 110 m; Facets (VHS); Battle of Eylau, 1807, and post-Napoleonic France.

The opening scene of *Colonel Chabert* exemplifies the emotional power of the cinema when it recreates the past. Beethoven's eloquent "Ghost Trio" (*Piano Trio in D Major Op. 70 No. 1*) accompanies a close-up image of hands unbuttoning another's coat. Imbued with strong tones of blue and black, punctuated by the dark red of blood and the bright red of Napoleonic uniforms and helmet plumes, more close-ups appear in succession. Sabers, breast plates, boots, pants, and rings are stripped from stiffening bodies. Piles of sorted materials grow higher. Bodies are dragged across frozen ground to carts and a horse is dragged to its place on a pyre. Then, a long shot of a desolate, snowy plain shows horsemen supervising the cleanup on this vast battlefield. Horses pull carts groaning with bodies, men pile men into mass graves. Close shots of these darkened piles show us the faces of these dead soldiers; they appear at rest, or tragically lost, depending on your sensibilities.

This recreation of the aftermath of the 1807 Battle of Eylau is stunning. It is rapturously beautiful and powerfully conveys information about the historical experience of the dead, as well as the surviving—whose practical and grim work is detailed in a way that allows viewers to reflect on the minutiae of war, rather than its grand outcomes.

Action shifts to Paris, where the character of Colonel Chabert alleges he is a survivor of this scene from Eylau, someone who was mistaken for dead and crawled his way out of the grave. The film follows his attempts to recover his earnings from his wife, who believing Chabert perished at Eylau, remarried a man set on achieving rank in Louis XVIII's new Chamber of Peers. Based on a Balzac story, *Colonel Chabert* is a highly evocative depiction of post-Napoleonic power relations, as the elite try to win back or maintain their wealth and status in a new political era of constitutional monarchy.

Colonel Chabert's wonderful performances, absorbing dialogue, and reflective narrative make it worthwhile viewing. It is recommended here especially for that opening scene of a battlefield—3 minutes in all—because it represents a poignant marriage of art and history.

Hanley, Sarah. "European History in Text and Film: Community and Identity in France, 1550–1945." *French Historical Studies* 25 (Winter 2002): 3–10.

Murray, Scott. "*Le Colonel Chabert.*" *Cinema Papers* 103 (March 1995): 48.

Neff, Renfreu. "*Colonel Chabert.*" *The Film Journal* 98 (January/February 1995): 50–51.

Reader, Keith. "*Le Colonel Chabert.*" *Sight & Sound* 5 (May 1995): 43.

Schama, Simon. "Clio at the Multiplex." *The New Yorker* 73 (January 19, 1998): 38–43.

Vincendeau, Ginette. "Unsettling Memories." *Sight & Sound* 5 (July 1995): 30–32.

Colonel Wolodyjowski / Pan Wolodyjowski

Colonel Wolodyjowski / Pan Wolodyjowski (1969) Jerzy Hoffman; Poland; Polish with English subtitles; Color; 147 m; Facets (DVD, VHS); Poland, 1668.

Colonel Wolodyjowski is based on the last in a historical novel trilogy by Henryk Sienkiewicz. A modest knight and his sidekick round up a fighting force against a formidable Turkish invasion of a fortress on the border of Eastern Poland in the seventeenth century. Unabashedly adventurous and nationalistic in spirit, *Colonel Wolodyjowski* is a celebratory marriage of history film and popular entertainment.

Mazierska, Ewa. "In the Land of Noble Knights and Mute Princesses: Polish Heritage Cinema." *Historical Journal of Film, Radio & Television* 21(2) (June 1, 2001): 167–82.

Come and See / Idi i smotri

Come and See / Idi i smotri (1985) Elem Klimov; Soviet Union; Russian/Belarusian with English subtitles; Color; 140 m; Kino (DVD, VHS); Byelorussia, WWII.

Adopting the familiar motif of a young boy's witness to the madness of war, Elem Klimov's *Come and See* uses astonishingly effective imagistic and aural effects to suggest Florya's experience of 1943 Nazi-occupied Byelorussia. Beginning with the boy's innocent and eager joining with the local partisans, and concluding with an expressionistic carnivalesque scene of Nazi atrocities in a small village, the film plunges viewers into the sensory bombardment Florya must endure.

In a key early scene, the novice Florya, told to remain at camp while the partisans leave the forest for a mission, is nearly killed in an aerial bombing. The noise seriously damages his hearing. His injury makes Florya a possibly unreliable historical witness for viewers, but it also attunes him to the sounds of his own deeply muffled breathing and voice. This sensation of muffled sound is frequently transmitted to the audience in the film's sound work, leading to their entrapment in Florya's own perceptions of his experience. The effects for some will be so histrionic as to be too much a departure from conventional cinematic realism; for others, Klimov's highly expressive method offers insight into the subjection of vulnerable people to war and occupation.

Le Fanu, Mark. "*Come and See.*" *Sight & Sound* 56 (Spring 1987): 140–1.

Stein, Elliot. "*Come and See* Indelible Images: The War at Ground Zero." *Film Comment* 34(5) (September/October 1998): 31–32.

Wrathall, John, and Julian Graffy. "Excursion to Hell." *Sight & Sound* 14(2) (February 2004): 28–30.

Youngblood, Denise J. "Post-Stalinist Cinema and the Myth of World War II: Tarkovskii's *Ivan's Childhood* (1962) and Klimov's *Come and See* (1985)." *Historical Journal of Film, Radio and Television* 14(4) (1994): 413–19.

———. "A War Remembered: Soviet Films of the Great Patriotic War." *American Historical Review* 106(3) (June 2001): 838–56.

Le Coup De Grâce / Der Fangschuß (1976) Volker Schlöndorff; France/West Germany; German and French with English subtitles; Black and White; 98 m; Facets (DVD; VHS); Latvia, 1919.

This adaptation of Marguerite Yourcenar's novel is the story of fictional characters Countess Sophie von Reval, her brother Konrad, and their childhood friend, Prussian Erich von Lohmond. The film is largely set at the sibling's ancestral estate Kratovice, near Riga. It is 1919, and the Russian civil war has brought the Bolsheviks to the brink of success against Latvian nationalist holdouts, despite the help of German officers like von Lohmond, who with "nothing to do" back in postwar Berlin has taken up the "lost cause" of the nobility's fight to preserve their homes and privileges in the Baltic States.

Le Coup de Grâce has many interesting elements: its performances, *mise en scène*, the narrative perspective provided by Erich—which audiences are forced to question—and the characterization of the female protagonist all make for a layered and textured film. From the point of view of its representation of the past, the film is equally rich. Erich's opening voiceover says, "Kratovice was in that last borderland of Eastern Europe where Russian or German place names no longer meant anything." The often shifting outlines of antagonists in the civil war is symbolized effectively here, especially in the character of Sophie. Despite her sentiments about the family estate, she sympathizes with the Latvian Bolsheviks in the village, and later—perhaps in reaction to her unrequited love for Erich and her discovery of his sexual relationship with Konrad—joins the revolutionaries on a campaign against the "white" holdouts. Consistent with the inversion trope that occupies much of *Le Coup de Grâce*, the final scene, where Sophie is eventually captured and shot by Erich, challenges any comfortable ideas about the inviolability of the boundaries of the personal and the political.

See also: *The Chekist*; *The Red and the White*

Corrigan, Timothy. "Types of History: Schlöndorff's *Coup De Grâce.*" In *New German Film: The Displaced Image*, rev. ed., 54–73. Bloomington: Indiana University Press, 1994.

Moeller, Hans-Bernhard, and George Lellis. "*Coup De Grâce.*" In *Volker Schlöndorff's Cinema: Adaptation, Politics, and the "Movie-Appropriate,"* 144–54. Carbondale: Southern Illinois University, 2002.

**The Courage of the People / The Night of San Juan / El coraje del pueblo /
La Noche de San Juan** (1971) Jorge Sanjinés; Italy/Bolivia; Spanish and Quechua
with English subtitles; Color; 90 m; Facets (VHS); Bolivia, 1942–1967.

In 1967 tin miners were massacred by the Bolivian army, the result of rising
fears of communist influence in the building protest by workers over working and
living conditions. Director Jorge Sanjinés makes no apologies for creating films
that defend the cause of Bolivian Indians, condemn American imperialism, and
criticize the role of the military in Bolivian history. These themes are taken up in
The Courage of the People; using a documentary–realist form, the film reconstructs
the event itself, and uses some of the participants as actors and narrators.

See also: *Blood of the Condor; The Principal Enemy*

n/a. "The Courage of the People: An Interview with Jorge Sanjines." *Cineaste* 5 (Spring
    1972): 18–20.
Schwartz, Ronald. "*El Coraje Del Pueblo (The Courage of the People).*" In *Latin American
    Films, 1932–1994: A Critical Filmography,* 70–71. Jefferson, NC: McFarland, 1997.

Cromwell (1970) Ken Hughes; United Kingdom; English; Color; 145 m;
Columbia/Tristar (DVD, VHS); Great Britain, 1640–1653.

Sometimes there are good lessons learned in the viewing of a bad historical film.
Cromwell might fit the bill, depending on one's patience with its errors of fact,
its stock characters, its lifeless directing, and the strained performances of Richard
Harris in the title role of Oliver Cromwell and Alec Guinness as King Charles I. For
forgiving viewers, posing questions like "why does the film show Cromwell as an
early opponent of King Charles, when he was not?" or "why does the film end with
Cromwell's dissolution of Parliament and his appointment as Lord Protector, and
not later?" might be a fruitful starting point in considering historical debates about
the English Civil War and Protectorate, or about the challenges of engaging the
past on screen. Some of the faults of *Cromwell,* and answers to such questions, are
found in the film's striving for heightened drama, its need to compress time, and
strong interest in characterizing Cromwell as a hero of early Western democracy.

See also: *Winstanley*

Herman, Gerald H., and Wendy S. Wilson. "Unit 7: The Crises of the Seventeenth Century.
    Teacher's Guide: *Cromwell.*" In *World History on the Screen: Film and Video Resources,*
    43–45. Portland, Maine: Walch, 1990.
Williamson, Hugh Ross. "Epistle Dedicatory: To Ken Hughes." In *Who Was the Man in
    the Iron Mask? And Other Historical Enigmas,* 9–11. London: Penguin, 1955.

Crows and Sparrows / Wuya yumaque (1949) Zheng Junli; China; Mandarin
with English subtitles; Black and White; 113 m; International Film Circuit (VHS);
Shanghai, China, 1948–1949.

Crows and Sparrows is set in late 1940s Shanghai, on the verge of the Communist takeover of power in China. The poor tenants of a building owned by a
Nationalist official about to flee the country for Taiwan worry about their fate.
With the pending sale of the tenement, they scheme to avoid eviction, but mistrust
among them complicates their plans. The arrival of the People's Liberation Army
in the city saves them from homelessness and destitution. As a relieved tenant,
Mr. Kong says, "This time the New Year brings a new society."

Crows and Sparrows is a wonderful work of social commentary, with vivid characterization and a neorealist approach that measures up to the best in European cinema of the era. Particularly striking is its portrait of the corrupt speculation running rampant on the eve of the Communist victory. Landlord Hou, for example, is dismayed that property prices are not rising like other goods, but he has a scheme to use a treasury bill to buy a cache of gold, convert the gold to rice, and then sell the rice to hoarders. The money he earns from the rice will be used to buy gold to secret away to Taiwan.

The production history of *Crows and Sparrows* was itself affected by the civil war between the Nationalist Government of Republican China and Chinese Communist forces, mirroring the themes of the film. When filming began in Shanghai in 1947, Zheng Junli adopted elaborate ruses to achieve the approval of Nationalist officials, including covertly working from a different shooting script than that passed by censors.

See also: *Farewell, My Concubine; Good Men, Good Women; Joyless Street; Record of a Tenement Gentleman*

Wang, Yiman. "*Crows and Sparrows*: Allegory on a Historical Threshold." In *Chinese Films in Focus: 25 New Takes*, edited by Chris Berry, 65–72. London: BFI, 2003.

Cry Freedom (1987) Richard Attenborough; United Kingdom; English; Color; 157 m; Universal Studios Home Entertainment (DVD, VHS); South Africa, 1970s.

Cry Freedom was deemed a failure by critics and box office figures. The film nevertheless contains so much (unrealized) potential to be a powerful and instructive story about 1970s South Africa that it warrants analysis.

It is difficult to assign a principle subject to *Cry Freedom*. The first half of this epic-length film is about Stephen Biko, the founder of the "black consciousness" movement. Audiences learn about Biko's ideas, activism, and his death in police custody through the story of his emerging friendship with Donald Woods, a white South African editor of a liberal newspaper. The second half of *Cry Freedom* offers brief retrospective glimpses of Biko. As Woods crusades for an inquest into the cause of Biko's death—officially regarded as the result of a hunger strike—Woods is declared a "banned person" and eventually chooses flight from the country in order to tell Biko's story to the world. In this half of the film, Woods occasionally recalls the words of his friend, Biko becoming a kind of muse that exhorts Woods to courage and a fight for justice.

But this ghostly Biko is little match for the emphasis on the suspense-filled story of the subterfuge of Woods and his family to reach neighboring Lesotho. *Cry Freedom* asks us to engage in the drama of the Woods family's principled flight to freedom. Compelling as that story of escape is, it is a pale shadow to earlier scenes of Biko, a poor, oppressed black South African, victim in the worst way of the official system of apartheid. Perhaps director Attenborough wants viewers to be consoled by the fact that Woods carries his manuscript *Biko* into exile. But it's not difficult to feel affronted by a narrative structure in which Biko's story is paralleled with scenes of an intact and reunited white family safely ensconced in an airplane—accompanied by a Lesotho official—that carries them far away from the mess of apartheid.

Looking beyond the problems in *Cry Freedom*'s narrative emphasis, one discovers some worthwhile elements. The scene of the bulldozing of the township during opening credits establishes journalistic and documentary authority for the film by combining live action and still photos. Woods' visit to the Minister of Police is chilling; the minister's "reasoned" defense of Afrikaner interests in South Africa and his concern about police brutality is soon realized as sinister in later scenes that describe his duplicity. And nothing captures Biko's helplessness, vulnerability, and victimization more than the scene of his beaten body—his brain badly damaged—dangerously bouncing about in the back of a police van en route via poor roads to a distant hospital. Apart from the tiresome anthemic score, there is a wonderful restraint in the performances and the execution of these scenes, and a relief to hear few histrionics in a polemical film.

As in so many historical films, *Cry Freedom* briefly engages our emotional interest in some of the individuals who make and are unmade by history. But while the film might also pique our curiosity about the historical context of the South African system, it offers virtually nothing in the form of explanation. Attenborough instructs us that apartheid is racist, that racism is unjust, that injustice caused a dilemma for white liberal South Africans, and that black activism was warranted and courageous. The simplicity of this message could be construed as dangerously reductive, or importantly consciousness-raising, for Western audiences.

See also: *A Dry White Season*; *Mapantsula*

Carchidi, Victoria. "Representing South Africa: Apartheid from Print to Film." *Film & History: An Interdisciplinary Journal of Film and Television Studies* 21(1) (1991): 20–27.

———. "South Africa from Text to Film: *Cry Freedom* and *A Dry White Season*." In *Literature and Film in the Historical Dimension: Selected Papers from the Fifteenth Annual Florida State University Conference on Literature and Film,* edited by John D. Simons, 47–61. Gainesville: University Press of Florida, 1994.

Gevisser, Mark. "Review of *Cry Freedom*." *The Nation* 246(1) (January 9, 1988): 30–32.

Nixon, Rob. "Cry White Season: Anti-Apartheid Heroism and the American Screen." In *Homelands, Harlem and Hollywood: South African Culture and the World Beyond,* edited by Rob Nixon, 77–97. New York: Routledge, 1994.

Whitely, A. "Apartheid Chic." *Film Comment* 23(6) (November/December 1987): 11–14, 16.

Daens (1993) Stijn Coninx; Belgium/France/Netherlands; Dutch with English subtitles; Color; 138 m; Fox Lorber (VHS); Flanders, Belgium, 1890s to 1907.

Similar to *Germinal* in its almost pedantic simplicity, *Daens* is an accessible overview of social and political conflict in late nineteenth-century Belgium. Pieter Daens, the real-life Catholic priest turned social and political reformer, is its subject. The film follows a chronological narrative of his advocacy of improved industrial working conditions in the Flemish town of Aalst, his eventual advocacy of universal suffrage, and his election as an independent to the Belgian parliament.

Typical of adulatory biopics, the film's narrative approach positions Daens as central to events in Belgian history at the turn of the twentieth century. For example, almost immediately following a scene devoted to Daens' preaching a sermon arguing the necessity of universal suffrage, viewers watch Belgium's Parliament pass such a bill. While such an interpretation of Daens' influence might be emotionally satisfying to audiences who become invested in Daens' passionate struggles on behalf of the working class, it is a simplification of history to isolate him as the sole force behind reform in an era when modern and traditional political systems and ideologies clashed in a prolonged period of transition. Explanation of the state of Belgium's constitutional monarchy in the late nineteenth century is provided in simply drawn characters representing conservative monarchists and clerics, timid and socially isolated liberals, rightist thugs, and well-meaning but too-rash socialists. A brief allusion to the Congo ventures of Belgian King Leopold II is provided in a royal banquet scene that introduces his African servants.

Director Stijn Coninx's fashioning of Pieter Daens' character is only slightly more dimensional. This is an exploration of the public persona of Daens; a few stock scenes depict a private side to the man when he anguishes with his brother—a local printer—about the personal toll of his actions. But the film assumes his motivations stem from moral conviction and an innate sense of justice stirred by his observation of the desperate plight of factory children. The Daens of this film is a public figure, an orator, and an icon of conviction in the face of threats from his church, opposition politicians, and street thugs.

See also: *Germinal*; *The Organizer*

Bright, Martin. "*Daens.*" *Sight & Sound* 4 (April 1994): 41–42.
Brown, Mark. "The Big Picture: *Daens.*" *Socialist Review* 211 (September 1997): 35.
Jenkins, Gareth. "The Workers' Friend: *Daens.*" *Socialist Review* 175 (May 1994): 24.

The Damned / La Caduta degli dei (1969) Luchino Visconti; Italy/Switzerland/West Germany; English with English-dubbed German and Italian; Color; 150 m; Facets (DVD, VHS); Germany, 1933–34.

News of the 1933 Reichstag fire arrives at an Essenbeck family dinner. The steel baron patriarch, Joachim von Essenbeck, professes to despise the Nazis, but in order to protect the family's assets decides that his new vice president should be cousin Konstantin, a factory manager whose association with the paramilitary *Sturmabteilung* places him in favor with the new Hitler regime. The drama that unfolds from the dinner party shows family members' involvement in murder, pedophilia, and other corrupt machinations for power. Those who protest the family's complicity with the Nazis are exiled and incarcerated. Visconti's highly stylized family drama places a damning lens on the corruption and moral decay of the German industrial elite, and the fatal consequences of its self-aggrandizement in the early years of the Third Reich. When Friedrich, the ambitious lover of Joachim's daughter Sophia, realizes his next task will be to assassinate Konstantin, he moans, "God, the complicity grows." Cousin Aschenbach, a member of the SS whose manipulation of Friedrich, Sophia, and others in the family suggests the foolishness of anyone who thinks they can manipulate the Nazis, comments, "They are using National Socialism as an instrument for their own ambitions. They still don't understand what National Socialism really is." By film's end, Visconti suggests the only winners among the von Essenbecks are those whose brutality, decadence, and submission to Hitler matches that of the Nazis themselves.

See also: *Mephisto*

Bacon, Henry. "Visconti and Germany." In *Visconti: Explorations of Beauty and Decay*, 139–87. Cambridge: Cambridge University Press, 1998.
Insdorf, Annette. "The Condemned and Doomed." In *Indelible Shadows: Film and the Holocaust*, 3rd ed., 125–36. New York: Cambridge University Press, 2003.
Mellen, Joan. "Fascism in the Contemporary Film." *Film Quarterly* 24(4) (Summer 1971): 2–19.
Ravetto, Kriss. *The Unmaking of Fascist Aesthetics*. Minneapolis, MN: University of Minnesota Press, 2002.

A Dance for Heroes / Finzan (1990) Cheick Oumar Sissoko; Mali/Germany; Bambara with English subtitles; Color; 107 m; California Newsreel (VHS); Mali, contemporary.

At turns comic and tragic, *A Dance for Heroes* follows the social upheaval in Sabugu and Konyumani, two Malian villages, when a widow resists her arranged marriage, and her niece resists a traditional clitoridectomy. This is an activist film, dedicated "To the African woman" and condemning patriarchal customs. It also shows many dimensions of modern Mali's history and modernization: the peasants protest the authoritarian government's millet pricing; widow Nanyuma's betrothed has returned to the village from France; and the village griot (oral historian) is now recording on paper the negotiations between the local chief and the government official.

DeLuca, Laura, and Shadrack Kamenya. "Representation of Female Circumcision in *Finzan, a Dance for the Heroes*." *Research in African Literatures* 26(3) (Fall 1995): 83–86.

Gugler, Josef. "*Finzan* (1990): Gender Conflict and Village Solidarity." In *African Film: Re-Imagining a Continent*, 160–67. Bloomington: Indiana University Press, 2003.

Danton (1983) Andrzej Wajda; France/Poland/West Germany; French and dubbed French with English subtitles; Color; 136 m; Facets (DVD), Home Vision Entertainment (VHS); France, 1793–1794.

On its surface, *Danton* tells the story of the conflict between two leading revolutionaries at the height of the French Revolution's "terror." Georges-Jacques Danton is the high-living and disillusioned populist. Robespierre is the grave, austere, and uncompromising ideologue whose commitment to the survival of the nascent Republic sanctions the investigation, trial, and execution of its enemies. These "great men" and their differences create a dramatically pleasing sparring match when Danton must now defend himself in front of the Revolutionary Tribunal. This "courtroom" scene pits the protagonist against Robespierre's apparently unyielding desire to rid the nation of the forces of counterrevolution. The performances of Gérard Depardieu in the title role and Wojciech Pszoniak as Robespierre elevate a somewhat formulaic narrative structure to an intense and engaging battle of wits and principles.

Danton also commissions the past to address the contemporary concerns of the filmmakers. The film is based on the 1931 play by Stanislawa Przybyszewska. Depending on one's interpretation, *Danton* is about the radical phase of the revolution, the Stalinist regime, the Polish Solidarity movement, or more generally, as Elaine McAllister says, "the nature of political power" and the "problem of idealism gone astray." The film also engages contemporary debate about national myths. Director Wajda's interpretation of one of the most important episodes in French history aroused Mitterand-era leftists to paroxysms of protest: how could *Danton* so misread the past by portraying Robespierre as virtually totalitarian in his actions? No less interesting is the film's opposite, enthusiastic, reception in Poland.

See also: *La Marseillaise; Napoléon; The Night at Varennes; Ridicule*

Darnton, Robert. "*Danton*." In *Past Imperfect: History According to the Movies*, edited by Mark C. Carnes, 104–09. New York: Henry Holt, 1995.

———. "Film: *Danton* and the *Double Entendre*." In *The Kiss of Lamourette: Reflections in Cultural History*, 37–52. New York; London: W.W. Norton, 1990.

Falkowska, Janina. *The Political Films of Andrzej Wajda: Dialogism in Man of Marble, Man of Iron,* and *Danton.* Oxford: Berghahn Books, 1996.

Hunt, David. "Andrzej Wajda and the 'Reign of the People.'" *Radical History Review* 28(30) (1984): 141–50.

McAllister, Elaine. "Film as Historical Text: *Danton.*" In *Literature and Film in the Historical Dimension: Selected Papers from the Fifteenth Annual Florida State University Conference on Literature and Film,* edited by John D. Simons, 63–73. Gainesville: University Press of Florida, 1994.

Day of Wrath / Vredens Dag (1943) Carl Theodor Dreyer; Denmark; Danish with English subtitles; Black and White; 97 m; Criterion (DVD), Facets (VHS); Denmark, 1623.

Adapted from the play *Anne Pedersdotter* by Hans Wiers-Jenssen, *Day of Wrath* is set in a village of Denmark in the early seventeenth century. The fictional story of the prosecution of an older woman, Marthe, as a witch, becomes the catalyst for a study of secrets and denunciation in this morally upright Protestant society. The film has a very distinctive, austere style: its lighting, camerawork, and interiors create the effect of characters being under intense scrutiny and personal constraint. The local pastor, Absalon, must live with the knowledge of his false testimony at a witch trial some years before, when he attempted to secure the affections of Anne, the daughter of the accused. Now his second wife, Anne confesses her love for stepson, Martin.

Produced as it was in Nazi-occupied Denmark, the film is often interpreted as an allegory of the persecution of the innocent in a dictatorial society. *Day of Wrath* is also of interest for its incorporation of written documents in scenes, such as the records of Marthe's confession. The disjunction between written record and historical truth or meaning is an important theme in the film. The film is also a close study of gender and family relations in early modern Denmark, considering in addition to the religious context of the European witch hunts, its social underpinnings as well.

See also: *Anna Göldin, the Last Witch; The Passion of Joan of Arc*

Coiner, Miles. "Dramaturgy and Theme: A Comparison of *Day of Wrath* and *Anne Pedersdotter.*" *Literature/Film Quarterly* 17(2) (1989): 123–28.

Davis, Natalie Zemon. "'Any Resemblance to Persons Living or Dead': Film and the Challenge of Authenticity." *The Yale Review* 76(4) (1987): 457–82.

Pipolo, Tony. "Historical Consciousness in Carl Dryer's *Day of Wrath.*" *Persistence of Vision: The Journal of the Film Faculty of the City University of New York* 8 (1990): 15–28.

Dersu Uzala (1975) Akira Kurosawa; Japan/Soviet Union; Russian with English subtitles; Color; 140 m; Facets (DVD; VHS); Eastern Siberia, 1902–1910.

This story of a Russian army officer commissioned to explore and map the wilds of Eastern Siberia begins in 1910. Arseniev is searching for the gravesite of an "old friend" but clearing for a settlement has made the cedar trees that mark the spot unrecognizable. Flashback to the chronological beginning of the friendship: an intertitle describes the year as 1902, and a voiceover lends the narrative a historical authority, residing in the semi-fictional memoirs of Vladimir Arseniev. "That year, my assignment was to go to the Shkotovo area in the Ussuri region to make a topographic survey." Soon, Arseniev and his party meet Dersu

Uzala, a Nanai hunter who agrees to be their guide. A deep friendship develops between Arseniev and Dersu, whose family was the victim of a smallpox epidemic. The dramatic exploits of the explorers under the demanding natural conditions, the film's cinematography, and the characterization are only a few of the many highlights of the film. *Dersu Uzala* captures an intimate cross-cultural relationship in a landscape on the verge of exploitation by Western civilization.

Daney, Serge. "One More Bear (*Dersu Uzala*)." In *Cahiers Du Cinéma: Vol. 4, 1973–1978: History, Ideology, Cultural Struggle: An Anthology from Cahiers Du Cinéma Nos. 248–292, September 1973-September 1978*, edited by David Wilson and Bérénice Reynaud, 289–95. London: Routledge, 2000.

Nichols, Johanna. "Stereotyping Interethnic Communication: The Siberian Native in Soviet Literature." In *Between Heaven and Hell: The Myth of Siberia in Russian Culture*, edited by Yuri Slezkine and Galya Diment, 185–214. New York: St. Martin's Press, 1993.

Prince, Stephen. *The Warrior's Camera: The Cinema of Akira Kurosawa*. Princeton, NJ: Princeton University Press, 1991.

Prynn, David. "Biographical Sketch of Vladimir Arsenev." In *Amur Tiger*, 11–13. Edinburgh: Russian Nature Press, 2004.

Richie, Donald. "*Dersu Uzala*." In *The Films of Akira Kurosawa*, 195–203. Berkeley, CA: University of California Press, 1996.

Diên Biên Phu (1992) Pierre Schoendoerffer; France; French with English subtitles; Color; 125 m; TFI (France), (DVD); Vietnam, 1954.

Diên Biên Phu's director Schoendoerffer was a corporal in the French army's film service. This feature draws from his experience of the 1954 siege of a French garrison by the Viet Minh in the waning days of French power in Indochina. *Diên Biên Phu*, adopting the spectacle associated with narrative cinema's war epics, is also a very personal film, engaging the perspective of common French soldiers and the character of an army cameraman.

Norindr, Panivong. "Filmic Memorial and Colonial Blues: Indochina in Contemporary French Cinema." In *Cinema, Colonialism, Postcolonialism: Perspectives from the French and Francophone World*, edited by Dina Sherzer, 120–46. Austin: University of Texas Press, 1996.

———. *Phantasmatic Indochina: French Colonial Ideology in Architecture, Film and Literature*. Durham, NC: Duke University Press, 1997.

Distant Thunder / Ashani Sanket (1973) Satyajit Ray; India; Bengali with English subtitles; Black and White; 101 m; Facets (VHS); Bengal, 1943.

In Satyajit Ray's film about the 1943 Bengal famine, the newly-arrived Brahmin of the small village is the "jewel in [its] crown." His education and experience provide the village with a new priest, doctor, and schoolteacher. Knowledgeable Gangacharan Chakravarti is also a conduit to events beyond the isolated world of the villagers. With the price of rice soaring, the villagers try to make sense of vague news about India's involvement in World War II. One villager confuses the "German" invasion of Singapore with a more immediate threat: "Which province is Singapore in?" he asks. Gangacharan explains, "Our king is fighting the Germans and Japanese," and clarifies the relationship of Singapore's capture to the requisitioning of Bengali rice for Indian troops serving the British Army.

Distant Thunder says little more about the war. Instead, it graphically chronicles the changes in the social relations of the villagers as hunger creates a tragic leveling effect on all. Warplanes occasionally fly overhead, signifying the power politics that are ultimately responsible for what an intertitle at the end of the film describes as a "man-made" famine.

See also: *The Home and the World; Spices*

Cooper, Darius. "From Gazes to Threat: The Odyssean *Yatra* (Journey) of the Ray Woman." In *The Cinema of Satyajit Ray: Between Tradition and Modernity*, 75–133. Cambridge: Cambridge University Press, 2000.

———. "The Reponses, Trauma, and Subjectivity of the Ray *Parush* (Man)." In *The Cinema of Satyajit Ray: Between Tradition and Modernity*, 134–176. Cambridge: Cambridge University Press, 2000.

Polt, H.R. "Review of *Distant Thunder*." *Film Quarterly* 27(2) (Winter 1973/74): 57–58.

Rosenbaum, Jonathan. "Review of *Distant Thunder*." *Sight & Sound* 44(2) (Spring 1975): 123–4.

Schemering, C. "Review of *Distant Thunder*." *Cineaste* 7(2) (Spring 1976): 38–39.

A Dry White Season (1989) Euzhan Palcy; United States; English; Color; 107 m; MGM (DVD); South Africa, 1976–1977.

The protagonist of this ostensibly anti-apartheid film is a white Afrikaner teacher, the character Ben du Toit. Early in the film one of his students recites in class the "great" story of Boer freedom from the British, the conquest of the natives, and the Boer settlement of vast lands. Ben's awakening to the injustice of this racially segregated South Africa arrives through the suspicious death in police custody of a boy named Jonathan Ngubene, who had participated in the beginning of the Soweto township uprising. Later the boy's father, Gordon, dies under similar circumstances in jail. Ben's long quest to see the conviction of members of South Africa's Internal Security Forces for the murder of Jonathan and Gordon involves two trials, the interest of a liberal journalist, the surveillance of his home, the loss of his job, and the disintegration of his family. Ben's wife warns that if "the blacks" win, they "will swallow us up" and their "nice, peaceful lives" will be destroyed. "... you have to choose your own people," she says.

Surely Ben's world has been turned upside down by his rejection of the "lies" to which he had formerly subscribed. The development of his convictions are made believable in the film, and the large amount of dialogue—much of it overtly didactic—makes clear the film's assessment of apartheid South Africa as corrupt, brutal, and fundamentally unjust.

A Dry White Season is ultimately about Ben du Toit, a white man seemingly alone in all of the country in his fight for justice, and a white man pitted against villainous Captain Smits, the man responsible for Gordon's death. A subplot involving the victimization of Gordon's wife Emily is insufficient to draw the story about the victims of apartheid beyond the focus of its principal white victim, du Toit. The film largely ignores the structural foundations of apartheid, and it constructs the anti-apartheid movement as consisting of little more than the ill-advised march of schoolchildren in Soweto; the protest of a white teacher, a journalist, and a lawyer; and the help of their trusty black sidekick, Stanley.

See also: *'Breaker' Morant; Cry Freedom; The Making of the Mahatma; Mapantsula*

Carchidi, Victoria. "Representing South Africa: Apartheid from Print to Film." *Film & History: An Interdisciplinary Journal of Film and Television Studies* 21(1) (1991): 20–27.
———. "South Africa from Text to Film: *Cry Freedom* and *A Dry White Season.*" In *Literature and Film in the Historical Dimension: Selected Papers from the Fifteenth Annual Florida State University Conference on Literature and Film*, edited by John D. Simons, Gainesville, FL, 1994.
Gill, June M. "The Films of Euzhan Palcy: A Voice for Black History." *Quarterly Review of Film and Video* 17(4) (November 2000): 371–82.
Gugler, Josef. "*A Dry White Season* (1989): A White Awakening." In *African Film: Re-Imagining a Continent*, 80–90. Bloomington: Indiana University Press, 2003.
Nixon, Rob. "Cry White Season: Anti-Apartheid Heroism and the American Screen." In *Homelands, Harlem and Hollywood: South African Culture and the World Beyond*, edited by Rob Nixon, 77–97. New York: Routledge, 1994.

Drylanders (1962) Don Haldane; Canada; English; Black and White; 69 m; National Film Board of Canada (VHS); Saskatchewan, Canada, 1907–1938.

The first feature film produced by Canada's National Film Board, *Drylanders* is the fictional story of Dan and Elizabeth Greer and their two sons Colin and Russell. We meet them in 1907, crossing the barren Saskatchewan prairie with an oxen-pulled wagon. Lured by the promise of plentiful and inexpensive farmland in— as the opening intertitle suggests—an "almost empty" early twentieth-century Prairies, Dan Greer is anxious for the independence and economic mobility he could never hope to achieve as a clerk in Montreal.

Drylanders' story moves rapidly through the Greers' early adjustments to homesteading. Elizabeth's loneliness, Dan's exhaustion and near-death in a blizzard, and the destruction of their first wheat crop by a hailstorm, are dispatched quickly enough for the story to arrive at the point, just prior to World War I, when they have arrived at prosperity, symbolized by the purchase of a car.

The second half of the film provides a less breathless account, this time enacting the advent of the drought and Great Depression, which lead to a complete cessation of the Greers' agricultural production, the departure of neighbors and Russell for better prospects in the city, and the increasing despair and desolation of Dan as his independence and attainments are lost in the dust of his formerly fertile farm.

Drylanders presents an interpretation of white Prairie settlers that stresses their resiliency, work ethic, and mutual support mechanisms. The universality of farmers' reliance on the cycles of the seasons and weather is stressed. In Dan's case, it will be his progeny that stay on the farm—son Colin and family—who will enjoy the fruits of the rains that finally arrive after his death. Reinforcing the Canadian farmer's relationship to nature are the lovely wide shots of the vastness of the prairie, those often framing more of the sky—and its ominous and promising clouds—than the land. This is also an interpretation that ignores the existence of native people on the same landscape, and eschews any discussion of the human origins of the Depression. As Don Kerr says, "*Drylanders* is a film about farmers and nature, not about farmers and markets."

Almost a half century after its release, the narrative control given to Elizabeth Greer in *The Drylanders* is one of its most interesting aspects. Her voiceovers guide us through the story; through her explanation we learn of women's feelings of isolation and gradual empowerment, of her adoption of the values and norms of her husband over time, and of her characterization of the fates that befall her family as cyclical. Offering the main female character in *Drylanders* the control of the narrative is logical given that the film is in effect a retrospective that follows Dan's death. Elizabeth's voice here honors the matriarch's role as the keeper of the family history. Whether in this role she tends to echo and buttress the patriarch's story is a matter of debate.

Gittings, Christopher E. *"Drylanders."* In *Canadian National Cinema: Ideology, Difference and Representation*, 15–21. London: Routledge, 2002.

Kerr, Don. *"Drylanders."* In *Encyclopedia of the Great Plains*, edited by David J. Wishart, 265–66. Lincoln: University of Nebraska Press, 2004.

Moen, Kristian. "The Polyphonic Prairies: The Creation and Re-Creation of *Drylanders*." *Canadian Journal of Film Studies* 10(1) (Spring 2001): 28–47.

The Dupes / al-Makhdu'un (1972) Tewfik Saleh; Syria; Arabic with English subtitles; Black and White; 107 m; Facets (VHS); Iraq, early 1950s.

Based on the novel *Men in the Sun* by Ghassan Kanafani, *The Dupes* is a close study of three fictional Palestinian men in the early 1950s who each decide to seek a new life in Kuwait. A series of flashbacks examine the circumstances that have led these men—representing three generations—to their individual decisions to leave their families and risk an illegal border-crossing. Each has experienced some form of displacement, loss of livelihood, and family strife as a result of the Arab-Israeli war. The oldest reproaches himself for his earlier lack of resolve in leaving Palestine, and for his faith in the proponents of the Palestinian cause: "What did you expect? Talks, talks . . . arguing nonsense. They've sold you and bought you again. You have been brooding ten years over their words. . . . You've the Zionists before and the traitors behind. . . ."

The three strangers cross paths in Basra, and resolve to travel together. The illegal and covert transport of the increasingly bonded group of strangers in a former oil transport truck, now water carrier, is portrayed in a series of simple, and harrowing, scenes. By the time these men for the first time in the journey descend into the inhuman heat of the steel tank for travel over a border checkpoint, they have also come to know their driver/smuggler, whose own physical wounds from the war are masked by his affected self-assurance. Emerging from their first stint inside the tank, they are practically overcome. The dazed youngest traveler says, with no irony, "I think we shouldn't have come. I feel like we're all going backward."

With their past offering no better option than this horrifying gambit, the travelers face an almost unbearably harsh tableau in the barren desert. The next checkpoint looming, the tank occupants are reassured that this stage should last only seven minutes. In this scene of the driver again desperately hurtling the lone truck ahead, there seems to be nothing more important than the human dimension of the aftermath of the Arab-Israeli War of 1948–9. The tragedy of the death of the men in the delayed transport across the second checkpoint is magnified by the driver's sorrow and by the final image of the men's bodies lying in an undignified heap amid a pile of garbage in what appears to be nothing but the middle of the desert.

See also: *Boat People; The Boat Is Full; Journey of Hope; Welcome to Canada*

Cleary, Joe. "The Meaning of Disaster: The Novel and the Stateless Nation in Ghassan Kanafani's *Men in the Sun*." In *Literature, Partition and the Nation-State: Culture and Conflict in Ireland, Israel and Palestine*, 186–225. Cambridge: Cambridge University Press, 2002.

Harlow, Barbara. "History and Endings: Ghassan Kanafani and the Politics of Terminations in Palestine." In *After Lives: Legacies of Revolutionary Writing*, 45–75. London: Verso, 1996.

Shafik, Viola. *Arab Cinema: History and Cultural Identity*. Cairo: American University in Cairo Press, 1998.

Earth / Zemlya (1930) Alexander Dovzhenko; Soviet Union; Silent with Russian intertitles and English subtitles; Black and White; 70 m; Kino (DVD, VHS); Ukraine, 1929.

This is the story of the arrival of collective farming and modernization in a small Ukrainian farming village. Exalting the socialist spirit of farmers in pre-Stalinist Ukraine, *Earth* also examines the conflict that results from generational and social class differences over state collectivization policy. Many of the images in *Earth*—medium close-ups of the peasants' faces, the play of light on undulating fields of wheat, a tractor arriving on the horizon—are very beautiful. These images are also monumental, glorifying the farmers and their connection to the land, and their contribution to the building of socialist society.

Burns, Paul E. "Cultural Revolution, Collectivization, and Soviet Cinema: Eisenstein's *Old and New* and Dovzhenko's *Earth*." *Film & History: An Interdisciplinary Journal of Film and Television Studies* 11(4) (1981): 84–96.

Kepley Jr., Vance. *In the Service of the State: The Cinema of Alexander Dovzhenko*. Madison: University of Wisconsin Press, 1986.

Liber, George O. *Alexander Dovzhenko: A Life in Soviet Film*. London: BFI, 2002.

Earth (1998) Deepa Mehta; India/Canada; Hindi, English, Parsee, Punjabi, and Urdu with English subtitles; Color; 110 m; Facets (DVD, VHS); Lahore, Punjab, 1947.

Earth is a serviceable introduction to the complex class, gender, and religious divisions that afflicted the process of India's decolonization and partition in 1947. The film's protagonist, a young Parsee girl, Lenny, is a somewhat distant witness to events, retrospectively narrating the fate of her beautiful nanny, Shanta, whose suitors represent competing religious and political perspectives.

Viewers will either love or loathe the film's conventional portrayal of love in the midst of civil war, but the story Lenny tells efficiently coordinates the points of view of diverse interests in the days leading up to partition. *Earth*'s multiple points of view are contrived, but what makes for awkward cinema in this case nevertheless provides an instructive lesson in the positions of British, Hindu, Muslim, Sikh, and Parsee neighbors in 1947 Lahore. The local park becomes symbolic of changing relations as residents begin to debate British plans for Lahore. Once hosting casual mixed gatherings of Shanta's diverse friends, the park increasingly becomes the venue for segregated political meetings, with tense interactions between those characters representing the Muslim majority, the prosperous Hindu business community, and the Sikh landholders. Good-natured religious jokes—one of Shanta's suitors, the charismatic Muslim Dil Navaz, masquerades as a holy man who talks to Allah on the telephone—give way to increasing politicization and emotional hardening by the end of the film, as when Dil Navaz jeopardizes Shanta's life by reporting her whereabouts to a Muslim mob.

Earth is based on Bapsi Sidhwa's autobiographical novel *Cracking India*. The film's audience is asked to accept Lenny's historical account as credible, because her family is neutral Parsee. The Parsees are, as her mother says, chameleons, who change colors to survive their historic migration. Over time, Lenny's mother argues to her husband that "this neutral position isn't comfortable," but he stands firm: "If the Swiss can do it, so can we Parsees." That the family is also clearly Anglicized places Western audiences in a position of familiarity and identification with Lenny and her family as well.

See also: *Gandhi*; *Hot Winds*

Levitin, Jacqeline. "Deepa Mehta as Transitional Filmmaker, or 'You Can't Go Home Again.'" In *North of Everything: English Canadian Cinema since 1980*, edited by William Beard and Jerry White, 270–293. Edmonton, AB: University of Alberta Press, 2002.

Levitin, Jacqueline. "An Introduction to Deepa Mehta: Making Films in Canada and India." In *Women Filmmakers: Refocusing*, edited by Jacqueline Levitin, Judith Plessis, and Valerie Raoul, 273–83. Vancouver: UBC Press, 2003.

Effi Briest (1974) Rainer Werner Fassbinder; West Germany; German with English subtitles; Black and White; 135 m; Facets (DVD, VHS); Germany, 19th century.

Based on the novel by Theodor Fontane, this story is set in imperial Germany, where a lively and precocious seventeen-year-old girl, Effi, marries an ambitious baron. When her adultery is discovered, her husband and family react in accordance with the social codes of the day, which demand their condemnation of Effi's actions.

See also: *Girls in Uniform*

Borchardt, E. "Leitmotif and Structure in Fassbinder's *Effi Briest*." *Literature/Film Quarterly* 7(3) (1979): 201–07.

Krause, Edith H. "Effi's Endgame." *Oxford German Studies* 32 (2003): 155–84.

Plater, Edward M.V. "Reflected Images in Fassbinder's *Effi Briest*." *Literature/Film Quarterly* 27(3) (July 1999): 178–88.

Eijanaika (1981) Shohei Imamura; Japan; Japanese with English subtitles; Color; 151 m; Facets (DVD; VHS); Japan, 1860s.

The Meiji Restoration of 1868 returned a form of imperial rule to Japan after the period of the Tokugawa Shogunate, although the reforms of the Meiji era would be squarely directed by a group of Japanese nobles and samurai to whom the Meiji emperor owed his position. *Eijanaika* is set in 1867–68, the eve of the restoration. The story is ostensibly about, or inspired by, a real event: an outburst of prolonged popular revelry that spread through Japanese urban centers. Dancing and singing "eijanaika!" ("why not?!"), commoners engaged in what has been variously described as a form of popular protest, an apolitical carnivalesque ritual, or a millenarian pilgrimage.

The film begins with an intertitle that describes the 1860s as a period characterized by Japan's opening to the West, the struggle for power between pro-restoration and pro-Shogunate forces, and those "hundred factions" behind the scenes seeking to profit from the conditions. "Beneath these," the intertitle ends, "the people: heedless, unmindful, frivolous, and strong." Imamura's story of "the people" revolves around Genji and his wife Iné. Genji has just returned to Ryōgoku from years away—including time spent in America—and discovers Iné has been contracted as a performer (and prostitute) for the carnival. Soon Genji and his friend Itoman find work thieving for the carnival owner, Kinzō. Genji tries unsuccessfully to find a return voyage to America, and to convince Iné to travel with him. Kinzō, the local pimp and effective ruler of Ryōgoku, is seen playing both sides of the political factions of the time, much to the bewilderment of his henchmen, who must obey orders that seem to contradict others given.

Imamura's cinematic enactment of this event is unconventional, not the least because events of what might be deemed "historical" significance are often given little emphasis and explanation, and those traditionally demoted as peripheral or irrational are given weight. One example of this emphasis would be a scene that devotes more attention to the unprecedented spectacle of an elephant in Ryōgoku than to the problem of the spiraling price of rice. In *Eijanaika* the spirited—and seemingly uncontrollable—popular cry of "why not?!" is placed in relief with the sober, rational master narratives of nation-building at the dawn of the Meiji era.

Casebier, Allan. "Images of Irrationality in Modern Japan: The Films of Shohei Imamura." *Film Criticism* 8(1) (Fall 1983): 42–49.

Keirstead, Thomas, and Deidre Lynch. "*Eijanaika*: Japanese Modernization and the Carnival of Time." In *Revisioning History: Film and the Construction of a New Past*, edited by Robert A. Rosenstone, 64–76. Princeton, NJ: Princeton University Press, 1995.

Quandt, James, ed. *Shohei Imamura*. Waterloo, ON: Wilfred Laurier University Press, 1997.

Elizabeth (1998) Shekhar Kapur; United Kingdom; English; Color; 124 m; Universal Studios Home Entertainment (DVD, VHS); England, 1558–c.1563.

As much a time piece of the twentieth century as it is of the sixteenth, Shekhar Kapur's film version of the life of English Queen Elizabeth I is a perfect example of historical films' preoccupation with themes that are essentially presentist rather than historical. *Elizabeth*'s entertaining visual and narrative storytelling also makes the film immensely engaging, and successful in its communicating to a popular audience its (not particularly imaginative or demanding) themes of power, identity, and gender. Some experts on the Elizabethan era have raised objections about the many omitted or erroneous details in the film, as well as its inclusion of events that followed later in Elizabeth's reign. As such, *Elizabeth* raises questions about where the particular virtues of historical films lie: perhaps the neglect of historical explanation in a historical film should not be mourned when the past is instead such a successful forum for robust entertainment and modest reflection.

Levin, Carole. "Elizabeth: Romantic Film Heroine or Sixteenth-Century Queen?" *Perspectives Online (American Historical Association)* 37(4) (April 1999), http://www.historians.org/perspectives/issues/1999/9904/9904FIL5.CFM (accessed May 30, 2006).

McKechnie, Kara. "Taking Liberties with the Monarch: The Royal Bio-Pic in the 1990s." In *British Historical Cinema: The History, Heritage, and Costume Film*, edited by Claire Monk and Amy Sargeant, 217–36. London: Routledge, 2002.

Pigeon, René. "No Man's Elizabeth: The Virgin Queen in Recent Films." In *Retrovision: Reinventing the Past in Film and Fiction*, edited by Deborah Cartmell, I.Q. Hunter, and Imelda Whelehan, 8–24. London: Pluto Press, 2001.

Sweet, Rosemary. "Review of *Elizabeth*." *American Historical Review* 104(1) (February 1999): 297–198.

Emitai / God of Thunder (1971) Ousmane Sembène; Senegal; Diola and French with English subtitles; Color; 103 m; Facets (VHS); West Africa, early 1940s.

Emitai is about a real event that occurred in the southern Senegalese village of Effok in the Second World War. Senegal, a colonial possession of France, was a source of soldiers for the French army. The film reconstructs the refusal of women of the village to yield up the kilos of rice per villager mandated by the local French colonel who commands a company of native soldiers. Having already experienced such tactics as the hostage-taking of family members to forcibly recruit their young males for army duty, the women execute a plan of defiance, hiding the rice harvest. Meanwhile, male village elders meet and engage in what appear to be unprofitable debates about the best course of action in response to the women's actions and French demands. Consulting the gods is one aspect of the attempts to divine the decision. The chief decides to lead an attack on the French forces; it is repelled and he is killed. The women are rounded up by soldiers and forced into the sun, a tactic aimed to break their will. Men at the chief's funeral receive French threats of the village's destruction or their imprisonment. The elders choose a new chief, pray, and perform a rite of animal sacrifice to the god of thunder embodied in a great baobab tree. In a remarkable scene, some of the male villagers decide to guide the colonel to the rice's location; when the women call on them to stop, the men hesitate. Soldiers open fire and the men are killed.

Emitai's picture of anticolonial resistance suggests, respectfully, some of the limitations of the traditional Diola religious practices in meeting the overwhelming force of colonialism. Women of the village—in the absence of the conscripted men—seed, gather wood, plant rice shoots, resist their oppressors, and lead their men to do so as well.

See also: *The Camp at Thiaroye; Spices*

Iyam, David Uru. "The Silent Revolutionaries: Ousmane Sembene's *Emitai, Xala*, and *Ceddo*." *African Studies Review* 29(4) (December 1986): 79–87.

Kindem, G., and M. Steele. "*Emitai* and *Ceddo*: Women in Sembene's Films." *Jump Cut: A Review of Contemporary Media* 36 (May 1991): 52–60.

Murphy, David. "Dis-Membering Empire, Re-Membering Resistance: The Memory of Colonialism in *Emitai, Ceddo* and *Camp De Thiaroye*." In *Sembene: Imagining Alternatives in Film and Fiction*, edited by David Murphy, 151–85. Oxford: James Currey, 2000.

———. "Mothers, Daughters and Prostitutes: The Representation of Women in Sembene's Work." In *Sembene: Imagining Alternatives in Film and Fiction*, edited by David Murphy, 124–50. Oxford: James Currey, 2000.

Pfaff, Françoise. *The Cinema of Ousmane Sembene, a Pioneer of Black African Film*. Westport, CT: Greenwood Press, 1984.

The Emperor's New Clothes (2001) Alan Taylor; United Kingdom/Italy/Germany; English; Color; 107 m; Facets (DVD, VHS); France, early 19th century.

This is a gentle comedy belonging to the category of "counterfactual history." Adapted from the novel *The Death of Napoleon* by Simon Leys, the film follows the imaginative premise that Napoleon, using a substitute double, escaped from imprisonment on St. Helena. When his plans to meet with loyalists in Paris go awry, he must adapt to the virtues of a commoner's life.

See also: *It Happened Here*

Elley, Derek. "The Emperor's New Clothes." *Variety* 384 (August 20/26, 2001): 25–26.
Kauffmann, Stanley. "Appreciation, Please." *New Republic* 227(1) (July 1, 2002): 24–25.
Vineberg, Steve. "Napoleon's Return." *Christian Century* 119(1)6 (July 31, 2002): 43–44.

Empire of the Sun (1987) Steven Spielberg; United States; English; Color; 154 m; Facets (DVD); China, 1941–45.

Empire of the Sun is an amalgam of action-adventure film, memoir of childhood, and historical drama. The story, adapted from J.G. Ballard's autobiographical novel, follows the Second World War era experiences of young Briton James Graham. In early scenes, we observe his comfortable childhood in cosmopolitan Shanghai. Glimpses of the city he snatches through the view from his comfortable seat in a car are Jamie's only contact with the social and racial disparities of Republican China. This privileged life is abruptly ended when the Japanese army invades Shanghai in December of 1941. Separated from his parents, and learning survival from the likes of an American street hustler, Jamie is eventually captured by the Japanese, and interned at Suzhou until 1945. While the conditions at Suzhou could hardly be described as comforting, the camp provides for Jamie a semblance of safety and family.

Empire of the Sun delivers on one level a basic history lesson about the wartime invasion of China and the consequences for its residing foreigners. But delivered as it is in the sometimes dreamlike ecstasies of a traumatized child, the lesson is romanticized. The film delivers what could only be charitably described as interesting messages about relations of race, nation, and empire in wartime Asia. Jamie has never lived in Britain, and his admiration for the Americans—portrayed as plucky, inventive, and even cocky in the face of their often cruel captors—and the Japanese, who are implied to have "liberated" the impoverished Chinese from the inequalities and cowardice of the Republican government of Chiang Kai-Shek, is arguably a reasonable window into the nature of childhood and national identity in the colonial era. At the same time the film's troubling assignment of positive value to militarism and conquest is not entirely confined to the awed gaze of a child; liberty and reunion with family—suggested symbolically in Jamie's love of aircraft—come with American bombers, and with the flash of the atomic bomb.

Gordon, Andrew. "Steven Spielberg's *Empire of the Sun*: A Boy's Dream of War." *Literature/Film Quarterly* 19(4) (1991): 210–21.
Riet, Fred van. "Teaching *Empire of the Sun*." *New England Journal of History* 2 (Autumn 1990): 29–36.

The End of St. Petersburg / Konets Sankt-Peterburga (1927) Vsevolod Pudovkin; Soviet Union; Silent with English intertitles; Black and White; 89 m; Kino (DVD, VHS); Russia, WWI.

The End of St. Petersburg was commissioned by the Soviet state to commemorate the 10-year anniversary of the October, or Bolshevik, revolution of 1917. The story revolves around a fictional young peasant from Penza Province. Upon arriving in the city he performs work as a strikebreaker, but in a reversal of his political judgments, then attacks the factory owners and is jailed. When he is conscripted into the army, scenes of the World War I battlefield are intercut with those of the stock market, where high capitalists enjoy the fruits of their exploitation of the war economy. A subplot involving the wife of a relative in the city, who opposes her husband's radicalism, is resolved when both characters—and their mutual revolutionary convictions—converge at the site of the 1917 storming of the Winter Palace.

See also: *The Battleship Potemkin*; *Earth* (Dovzhenko); *October* (*Ten Days That Shook the World*)

Corney, Frederick C. *Telling October: Memory and the Making of the Bolshevik Revolution.* Ithaca, NY: Cornell University Press, 2004.

Kepley, Vance Jr. "Pudovkin and the Continuity Style: Problems of Space and Narration." *Discourse* 17(3) (Spring 1995).

Smith, Murray. "The Influence of Socialist Realism on Soviet Montage: *The End of St. Petersburg*, *Fragment of an Empire* and *Arsenal*." *Journal of Ukrainian Studies* 19(1) (1994): 45–65.

Enemy at the Gates (2001) Jean-Jacques Annaud; United States/United Kingdom/Germany; English; Color; 131 m; Paramount Home Entertainment (DVD, VHS); Soviet Union, 1942.

Enemy at the Gates introduces us early on to its protagonist, Vassily Zaitsev, a young and prodigious Red Army marksman. A flashback that shows Vassily as a young boy, learning to hunt from his grandfather, reinforces his status as an ordinary hero. A brief and stylish allusion to wartime newsreels shows a map animating the spreading shadow of Nazism across Europe and the need for the German army to use Stalingrad as the base from which to access Caucasus oil fields. With this limited explanation of the film's context, viewers join Vassily as he participates in the Russian defense of the city.

Another ambitious drama in the historical film oeuvre of director Jean-Jacques Annaud, *Enemy at the Gates* conflates verifiable fact and legend to tell an interesting and suspenseful story of two competing snipers in the ruins of German-occupied Stalingrad in 1942. Vassily, a real-life figure, will meet his match in Major Ernst König, a German marksman whose existence is disputed by experts. Popular film conventions—improbable romance, transparent dialogue, a cloying child, and a derivative musical score—are adopted with abandon here. The film reduces the history of Stalingrad to the battle of two men, thus personalizing but limiting viewers' understanding of the scope and importance of what has been described as a turning point in World War II.

See also: *Stalingrad*

Tibbetts, John C. "Review of *Enemy at the Gates*." *American Historical Review* 106(3) (June 2001): 1107–08.

Europa, Europa / Hitlerjunge Salomon (1990) Agnieszka Holland; Germany/France/Poland; German, Russian, Polish and Hebrew with English subtitles; Color; 112 m; Facets (DVD); Germany, Soviet Union and Poland, 1938–1945.

The memoirs of Salomon Perel are the basis of this story of a German Jewish teenager who masquerades as first a Stalinist and then a Nazi in order to survive. Hiding the fact of his circumcision is a crucial part of his masquerade as a "pure-blood" German war hero and SS trainee. Weighted with the theme of religious, racial, and national identity, *Europa, Europa* conveys Solly through a series of experiences in which his survival depends on convincing others he is just like them. But a crisis of conscience about his relationship to the murderous Nazis leaves him to ask: "Who was my friend? Who was my enemy? How could they be kind to me and at the same time kill others so horribly? What set us apart? A simple foreskin?" The film is unabashed in making generous use of humor—much of it gently ironic in tone—in its depiction of the grave situations facing Solly. The humor is one way for filmmaker Holland to openly confront what she expects will be audience's disbelief at the many coincidences and near-misses that characterize Solly's survival. Meeting their incredulity with this exuberance also creates a tonal counterpoint to other Holocaust films.

See also: *Swing Kids*

Everett, W. "The Autobiographical Eye in European Film." *Europa: An International Journal of Language, Art and Culture* 2(1) (1995): 3–10.

Linville, Susan E. "Agnieszka Holland's *Europa, Europa*: Deconstructed Humor in a Holocaust Film." *Film Criticism* 29(3) (Spring 1995): 44–53.

———. "*Europa, Europa*: A Test Case for German National Cinema." *Wide Angle* 16(3) (February 1995): 39–51.

Lungstrum, Janet. "Foreskin Fetishism: Jewish Male Difference in *Europa, Europa*." *Screen* 39(1) (Spring 1998): 53–66.

Reimer, Robert C., and Carol J. Reimer. "*Europa, Europa*." In *Nazi-Retro Film: How German Narrative Cinema Remembers the Past*, 145–47. New York: Twayne, 1992.

Exodus (1960) Otto Preminger; United States; English; Color; 208 m; Facets (DVD); Cyprus and Palestine, 1947–1948.

Based on the novel by Leon Uris, *Exodus* is a technicolor epic about the founding of the state of Israel. The film offers a fascinating study of the adaptation of historical novels for the screen, and the ways in which cinematic melodramas construct historical interpretation.

The film begins in Cyprus in 1947, where British authorities are trying to manage the mass migration of European Jews to the British mandate of Palestine. Caught between the aspirations of Zionists and Arabs in Palestine, and facing an unprecedented influx of Jewish immigrants, the British have set up temporary camps in Cyprus from which intercepted Jews will be deported back to Europe. The character of *Haganah* leader Ari Ben Canaan—the personification of what the film wishes to present as the "good" Zionist—plots the escape to Palestine of over six hundred detainees who have recently arrived on the ship *Star of David*. The second half of the film follows the main characters involved in the escape—Ari, an American (Presbyterian) nurse who becomes his love interest, and two young Auschwitz survivors (Dov, once in Haifa, joins the *Irgun*, and Karen joins other Jewish children at the fictional kibbutz Gan Dafna), as they participate in attempts to found a national state. The few Palestinian Arabs in the film who are given individual characterization, such as Ari's friend Taha, son of the Mukhtar of Abu Yesha who has donated land for Gan Dafna, are generally portrayed as sympathetic to their Zionist "brethren," but conflicted by the implications of their minority status when the British pull out and the United Nations vote in favor of Palestine's partition.

Covering a staggering amount of chronological ground in just over three hours of screen time, the film earnestly develops—in plot, dialogue, characterization, and landscape—an interpretation of events in postwar Palestine that is palatable to audiences, one which is especially laden with the theme of reconciliation. Holocaust survivors like Dov and Karen must reconcile themselves to the past and commit to the construction of the new Israel; *Haganah* and *Irgun* must iron out their differences; and Jews and Arabs of Palestine must reconcile in order to prevent their future colonization. As Ari implores of Taha: "Don't you see? We have to prove to the world that we can get along together. . . ." While the theme of peace and reconciliation might be a powerful balm to postwar audiences in the United States, it is thin as a form of historical explanation. That the film ends before the major events of the 1948 war somewhat disingenuously obscures the fact of violent and sustained conflict that is as much a feature of the region's history as its attempts at coexistence.

The character of nurse Kitty Fremont is one of the most interesting features of *Exodus*. Kitty is the audience's intermediary—a familiar, white, Gentile American—who will make less foreign the experience of European Jews and the Zionist position. The scene of a crowd rejoicing at the news of the United Nations vote is intersected with that of Kitty, Ari, and Taha listening to a radio broadcast of the news. Before professing that he loves her, Ari says to Kitty, "You know, you're wonderful. I look at you and I ask myself, what are you doing here in the middle of somebody else's fight?" Kitty protests that she'll stay as long as he'll have her. Indeed, as much as the film supports the historical claims of the Jews to the "land of Canaan," *Exodus* argues that the Zionist cause is also a universal one: Kitty's relationship with Ari, and sense of belonging, in Palestine is a reassuring humanistic model for audiences.

See also: *Hill 24 Doesn't Answer*; *Kedma*

Loshitzky, Yosefa. "Screening the Birth of a Nation: *Exodus* Revisited." In *Identity Politics on the Israeli Screen*, 1–14. Austin: University of Texas Press, 2001.

Loshitzky, Yosefa. "National Rebirth as a Movie: Otto Preminger's *Exodus*." *National Identities* 4(2) (July 2002): 119–31.

Salt, Jeremy. "Fact and Fiction in the Middle Eastern Novels of Leon Uris." *Journal of Palestine Studies* 14(3) (Spring 1985): 54–63.

Weissbrod, Rachel. "*Exodus* as a Zionist Melodrama." *Israel Studies* 4(1) (Spring 1999): 129–52.

Fall of Otrar / Gibel Otrara (1990) Ardak Amirkulov; Soviet Union/Kazakhstan; Mandarin, Kazakh, and Mongolian with English subtitles; Black and White; 165 m; Seagull Films (theatrical); Central Asia, 13th century.

The early thirteenth century invasion of the Central Asian empire of Khwarezm—associated with present-day Kazakhstan—is the subject of this extremely violent, tightly-framed, and at times expressionistic film. The character of Unzhu is a Kipchak (Turkic nomad) who, after spending years with the army of Genghis Khan, returns to Khwarezm to warn of the Mongol threat. While most of Khwarezm quickly succumbs to foreign invasion in the early 1220s, the city of Otrar, under the command of its governor, Kairkhan, puts up greater resistance.

Jones, Kent. "Lone Wolves at the Door of History." *Film Comment* 39(3) (May/June 2003): 54–57.

Rapfogel, Jared. "Central Asian Films." *Senses of Cinema: An Online Film Journal Devoted to the Serious and Eclectic Discussion of Cinema*, http://www.sensesofcinema.com/contents/03/27/central_asian_films.html (accessed May 30, 2006).

The Family / La Famiglia (1987) Ettore Scola; Italy/France; Italian and English with English subtitles; Color; 127 m; Facets (VHS); Rome, Italy, 1906–1986.

In this work of cinematic family history, patriarch Carlo reminisces about his life from his 1906 baptism to his eightieth birthday. All of *The Family*'s scenes are staged within the walls of the family's Rome apartment. While the events of Italian political history impact the family, Carlo's personal, familial, and generational history is the locus of the story.

See also: *1900*; *The Garden of the Finzi-Continis*; *The Tree of Wooden Clogs*

Landy, Marcia. "*La Famiglia*: The Cinematic Family and the Nation." In *Italian Film*, 205–33. Cambridge: Cambridge University Press, 2000.

Family / Jia (1957) Chen Xihe and Ye Ming; China; Mandarin with English subtitles; Black and White; 111 m; no current; China, 1916–1920.

This melodrama opens with an intertitle quoting novelist Ba Jin: "I'll shout my accusation against this dying system." Ba Jin's 1931 saga of a traditional multigenerational Chinese family and its struggle with the modernization of social values in the early Republican era has become a literary classic. At its publication, *Family* was a critical success and enjoyed by the literate public. Several stage and screen adaptations have been produced since, including this Shanghai Film Studios version; these have broadened the appeal of the novel to a wider audience in China, and abroad.

Family is a study of four generations of the Gao clan, who reside in a traditional family compound in an indeterminate city "on the upper reaches of the Yangtze River." The patriarch grandfather is unequivocal: "I'm the master of the family. My word is law!" But the three male grandchildren, and their female cousin Qin, each have independent desires, very often in the form of romantic partners who are out of reach in a system of arranged marriage. These thwarted love stories form much of the melodramatic centerpiece to the plot. Ming-feng is the "ill-fated girl" whose servant status makes her ineligible for marriage to middle grandson Juehui. His protest that "we're all human beings" can do little to address her station, and she drowns herself in the lake on the family estate. The tortured progress of eldest grandson Juexin's love for Mei is informed by his respect for his wife and his obligation to exercise filial piety. Looming in the background are brief glimpses of the political context; while these are less pronounced than in Ba Jin's novel, there are allusions to the May Fourth Movement (1919) and the political strife caused by competing warlords.

This Maoist-era film reflects Chinese artists' attempts before the "anti-rightist" campaign of 1959 to portray pre-1949 Chinese society as corrupted by feudal gender and class relations, and its members suffering a staggering lack of individual freedom—especially in the areas of marital choice and further education for both men and women. The villains of *Family* are those members of the older generation who resist change; its heroes are those who determine to act. In the middle are the many characters who could be described as victims—often desperate and tearful—who lack power or resolve.

This sentimental and melodramatic family saga ends with a scene of Juehui heading downstream on a boat bound for Shanghai; he has defied Grandfather Gao's warning that his departure is "a blow to our family's honor and discipline!" *Family* argues that there was little true honor or dignity in the traditional Chinese family in the Republican era. Juehui's departure for the city in which the Chinese Communist Party was founded in 1921 signals the direction of Chinese society's renewal.

Leyda, Jay. *Dianying: An Account of Films and the Film Audience in China.* Cambridge, MA: Harvard University Press, 1967.

Robinson, Lewis. "*Family*: A Study in Genre Adaptation." *Australian Journal of Chinese Affairs* 12 (1984): 35–57.

Farewell My Concubine / Ba wang bie ji (1993) Chen Kaige; China/Hong Kong; Mandarin with English subtitles; Color; 157 m; Facets (DVD; VHS); China, 1920s–1970s.

Farewell My Concubine is an opulent love story, and a study of much of China's twentieth-century political history. Combining elements of art house and commercial cinema, the film has managed to find considerable popular success. The film is about three fictional characters who essentially constitute a love triangle: Dieyi and Xiaolou establish a friendship as childhood classmates at an opera school in the 1920s, and Juxian is a prostitute who becomes Xiaolou's wife. Dieyi and Xiaolou become stars of the Beijing opera; Dieyi, having been trained as a *dan* (female impersonator) assumes the role of the concubine in a traditional opera, while Xiaolou is his/her king. The three characters endure the warlord era, Japanese invasion, civil war, and the consolidation of Communist rule. Over the decades, the personal turmoil of Dieyi over his unrequited love for Xiaolou takes place in the context of almost unrelenting turmoil in the public sphere, culminating in the devastating loss of the characters' status as artists in the Cultural Revolution, and their submission to the games of violence, suspicion, and denunciation demanded by the Communist State to prove one's loyalty.

Interesting with respect to *Farewell*'s construction of history is its use of the eponymous *Farewell My Concubine*—an ancient Chinese opera—as an allegory for China's own modern (and operatic) history. In the key scene of the opera, Xiang Yu, a king of the third century BCE, has failed to unite the kingdoms of China and is now surrounded by the armies of his victorious enemies. His beloved concubine, Lady Yu, is one of his only remaining loyalists. She performs one last dance for him, then slits her own throat. Soon Xiang Yu has used his own sword to join her in death. Defeated, alone, and having lost his stature, the king is resigned to his fate. *Farewell My Concubine* is a grandiose and pessimistic tale, and a damning interpretation of the fate of identity, art, and love in the political upheaval of modern China.

Lau, Jenny Kwok Wah. "*Farewell My Concubine*: History, Melodrama, and Ideology in Contemporary Pan-Chinese Cinema." *Film Quarterly* 49 (Fall 1995): 16–27.

Silbergeld, Jerome. "A Farewell to Arts: Allegory Goes to the Movies (*Farewell My Concubine* and *The Story of Qiu Ju*)." In *China into Film: Frames of Reference in Contemporary Chinese Cinema*, 96–131. London: Reaktion Books, 1999.

Xiao, Zhiwei. "Review of *Farewell My Concubine.*" *American Historical Review* 100(4) (October 1995): 1212–14.

Xu, Ben. "*Farewell My Concubine* and Its Nativist Critics." *Quarterly Review of Film and Video* 16(2) (1997): 155–70.

Zhang, Benzi. "Figures of Violence and Tropes of Homophobia: Reading *Farewell My Concubine* between East and West." *Journal of Popular Culture* 33(2) (Fall 1999): 101–09.

Fever / Goraczka (1981) Agnieszka Holland; Poland; Polish with English subtitles; Color; 122 m; Polart (VHS); Poland, 1905.

The opening credit sequence of *Fever* shows a darkly lit close-up of hands carefully making a bomb. The process causes a character called "the chemist" to prick his finger. His face is revealed when the camera follows injured finger to mouth, and the symbolism of the blood is clear: the bomb is capable of violence against its possessor. This victimization of the bomb's maker—he will soon be apprehended by the Russian authorities and executed—establishes the intriguing theme of Agnieszka Holland's film. An intertitle near the beginning of the film describes the story's "heroes" as "militants of the Socialist Party." Yet these are not typical cinematic heroes who overcome adversity to achieve their goals. The Socialist Revolutionaries who aim to use their "last" bomb to assassinate the Russian governor of partitioned Poland experience little success in two years of trying. By film's end, the protagonists are all dead or jailed; the bomb, failing to explode when thrown into a meeting room of Russian authorities, is finally detonated in a river by demolition experts. "A lovely bang!" watching soldiers comment.

The apparent futility of the revolutionary's actions makes *Fever* a resonant history lesson. As one revolutionary's father cautions: "You have unchained the emotions of the mob.... Your reply to social justice is to incite violence! But you will be their first victims! It is a law of history!"

See also: *Rosa Luxemburg*

Jameson, Frederic. "On Magic Realism in Film." *Critical Inquiry* 12(2) (1986): 301–25.

Lugo de Fabritz, B. Amarillis. "Agniezska Holland: Continuity, the Self, and Artistic Vision." In *Women Filmmakers: Refocusing,* edited by Jacqueline Levitin, Judith Plessis, and Valerie Raoul, 96–108. Vancouver: UBC Press, 2003.

Fires on the Plain / Nobi (1959) Kon Ichikawa; Japan; Japanese with English subtitles; Black and White; 108 m; Facets (VHS); Philippines, 1945.

Fires on the Plain is the cinematic adaptation of the highly acclaimed and popular novel by Ōoka Shōhei. The protagonist of novel and film is Tamura, a tubercular Japanese army private who tries to survive with a few other remaining soldiers—rejected from both their unit and a hospital because they are weak from starvation and have no rations to offer as currency for treatment—in the jungle and plains of Leyte Island, the Philippines, at the end of the Pacific War. Trying to reach the port of Palompon, where the group can be evacuated to Cebu, they encounter food hoarders, masses of dead, and American truck convoys. As one of Tamura's group comments of these foreigners: "They're fat as pigs!" This attention to hunger and food is unrelenting: the imminent threat of starvation, killing for a stash of salt, and cannibalism are the basic events of the film.

Fires on the Plain privileges the experience of ordinary soldiers over rational explanation of the broader context of events. The closer Tamura comes to delirium and death, the more openly, through extensive use of voiceover, he asks why his emperor has asked him to die. But Tamura's story is recollective, told from his perspective six years later in a Tokyo hospital for the mentally ill. This dimension of the storyteller's voice is central to the narrative, leaving viewers to decide whether such retrospect has as much to say about the legacy of Tamura's experience as about the experience itself.

See also: *Burmese Harp*; *The Human Condition*

Hauser, William B. "*Fires on the Plain*: The Human Cost of the Pacific War." In *Kon Ichikawa*, edited by James Quandt, 205–16. Waterloo, ON: Wilfrid Laurier University Press, 2001.

Masters, Patricia Lee. "Warring Bodies: Most Nationalistic Selves." In *Colonialism and Nationalism in Asian Cinema*, edited by Wimal Dissanayake, 1–10. Bloomington: Indiana University Press, 1994.

Washburn, Dennis. "Toward a View from Nowhere: Perspective and Ethical Judgment in *Fires on the Plain*." *Journal of Japanese Studies* 23(1) (Winter 1997): 105–31.

The First Charge of the Machete / La primera carga al machete (1969)

Manuel Octavio Gómez; Cuba; Spanish with English subtitles; Black and White; 80 m; Tricontinental Film Center (theatrical); Cuba, 1868.

The defense by Cuban rebels of the town of Bayamo against the Spanish army during the War of Independence is framed around multiple perspectives and a nonlinear time frame. *The First Charge of the Machete* also uses a documentary style, making a fictional reconstruction of an actual event look akin to newsreel footage.

Myerson, Michael. "*The First Charge of the Machete/La Primera Carga Al Machete*." In *Memories of Underdevelopment: Three Revolutionary Films of Cuba*, 167–70. New York: Grossman, 1973.

Quiros, Oscar. "Critical Mass of Cuban Cinema: Art as the Vanguard of Society." *Screen* 37(3) (1996): 279–93.

Schwartz, Ronald. "*La Primera Carga Del Machete (The First Charge of the Machete)*." In *Latin American Films, 1932–1994: A Critical Filmography*, 205. Jefferson, NC: McFarland, 1997.

Flame (1996) Ingrid Sinclair; Zimbabwe; English; Color; 85 m; California Newsreel (VHS); Rhodesia/Zimbabwe, 1970s.

The production history of *Flame* is a fine example of the politics of historical film. When individual, collective, and official historical memory collide in a popular medium like the movies, stakeholders in the interpretation of the past can be aroused to defend their version of the past, in sometimes dramatic ways.

According to director Ingrid Sinclair—a white, female Zimbabwean—*Flame's* story of two friends "is only one of many" arising from the Second Chimurenga. This war of resistance against white rule in Rhodesia ended in 1980 with the victory of African forces and the establishment of Zimbabwe. Florence and Nyasha reunite 15 years after their participation in the struggle. Nyasha has worked hard to establish a career in the new, urban Zimbabwe. Initially reluctant to revisit the past, she soon becomes our conduit to events. As narrator, she tells the story of

Florence, whose difficult post-liberation life in a small village has finally led her to seek help from Nyasha to find a "city job."

Using extended flashbacks, *Flame* follows the young women as they join the resistance movement in 1975 and receive training in a remote camp. Nyasha is happiest producing educational literature for the cause. Florence, who adopts the revolutionary identity of "Flame," becomes a skilled combatant and is promoted to detachment commander.

Flame, the first Zimbabwean feature film to explore the Chimurenga, is a visually and narratively powerful depiction of women's experience as participants. The gender politics in the movement are vividly described. Young women are trained as combatants, and by 1979 are praised by male commanders for their essential contribution to the victory: "It is women like this," says one, pointing to Florence, "to whom they [Zimbabweans] owe their freedom. They fought with us, they fed us...." But the women's position is also vulnerable. Sinclair shows young women in the camps at times serving as sexual comfort for the men; Flame's rape by Captain Danger is a manifestation of the women's exploitation. Flame's later acceptance of her rapist's apology and adoption of him as her lover (the union produces a child) is an example of Sinclair's fairly effective—if controversial—consideration of the male perspective. Characters like Captain Danger—who later marries Florence and fails to adjust to civilian life—seem also to have entered a world where ideology and conviction do not always compensate for their isolation and the danger of combat.

In 1996 the rough cut of *Flame* was seized by Zimbabwean police after the Ministry of Information failed to secure the producers' agreement to changes demanded by the Zimbabwean War Veterans' Association. The ministry argued that a script approved for its contribution to the "record of the war" had been corrupted, as (quoted by Tafataona Mahoso) "undue prominence has been given to certain aberrations and misdemeanors in which young women were abused, brutalized or raped...." The conflict was eventually resolved with the permission to release the film with minor changes. Consistent with official concern was a more general dismay among contemporary Zimbabwean military leaders that the memory of male heroism had been permanently blighted by the scenes of sexual exploitation.

Arguably, the Zimbabwean leadership was even more discomfited by Sinclair's treatment of the postwar era. Refusing to end the film with the independence movement's victory, she extends her look at gender and class relations after the struggle has been won. The economic and social conditions of both male and female peasants, who formed the ranks of the soldiers, are not immediately improved at liberation. Flame and Danger struggle to make ends meet in Flame's home village, and Danger joins other unemployed men in the local bar. In a highly effective melding of documentary and invented footage, Flame—now reunited with Nyasha in the city—joins a group of former comrades in an apartment on Heroes' Day. Their role in Zimbabwean national politics is now as observers, watching—some bitterly, some resignedly—the festivities on television. The TV camera pans the grandstand at a sports stadium, the site of the national celebrations, and pauses at a row of men in military dress, presiding over their version of remembrance. When Flame argues their group has a rightful place at the stadium, Nyasha insists to her old friend and comrade: "No Flame. We're just women." On their way to the private party, the women hail bystanders with the cry, "*A luta continua*": the struggle continues.

See also: *Tjoet Nja' Dhien; Those Whom Death Refused*

Bryce, Jane. "Incendiary Interpretations and the Patriotic Imperative: The Case of *Flame*." In *Versions of Zimbabwe: New Approaches to Literature and Culture*, edited by Robert Muponde and Ranka Primorac. Harare, Zimbabwe: Weaver Press, 2006.

Gugler, Josef. "*Flame* (1996): A Twofold Struggle." In *African Film: Re-Imagining a Continent*, 57–63. Bloomington: Indiana University Press, 2003.

Mahoso, Tafataona. "Unwinding the African Dream on African Ground." In *African Experience of Cinema*, edited by Imruh Bakari and Mbye B. Cham, 197–226. London: BFI, 1996.

Floating Life (1996) Clara Law; Australia; English, German, and Cantonese with English subtitles; Color; 95 m; Southern Star, Australia (VHS); Hong Kong, Australia, Germany, 1990s.

Floating Life is a funny and poignant look at the modern Chinese diaspora through the story of several members of a Hong Kong family who migrate to Australia and Germany in the 1990s. As the successful second daughter impatiently tells her newly arrived parents in suburban Australia: "You're here as migrants, not here to enjoy life."

Heo, Stephen. "*Floating Life*: The Heaviness of Moving." *Senses of Cinema: An Online Film Journal Devoted to the Serious and Eclectic Discussion of Cinema* 12 (February/March 2001), http://www.sensesofcinema.com/contents/01/12/floating.html (accessed May 30, 2006).

Mitchell, Tony. "Clara Law's *Floating Life* and Hong Kong-Australian 'Flexible Citizenship.'" *Ethnic & Racial Studies* 26(2) (March 2003): 278–300.

A Funny, Dirty Little War / No habrá más penas ni olvido (1983) Héctor Olivera; Argentina; Spanish with English subtitles; Color; 80 m; Vanguard (DVD), Connoisseur/Meridian (VHS); Argentina, 1970s.

In this black comedy set in the third presidency of Juan Perón (1973–1974), the fictional town of Colonia Vela is the site of internal warfare in 1974. *A Funny, Dirty Little War* offers a scathing critique of the betrayal of left wing Perónists by a presidency that increasingly secured its support from its conservative wing, and used a paramilitary (the "Triple A" or Argentine Anticommunist Alliance) to quell dissent. Slapstick, absurd situations, and parody are major elements of this critique, as Olivera tells the story of the left wing mayor, Fuentes—a Perónist—who gathers a motley band of citizens to defend the town hall against the opposing faction, which is supported handsomely by armored vehicles.

For all the comic situations—Fuentes' group is defended by a local crop duster spraying DDT, and then manure—*A Funny, Dirty Little War* shifts gradually to a more serious tone. Audiences must confront the loss of life graphically laid out before them, and the terrible costs to a small community of political divisions writ at the level of high politics. When two survivors of the battle insist to each other that Perón "will come," because he'll care about how Fuentes and the others "died for him," the distance between the Argentinians' hopefulness at the return of Perón and the reality is clearly observed.

See also: *The Traitors*

Pellón, Gustavo. "The Spanish American Novel: Recent Developments 1975–1990." In *The Cambridge History of Latin American Literature*, edited by Roberto González Echevarría and Enrique Pupo-Walker, 279–302. Cambridge: Cambridge University Press, 1996.

Weinberger, P. *"Funny Dirty Little War."* *Cinema Papers* 49 (December 1984): 464–65.

Gaijín: A Brazilian Odyssey / Gaijín, Caminhos da Liberdade (1980) Tizuka Yamasaki; Brazil; Portuguese and Japanese with English subtitles; Color; 112 m; Unifilms (theatrical); Japan and Brazil, early 20th century.

Director Tizuka Yamasaki's first feature film is based on the accounts of her Japanese grandmother and Brazilian-born mother. In 1908, a young Japanese woman arrives in São Paulo, Brazil, joining other migrant workers from Brazil, Italy, and Japan on a coffee plantation. Titoé's experiences—including an arranged marriage, growing politicization, and factory labor—provide a telling description of the gender, class, ethno-linguistic, and increasingly globalized dimensions of the migrant experience in the early twentieth century.

See also: *Aya*

Moniz, Naomi Hoki. "Race, Gender, Ethnicity, and the Narrative of National Identity in the Films of Tizuka Yamazaki." In *New Worlds, New Lives: Globalization and People of Japanese Descent in the Americas and from Latin America in Japan*, edited by James A. Hirabayashi, Lane Ryo Hirabayashi, and Akemi Kikumura-Yano, 221–36. Palo Alto, CA: Stanford University Press, 2002.

Gallipoli (1981) Peter Weir; Australia; English; Color; 110 m; Paramount Home Entertainment (DVD, VHS); Australia, Egypt, and Dardanelles, Ottoman Empire, 1914–1915.

Frank Dunne and Archy Hamilton are two (fictional) Australian men who enlist in the Australian Imperial Force. They train in Cairo and participate in the Gallipoli campaign of August 1915. Members of the 10th Light Horse Regiment of Western Australia (with their horses left behind in Egypt), these infantrymen charge the Turkish lines at the Nek. Hamilton dies, as do hundreds of other Australian soldiers in three waves of attack, in what the film describes as an ill-conceived assault that was fatally marred by miscommunications and the alleged indifference of British commanders.

The original screenplay of *Gallipoli*, coauthored by director Peter Weir and David Williamson, draws from C.E.W. Bean's *The Story of Anzac* (1934) as well as Bill Gammage's 1971 *The Broken Years*, a history of the event told through soldiers' letters and diaries. The film is flexible enough in its message that it has been read variously as a work that honors the sacrifice of Australian youth in wartime, celebrates "Australianness"/Australian identity, makes an antiwar statement, or produces a moving buddy-adventure film. Some analysts note a measure of internal conflict underlying the film's interpretation of Australia's role in World War I, suggesting that Weir is undecided whether *Gallipoli* should be nostalgic about the past, or horrified. Matthew Stewart argues the film "largely adheres to the ANZAC myth, both lamenting the death of lads such as Archy, and honouring that which their deaths occasioned."

Gammage, Bill. "Working on *Gallipoli*." In *The First Australian History and Film Conference Papers*, edited by Anne Hutton, 67–72. New South Wales, Australia: Australia Film and Television School, 1982.

Haltof, Marek. "In Quest of Self-Identity: *Gallipoli*, Mateship and the Construction of Australian National Identity." *Journal of Popular Film and Television* 21(1) (1993): 27–36.

Jackson, Kenneth T. "*Gallipoli*." In *Past Imperfect: History According to the Movies*, edited by Mark C. Carnes, 182–85. New York: Henry Holt, 1995.

Macleod, Jenny. "Post-Participant Historiography of Gallipoli." In *Reconsidering Gallipoli*, 209–38. Vancouver: UBC Press, 2004.

n/a. "'I Felt Somehow I Was Touching History': Interview with Peter Weir." *Literature/Film Quarterly* 9(4) (1981): 213–17.

Stewart, Matthew. "*Gallipoli*." *History Today* 53(2) (February 2003): 45–51.

Travers, T.H.E. "*Gallipoli*: Film and the Traditions of Australian History." *Film & History: An Interdisciplinary Journal of Film and Television Studies* 14(1) (1984): 14–20.

Gandhi (1982) Richard Attenborough; United Kingdom/India; English; Color; 188 m; Columbia/TriStar (DVD, VHS); India and South Africa, 1893–1948.

It is impossible to deny that *Gandhi*'s release brought a significantly greater awareness among mainstream Western audiences of its title subject, as well as the history of British colonial India on the eve of partition. For many, Gandhi "is" the Ben Kingsley-performed historical figure, a man whose political activism originated in racial inequalities witnessed in South Africa in the 1890s and who led Indians on a salt march to protest British rule. He is the primary exponent and cause of Indian independence, and a martyr to nonviolence and freedom as a result of his assassination in 1948. Audiences could arguably fare worse than this cinematic lesson about Gandhi. While the film predictably compresses events and over-narrows its focus to a single man's relationship to the cause of historical events, *Gandhi* competently handles the chronology it engages, and provides a reasonable portrait of Gandhi's actions in the political sphere and the context of British imperialism.

At the same time, there are many egregious aspects of *Gandhi*, leaving one to wonder whether the lessons of the film, given their impact, are more dangerous than benign. Regardless of one's judgment in that regard, there is no doubt that *Gandhi* offers a marvelous opportunity to study popular interpretations of Gandhi, Indian history, and the history of British imperialism, in this biographical film.

From its start, *Gandhi* signals that its medium for understanding the man will be western European and American observers, commentators, and interpreters. His funeral procession is narrated by a broadcaster who excitedly says this "little brown man in a loincloth" gave India its freedom. In a conventional gambit that asks Western audiences to recognize the film's subject as important because other Westerners think so, the film privileges the perspective of these foreign observers. Upon meeting American journalist Vince Walker, Gandhi says, "Without a journal of some kind, a newspaper, you cannot unite a community. You belong to a very important profession."

"Western" ideas, values, and texts will also be echoed in Gandhi's precepts, thus finding their way back to us with such familiarity that we not only understand what he believes and wants, but we're already convinced of these ourselves and can only hope Gandhi sees through their entrenchment in India. In South Africa, Gandhi demonstrates to Anglican clergyman Charlie Andrews he knows the New Testament as well as a Christian. And Gandhi's Hinduism is essentially explained as Indo-Christianity, with the theme "love thy neighbor" identified as the heart of Gandhi's philosophy.

Gandhi is beautiful as mass spectacle, reasonably interesting as drama, and superficial and unimaginative as history. Perhaps all could be forgiven if the film wasn't also so all-encompassingly Western-centric in its interpretation of Gandhi, where, to quote George Fischer, we receive "a George Washington with brown skin and few clothes."

See also: *The Making of the Mahatma*

Chakravarty, Sumita S. "The Recuperation of History and Memory." In *National Identity in Indian Popular Cinema 1947–1987*, 157–95. Austin: University of Texas Press, 1993.
Cooper, Darius. "Review of *Gandhi*." *Film Quarterly* 37 (Winter 1983/84): 46–50.
Fischer, George. "The 'New Politics' of *Gandhi*." *Social Policy* 13 (Spring 1983): 61–64.
Grenier, Richard. "The Gandhi Nobody Knows." *Commentary* 73 (March 1983): 59–64.
Jeffery, Peter. "Gandhi: Documentary and Epic Feature Film (Problematics of Representation)." *SPAN: Journal of the South Pacific Association for Commonwealth Literature and Language Studies* 34–35 (October/May 1992/93): 82–96.
Rajadhyaksha, Ashish. "Gandhiana and Gandhiology." In *The Media Reader*, edited by Manuel Alvarado and John O. Thompson. London: BFI, 1990.
Ward, Geoffrey C. "*Gandhi*." In *Past Imperfect: History According to the Movies*, edited by Mark C. Carnes, 254–57. New York: Henry Holt, 1995.

The Garden of the Finzi-Continis / Il Giardino dei Finzi-Contini (1970)

Vittorio De Sica; Italy/West Germany; Italian with English subtitles; Color; 94 m; Columbia/Tristar (DVD, VHS); Italy, 1938–1943.

With the introduction of Mussolini's racial laws, the estate of an aristocratic Italian Jewish family is less and less a site of privilege and pleasure and increasingly one of isolation and refuge. A family friend, middle-class Giorgio, is at once drawn to and repulsed by the false sanctuary of the estate as his own fate is increasingly affected by his Jewish identity.

Davis, Harry. "Narrated and Narrating I in *Il Giardino Dei Finzi-Contini*." *Italian Studies* 43 (1988): 117–29.
Eskin, S.G. "*The Garden of the Finzi-Continis*." *Literature/Film Quarterly* 2(2) (Spring 1973): 170–75.
Marcus, Millicent. "De Sica's *Garden of the Finzi-Continis*: An Escapist Paradise." In *Vittorio De Sica: Contemporary Perspectives*, edited by Howard Curle and Stephen Snyder, 258–79. Toronto: University of Toronto Press, 2000.

Gate of Hell / Jigoku mon (1953) Teinosuke Kinugasa; Japan; Color; Japanese with English subtitles; 89 m; Facets (VHS); Japan, 12th century.

The protagonist of *Gate of Hell* is a twelfth-century samurai, Moritoh. He proves his loyalty to the Taira clan Emperor Goshirakawa during a challenge from the rival Genji, but his pursuit of Kesa, lady-in-waiting to the Empress, is unsuccessful. From the outset, the film argues its historical authority: as a voiceover explains the background to the Heiji revolt, the camera slowly pans the images of battle depicted on an unfurled scroll.

Gate of Hell is an entertaining film whose high production values are often targeted for more praise than its storyline. The film is cited here primarily because of its close analysis by Darrell Davis, whose seminal study of the relationship of *Gate of Hell* to Westerners' constructions of their concepts of "Japaneseness" suggests the ways historical films are received by foreign audience. Davis describes *Gate of Hell* as "a shorthand stylization of things Japanese for Western consumption."

See also: *Rashomon*; *Taira Clan Saga*

Davis, Darrell William. "Monumentalism, Orientalism, and *Gate of Hell* (1953)." In *Picturing Japaneseness: Monumental Style, National Identity, Japanese Film*, 219–27. New York: Columbia University Press, 1996.

A Generation / Pokolenie

A Generation / Pokolenie (1954) Andrzej Wajda; Poland; Polish with English subtitles; Black and White; 90 m; Criterion (DVD), Facets (VHS); Warsaw, Poland, 1942.

Stach and other Polish youth live a meager existence in an impoverished neighborhood of Warsaw during the German occupation. Their only act of defiance is the theft of coal from passing German transport trains. But Stach's apprenticeship at a carpentry workshop exposes him to the covert world of the Polish resistance. Stach also learns the Marxist theory of surplus value as his own experience as a worker is illuminated by the lessons from Sekura, a shop steward. Joining the leftist Youth Underground, Stach has an affair with one of its leaders, Dorota, and recruits friends to the cause. The decision to aid fellow Poles, Jews in the Warsaw Ghetto, leads to the death of Janek, one of the reluctant converts to the cell. Wajda's first feature film, the first of what is known as his war trilogy (with *Canal* and *Ashes and Diamonds*), is an adaptation of Bohdan Czeszko's novel.

Mazierska, Ewa. "The Exclusive Pleasures of Being a Second Generation *Inteligent*: Representation of Social Class in the Films of Andrzej Wajda." *Canadian Slavonic Papers* 44(3/4) (September 1, 2002): 233–249.

Stevenson, Michael. "Wajda's Filmic Representation of Polish-Jewish Relations." In *The Cinema of Andrzej Wajda: The Art of Irony and Defiance*, edited by John Orr and Elzbieta Ostrowska, 76–92. London: Wallflower Press, 2003.

Germany, Pale Mother / Deutschland, bleiche Mutter

Germany, Pale Mother/Deutschland, bleiche Mutter (1980) Helma Sanders-Brahms; West Germany; German with English subtitles; Color; 123 m; Facets (VHS); Germany, 1930s and 1940s.

Germany, Pale Mother is based on filmmaker Helma Sanders-Brahms's own family history. The film describes the love affair of a mother (the character Lena) and father (Hans) and his departure with the German army in 1939. Anna is born during his absence. She and her mother must survive the war and the effects of its traumas in the postwar period when the family is reunited.

Anna announces near the beginning of the film: "It is a conventional love story, except that it happened in that time and that place." The film that follows, both in its style and themes, strongly counters this claim of conventionality, suggesting the impossibility of "that time and that place" permitting a "normal" life or discourse about it—even if Anna longs for that to be true. As a work of autobiography, *Germany, Pale Mother* can be studied for its construction of personal memory and history. But as personal a subject as Anna's life is, its intersection with the political "master" history of Nazi and post-Nazi Germany is unmistakable; the result is a very incisive interpretation of the historical private and public spheres in this period.

Germany, Pale Mother is in some ways a stark, honest, and even "distanced" treatment of its subject, which refuses to succumb to simplistic explanations of

Germans' behaviors during and after the Third Reich, and the relationship of contemporary Germans to their past. As Robert and Carol Reimer state, the film helps "viewers experience and thereby gain insight into why they—the film characters, the German people, and, perhaps, viewers in the movie audience— acquiesced so readily to policies that denied humanity."

Bammer, Angelika. "Through a Daughter's Eyes: Helma Sanders-Brahms' *Germany, Pale Mother*." *New German Critique* 36 (Fall 1985): 91–109.

Caplan, Jane. "Review of *Deutschland, Bleiche Mutter*." *American Historical Review* 96(4) (1991): 1126–28.

Cook, Roger F. "Melodrama or Cinematic Folk Tale?: Story and History in *Deutschland, bleiche Mutter*." *Germanic Review* 66(3) (Summer 1991): 113–129.

Kaes, Anton. "Our Childhoods, Ourselves: Helma Sanders-Brahms's *Germany, Pale Mother*." In *From Hitler to Heimat: The Return of History as Film*, 137–60. Cambridge, MA: Harvard University Press, 1989.

Keene, Judith. "Mothering Daughters: Subjectivity and History in the Work of Helma Sanders-Brahms's *Germany Pale Mother* (1979–1980)." *Film-Historia* 7(1) (1997): 3–12.

Liebman, Stuart. "*Germany, Pale Mother*." *Cineaste* 25(1) (1999): 51–52.

Naughton, Leonie. "*Germany Pale Mother*: Screen Memories of Nazism." *Continuum* 5(2) (1992): 141–58.

Reimer, Robert C., and Carol J. Reimer. "*Germany, Pale Mother*." In *Nazi-Retro Film: How German Narrative Cinema Remembers the Past*, 201–04. New York: Twayne, 1992.

Germinal (1993) Claude Berri; France/Belgium/Italy; French with English subtitles; Color; 160 m; Sony Pictures Home Entertainment (VHS); France, 1860s.

With a budget of over 160 million francs, *Germinal* was in 1993 the most expensive French film ever produced. Premiering in France the same autumn as Hollywood's own budget-devouring *Jurassic Park*, Germinal carried the burden of expectations it would appeal to critics and audiences, as well as symbolize French national cultural sovereignty. Director Claude Berri's answer to American blockbusters was that the French were capable of making crowd-pleasing epics that told their own stories, and which could rally citizens to political and social justice issues. As Donald Reid argues, this was a point repeatedly emphasized in the film's marketing, and which made the decision to purchase a ticket for *Germinal* an almost political act: "No one who saw *Germinal* in France in the fall of 1993 did so outside of the context of vanishing coal mines, a media barrage focused on the actors and director more than the film, and the GATT negotiations." (After intense French lobbying, the General Agreement on Tariffs and Trade excluded French farm products and cultural goods.) Judging from the critics on both sides of the Atlantic, though, Berri had perhaps achieved the same critical ambivalence that attends Hollywood's commercial successes. As Anthony Lane judged, "the lasting impression is of something long and boring and good for you, like celery. . . ."

Germinal is set in the industrial north of France in the 1860s, its plot revolving around the extensive Maheu family, generations of whom work at the Voreux coal mine in the town of Montsou. Newcomer Etienne Lantier arrives in town, boards with the Maheu's, and soon introduces the workers to his own burgeoning understanding of socialism. A surplus of coal has affected its market price; managers at Voreux announce that workers' wages will be recalculated in a new system that does not recognize the hours spent timbering the mine wall. Lantier initiates Maheu and other workers into the world of strike funds and mass action. The strike soon pits workers against capitalists in sometimes violent confrontation, divides the Voreux workers—some become "scab" laborers at the nearby Jean-Bart mine, which has remained open—and causes familial strife. The Maheu patriarch, characterized as a populist innocent awakened by injustices that harm his family, becomes a convinced unionist. Since the audience is asked to engage emotionally with his character and those in his family, his fate is the catalyst for the dramatic tension in the film.

Germinal includes an extensive range of characters, each representing in somewhat caricatured fashion the industrial and working classes, socialists, and anarchists. The wealth and ease of the Gregoire and Hennebeau families—the mine's principal shareholders and managers—is often starkly contrasted with the crowded living conditions and poor health of the Maheu's. The charity efforts of young Cécile Gregoire seem ineffective and condescending. That her betrothed, a nephew of mine manager Hennebeau, is having a sexual affair with his aunt, casts the upper class families as morally bankrupt. The repetition of these contrasts echoes the structure of Zola's nineteenth-century novel, upon which *Germinal* is based.

Its lack of subtlety makes *Germinal* sometimes irritatingly pedantic. As Lane says, "Claude Berri's overriding ambition is to insure that we will, at all costs, get the point." For those with little knowledge of the industrial era, however, this approach has its virtues. Berri has stuffed much valuable visual and empirical data into the film. The competing interests of industrialists and workers, the effect of industrial capitalism on labor conditions and labor relations, the character of early labor organization and organized labor activity, even gender roles of the era, are all, if briefly, "covered" in *Germinal*.

Viewers should be wary, however, of Berri's intentions with *Germinal*. The film is a paean to the past, a depiction of failed but seminal labor activism and working class heroes of France, intended to inspire modern French audiences. The film does not provide analysis of the roots of labor strife, or meaningfully situate these isolated events in the broader context of nineteenth-century social history. As Donald Reid says of Berri: "His goal was to evoke a collective memory of the world of manual labor. . . . Berri was not seeking to re-create a specific historical reality; he rejected out of hand the idea of bringing a historical consultant on board. Although the film is clearly set in the past, Berri went out of his way to insure that the viewer could not situate the period in which the action took place; great effort was taken to see that the costumes looked right, not that they were specific to an era. Berri reiterated that he wanted 'truth' rather than exactitude; a reinvention, not a reconstitution of the past. . . ."

See also: *Daens*; *The Organizer*

Cohen-Solal, Annie. "Coal Miners and Dinosaurs." *Media Studies Journal* (Fall 1995): 125–36.

Cousins, Russell. "The Heritage Film and Cultural Politics: Berri's *Germinal*." In *French Cinema in the 1990s: Continuity and Difference*, edited by Phil Powrie, 25–36. Oxford: Oxford University Press, 1999.

Murray, Alison. "Film as National Icon: Claude Berri's *Germinal*." *The French Review* 76(5) (April 2003): 906–16.

Reid, Donald. "Claude Berri's *Germinal*." *Radical History Review* 66 (Fall 1996): 146–62.

Siegel, Mona L. "*Germinal*: Teaching About Class and Industrial Capitalism through Film." *Radical History Review* 83 (Spring 2002): 180–185.

Zaniello, Tom. "*Germinal*." In *Working Stiffs, Union Maids, Reds, and Riffraff: An Organized Guide to Films About Labor*, 91–93. Ithaca, NY: ILR Press/Cornell University Press, 1996.

Girls in Uniform / Mädchen in Uniform (1931) Leontine Sagan; Germany; German with English subtitles; Black and White; 87 m; Home Vision Entertainment (VHS); Prussia, Germany, 1913.

The *Girls in Uniform* of the film's title are students of a Prussian girls' school in 1913, daughters of army officers. The strict rules and regimen of the institution mirror the militaristic values of the Prussian society. When it is reported to the dour principal, Frau Oberin, that confiscated letters to family contain students' complaints of hunger, she exclaims, "Hunger! We Prussians know how to hunger. Soldiers' children—and God willing, soldiers' mothers—we need discipline here, not luxury."

Frau Oberlin's view that discipline is the best form of schooling is soon contrasted with the methods of beloved teacher Fraulein von Bernburg, who professes the girls are more studious and well-adjusted when they receive love akin to "a mother's care."

In this setting—the camera only briefly moves beyond the walls of the institution—a lonely student named Manuela develops a close relationship with von Bernburg. Scenes of goodnight kisses and tearful meetings adopt a sensual tone, and viewers, like Frau Oberlin and the students, might wonder about the nature of the friendship.

A rare cinematic evocation of the private world of German girls and women in the imperial era, the film is often interpreted as a meditation on pre-Nazi German authoritarianism.

See also: *Effi Briest*

McCormick, Richard W. "Coming out of the Uniform: Political and Sexual Emancipation in Leontine Sagan's Film *Mädchen in Uniform*." In *Gender and Sexuality in Weimar Modernity: Film, Literature, and "New Objectivity,"* 146–62. New York: Palgrave, 2001.

Ohm, Lisa. "The Filmic Adaptation of the Novel *The Child Manuela*: Christa Winsloe's Child Heroine Becomes a *Girl in Uniform*." In *Gender and German Cinema: Feminist Interventions, Vol. II: German Film History/German History on Film*, edited by Sandra Frieden, Richard W. McCormick, Vibeke R. Petersen, and Laurie Melissa Vogelsang, 97–104. Providence, RI: Berg, 1993.

Rich, B. Ruby. "*Maedchen in Uniform*: From Repressive Tolerance to Erotic Liberation." *Jump Cut: A Review of Contemporary Media* 24/25 (March 1981): 44–50.

The Gleiwitz Case / Der fall Gleiwitz (1961) Gerhard Klein; East Germany; German with English subtitles; Black and White; 70 m; DEFA Film Library (VHS); Poland, 1939.

In 1939, a radio station at the German–Polish border at Gleiwitz suffered a surprise attack by "Polish" forces. Actually a staged operation by Nazis disguised as Poles, the attack was designed to create a pretext for the invasion of Poland.

The Gleiwitz Case—also known as *The Gleiwitz Affair*—recreates the events in a documentary style that incorporates elements of modernist experimentation.

Allan, Seán, and John Sandford, eds., *DEFA: East German Cinema, 1946–1992*. New York: Berghahn, 1999.

God's Gift / Wend Kuuni (1982) Gaston Kaboré; Burkina Faso; More with English subtitles; Color; 70 m; California Newsreel (VHS); Mossi village, Africa, mythic.

Its story rooted in the oral tradition of the Mossi of the western Sudan, the setting of *God's Gift* is a village that discovers and adopts a mute and memoryless boy. As a harvest scene unfolds, a voiceover says, "This was long ago, long before the white man came. The Mossi Empire was in its days of splendor." The recovery of the speech and memory of the boy, who has been interpreted as "God's Gift" to the villagers, provides the narrative tension in the story. Through flashbacks, the tragic circumstance of the boy's history unfolds. In addition, the depiction of villagers—tending goats, selling cloth in the market, sweeping the houseyard, or making small talk—introduces the social rhythms of daily life in the village.

See also: *Atanarjuat*; *Keïta! The Heritage of the Griot*; *Yeelen*

Andrade-Watkins, Claire. "Review of *Wend Kuuni, Zan Boko, Yaaba,* and *Tilai*." *American Historical Review* 97(4) (October 1992): 1143–46.

Andrew, Dudley. "The Roots of the Nomadic: Gilles Deleuze and the Cinema of West Africa." In *The Brain Is the Screen: Deleuze and the Philosophy of Cinema*, edited by Gregory Flaxman, 215–49. Minneapolis, MN: University of Minnesota Press, 2000.

Diawara, Manthia. "Oral Literature and African Film: Narratology in *Wend Kuuni*." In *Questions of Third Cinema*, edited by Jim Pines and Paul Willemen, 199–211. London: BFI, 1989.

Gone, Gone Forever Gone / Gate, gate paragate (1996) Hô Quang Minh; Vietnam/Switzerland; Vietnamese with English subtitles; Color; 85 m; no current; Vietnam, 1940s–1980s.

Gone, Gone Forever Gone begins in 1985 with the plans of a sister to reunite her estranged brothers, whose polarized politics were fashioned during the war between North and South Vietnam. *Gone, Gone Forever Gone* looks back to 40 years of family—and Vietnamese national—history. Its modest production values, leisurely pace, and invocation of a Buddhist sensibility might alienate some viewers, but its perspective on the effects of civil, colonial, and international strife is a necessary complement to more familiar productions that emphasize the historical American or French presence in Indochina.

See also: *Diên Biên Phu*; *Indochine*

Elley, Derek. "*Gone, Gone, Forever Gone (Gate, Gate, Paragate)*." *Variety* 364 (October 21/27, 1996): 100.

Good Men, Good Women / Haonan haonu (1995) Hou Hsiao-hsien; Taiwan; Taiwanese, Mandarin and Cantonese with English subtitles; Color, Black and White; 108 m; Facets (DVD; VHS); Taiwan and China, 1940s and 1990s.

The relationship of Taiwan's present and past is explored in this multi-layered film. The character of a young actress, Liang Ching, is rehearsing her role for a film about a Taiwanese couple who participated in the anti-Japanese movement in China in the 1940s and who were arrested as communists in Taiwan.

See also: *City of Sadness; The Puppetmaster; A Time to Live and a Time to Die*

Yip, June Chun. "Remembering and Forgetting Part II: Hou Hsiao-hsien's Taiwan Trilogy." In *Envisioning Taiwan: Fiction, Cinema, and the Nation in the Cultural Imaginary*, 85–130. Durham, NC: Duke University Press, 2004.

Goodbye, Children / Au revoir les enfants (1987) Louis Malle; France/West Germany; French with English subtitles; Color; 104 m; Criterion (DVD), MGM (VHS); France, 1944.

Child protagonists are a stock-in-trade of the movies. Historical films are no exception, frequently placing children in the role of witness to the past. In the process these films commonly narrate a passage from innocence to experience in the midst of overwhelming events. The best of these, a class that includes Louis Malle's autobiographical *Goodbye, Children*, interrogate the nature of historical memory and reconstruction.

Goodbye, Children is the gripping story of Julien Quentin, a student at a Catholic boarding school in Vichy France. In early 1944 a new student, Jean Bonnet, arrives. The film traces a year in these students' lives, one that we eventually discover is Jean's last. The social world of the school, with its pranks, cruelties, adolescent preoccupation with sex, and competing loyalties and friendships is increasingly penetrated by the realities of the German occupation and war. Food and fuel shortages become the basis for the enterprise (and later firing) of cook's helper Joseph, and militia searches seek a school monitor allegedly evading forced labor. As Julien's sometimes uneasy relationship with Jean grows into real friendship, and he attains knowledge of Jean's Jewish identity, his questions about racial politics emerge: Why must Jews wear stars? What is a Jew and what have they done that's so bad?

The film also very effectively depicts, in scenes of the provincial life of Julien's mother, the stubborn, and perhaps indictable continuation of the veneer of French social convention in the period of occupation. The wealthy enjoy fine restaurants where their rhetorical criticism of the French militia's collaboration with the Nazis is the weakest form of resistance.

Julien's own "collaboration"—linked to a Catholic Sister who reveals a Jewish child in the infirmary—is profoundly and irrevocably vulnerable to the personal judgment that will consume his whole life. As Louis Malle tells the story—as his memory insists—Julien sneaks one quick, worried glance at Jean, and exposes to the searching Gestapo his friend Jean Kippelstein, who is then taken away to his death at Auschwitz. Malle's voiceover at the film's conclusion, devastatingly connects past actions to a lifetime of personal regret: "More than forty years have passed, but I will remember every second of that January morning until I die."

Viewers' own estimation of Julien's responsibility, however, may differ. They know—because Malle shows them—that Joseph had earlier informed the authorities of Jean's real identity. The tension between viewers' own analysis of events, and that of Jean's, reveals history's multi-dimensional reality and its sometimes irreconcilable personal and collective retellings. Malle's assertion that even memory can be fractured by historical experience is the ultimate lament for the devastation wrought by history. As Elisa New says, Malle's story is thus "not a solution" to, but a "symptom of," the "brokenness" of his memory.

See also: *Border Street*; *Europa, Europa*; *Korczak*; *Empire of the Sun*

Corbitt, J.C. "Au Revoir to Film Illiteracy: An Interdisciplinary Exploration of *Au Revoir Les Enfants.*" *English Journal* 87(1) (1998): 83–87.

Ehrlich, Linda C. "The Name of the Child: Cinema as Social Critique." *Film Criticism* 14(2) (Winter 1989–90): 12–23.

Everett, W. "The Autobiographical Eye in European Film." *Europa: An International Journal of Language, Art and Culture* 2(1) (1995): 3–10.

Greene, Naomi. "Battles for Memory: Vichy Revisited." In *Landscapes of Loss: The National Past in Postwar French Cinema, 64–97*. Princeton, NJ: Princeton University Press, 1999.

Higgins, Lynn A. "If Looks Could Kill: Louis Malle's Portraits of Collaboration." In *Fascism, Aesthetics, and Culture*, edited by Richard J. Golsan, 198–211. Hanover, NH: University Press of New England, 1992.

New, Elisa. "Good-Bye, Children; Good-Bye, Mary, Mother of Sorrows: The Church and the Holocaust in the Art of Louis Malle." *Prooftexts* 22(1 and 2) (2002): 118–40.

Shorley, Christopher. "History, Memory and Art in Louis Malle's *Au Revoir Les Enfants.*" In *The Seeing Century: Film, Vision and Identity*, edited by Wendy Everett, 49–59. Amsterdam: Rodopi, 2000.

The Great White Man of Lambaréné / Le grand blanc de Lambaréné (1995)

Bassek Ba Kobhio; Gabon/Cameroon/France; French with English subtitles; Color; 94 m; California Newsreel (VHS); Gabon, 1944–1965.

The Great White Man of Lambaréné is about Alsatian doctor and Nobel Peace Prize winner Albert Schweitzer (1875–1965), who founded a hospital in French Equatorial Africa (present-day Gabon) in 1913.

The film is so genuinely beautiful and engaging that a viewer unfamiliar with the life of its subject might be left with questions about the veracity of the story. In many ways the film is faithful to the historical record. The setting is quite authentic; an intertitle describes the film as "made where Dr. Schweitzer lived and worked," a small hospital in the village of Lambaréné, on the Ogooué River. As the story suggests, Gabon did become an independent republic in 1960, and true to the film, Schweitzer was highly celebrated throughout the Western world for his humanitarian work in Africa, and heralded with the Nobel. In addition—as scenes showing the visit of an uncomfortably probing journalist suggest—questions about whether his treatment of the locals was abusive were in fact voiced in contemporary press articles. (Such questions have not, however, dimmed Schweitzer's continuing popular reputation as a humanitarian.) The doctor's prodigious knowledge of medicine, philosophy, Christianity, and music has been well documented. Finally, the film's revisionist representation of Schweitzer as testy, paternalistic, and culturally arrogant is consistent with credible postcolonial interpretations of the Europeans in Africa. In other words, canonization of Schweitzer here is, reasonably, rejected.

But Cameroonian director Ba Kobhio refuses to quantify this European's life in merely heroic or villainous terms. Schweitzer's encounters and relationships with such invented characters as Bissa—portrayed as a confidant and lover—provide an avenue for the film to create a subtle and profound verdict on the man. When Schweitzer first resists Bissa's advances, he protests, "because I mustn't." Bissa's reply is a lament for those lost opportunities for a truly cross-cultural encounter in Africa: "Perhaps you give," she says, "but you don't share."

See also: *Bethune: The Making of a Hero*

Foster, Gwendolyn. "The Post-Colonial Vision of the 'Great White' of Lambaréné." *Popular Culture Review* 11(2) (Summer 2000): 113–119.

Foster, Gwendolyn. *Performing Whiteness: Postmodern Re/Constructions in the Cinema.* Albany, NY: Suny Press, 2003.

Rocchio, Vincent F. "*The Great White Man of Lambaréné* and the Limits of Representation." In *Reel Racism: Confronting Hollywood's Construction of Afro-American Culture,* 191–210. Boulder, CO: Westview, 2000.

Hamsin / Eastern Wind / Hot Wind (1982) Daniel Wachsmann; Israel; Hebrew with English subtitles; Color; 90 m; Facets (VHS); Israel, 1982.

Daniel Wachsmann's film is set in an agricultural community in 1980s Galilee, where both Arabs and Jews are settled and enjoy friendships that reach back generations. The Israeli state's plans to confiscate some Arab-owned lands produce unease, and when Abu Yussuf agrees to sell to his neighbor, Gedaliah, and enjoy a profit-sharing scheme, not all his family members or Jewish and Arab neighbors approve. In the mix of these tensions is Khaled, a Palestinian employee of Gedaliah, who has begun a covert relationship with Gedaliah's sister, Hava.

Hamsin is an example of the (many) historical films that place a story of forbidden love in the context of civil conflicts. Such lovers can convey the perspective of partisan factions, and yet at the same time construct a bridge that reconciles these historic factions, or establish significant shared values or norms that transcend difference and signal a means of coexistence. In turn, the personal and emotional dimensions of romantic love depicted in the film can engage the audience in the fate of the couple, and by association, in the fate of the conflict. In the case of *Hamsin*, the lovers find no supporters from either Jewish or Arab quarters, suggesting not only the power of interracial taboos in this Israeli society, but also the intransigence of those modern Israelis, like Gedaliah, who seem on other grounds to have accepted the economic interrelationships of Jews and Arabs.

Loshitzky, Yosefa. "Forbidden Love in the Holy Land: Transgressing the Israeli-Palestinian Conflict." In *Identity Politics on the Israeli Screen,* 112–53. Austin: University of Texas Press, 2001.

Naaman, Dorit. "Orientalism as Alterity in Israeli Cinema." *Cinema Journal* 40(4) (2001): 36–54.

Yosef, Raz. "Homoland: Interracial Sex and the Israeli/Palestinian Conflict." In *Beyond Flesh: Queer Masculinities and Nationalism in Israeli Cinema,* 118–41. New Brunswick, NJ: Rutgers University Press, 2004.

Harvest 3000 Years / Mirt sost shi amit (1976) Haile Gerima; Ethiopia; Amharic with English subtitles; Black and White; 150 m; Mypheduh Films (VHS); Ethiopia, contemporary.

The relationship of a poor Ethiopian farm family and their wealthy landlord is examined in this meditative drama whose plot revolves around the resistance of teenage siblings to their expected roles.

Gerima, Haile. "Visions of Resistance." *Sight & Sound* 5 (September 1995): 32–33.

Quam, Michael D. "*Harvest: 3000 Years*: Sowers of Maize and Bullets." *Jump Cut: A Review of Contemporary Media* 24/25 (March 1981): 5–7.

Heimat / Heimat: Eine deutsche Chronik (1984) Edgar Reitz; West Germany; German with English subtitles; Black and White, Color; 924 m; Facets (DVD, VHS); Germany, 1918–1982.

Heimat, roughly translated as "homeland," is an epic but intimate chronicle of the lives of several generations of members of the fictional village of Schabbach over much of the twentieth century. Originally conceived as a feature film, *Heimat* premiered in serial form on West German television and became something of a popular phenomenon. Many of the great events of German and world history are in the distant background of *Heimat*, which privileges scenes of everyday life, such as the arrival of the telephone or highway, personal ambition and family gatherings, and the absence of villagers during their army service or visits in the city. Nostalgic in tone, the film explores the seemingly inexorable change of the physical environment and social mores over time, and the relationship of memory to personal and political history. *Heimat* has been both praised and criticized for "normalizing" the period of the Third Reich through this foregrounding of everyday life.

See also: *The Family* (Scola); *Siberiade*; *Sunshine*

Barkin, Kenneth. "Review of *Heimat*." *American Historical Review* 96(4) (October 1991): 1124–26.

Barta, Tony. "Recognizing the Third Reich: *Heimat* and the Ideology of Innocence." In *History on/and/in Film: Selected Papers from the Third Australian History and Film Conference*, edited by Brian Shoesmith and Tom O'Regan, 131–39. Perth: History and Film Association of Australia, 1985.

Elsaesser, Thomas. "Subject Positions, Speaking Positions: From *Holocaust, Our Hitler*, and *Heimat* to *Shoah* and *Schindler's List*." In *The Persistence of History: Cinema, Television, and the Modern Event*, edited by Vivian Sobchack, 145–83. New York: Routledge, 1996.

Kaes, Anton. "Germany as Memory: Edgar Reitz's *Heimat*." In *From Hitler to Heimat: The Return of History as Film*, 161–192. Cambridge, MA: Harvard University Press, 1989.

Reimer, Robert C., and Carol J. Reimer. "*Heimat*." In *Nazi-Retro Film: How German Narrative Cinema Remembers the Past*, 188–92. New York: Twayne, 1992.

Hill 24 Doesn't Answer / Giv'a 24 Eina Ona (1955) Thorold Dickinson; Israel; English and Hebrew with English subtitles; Black and White; 101 m; Sisu (DVD), Facets (VHS); Palestine, 1948.

An example of what Ella Shohat describes as Israeli cinema's "heroic-nationalist" phase, *Hill 24 Doesn't Answer* is about four fighters who are assigned to defend a strategic point outside of Jerusalem during the 1948 Arab-Israeli War. The characters comprise a multinational cross-section of Zionists: a Sephardic woman from Yemen, an Ashkenazi man, an Irishman, and an American. The film opens with shots of their dead bodies, then reaches back to the stories of each, in effect explaining how their fates converge on the hill. Little attention is given to the woman's story, but each of the other characters appear in extended flashbacks, their personal stories becoming the agent of *Hill 24*'s explanation of the creation of the Israeli state.

See also: *Exodus*; *Kedma*

Quart, Leonard. "*Hill 24 Doesn't Answer.*" *Cineaste* 16(3) (1988): 57.

Shohat, Ella. "*Hill 24 Doesn't Answer (Giv'a 24 Eina Ona, 1955).*" In *Israeli Cinema: East/West and the Politics of Representation*, 58–76. Austin: University of Texas Press, 1989.

Hiroshima, My Love / Hiroshima, mon amour (1959) Alain Resnais; Japan/France; French with English subtitles; Black and White; 91 m; Facets (DVD; VHS); Japan, 1959.

Marguerite Duras wrote the screenplay for this enigmatic work, in which a French actress in Hiroshima in 1959 to shoot a film spends the night with a Japanese man. Their relationship becomes a confessional one, as the actress begins to relate her story of a wartime love affair with a German soldier and its traumatic outcome. But for its scenes of the woman's recalled experiences in France, *Hiroshima, mon amour* takes place in a city that was obliterated by the atomic bomb, and whose traces of that event are (at least superficially) being lost to reconstruction. In this setting, the lovers question their fidelity to their own traumatic experiences: reintegration into society, the loss of memory, physical alterations over time—all threaten their hold on the realness of the past. The terrible implications of the past's ephemerality is a desolating theme. As the Japanese lover insists, "You saw nothing in Hiroshima, nothing."

See also: *Ararat*; *Black Rain*

Baker, Deborah Lesko. "Memory, Love, and Inaccessibility in *Hiroshima Mon Amour*." In *Marguerite Duras Lives On*, edited by Janine Ricouart, 27–37. Lanham, MD: University Press of America, 1998.

Lane, Nancy. "The Subject in/of History: *Hiroshima Mon Amour*." In *Literature and Film in the Historical Dimension: Selected Papers from the Fifteenth Annual Florida State University Conference on Literature and Film*, edited by John D. Simons, 89–100. Gainesville: University Press of Florida, 1994.

Maclear, Kyo. "The Limits of Vision: *Hiroshima Mon Amour* and the Subversion of Representation." In *Witness and Memory: The Discourse of Trauma*, edited by Ana Douglass and Thomas A. Vogler, 233–48. London: Routledge, 2003.

Ropars-Wuilleumier, Marie-Claire. "How History Begets Meaning: Alain Resnais' *Hiroshima Mon Amour*." In *French Film: Texts and Contexts*, edited by Susan Hayward and Ginette Vincendeau, 173–86. London: Routledge, 1990.

Roth, Michael S. "*Hiroshima Mon Amour*: You Must Remember This." In *Revisioning History: Film and the Construction of a New Past*, edited by Robert A. Rosenstone, 91–101. Princeton, NJ: Princeton University Press, 1995.

The Home and the World / Ghare-Baire (1984) Satyajit Ray; India; Bengali with English subtitles; Color; 140 m; Columbia/Tristar (VHS); Bengal, 1907–8.

The Home and the World is narrated by the female protagonist Bimala, whose fate is described at the film's outset in a roaring wall of flames that frame opening credits. Bimala draws viewers into an extended flashback, recalling her arranged marriage 10 years earlier to the son of a nobleman. As the scene unfolds, we learn Bimala was raised in a traditional Bengali family. Her husband, however, has a modern outlook; the first in his family to have a Western education, Nikhil owns a large estate and prides himself on treating his tenants humanely. Nikhil also decries the custom of cloistering women (*purdah*), and encourages a reluctant Bimala to learn English and—fatefully—to meet Sandip, a friend and leader of the *swadeshi* movement. Soon, Bimala is increasingly discomfited by her emergence from social isolation, just as Bengal is more deeply immersed in the conflicts of the emerging anticolonial movement.

See also: *Distant Thunder; Spices*

Banerjee, Arundhati. "The Indian Woman's Dilemma: A Study of Formation in Gender Construct through Mediation of Western Culture in Tagore's *Ghare Baire* and Ray's Film Version." In *Gender and Culture in Literature and Film East and West: Issues of Perception and Interpretation: Selected Conference Papers*, edited by Nitaya Masavisut, George Simson and Larry E. Smith, 207–24. Honolulu, HI: University of Hawaii: East-West Center, 1994.

Cooper, Darius. "From Gazes to Threat: The Odyssean *Yatra* (Journey) of the Ray Woman." In *The Cinema of Satyajit Ray: Between Tradition and Modernity*, 75–133. Cambridge: Cambridge University Press, 2000.

———. "Review of *The Home and the World*." *Film Quarterly* 43(2) (1989–90): 40–43.

Dirks, Nicholas B. "Review of *The Home and the World*." *American Historical Review* 95 (1990): 1119–21.

———. "*The Home and the World*: The Invention of Modernity in Colonial India." In *Revisioning History: Film and the Construction of a New Past*, edited by Robert A. Rosenstone, 44–63. Princeton, NJ: Princeton University Press, 1995.

Ghosh, Bishnupriya, and Bhaskar Sarkar. "Contested Boundaries: Anti-Colonial Struggles and Postcolonial Negotiations in *Ghare Baire*." *Journal of Commonwealth and Postcolonial Studies* 6(1) (1997): 74–90.

Leenerts, Cynthia A. "Rabindranath Tagore's and Satyajit Ray's 'New Woman': Writing and Rewriting Bimala." In *Rabindranath Tagore: Universality and Tradition*, edited by Patrick Colm Hogan and Lalita Pandit, 129–40. Madison, NJ: Fairleigh Dickinson University Press, 2003.

Hot Winds / Garam Hava / Garm Hawa (1973) M.S. Sathyu; India; Urdu and Hindi with English subtitles; Color; 136 m; Facets (DVD); India, late 1940s.

In 1947 the British colony of India was divided into the two sovereign states of India and Pakistan. The accompanying violence, migration, and dislocation of Hindus and Muslims was massive. The dilemmas of families who found themselves an ethnic or religious minority in the newly-constituted states is dramatized in *Hot Winds*, often described as a classic of "partition drama." Patriarch Salim Mirza, of a fictional Muslim family in the northern Indian town of Agra, must decide whether to abandon the generations-old family shoe-making business and migrate to Pakistan. The implications of his decision suggest some of the experiences of other Muslim Indian families. These include family division, economic decline, and the growing attraction of ideological solutions (such as found in the communist movement) to the historical ethnic, religious, and class strife.

See also: *Earth* (Mehta); *Cloud-Capped Star*

Chakravarty, Sumita S. "Redefining the Nation: *Garm Hawa*." In *National Identity in Indian Popular Cinema 1947–1987*, 248–52. Austin: University of Texas Press, 1993.

Datta, Sangeeta. "*Garam Hawa*." *Cinema in India* 4(1) (1993): 107–8.

The House on Chelouche Street / Ha-Bayit Berechov Chelouche / Habayit B'Rechov Chelouche (1973) Moshé Mizrahi; Israel; Hebrew with English subtitles; Color; 110 m; Facets (VHS); Tel Aviv, 1946–1948.

The House on Chelouche Street is at turns a nostalgic coming-of-age film, and a dramatic invocation of the fear and violence experienced everyday by Sephardim in late 1940s Palestine. A poor Sephardi family lives on Chelouche Street, in Tel Aviv, during the end of the British mandate in Palestine. "How did we come to this?" Aunt Mazal says, recalling their better days in Egypt, where they enjoyed paid help. Now Clara, her widowed sister, cleans for rich households in the city. Clara's eldest son, 15-year-old Sami, has so far avoided joining the Zionist militant anti-British organization, the *Irgun*. His association with a young communist coworker leads to his beating by local thugs, and British raids seeking out *Irgun* members reach closer and closer to home.

See also: *Exodus; Kedma; Hill 24 Doesn't Answer; The Wooden Gun*

Lubin, Orly. "Nationality, Ethnicity and Women." *Cinemateque* 75(16–9) (September/October 1994): 16–29.

Shohat, Ella. "*The House on Chlouch Street (Habait Birkhov Chlouch*, 1973)." In *Israeli Cinema: East/West and the Politics of Representation*, 166–72. Austin: University of Texas Press, 1989.

How Tasty Was My Little Frenchman / Como era gostoso o meu francês (1971) Nelson Pereira dos Santos; Brazil; Portuguese, Tupi, and French with English subtitles; Color; 84 m; Facets (VHS); Brazil, 16th century.

The history of the Columbian era of expansion has inspired films that are unambiguous in their praise of heroic and triumphant conquerors. *How Tasty Was My Little Frenchman* offers a counter-discourse. The film revisits the Portuguese and Dutch contest in sixteenth-century Brazil as farce, where the roles of victim and protagonist are inverted and the distinctions between document and fiction are questioned.

Director Nelson Pereira dos Santos portrays Brazilian natives as keenly otherwise than conquistadors' historical documents suggest, challenging traditional claims of history and simplistic images of colonial natives. In the opening scene, images of the Tupinamba natives greeting Europeans contrast with the claims of the voice of a letter reader: "The country is a barren desert ... the natives are barbarous savages."

The story follows an explorer in Portuguese Brazil who claims to be French but whose inability to prove this ultimately leads to his death in a cannibal ritual of the Tupinamba. Using identity as a tool of survival and potential escape, the captive "Frenchman" Jean integrates with the tribe, adopting Tupi dress, accepting a Tupi wife, acting to secure a cache of gunpowder coveted by the tribe, and teaching them the use of captured Portuguese cannons. Jean's relationship to his captors allows viewers a representation of the Tupi as both "other" and inexorably affected by contact, as is Jean.

See also: *1492: Conquest of Paradise; Aguirre; Cabeza de Vaca; Jericho*

Burton, Julianne. "Interview with Nelson Pereira Dos Santos." In *Cinema and Social Change in Latin America: Conversations with Filmmakers*, edited by Julianne Burton, 133–41. Austin: University of Texas Press, 1986.

Davis, Darien J. "Review of *Hans Staden* and *How Tasty Was My Little Frenchman*." *American Historical Review* 106(2) (2001): 695–97.

Gordon, Richard. "Exoticism and National Identity in *Cabeza De Vaca* and *Como era gostoso o meu francês* [*How Tasty Was My Little Frenchman*]." *Torre de Papel* 10(1) (2000): 77–119.

Peña, Richard. "*How Tasty Was My Little Frenchman*." In *Brazilian Cinema*, edited by Randal Johnson and Robert Stam, 191–99. Rutherford, NJ: Associated University Press, 1982.

Sadlier, Darlene J. "The Politics of Adaptation: *How Tasty Was My Little Frenchman*." In *Film Adaptation*, edited by James Naremore, 190–205. New Brunswick, NJ: Rutgers University Press, 2000.

The Human Condition: No Greater Love / Ningen no joken I (1958) Masaki Kobayashi; Japan; Japanese with English subtitles; Black and White; 208 m; Image Entertainment (DVD, VHS); Manchuria, 1943.

The Human Condition: Road to Eternity / Ningen No Joken II (1959) Masaki Kobayashi; Japan; Japanese with English subtitles; Black and White; 180 m; Image Entertainment (DVD, VHS); Manchuria, 1944–1945.

The Human Condition: A Soldier's Prayer / Ningen No Joken III (1961) Masaki Kobayashi; Japan; Japanese with English subtitles; Black and White; 190 m; Image Entertainment (DVD, VHS); Siberia and Manchuria, 1945.

The Human Condition is a film trilogy of over nine hours in length, based on a 6-volume novel by Junpei Gomikawa. The setting is Manchuria beginning in 1943, where Kaji has come to work in the Japanese management of a prison camp for the Chinese. He has many modern ideas about making operations at the camp humane and efficient, derived from his university studies and his work at a steel company. His supervisors are doubtful about his plans, and when a successful prison escape occurs, Kaji is suspected as having played a role. Events place Kaji more squarely in the experience of the war than he, an intellectual opposed to imperial Japan's militarism, would choose. He becomes a combatant soldier for the Kwangtung army, is captured and imprisoned in Siberia, and eventually dies in the snow on his escape home to his wife.

In the same vein of other 1950s Japanese cinematic efforts at coming to terms with the recent past, the film relies upon a single character's experience of the war to convey an antiwar message. Unlike films like *Fires on the Plain*, however, *The Human Condition* provides the perspective of a Japanese man whose sense of patriotic duty is conceived in economic, not militaristic, terms, but who is powerless to avoid participation in the war.

See also: *Burmese Harp*; *Fires on the Plain*; *Stalingrad*

Gluck, Carol. "*The Human Condition*." In *Past Imperfect: History According to the Movies*, edited by Mark C. Carnes, 250–53. New York: Henry Holt, 1995.

Hyenas / Hyènes (1992) Djibril Diop Mambety; Senegal; Wolof with English subtitles; Color; 110 m; California Newsreel (DVD, VHS); Senegal, contemporary.

A woman returning to her native village after an absence of 30 years offers to share her immense riches if the villagers commit a murder. A satirical fable about consumerism in postcolonial Africa, *Hyenas* is an adaptation of Swiss playwright Friedrich Dürrenmatt's *The Visit of the Old Woman*.

Mermin, Elizabeth. "A Window on Whose Reality? The Emerging Industry of Senegalese Cinema." *Research in African Literatures* 26(3) (1995): 120–33.

Morganti, Nike. "Djibril and Myth: Anta and Linguère: Portraits of Ladies." *Écrans d'Afrique* 7(24) (1998): 54–67.

Porton, Richard. "*Hyenas.*" *Cineaste* 23(2) (1997): 51.

———. "Mambety's *Hyenas*: Between Anti-Colonialism and the Critique of Modernity." *Iris* 18 (Spring 1995): 95–103.

Racevskis, Maija. "Applications of African Cinema in the High School Curriculum: A Secondary Teacher's Views of *Three Tales from Senegal, Ca Twiste À Poponguine, Udju Azul Di Yonta, Hyenas,* and *Keïta.*" *Research in African Literatures* 27(3) (1996): 98–109.

Ukadike, N. Frank. "The Hyena's Last Laugh." *Transition: An International Review* 8(2) (1999): 136–53.

I, Pierre Rivière, Having Slaughtered My Mother, My Sister and My Brother... / Moi, Pierre Rivière, ayant égorgé ma mère, ma soeur et mon frère... (1974) René Allio; France; French; Color; 130 m; no current; France, 1835.

In 1835 a peasant in Normandy murdered three family members. His story is recreated here—largely using locals as actors—on the basis of extant records, including a prison confession. *I, Pierre Rivière* is based on the document analysis of the same name produced by Michel Foucault.

See also: *The Return of Martin Guerre*

Benson, Ed. "*Martin Guerre,* the Historian and the Filmmakers: An Interview with Natalie Zemon Davis." *Film & History: An Interdisciplinary Journal of Film and Television Studies* 13(3) (1983): 49–65.

Jenkins, S. "*Moi, Pierre Rivière, Ayant égorgé ma Mère, Ma Soeur Et Mon Frère....*" *Monthly Film Bulletin* 47 (December 1980): 238–39.

Jourdheuil, Jean, Serge Toubiana, Pascal Bonitzer, René Allio, Pascal Kané, and Michel Foucault. "*I, Pierre Rivière, Having Slaughtered My Mother, My Sister and My Brother...* By René Allio." In *Cahiers Du Cinéma: Vol. 4, 1973–1978: History, Ideology, Cultural Struggle: An Anthology from Cahiers Du Cinéma Nos. 248–292, September 1973-September 1978,* edited by David Wilson and Bérénice Reynaud, 173–85. London: Routledge, 2000.

I, the Worst of All / Yo, la peor de todas (1990) María Luisa Bemberg; Argentina; Spanish with English subtitles; Color; 105 m; Facets (DVD, VHS); Mexico, 17th century.

I, the Worst of All takes viewers into the cloistered and accomplished life of Sor Juana—a seventeenth-century poet and scholar—and at the same time connects that life to the context of international politics. The story is based on Octavio Paz's 1982 book *Sor Juana Inés de la Cruz, o, Las trampas de la fe.* Juana Inés de la Cruz enters a convent as a young adult in order to be free to pursue her studies. But Sor Juana's tightly framed world is not as insulated from society as one might first expect. Director Bemberg suggests there is sexual intimacy behind Sor Juana's friendship with the Vicereine, and she is interpreted as a pawn in the power struggle between the Spanish crown, the Viceroy, the Catholic Archbishop, and the Jesuit order.

See also: *Camila*

Bach, Caleb. "Maria Luisa Bemberg Tells the Untold." *Americas* 46(2) (March–April 1994): 20–27.

Falicov, Tamara. "Argentina's Blockbuster Movies and the Politics of Culture under Neoliberalism, 1989–98." *Media, Culture & Society* 5(22) (2000): 327–42.

Miller, Denise. "María Luisa Bemberg's Interpretation of Octavio Paz's *Sor Juana*." In *An Argentine Passion: María Luisa Bemberg and Her Films*, edited by John King, Sheila Whitaker, and Rosa Bosch, 137–73. London: Verso, 2000.

Ramírez, Susan E. "*I, the Worst of All*: The Literary Life of Sor Juana Inés De La Cruz." In *Based on a True Story: Latin American History at the Movies*, edited by Donald F. Stevens, 47–62. Wilmington, DE: Scholarly Resources, 1997.

———. "Review of *I, the Worst of All*." *American Historical Review* (October 1991): 1161–62.

Identity Pieces / Pièces d'identités (1998) Mweze Ngangura; Congo/Belgium; French with English subtitles; Color, Black and White; 93 m; California Newsreel (VHS); Belgium and Congo, contemporary.

In a fable-like story, the king of the Bakongo people of modern Congo travels to Brussels to find his grown daughter. Despite his people's claim that "Our King will live everywhere as King," his travels expose his irrelevance in the modern world and the loss of his culture to westernization.

Georges, Genevieve. "*Pieces d'identités*, Un Africain a Bruxelles." *Écrans d'Afrique* 6(20) (1997): 10–13.

Ukadike, N. Frank. "Ngangura Mweze (Congo)." In *Questioning African Cinema: Conversations with Filmmakers*, 133–50. Minneapolis, MN: University of Minnesota Press, 2002.

In the Heat of the Sun / Yangguang canlan de rizi (1994) Jiang Wen; China/Hong Kong; Mandarin with English subtitles; Black and White, Color; 134 m; no current; China, 1970s.

Challenging viewers to accept memories of childhood as veracious, *In the Heat of the Sun* is a stylistic counterpoint to films about the Chinese Cultural Revolution that adopt a realist mode. Based on a novel by Wang Shuo, the film is about a group of teenagers who seem at liberty to enjoy their privileges and freedom in a city that has become their playground since the revolution's closure of schools and forced exodus of adults to the countryside.

See also: *The Blue Kite*; *Farewell My Concubine*; *King of the Children*

Berry, Chris. "*Yangguang Canlan De Rizi*." *Cinemaya: The Asian Film Quarterly* 31 (Winter 1995): 23–24.

Braester, Yomi. "Memory at a Standstill: From Maohistory to Hooligan History." In *Witness against History: Literature, Film, and Public Discourse in Twentieth-Century China*, 192–205. Stanford: Stanford University Press, 2003.

Liu, Xinmin. "Play and Being Playful: The Quotidian in Cinematic Remembrance of the Mao Era." *Asian Cinema: a Publication of the Asian Cinema Studies Society* 15(1) (Spring 2004): 73–89.

Lu, Tonglin. "Fantasy and Ideology in a Chinese Film: A Žižekian Reading of the Cultural Revolution." *Positions: East Asia Cultures Critique* 12(2) (Fall 2004): 539–64.

Indochine (1992) Régis Wargnier; France; French and Vietnamese with English subtitles; Color; 155 m; Columbia/TriStar (DVD, VHS); Indochina, 1930–1954.

The affair between a French rubber plantation owner and a French naval officer in Indochina in the 1930s is complicated when her adopted Annamese daughter falls in love with the same man. This romantic historical drama describes the waning of the French colonial era.

Heung, Marina. "The Family Romance of Orientalism: From *Madame Butterfly* to *Indochine*." In *Visions of the East: Orientalism in Film*, edited by Matthew Bernstein and Gaylyn Studlar, 158–83. New Brunswick, NJ: Rutgers University Press, 1997.

Murray, Alison. "Women, Nostalgia, Memory: *Chocolat, Outremer*, and *Indochine*." *Research in African Literatures* 33(2) (Summer 2002): 235–44.

Nicholls, David. "*Indochine*." *History Today* 46(9) (September 1996): 33–38.

Norindr, Panivong. "Filmic Memorial and Colonial Blues: Indochina in Contemporary French Cinema." In *Cinema, Colonialism, Postcolonialism: Perspectives from the French and Francophone World*, edited by Dina Sherzer, 120–46. Austin: University of Texas Press, 1996.

———. *Phantasmatic Indochina: French Colonial Ideology in Architecture, Film and Literature*. Durham, NC: Duke University Press, 1997.

The Inner Circle / Blizhniy krug (1991) Andrei Konchalovsky; Italy/United States/Russia; English; Color; 137 m; Sony Pictures Home Entertainment (VHS); Soviet Union, 1939–1953.

Despite the drubbing given *The Inner Circle* by most North American critics, Andrei Konchalovsky's tale of romance and persecution in the Stalinist era is worthwhile viewing. An American, Russian, and Italian coproduction, the film was shot on location in Moscow, including the Kremlin. Intended for both American and Russian audiences, it was the first post-USSR film to examine the Stalinist era. Despite the sometimes laughable Russian accents of its largely English-speaking cast, and the sentimentalization of its love story, *The Inner Circle* provides in its better moments an interpretation of the nature of the regime and its relationship to ordinary people. That interpretation is simplistic, but is nevertheless the one to (briefly) grace the screens of North American and Russian cinemas early in the post-Soviet era.

The "inner circle" of the title is the locus of power in the Kremlin, consisting of a small group of men including Comrades Stalin, Beria (head of the NKVD), Molotov (foreign minister), and Voroshilov (defense minister). Viewers' glimpse into that world is through the window of a projectionist's room, from which we see Stalin's personal screening theater, where he enjoys fare as diverse as *The Great Waltz*, Chaplin, and Soviet propaganda newsreels. We meet Ivan Sanshin, the protagonist and soon-to-be Kremlin projectionist, in 1939; he is celebrating his marriage to Anastasia, and enjoys a secure job showing films at KGB headquarters. (The film prefers to identify the NKVD as its later incarnation, the KGB.) The character of Sanshin is based on real Kremlin projectionist Aleksandr Ganshin, who served as a consultant on the film. Like Ganshin, the film's Sanshin holds his job until Stalin's death in 1953. During this period he enjoys the benefits of his association with Stalin, including a healthy salary and a modest basement apartment that is superior to the crowded rooms others in Moscow are forced to share. Sanshin also enjoys some limited interaction with his "boss," but is sworn to secrecy about where he works.

Sanshin's inability to keep that secret soon implicates his wife in this world of privileges, and their costs. Her eventual seduction by Beria not only casts him as the main villain of the film (and thereby the period), but leads to her suicide and Sanshin's epiphany about the unethical and tragic consequences of his allegiance to his revered Stalin. By film's end, Sanshin has begun to redeem himself by vowing to protect Katya Gubelman, a young Jewish woman who was orphaned and institutionalized at the age of three when her parents—Sanshin and Anastasia's neighbors—were arrested as "traitors to the Motherland." The danger of Anastasia's affection for poor Katya—she insists on visits to the orphanage as Katya's "aunt"—are not lost on Sanshin, and his forbiddance of such visits is the catalyst for a series of events that lead to his wife's death.

The resonant scenes of *The Inner Circle* are not those that chronicle this story of love and redemption, nor the character arcs traversed by Ivan and Anastasia, he from political savvy to deliberate abandon, she from political naivety to tragic awareness and complicity. Instead, it is the abject fear shown by three peripheral characters that is most successful in suggesting that beneath the surface of the socialist masses working toward the dream of communism is the manipulation of those people through terror. The head of the KGB orphanage discovers that Anastasia's motive to apply for a job to help oversee the orphaned children of political enemies is only to find Katya. The orphanage director's paralyzing fear of her mistake and being implicated by Anastasia's foolishness is palpable in her nervous smoking and pacing. The Cinema Minister is equally fear-stricken when Sanshin's naive criticism of a Soviet-produced portable projector takes place in front of Stalin. And Professor Bartnev, a tenant in Sanshin's building, simply wants to be left alone; having not succumbed to Stalin's cult of personality, he wishes to observe and hear nothing.

See also: *Repentance*

Boym, Svetlana. "Stalin's Cinematic Charisma: Between History and Nostalgia." *Slavic Review* 51(3) (Fall 1992): 537–45.

Michalski, Milena. "Review of *Inner Circle*." *Slavonic & East European Review* 72(3) (July 1994): 591–93.

Philip, J.V.N. "Hollywood Discovers the Gulag: *The Inner Circle*." *Policy Review* 92(60) (1992).

Youngblood, Denise J. "The Cosmopolitan and the Patriot: The Brothers Mikhalkov-Konchalovsky and Russian Cinema." *Historical Journal of Film, Radio and Television* 23(1) (2003): 27–42.

It Happened Here (1966) Kevin Brownlow and Andrew Mollo; United Kingdom; English and German with English subtitles; Black and White; 97 m; Milestone (DVD, VHS); England, 1944.

This imaginative, and disconcerting, rewrite of the outcome of World War II imagines England ruled by victorious Nazi Germany. The story of the film's main character, an English nurse, invites ethical questions about the nature of complicity and resistance.

See also: *The Emperor's New Clothes*

Rosenfeld, Gavriel D. *The World Hitler Never Made: Alternate History and the Memory of Nazism*. Cambridge: Cambridge University Press, 2005.

Tibbetts, J.C. "Between the Map and the Painted Landscape: Kevin Brownlow's Historical Films: *It Happened Here* (1965) and *Winstanley* (1975)." *Historical Journal of Film, Radio and Television* 20(2) (2000): 227–51.

It's Raining on Santiago / Il pleut sur Santiago (1976) Helvio Soto; France/Bulgaria; French and Spanish with English subtitles; Color; 112 m; Image Entertainment (DVD, VHS); Chile 1970–1973.

It's Raining on Santiago ambitiously interprets the events surrounding the overthrow and death of Chile's President Salvador Allende on September 11, 1973. A flashback to the presidential election of 1970 shows the announcement of Allende's victory was delayed by the conservative incumbent's nervous consultation with the army and CIA. And a scene of May Day celebrations in 1971 symbolizes the pro-labor policies of Allende's Unidad Party. Director Helvio Soto weaves several personal stories into the framework of power politics in early 1970s Chile. While the cinematic Allende is a rarely seen and idealized figure, three supporters of the Left whose personal lives are sacrificed are followed: a journalist, a close Allende advisor, and a labor leader.

Pick, Zuzana M. "Chilean Cinema: Ten Years of Exile: 1973–1983." *Jump Cut: A Review of Contemporary Media* 32 (April 1986): 66–70.

Ivan the Terrible, Part One / Ivan Groznyj I (1945) Sergei M. Eisenstein; Soviet Union; Russian with English subtitles; Black and White; 95 m; Criterion (DVD), Home Vision Entertainment (VHS); Russia, 1547–1564.

Ivan the Terrible, Part Two / The Boyars' Plot / Ivan Groznyj II: Boyarsky zagovor (1958) Sergei M. Eisenstein and M. Filimonova; Soviet Union; Russian with English subtitles; Black and White with color segments; 88 m; Criterion (DVD), Home Vision Entertainment (VHS); Russia, 1560s.

This magnificent work of Eisenstein's sound film period is comprised of two parts, the first beginning with the 1547 crowning of the archduke of Moscow, as Ivan IV, Tsar of Russia, the second ending in the late 1560s. Originally conceived as having a third segment, the plot of the extant films focuses on Ivan's empire-building, and his need to consolidate his power in the face of the opposition of the Boyars. His increasingly ruthless tactics (including the creation of his special guards, the *oprichniki*) are directed against formerly loyal advisors like Prince Kurbsky, who has defected to the court of King Sigismund II of Poland–Lithuania. Ivan's actions leave him powerful, isolated, and subject to bouts of melancholy and despair.

The opening intertitle of *Ivan* describes the film's subject as "a Prince of Moscow who created a single and powerful state from a hodgepodge of divided and self-seeking principalities; a warlord who heralded the military glory of our Motherland...." While the story that follows might have some ambiguities that counter this claim, *Part I* met with the approval of Josef Stalin, for whom the fashioning of the historical Ivan in the image of a heroic unifier was an element in the creation of his own cult of personality. *Part II*, however, was never released in Eisenstein's lifetime. Stalin is reputed to have taken issue with many elements of the film, including its portrayal of Ivan's "Hamlet-like" anxieties and indecision. He was also concerned that some of the formalist cinematic elements distracted from the history of Ivan. There is little doubt he read correctly that for Eisenstein, *Ivan the Terrible* was as much (or more) a commentary on dictatorship as it was a historical biopic.

See also: *Alexander Nevsky*

Goodwin, James. "*Ivan the Terrible*: An Inversion of History." In *Eisenstein, Cinema, and History*, 179–209. Urbana: University of Illinois Press, 1993.

Neuberger, Joan. "The Politics of Bewilderment: Eisenstein's *Ivan the Terrible* in 1945." In *Eisenstein at 100: A Reconsideration*, edited by Al La Valley and Barry P. Scherr, 227–52. New Brunswick, NJ: Rutgers University Press, 2001.

Tsivian, Yuri. *Ivan the Terrible*. London: BFI, 2002.

Zholkovsky, Alexander. "The Power of Grammar and the Grammar of Power: The Childhood Scenes in *Ivan the Terrible*." In *Eisenstein at 100: A Reconsideration*, edited by Al La Valley and Barry P. Scherr, 252–67. New Brunswick, NJ: Rutgers University Press, 2001.

Jericho / Jericó (1991) Luis Alberto Lamata; Venezuela; Spanish with English subtitles; Color; 85 m; Latin American Video Archives (VHS); Amazon region, 16th century.

Jericho tells the fictional story of a sensitive Dominican friar, Santiago, who is repulsed by the inhumanity of the Spanish conquistadors he accompanies on their mission in the Amazon region of South America. When he is captured by an indigenous tribe, Santiago adopts the habits and perspective of his captors—literally shedding his clothes in a coca ceremony—and marries within the tribe. Director and screenwriter Lamata, who studied history at university, has been praised for his careful research of the languages and cultures of the indigenous peoples represented in the film. *Jericho* claims itself as history in its narration of Santiago's (invented) diary account. But the film is unambiguously allegorical and metaphorical as well, inverting biblical and utopian ideas to build its revisionist version of the era of conquest.

See also: *Aguirre*; *Black Robe*; *Cabeza de Vaca*; *How Tasty Was My Little Frenchman*; *The Mission*; *At Play in the Fields of the Lord*

Alvaray, Luisela. "Imagi(ni)ng Indigenous Spaces: Self and Other Converge in Latin America." *Film & History: An Interdisciplinary Journal of Film and Television Studies* 34(2) (2004): 58–64.

Schwartz, Ronald. "*Jericó*." In *Latin American Films, 1932–1994: A Critical Filmography*, 126–27. Jefferson, NC: McFarland, 1997.

Stone, Cynthia Leigh. "The Filming of Colonial Spanish America." *Colonial Latin American Historical Review* 5(2) (December 1996): 315–20.

José Rizal (1998) Marilou Diaz-Abaya; Philippines; Tagalog with English subtitles; Color; 178 m; GMA Network Films, Philippines (DVD, VHS); Philippines and Belgium, 1890–1898.

Biographical films about intellectuals and artists often struggle to find in their subjects' ideas or work the same sort of drama inherent in historical figures whose actions allow for spectacular scenes of battle, mass protest, or high passion. Effective reconstruction of the process of artistic creation can fall into clichés. A typical approach uses montage to suggest the path from a blank page or canvas to a full one; another is to make tortured romance the centerpiece of the drama. (Three films with artistic female protagonists—*Camille Claude, Bride of the Wind*, and *Artemisia*—are a case in point.)

José Rizal is a lucky "find" for a filmmaker: Rizal was not only an adored novelist, physician, and engineer who was a voice for Philippines nationalism, but was also subject to a sensational trial in which he had to defend himself against charges of being the soul of the anticolonial revolution in 1896. (Rizal, who had no direct involvement in the rebellion, was convicted of the charge of sedition and rebellion and executed in 1898). Using the pretext of Rizal's need to make an account of his life for his defense lawyer and later his trial, the film is constructed around extended flashbacks that reconstruct his memories. Another method through which Rizal is given voice is the interweaving enactments of scenes from his iconoclastic anticolonial novel, *Noli Me Tangere*. Strained in its ambitions, the film nevertheless delivers a sweeping synthesis of nineteenth-century Philippine politics and society through the story of this one man.

Vera, Noel. "The Many Faces of Jose Rizal." *Cinemaya: The Asian Film Quarterly* 44 (1999): 9–11.

Journey of Hope / Reise der Hoffnung (1990) Xavier Koller; Switzerland/Turkey/United Kingdom; Turkish and Kurdish with English subtitles; Color; 109 m; HBO Home Video (VHS); Turkey, Italy, and Switzerland, 1980s.

The pastoral life of the Sener family in Turkey might look idyllic to North American eyes, but the patriarch Haydar clearly longs for a better life than he can achieve as a small farmer. After a field is sold, and arrangements for busing to Istanbul and hidden passage in the container of a cargo ship, Haydar, wife Meryem, and son Mehmet are bound for Switzerland. The journey is long, and is complicated by the extortion of smugglers whose livelihood is designed around the exploitation of these people's longings. In order to evade Swiss border police, the physical barriers of mountains and snow must also be surpassed by the family and their fellow-travelers—in city dress and with suitcases, no less.

Inspiration for the story of *Journey of Hope* came from director Xavier Koller's reading of a very brief newspaper account of similar events. He then received permission from the family to use that account as the basis for this fictionalized film. For those viewers who become emotionally engaged in the fate of the characters so beautifully wrought in the performances in this film, *Journey of Hope* will be highly memorable. For those less willing to suspend their analytical faculties, the film will also deliver, as it produces out of the microcosm of a single Kurdish family's travails an explanation of the lived experience of being a modern refugee.

See also: *Boat People*; *The Boat Is Full*; *The Dupes*; *Welcome to Canada*

Basutcu, Mehmet. "The Power & the Danger of the Image." *Cinemaya: The Asian Film Quarterly* 17/18 (Autumn/Winter 1992): 16–19.

Charity, Tom. "*Reise der Hoffnung (Journey of Hope)*." *Sight & Sound* 1 (July 1991): 52–53.

Fenner, Angelika. "Traversing the Screen Politics of Migration: Xavier Koller's *Journey of Hope*." In *Moving Pictures, Migrating Identities*, edited by Eva Rueschmann, 18–38. Jackson: University Press of Mississippi, 2003.

Walker, Beverly. "Behind the Mountains." *Film Comment* 27 (May/June 1991): 2.

"Spain ends here: it's every man for himself now." Spanish conqueror Álvar Núñez Cabeza de Vaca (Juan Diego, center) and other survivors of a shipwreck in the Gulf of Mexico are on the verge of capture by natives: Texas/New Spain, 1528. *Cabeza de Vaca*, Nicolás Echevarría (1991). [Courtesy of Photofest]

"I am no man's Elizabeth." Elizabeth I, Queen of England (Cate Blanchett) and Robert Dudley, Earl of Leicester (Joseph Fiennes): England, 1550s. *Elizabeth*, Shekhar Kapur (1998). [Courtesy of Photofest]

"It's the white in me, sir." Half-caste Jimmie Blacksmith (Tom E. Lewis) reckons his white father was a hard worker. Here he builds a farmer's fence with his brother, Mort (Freddy Reynolds): Australia, turn of the twentieth century. *The Chant of Jimmie Blacksmith*, Fred Schepisi (1978). [Courtesy of Photofest]

"They are always telling me what to say." An eight-year-old boy retains the title of Qing Emperor Pu Yi (Tsou Tijger) in the early days of the Republican era: China, 1910s. *The Last Emperor*, Bernardo Bertolucci (1987). [Courtesy of Photofest]

"A Story From the Spanish Revolution." Englishman David Carr (Ian Hart) is restrained by commander Juan Vidal (Marc Martínez) as their POUM (Workers' Party of Marxist Unification) unit is disbanded by troops of the Popular Army: Spain, 1937. *Land and Freedom,* Ken Loach (1995). [Courtesy of Photofest]

"In Africa, there are Negroes, and in the army, discipline." At a transit camp on the eve of their demobilization, African soldiers of the French army confront their wartime experience in Europe and the racism of white commanders: Senegal, end of World War II. *The Camp at Thiaroye,* Ousmane Sembene and Thierno Faty Sow (1987). [Courtesy of Photofest]

"History will have its say one day." Congolese troops loyal to Colonel Joseph-Désiré Mobutu arrest Patrice Lumumba (Eriq Ebouaney), the first President of the Republic of Congo, here with wife Pauline Lumumba (Mariam Kaba): Congo, 1960. *Lumumba*, Raoul Peck (2000). [Courtesy of Photofest]

"Listen, Weinraub, this is war. Real war! And this time it's ours." Klausner (Uri Klauzner) and Weinraub (Liron Levo) retrieve a casualty of the Yom Kippur War as members of an Israeli army helicopter rescue unit: Golan Heights, 1973. *Kippur*, Amos Gitai (2000). [Courtesy of Photofest]

"Go easy. That's world history you're kicking on the floor." Chris (Chris Haywood), member of a Cinetone newsreel camera crew, and Ellie (Lorna Lesley): Australia, 1950s. *Newsfront*, Phillip Noyce (1978). [Courtesy of Photofest]

"We can't afford to get involved." Cameraman Billy Kwan (Linda Hunt) on the shoulders of journalist Guy Hamilton (Mel Gibson): Indonesia, 1965. *The Year of Living Dangerously*, Peter Weir (1982). [Courtesy of Photofest]

Journey to the Sun / Günese yolculuk (1999) Yesim Ustaoglu; Turkey/ Netherlands/Germany; Turkish and Kurdish with English subtitles; Color; 104 m; Facets (DVD, VHS); Turkey, contemporary.

Mehmet is a young, somewhat naive Turkish man who has come from the village of Tire to Istanbul. He works earnestly at his new job as a leak detector for the water department, has a girlfriend, Arzu, and strikes up an acquaintance with a street peddler, Berzan. In a somewhat elliptical conversation, Mehmet learns that Berzan is from "Kurdistan," but there is no other explicit reference to the Kurds in the film. A late-night police check on a city bus leads to the false accusation that Mehmet possesses a gun. He is briefly incarcerated, and beaten by the police. His wounds and association with police custody mark him, and the film follows his eventual estrangement from his former ties in Istanbul, and the increasing support of Berzan and his associates. By film's end, Mehmet is journeying with the body of Berzan to his dead friend's family village, where he discovers nothing but a ruined shell evacuated of any of the inhabitants with whom he has developed—through his relationship to Berzan—an unorthodox type of belonging.

Journey to the Sun is a disconcerting film, demanding that its audience accept a new political and ethnic identity for its main character. In addition to its successes in making the character's identity-shift plausible, the film's major feat is to use Mehmet's transformation from a Turkish insider to a "Kurdish" outsider as the vehicle to make tangible the response of the Turkish military to the Kurdish-nationalist cause in the 1990s.

Dönmez-Colin, Gönül. "The Journey Must Go On." *Cinemaya: The Asian Film Quarterly* 44 (Summer 1999): 4–6.

Khoshchehreh, Mahmood, and Levon Haftvan. "The Drowned Culture of the Kurds." *Film International: Iranian Film Quarterly* 7(4) (2000): 43–44.

Monceau, Nicolas. "Confronting Turkey's Social Realities: An Interview with Yesim Ustaoglu." *Cineaste* 26(3) (2001): 28–30.

Mookas, Ioannas. "Homeward Bound." *Afterimage* 28(4) (January/February 2001): 34–5.

The Joyless Street / Die freudlose Gasse (1925) G.W. Pabst; Germany; Silent with English intertitles; Black and White; 96 m; Facets (VHS); Vienna, Austria, early 1920s.

Hugo Bettauer's serialized novel is the basis for this realist-style melodrama that presents a devastating critique of Viennese society during the severe postwar inflation of the early 1920s. Two women living in the same building on the same street represent the experience of different social classes: Maria of the "miserable" Lechner family in the basement, and Greta of the Rumforts on the first floor, the daughter of a civil servant who was once "well-to-do" but now faces destitution. *The Joyless Street* creates—with powerful images, vivid characters, and a plot that enjoys its fair share of murder, romance, and intrigue—a bleak picture of poverty, corruption, sexual exploitation, and brutality.

Horak, Jan-Christopher. "Film History and Film Preservation: Reconstructing the Text of *The Joyless Street* (1925)." *Screening the Past:* 5 (1988): http://www.latrobe.edu.au/screeningthepast/firstrelease/fir1298/jhfr5b.html (accessed May 30, 2006).

Myers, Tracy. "History and Realism: Representations of Women in G.W. Pabst's *The Joyless Street*." In *Gender and German Cinema: Feminist Interventions, Vol. II: German Film History/German History on Film*, edited by Sandra Frieden, Richard W.

McCormick, Vibeke R. Petersen, and Laurie Melissa Vogelsang, 43–59. Providence, RI: Berg, 1993.

Petro, Patrice. *Joyless Streets: Women and Melodramatic Representation in Weimar Germany*. Princeton, NJ: Princeton University Press, 1989.

Judgment at Nuremberg (1961) Stanley Kramer; United States; English and German with English subtitles; Black and White; 178 m; MGM (DVD, VHS); Germany, 1948.

Judgment at Nuremberg provides many excellent lessons. Screenwriter Abby Mann's choice of dramatizing the trial of Nazi-era judges by the U.S. Military Tribunal in 1948 reveals much about the thematic emphasis of *Judgment at Nuremberg*, and thus its approach to the past. This is as much a movie about "judges judging judges" as a movie about the trial of German judges who carried out Nazi policies in the (pseudo) legal system of the Third Reich. Here the chief prosecutor, Haywood, must confront his own professional and personal ethics as he weighs the defense and prosecution cases for the four judges accused. The character of German judge Ernst Janning—a man who refuses to participate in his own defense because his integrity allows him to acknowledge his own guilt—mirrors that of the American prosecutor, emphasizing for the film audience the type of man and judge Haywood is and wants to remain. By the end of the film, the prosecutor refuses to bow to American military officials and politicians who insinuate that in the context of the emerging Cold War, a verdict against the judges would imperil important West German–American relations. In a two to one decision, the judges are judged to have committed the crime, and audiences are reassured that there exists at least one man whose commitment to truth can model ethical behavior and save them from their own weaknesses or their vulnerability to totalitarian regimes.

Despite clothing itself in the story of a historical tribunal, this is a movie that less invites analysis of the nature of complicity in the Third Reich than reflection on troubling universal issues of individual responsibility and conscience. This interest in the behavior of humans in the context of overwhelming events is a conventional feature of historical films, not to be mistaken as careful analysis of a particular historical event.

At a superficial level *Judgment* covers useful historical ground for those interested in the relationship of the German people to the Third Reich. Prosecuting attorney Colonel Lawson ironically offers: "There are no Nazis in Germany. Didn't you know that, Judge?" The contentious issue of "ordinary" Germans' knowledge, participation, and culpability is effectively introduced here, and suggested in Haywood's growing doubts. "I don't know what to believe," he says, as he wonders how he can find, in both his informal interrogation of his housekeepers and his formal tribunal investigation, no one who professes to have supported the Nazis ideologically, or who had knowledge of the mass murder of European Jews.

Judgment at Nuremberg also provides some contextual explanation for the advent of the Nazi era, and some of its policies. Most striking is the passionate and almost desperate attempt to defend German dignity and the rationality and justice of the trial on the part of Janning's lawyer, Hans Rolfe. When he objects to the prosecution's inclusion of devastating footage of the victims of Nazi concentration and death camps, he admits that the Nazi actions are indefensible, but that the evidence submitted is irrelevant to the specific charges against his client. Viewers might be uncomfortable with the double game director Kramer and screenwriter Abby Mann play here, at once resorting to the graphic evidence to arouse the emotions of their audience and at the same time using Rolfe to protest its use. That the actual tribunal presented this footage should cause the same viewers their own reflection on the nature of justice, human behavior, and the ethics of investigating the past.

See also: *'Breaker' Morant*; *Paths of Glory*

Asimow, Michael. "Judges Judging Judges: *Judgment at Nuremberg*." *Picturing Justice: The On-Line Journal of Law and Popular Culture*, http://www.usfca.edu/pj/articles/Nuremberg.htm (accessed May 30, 2006).

Clover, Carol J. "Judging Audiences: The Case of the Trial Movie." In *Reinventing Film Studies*, edited by Christine Gledhill and Linda Williams, 244–64. London: Arnold, 2000.

Doneson, Judith E. "Eichmann and *Nuremberg*: Nazis on Trial in the 1960s." In *The Holocaust in American Film*, edited by Judith E. Doneson, 87–107. Syracuse, NY: Syracuse University Press, 2002.

Insdorf, Annette. "The Hollywood Version of the Holocaust." In *Indelible Shadows: Film and the Holocaust*, 3rd ed., 3–25. New York: Cambridge University Press, 2003.

Mintz, Alan. "The Holocaust at the Movies: Three Studies of Reception." In *Popular Culture and the Shaping of Holocaust Memory in America*, 85–158. Seattle: University of Washington Press, 2001.

Shale, Suzanne Gibson. "The Conflicts of Law and the Character of Men: Writing *Reversal of Fortune* and *Judgment at Nuremberg*." *University of San Francisco Law Review* 30(4) (1996): 991–1102.

Junoon (1978) Shyam Benegal; India; Hindi and English with English subtitles; Color; 141 m; Eros Entertainment (DVD); India, 1857–1858.

Junoon is a fictionalized drama set during the nineteenth-century rebellion of Indian units of the East India Company's army. The film begins with a voiceover describing the 1857 rebellion and execution of Sepoy Mangal Pandey, the revolt of the Sepoy garrison at Meerut, and the May 1857 proclamation in Delhi of Bahadur Shah Zafar as the emperor of Hindustan. The voiceover then introduces us to the first scene: "May 24, 1857, a small British cantonment town in the North Indian plains. . . ." Thus we arrive at Shahjahanpur, and the story of Javed Khan, brother-in-law of one of the rebellion leaders, and the fate of the town and its residents during the popular uprising against British rule. A subplot—some might call it the primary plot—about the romance of Javed Khan (soon drawn into the conflict himself) and an Anglo-Indian woman, Ruth Labadoor, ties in melodramatic fashion the fate of the lovers to the fate of the uprising. Audiences might argue about whether *Junoon* is a historical film or a colonial-sexual fantasy. The film's screenplay is adapted from the novella *A Flight of Pigeons* by Ruskin Bond, which is itself based on the experiences of Ruth Labadoor and her family.

See also: *The Chess Players*

Bond, Ruskin. "Introduction." In *A Flight of Pigeons*. Bombay: IBH, 1980.

Coleman, J. "Besieged." *New Statesman* 98 (November 30, 1979): 869–70.

Datta, Sangeeta. "Histories and Epics." In *Shyam Benegal,* 120–44. London: BFI, 2002.
Khorana, Meena G. *The Life and Works of Ruskin Bond.* Westport, CT: Praeger, 2003.

Kadarwati / The Five Faces of Kadarwati / Kadarwati, wanita dengan lima nama (1983) Sophan Sophiaan; Indonesia; Indonesian with English subtitles; Color; 110 m; Between Three Worlds Video (VHS); Java and Singapore, 1942–1945.

During the Second World War, women of various social backgrounds in Japanese-occupied territories were exploited as sexual laborers by the Japanese military. *Kadarwati,* adapted from Pandir Kelana's 1982 popular novel of the same name, follows a fictional character, a young Javanese woman, who decides to study medicine in Singapore. While her parents worry about her marriage prospects, she says, "These days women also have to get ahead." In 1942 Singapore, Kadarwati discovers the educational scheme the Japanese have offered to Indonesian women is a cover for her enslavement as a "comfort woman."

The film follows Kadarwati's experiences to 1945, when, as Kadarwati says, "Sukarno and Hatta proclaimed independence for our beloved country." This is a melodramatic and accessible treatment of Kadarwati's harrowing experiences. Her story of submission and defiance is paralleled with that of Indonesia's colonization and resistance.

Heider, Karl G. *Indonesian Cinema: National Culture on Screen.* Honolulu, HI: University of Hawaii Press, 1991.

Kafr Kassem (1974) Borhane Alaouie; Syria/Lebanon; Arabic with English subtitles; Color; 120 m; National Film Organization, Syria (theatrical); Israel, 1956.

On an October afternoon in 1956, with the Sinai campaign about to be launched, Israeli border police imposed a dusk-to-dawn curfew on Arab villages near the Jordanian border. Arriving at their homes after work, many villagers of Kafr Kassem were unaware of their violation of the newly announced curfew. Forty-seven of these Israeli Arabs were killed when Israeli troops opened fire on the village. *Kafr Kassem,* directed by Lebanese-born Borhane Alaouie, reconstructs this much-remembered event in Arab and Israeli history, especially with an eye to detailing the life of the community before it suffered the massacre.

Narboni, Jean. "Blood into Sign." In *Cahiers Du Cinéma: Vol. 4, 1973–1978: History, Ideology, Cultural Struggle: An Anthology from Cahiers Du Cinéma Nos. 248–292, September 1973-September 1978,* edited by David Wilson and Bérénice Reynaud, 259–67. London: Routledge, 2000.
Shafik, Viola. *Arab Cinema: History and Cultural Identity.* Cairo: American University in Cairo Press, 1998.

Kameradschaft (1931) G.W. Pabst; Germany; French and German with English subtitles; Black and White; 80 m; Movies Unlimited (VHS); German–French border, 1919.

Nationalist frictions on the border between France and Germany after World War I are overcome when German coal miners attempt to rescue French "comrades" trapped in a mine explosion on the French side. Based on a mine disaster of 1906, director Pabst dedicated his film "to the miners of the world."

Carroll, Nöel. "Lang, Pabst and Sound." In *Interpreting the Moving Image*, 92–104. Cambridge: Cambridge University Press, 1998.

Hogencamp, Bert. "A Mining Film without a Disaster Is Like a Western without a Shoot-Out: Representations of Coal Mining Communities in Feature Films." In *Towards a Comparative History of Coalfields Societies*, edited by Stefan Berger, Andy Croll, and Norman LaPorte, 86–98. Aldershot, UK: Ashgate, 2005.

Kelly, Andrew. "From the Defeated: *Westfront 1918*, *Kameradschaft*, and *Niemansland*—the German Cinema and the War." In *Cinema and the Great War*, 82–100. London: Routledge, 1997.

Neville, Robert G. "The Courrières Colliery Disaster, 1906." *Journal of Contemporary History* 13 (1) (January 1978): 33–52.

Zaniello, Tom. "*Kamaradschaft*." In *Working Stiffs, Union Maids, Reds, and Riffraff: An Organized Guide to Films About Labor*, 131–33. Ithaca, NY: ILR Press/Cornell University Press, 1996.

Kedma (2002) Amos Gitai; Italy/Israel/France; Hebrew, Arabic, German, Polish, Russian, and Yiddish with English subtitles; Color; 100 m; Kino (DVD, VHS); Palestine, 1948.

Those crowded on board the freighter *Kedma* are bound for the British mandate of Palestine. It is the eve of Israel's independence, and these illegal immigrants have fled Europe for a dangerous introduction to Arab-Jewish politics in the Middle East.

Kedma is a film that writes its history by allowing its characters to literally tell their personal stories. They do so on the ship's deck, upon landing, and during their forced march eastward when members of the underground Jewish defense organization *Palmach* meet them on shore and British troops try to intercept them. One man, Janusz, reports his family is from Lodz, and fears they died in the ghetto revolt. Rosa, his companion, has survived Siberia. "If you want to survive," she says, "you must forget." A young Cantor, Menahem, a sad and angry man who has lost both his parents, is eager to join the armed effort of the Zionists.

The dramatic action of *Kedma* taking place alongside the storytelling sees the march of the immigrants with the Palmach, and their action in a military engagement with Arab forces that suggests the Battle of Latrun. Along the march, the group meets Arab refugees; after the battle, a displaced Palestinian farmer tells his own story, adding, "We'll remain here in spite of you. Like a wall."

Director Amos Gitai's cinematic approach reinforces the estrangement of the immigrants from their homes and their lack of bearings in Palestine. Shots generally frame the viewpoint of the characters rather than an omniscient eye, and much of the action takes place outside in a hilly desert landscape that has few distinguishing features.

Kedma lets the Jewish refugees claim their histories in speaking during their journey. But by the end of the film more Jews are dead in battle, including Menahem. And now an exhausted and traumatized Janusz performs a powerful monologue that decries the theme of these stories/histories. Invoking Yudke's words from Hayim Hazaz's story *The Sermon*, he says: "We don't have a history. That's a fact ... the goyim made a history for us.... Oppression, slander, persecution, martyrdom. Deadly boring! Totally uninteresting! No glory, no action, no heroes, no conquerors! Just poor wretches pursued, moaning, crying, always begging for their lives."

See also: *Berlin Jerusalem; Exodus; Hill 24 Doesn't Answer*

Ginsburg, Shai. "A Shared Exile." *Tikkun* 20(2) (March/April 2005): 72–74.

Keïta! The Heritage of the Griot / Keïta! L'héritage du griot (1994) Dani Kouyaté; France/Burkina Faso; French and Diola with English subtitles; Color; 94 m; California Newsreel (DVD, VHS); Mali, mythic, 13th and 20th centuries.

Mabo Keïta and his classmates, schoolchildren in 1990s Mali, are learning a history lesson. Many are eager to answer when the teacher asks, "When was America discovered?" *Keïta! The Heritage of the Griot* suggests the irony, or tragedy, of the children knowing the story of America's past, but being largely ignorant of their own. The film tells the story of the arrival at Mabo's home of a mysterious man who announces himself Djéliba, a bard/griot. Insisting his mission is to teach Mabo about his history, the film takes the boy and Djéliba to the thirteenth century, where a griot is invited to reside in the court of the kingdom of Mande. Through the course of the film, more stories are told, and disagreements arise between Mabo's traditionalist father and modern mother over this stranger in their home and his influence over Mabo. Mabo begins to realize his ancestral relation to the great founder of the Malian Empire, Sundjata Keïta. *Keïta* is a very accessible introduction to the Sundjata epic, and a glimpse of Malian history. It is also a very engaging discourse on modern Africans' relationship to their heritage, and the oral tradition's relationship to history in modernizing and westernized society.

See also: *God's Gift; Yeelen*

Gugler, Josef. "*Keïta!* (1985): Transmitting the *Sundjata* to the Next Generation." In *African Film: Re-Imagining a Continent*, 36–44. Bloomington: Indiana University Press, 2003.

Racevskis, Maija. "Applications of African Cinema in the High School Curriculum: A Secondary Teacher's Views of *Three Tales from Senegal, Ca Twiste À Poponguine, Udju Azul Di Yonta, Hyenas,* and *Keïta*." *Research in African Literatures* 27(3) (1996): 98–109.

Khartoum (1966) Basil Dearden and Eliot Elisofon; United Kingdom; English; Color; 128 m; MGM (DVD, VHS); Sudan, 1883–1885.

The caption of a 1966 poster promoting the theatrical release of *Khartoum* reads: "*Khartoum*: Where the Nile Divides, the Great Cinerama Adventure Begins!" This is surely a widescreen epic, set in nineteenth-century Sudan. The attempt by British General Charles Gordon and Egyptian Khedival forces to defend the city of Khartoum, however, might be conceived as heroic, or foolish, but neither Gordon, nor those who had Khartoum under siege, would have considered the event an adventure. The film's interpretation of "adventure" is more a boyish illusion about the history of imperialism than history itself. Indeed, after an almost year-long ordeal, Gordon, whose orders had been to evacuate the city of Egyptian and British residents, not protect it, was dead.

Khartoum does several things of interest in its engagement of the past. Most notably, it renders British imperialism as an act of humanitarianism, and Gordon its martyr. The general and his government are attempting to save the Egyptians from the "fanatical" uprising led by Sudanese Muhammad Ahmed (who claimed himself a *Mahdi,* or "expected one"). Only hinted at are the economic, strategic, and political implications for Britain, and Egypt, of control of Sudan. Prime Minister Gladstone's refusal to "assume a British obligation to police the world," underpins the depiction of Britain as trying to pursue an isolationist policy. This is a significant obscuration of what was in fact a division among British foreign policy makers about, as Gerald Herman describes it, the methods—not goals—of empire.

Khartoum also "softens" the imperial enterprise by granting it certain qualities (whether admirable or not) that are akin to those of the colonized. The parallels serve dramatic effect more than history. Gordon is stoic and mysterious, a military genius, and devoted to the people of Sudan and the end of slavery. The Mahdi's cause, inspired by his sense of destiny, is the liberation of the Sudanese from Egypt. (An ahistorical scene of their meeting reinforces the parallels in the missions of the two.) Most importantly, these are—in cinematic romantic-hero fashion—men alone, fighting for what is right against the grain of society and the politics of their day. As Gladstone says, incredulously, "A man, one man, in the middle of Africa, is blackmailing the British government into a course of action it wouldn't otherwise take." For the Mahdi, whose practical nemesis is Gordon, the prospect of British military intervention drives his urgency. While Gordon is defending Khartoum against the Mahdi, his enemy seems as much the British lack of will in supporting him there.

Khartoum is consumed with creating a dramatic confrontation between two heroic and "adventurous" men. The interpretation of the history of these men and events must conform to this creative conceit.

See also: *Zulu*

Herman, Gerald. "For God and Country: *Khartoum* (1966) as History and as Object Lesson for Global Policemen." *Film & History: An Interdisciplinary Journal of Film and Television Studies* 9(1) (1979): 1–15.

Lewis, David Levering. "*Khartoum.*" In *Past Imperfect: History According to the Movies,* edited by Mark C. Carnes, 162–65. New York: Henry Holt, 1995.

Richards, Jeffrey. "Imperial Heroes for a Post-Imperial Age: Films and the End of Empire." In *British Culture and the End of Empire,* edited by Stuart Ward, 128–44. Manchester: Manchester University Press, 2002.

The Killing Fields (1984) Roland Joffé; United Kingdom; English, French and Khmer; Color; 141 m; Warner Home Video (DVD, VHS); Cambodia and New York, 1970s.

Like his *The Mission,* Roland Joffé's first feature film uses the friendship of two men in a historical setting to explore universal themes. Based on *New York Times* correspondent Sydney Schanberg's accounts, *The Killing Fields* is set in Cambodia during its takeover by the Khmer Rouge. Schanberg is plagued by guilt for not discouraging his interpreter Dith Pran's decision to remain in Cambodia. The seemingly arbitrary actions of Cambodian soldiers during the revolution, and the genocidal policy of Pol Pot, endanger foreign journalists and jeopardize Dith Pran's survival in a labor camp and his journey to freedom.

See also: *Beyond Rangoon; Boat People; Circle of Deceit; Cry Freedom; A Single Spark; The Year of Living Dangerously*

Chandler, David P. "*The Killing Fields* and Perceptions of Cambodian History: Review Article." *Pacific Affairs* 59: 92–7.

Green, Norma Fay. "Press Dress: The Beige Brigade of Movie Journalists Outdoors." In *Beyond the Stars*, edited by Paul Loukides and Linda K. Fuller. Bowling Green, OH: Bowling Green State University Popular Press, 1990.

Greenfield, Fenella, and Nicolas Locke, eds. *The Killing Fields: The Facts Behind the Film*. London: Weidenfeld & Nicolson, 1984.

Jhirad, Susan. "Review of *The Killing Fields*." *Cineaste* 14(1) (1985): 50–51.

Park, James. "Bombs and Pol Pot." *Sight and Sound* (Winter 1984/1985): 14–16.

Sammon, Paul M. "Chris Menges and *The Killing Fields*." *American Cinematographer* 66 (1985): 64–70.

Young, Vernon. "*The Killing Fields*." *The Hudson Review* 38 (1985): 110–14.

A King and His Movie / La película del Rey (1986) Carlos Sorin; Argentina; Spanish with English subtitles; Color; 107 m; Facets (DVD); Argentina, 1860s and 1980s.

The opening scene of *A King and His Movie* captures brilliantly the logic of filmmakers who enthusiastically create historical films. The fictional character of Argentinian screenwriter and director David is the subject of a television interview, his two hosts convivially indulging his description of (real-life) Orelie-Antoine de Tounens, who will be the subject of a film currently in preproduction. David explains that de Tounens, a Frenchman who was in 1860 crowned king of Araucania and Patagonia, legitimized his (brief) rule over the natives of the region by issuing decrees that referred to government ministers Lachaise and Desfontaines. But these men did not exist; they were the king's invention. David, however, plans to make these nonexistent historical figures real in his recreation of the king's story; they will be two "unscrupulous traders" who form a kind of self-serving entourage. One of the interviewers offers, "That's pure fiction." David replies, "Like all movies."

Film directors self-referencing the creative process is a familiar motif in motion pictures. Director Carlos Sorin provides an extended gaze on the filmmaking process in *A King and His Movie*, devoting the whole story to David's passionate yet disaster-ridden production of King Orelie-Antoine's motion picture story. When financing for the film falls through, David and his hapless producer, Arturo, must relinquish unionized actors and crew, cast nonprofessional actors, and rely on an enthusiastic costume designer and a German expert on Araucanian language to perform as camera, light, and sound operators. The motley crew's arrival on location in Patagonia shows their dwindling resources, the gradual defection of most of the actors and assistants—eventually the actor portraying the king decamps as well—and their creative methods of staging scenes of mass spectacle such as the king's coronation, with at times as few as three local natives portraying their nineteenth-century forebears.

A King and His Movie is very entertaining. That the character David's movie is a historical feature film also provides a kind of classic instructional guide for students of history on screen. The film recreates (or parodies) the ways in which historical reconstruction in the movies is controlled by the exigencies of production. When supporting actors desert the set prior to filming of the king's capture and imprisonment, David invents a new, stylized, scenario for Orelie-Antoine. The king has gone mad, and has wild visions of being the captive, not of native Araucanians, but of sinister dress dummies scattered across the barren landscape. It doesn't seem problematic to David that his commitment to the history of Orelie-Antoine is being compromised by his artistic license. And, as he might argue, even his revered Orelie-Antoine wasn't immune to a little invention himself.

See also: *Ararat; Good Men, Good Women; Ulysses' Gaze*

Barnard, Timothy, and Peter Rist. "Argentina: *La Película Del Rey*." In *South American Cinema: A Critical Filmography, 1915–1994*, edited by Timothy Barnard and Peter Rist, 69–71. Austin: University of Texas Press, 1999.

Ciria, Alberto. "Argentine Commercial Cinema: Industry, Society and Aesthetics, 1983–1989." In *The Reordering of Culture: Latin America, The Caribbean and Canada in the Hood*, edited by Alvina Ruprecht and Cecilia Taiana, 457–76. Ottawa, ON: Carleton University Press, 1995.

King of the Children / Haizi wang (1987) Chen Kaige; China; Mandarin with English subtitles; Color; 95 m; no current; China, 1970s.

King of the Children is about a young man who is assigned the job of school teacher in a remote Chinese village in the waning days of the Cultural Revolution. His innovative methods ask students to think rather than learn by rote, and these place him in conflict with officials.

Chow, Rey. "Male Narcissism and National Culture: Subjectivity in Chen Kaige's *King of the Children*." *Camera Obscura* 25–26(1) (January–May 1997): 9–40.

Rayns, Tony. "Chinese Vocabulary: An Introduction to *King of the Children* and the New Chinese Cinema." In *King of the Children and the New Chinese Cinema*, edited by Chen Kaige and Tony Rayns, 1–58. London: Faber & Faber, 1989.

Silbergeld, Jerome. "The Children of Melodrama: No-Drama, Pseudo-Drama, Melodramatic Masquerade, and Deconstruction Drama." In *China into Film: Frames of Reference in Contemporary Chinese Cinema*, 234–304. London: Reaktion Books, 1999.

Kippur (2000) Amos Gitai; Israel/France; Hebrew with English subtitles; Color; 117 m; Kino (DVD, VHS); Israel, 1973.

Director Amos Gitai's own experiences as part of an army medical team form the basis of this story set in the Yom Kippur War of 1973. The film begins, and ends, with the scene of lovers covering each other in artist paints whose colors symbolize both Arab and Israeli flags. The outbreak of the war, prompted by a surprise attack of Israel by Egypt and Syria, demands that the main characters, Lieutenant Russo and his friend Sergeant Weinraub, report for duty. There is an air of unreality as the reservists career along a deserted highway under a brilliant blue sky. Reminds Russo, "Listen, Weinraub, this is war. Real war! And this time it's ours. We're the right age!" In *Kippur*, the prospect of "enjoying" their generation's contribution to the defense of Israel will soon be lost in the exhausting, deafening, dangerous, and horrifying work of evacuating the wounded.

Kippur is a visually and dramatically arresting film that, like many war films, universalizes the experience of soldiers. Foregoing overt explanation of the political context of the war, and any close representation of the Arab forces, the film suggests all participants of war are victims. One of *Kippur*'s most important features is the invitation for audiences to contemplate the experience of the protagonists during action that in mainstream cinema would likely be conveyed in emotionally-charged spectacle. Amos Gitai uses exceptionally long takes, where such actions as the medical unit slogging through mud with stretchers seems to play out in agonizingly real time. Conversations in the helicopter are similarly prolonged, and accompanied by the relentless and intrusive sound of the aircraft's whirling propeller.

Kippur is as insistent that viewers do not look away or cover their ears as is the Israeli army's demands on its fighters. By the film's near-end, the helicopter's pilot, who is recovering from wounds sustained in a terrible crash landing, tells Weinraub: "They wanted me to fly to Tel Aviv to take [defense minister] Moshe Dayan to the front. I told them that he should go to the nearest bus station." Echoing the Israeli public's outrage at what they judged as an ill-prepared Israeli defense, *Kippur* revisits this event as traumatic national history, and human tragedy.

Jacobowitz, Florence. "Amos Gitai's *Kippur*." *CineAction* 54 (2001): 60–63.
Michelson, Annette. "Filming Israel: A Conversation." *October* 98 (Fall 2001): 47–75.
Privett, Ray. "Broken Utopia, Masterful Cinema." *Cinema Scope* 5 (Fall 2000): 31–34.
Sklar, Robert. "In the Line of Fire." *Film Comment* 37(1) (January 2001): 50–53.
Yosef, Raz. "Spectacles of Pain: War, Masculinity and the Masochistic Fantasy in Amos Gitai's *Kippur*." *Shofar: An Interdisciplinary Journal of Jewish Studies* 24(1) (Fall 2005): 49–66.

The Kitchen Toto (1987) Harry Hook; United Kingdom; English; Color; 95 m; Warner Home Video (VHS); Kenya, 1950s.

The Kitchen Toto is a good example of a movie that presents the past in a work-manlike fashion, telling an interesting story well. It does not demand much of its audience besides their sympathy for the characters and mild revulsion for the distant wrongs of history. As such, it is representative of hundreds of similar, popular movies that (often briefly) grace theater screens and then become serviceable additions to video store shelves. Harry Hook's drama provides an introduction to the so-called "Mau Mau Rebellion," an important episode in British colonial and African history.

The Kitchen Toto uses the familiar device of a child's observation of the playing out of history, and his loss of innocence in the process. The film opens in "Kenya Colony 1950." An intertitle tells us "A movement had begun amongst the Kikuyu tribe to reclaim their land and achieve independence from the British." The internal divisions among natives of the Kenya colony—a theme the film invokes frequently as a central explanation for the difficult process of decolonization in Kenya—are quickly established. Two males make a threatening night visit to an African pastor and his family. The pastor refuses their entreaties to preach to his congregation that Europeans have robbed them of their land. His next sermon, in fact, preaches that all should speak out against "wickedness" in their midst, and any oath taken for the rebels should be renounced.

When the pastor is hacked to death in his bed, and his family terrorized, the son is taken in by the sympathetic white police chief. Employed as a "kitchen toto," or helper, at the family's lovely estate, the boy becomes witness to and participant in the escalating conflict between those Kikuyu who have taken the rebels, "Thenge Oath" and those Kikuyu—and especially British authorities and settlers—who oppose their tactics.

The Kitchen Toto explores characteristics of white rule in Kenya in memorable ways. The police chief's son Edward is fascinated with killing, dissecting a snake and its half-eaten rat—an allusion to the colonial treatment of nature as scientific, distanced, dissecting, and ultimately murderous. The immorality and deception of even apparently liberal whites is revealed in the chief's sexual relations with a niece. With the difficulty of attracting police from among the Kikuyu, Masai are recruited, again suggesting the complex colonial relationship between whites and blacks.

Fiorillo, C.M. *"The Kitchen Toto." Films in Review* 40 (January 1989): 46.

Kasfir, Sidney L. "Slam-Dunking and the Last Noble Savage." *Visual Anthropology* 15(3–4) (July/December 2002): 369–85.

Sibley, A. *"The Kitchen Toto." Films and Filming* 398 (November 1987): 32–33.

Korczak (1990) Andrzej Wajda; Poland/Germany/United Kingdom; Polish with English subtitles; Color; 115 m; Facets (VHS); Warsaw, Poland, 1930s and 1940s.

Janusz Korczak was a Polish doctor and educator who ran an orphanage for Jewish children in the 1930s. This film concentrates on the period from the Polish General Government's decree of 1939 of the "relocation" of Jews to the newly created Warsaw ghetto. Korczak accompanies his wards, about two hundred in number, to live in the ghetto. In 1942 he and the children were murdered at Treblinka.

There is no question that *Korczak* is an emotionally powerful film. The devotion of the Jewish doctor and his nurses to their charges, the extreme suffering of many other ghetto children outside the walls of the Korczak house, and the picture of inter-ghetto Jewish relations—where humanity, corruption, withdrawal, and resistance all emerge as survival responses—are all emotionally affecting.

As is technically true of all historical films, audiences "know" the outcome of this story. *Korczak* is not built around the suspense of the fate of the children, or of the doctor. Not trading in audiences' hopefulness about the fate of the characters, director Wajda instead is free to concentrate on the actions and character of Korczak. In this respect, the doctor is portrayed—in stark contrast with the behavior of Nazi captors and the characteristics of Nazi racial ideology—as deeply committed to humanity. This is demonstrated in Korczak's focus on maintaining a measure of well-being for his charges and dispelling their fear and pain. The characterization of Korczak's stoicism for the sake of the children has been described by some critics as very compelling; others argue the portrait tends toward the hagiographic.

See also: *Border Street; The Pianist; Schindler's List; Under the Domim Tree*

Barkan, Elazar, and Robert A. Rosenstone. "Review of *Korczac, Tango of Slaves*, and *Schindler's List." American Historical Review* 99(4) (October 1994): 1244–50.

Insdorf, Annette. "Rescuers in Fiction Films." In *Indelible Shadows: Film and the Holocaust*, 3rd ed., 258–75. New York: Cambridge University Press, 2003.

Mazierska, Ewa. "Non-Jewish Jews, Good Poles and Historical Truth in the Films of Andrzej Wajda." *Historical Journal of Film, Radio & Television* 20(2) (June 2000): 213–26.

Stevenson, Michael. "Wajda's Filmic Representation of Polish-Jewish Relations." In *The Cinema of Andrzej Wajda: The Art of Irony and Defiance*, edited by John Orr and Elzbieta Ostrowska, 76–92. London: Wallflower Press, 2003.

Todorov, Tzvetan. "The Wajda Problem." *Salmagundi* (92) (Fall 1991): 29–35.

Kristin Lavransdatter (1995) Liv Ullmann; Germany/Norway/Sweden; Norwegian with English subtitles; Color; 180 m; Home Vision Entertainment (DVD, VHS); Norway, 14th century.

Set in fourteenth-century Norway, this romantic melodrama is about a young woman who defies marriage traditions. Based on a popular novel trilogy by Sigrid Undset, the film tends to duplicate the ahistorical stereotypes found in medieval popular film more than providing an instructive dramatic reconstruction of medieval Norway.

See also: *The Seventh Seal*

Reese, Ellen. "Dreaming of the Medieval in *Kristin Lavransdatter* and *Trollsyn*." *Scandinavian Studies* 75(3) (2003): 399–416.

Woods, William F. "Authenticating Realism in the Medieval Film." In *The Medieval Hero on Screen: Representations from Beowulf to Buffy*, edited by Martha W. Driver and Sid Ray, 38–51. Jefferson, NC: McFarland, 2004.

Kundun (1997) Martin Scorsese; United States; English, Tibetan and Mandarin with English subtitles; Color; 128 m; Buena Vista Home Entertainment (DVD, VHS); Tibet, 1930s–50s; **Seven Years in Tibet** (1997) Jean-Jacques Annaud; United States; English, German, Mandarin, and Tibetan with English subtitles; Color; 139 m; Columbia/Tristar (DVD, VHS); Austria, India, and Tibet, 1935–1959.

"Do you think someday people will look at Tibet on the movie screen and wonder what happened to us?" asks a young Dalai Lama to Austrian mountaineer Heinrich Harrer in *Seven Years in Tibet*. Two recent films—*Seven Years* and *Kundun*—cinematically journey to the Tibet of the first half of the twentieth century, an era when its fabled physical and cultural isolation was literally assaulted by adventurers and armies. These films suggest to their audience that the movie screen can indeed record—even in "fictional" versions—the past. Both film's directors even devote scenes to the Dalai Lama's fascination with the West's cinema technology, presenting the constructive—even salvational—power of the West, as well as its dangers. The cinematic Dalai Lama's worry about Tibet's fate echoes with the political concerns of filmmakers Jean-Jacques Annaud (*Seven Years*) and Martin Scorsese (*Kundun*), who clearly aim their 1997 screen versions of Tibetan history at the cause of Tibet's cultural preservation and territorial recovery. The mixed critical and weak box office response to the films suggests the limits of cinematic activism. As Brian Taves concludes, "American filmgoers apparently prefer the Shangri-La that never existed over two generally accurate depictions of the traditions, beliefs, and modern history of the country that ostensibly inspired the legend."

The release dates of *Seven Years* and *Kundun* coincide so closely that the two films have been unable to escape comparison. Both portray the character and actions of the fourteenth Dalai Lama, the occupation of Tibet by Communist China's People's Liberation Army beginning in 1950, and aspects of Tibetan culture. Both filmmakers were refused permission to film in India, its government—the current host of the exiled Dalai Lama—facing pressure from a China sensitive to the portrayal of its relations with what it terms the Tibetan Autonomous Region of the People's Republic. The Argentine Andes stand in for the Himalayas in *Seven Years*; *Kundun* recreated Tibet on location in Morocco's Atlas Mountains.

Seven Years in Tibet, after a brief scene of Tibetans bringing offerings to a child Dalai Lama, quickly shifts to 1939 Austria. Heinrich Harrer is about to embark from Graz with other members of a German national mountaineering team for an expedition to climb Nanga Parbat. Annaud positions Harrer as lacking in enthusiasm for Nazism, and even Germany, but a man whose passion for climbing outweighs politics—and concern for Ingrid, his pregnant wife. (During the production of *Seven Years* an investigation by Germany's *Der Stern* concluded that Harrer had been a member of the Nazi Party and later joined the SS.)

Harrer is a man of action, not contemplation: "So much time to question myself is not good," we hear in one of many voiceovers whose source is attributed to Harrer's journal. These voiceovers, a form of "authentication" bolstered by frequent intertitles that describe precise dates, must be considered cautiously. Voiceovers often recite invented journal entries, an example being Harrer's recorded anguish about his physical and emotional distance from his son.

Harrer's subsequent experiences—climbing in the Himalayas, incarceration in a British (wartime) prison camp in India, and his eventual tenure in Lhasa from 1942—are beautifully filmed and engagingly plotted. Comedic "buddies" (Harrer and fellow-climber Peter Aufschnaiter), a love triangle, and a measure of frontiersmen gun play complete the sense that this is largely a romance–adventure film. But Annaud suggests a more soulful dimension to Harrer's tale. The adventurer becomes a pilgrim, his travels inexorably offering a form of purification. His discovery of Tibet, Tibetans, and Buddhism transform him from an egotistic man who had made "miserable company" for Aufschnaiter, to a treasured confidant of the Dalai Lama, an engineer committed to Tibet's improvement, and finally a devoted father. Harrer even reflects on how he once was "no different from these intolerant Chinese" who by the late 1940s are threatening military occupation.

While Harrer's character arc might be emotionally satisfying for viewers, all must be aware that this interpretation of his personal journey is invention. His own memoir, upon which the film claims to be based, is not the source for these aspects of Harrer's portrayal: Harrer makes virtually no mention of anything other than his public exploits.

The historical context of Harrer's adventure receives a similarly problematic treatment in *Seven Years*. Collapsing of events and dramatic license tend to oversimplify the causes of China's annexation of Tibet. The process by which the People's Republic lay claim to control of Tibet, which involved years of negotiation and Sino–Tibetan battles, is given little scope here. The ambition, avarice, and duplicity of a single historic figure, provincial governor Ngapoi Ngawang Jigme, becomes the main catalyst of Tibet's fate in this film. Embodying the values of the Chinese, rather than of his own "peace-loving" people, Ngapoi sells Tibet out, ultimately issuing what the film implies is a premature surrender to the Chinese. As he says, Tibetan soldiers could have held off the Chinese for years, if they had adopted guerilla warfare from the mountains: "It would have bought us time to make appeals for help to other nations. Now it's lost." Historical films typically analyze causation as the product of personal forces, and the "what ifs?" that are rooted in the wrong actions of men commonly inhabit their approach to the past. *Seven Years in Tibet* does not break this mold, giving this Tibetan official—who some historians suggest had few other options—a villainous role.

In *Seven Years*, the audience sees Tibet through Harrer's eyes. *Kundun* asks audiences to understand the Dalai Lama's life as a metaphor for the experience of his country. *Kundun*'s opening intertitles position Tibetan belief in concrete terms. Referring to the death of the Thirteenth Dalai Lama in 1933 and the subsequent search of a holy man for the Fourteenth, they say: "His search was almost at an end. A Buddha had been reborn." There are no qualifying terms such as "according to" here. Western standards of historical veracity are only found in director Scorsese's provision of dates for the sequence of events.

The otherworldliness of Tibet is carefully conveyed in dream-like sequences and the depiction of the Potala Palace and its inhabitants as physically and spiritually removed from the outside world. Even surrounding Lhasa is barely seen, and the economic and social life of Tibetans ignored. While the director and screenwriter Melissa Mathison clearly decry the Chinese occupation as tragic, significant screen time is devoted to explaining the process by which this tragedy unfolded. For students of history, this attention is welcome, and offers a reasonably thorough and balanced treatment of events. Scorsese interprets China's actions as inexorably leading the Tibetan government to strategize according to the terms of the modern political and military norms of its foes. The invasion of the PLA in 1949 even appears as a slow motion march, with a radio voice intoning China's commitment to "liberating" Tibetans from the feudal tyranny of the Dalai Lama.

In *Kundun*, the Dalai Lama is the bridge between remote and integrated Tibet. As his Lord Chamberlain comments, "He's a modern man, just like he was last time." Not only is the Dalai Lama fascinated by Western technology, history, and belief systems, he is a pragmatic politician—despite warnings that he should not let the Chinese get a monk "entangled in politics." He refuses to leave Tibet in 1950, calculating Tibet's historical ability to "manage" the Chinese, and even appearing to accept, on a visit to Beijing, Mao's claims to respecting Tibet's pace of progress. This rapprochement is abruptly severed when on the following day Mao tells the Dalai Lama: "Religion is poison." With that, Scorsese has completed his measuring of perspectives. The film suggests China's ultimate disrespect for Tibetan values and beliefs cannot be anything but sinister, and potentially annihilating. As the film concludes with the Dalai Lama's harrowing journey into Indian exile, viewers are led to conclude that the director is correct: China's position is irredeemable.

Unlike *Seven Years*, which introduces Tibetan history to audiences with the varnished story of Harrer's self-actualization, *Kundun* ventures into more interesting territory narratively and stylistically. The power and vulnerability of memory and myth—and their preservation and abuse on film—haunt these two films. Neither *Seven Years* nor *Kundun* can escape the intrusion of the present. Contemporary politics, the spiritual longing of the modern West, and the exigencies of popular filmmaking all have their moment in the finished reels.

See also: *Red River Valley*

Abramson, Marc. "Mountains, Monks, and Mandalas: *Kundun* and *Seven Years in Tibet.*" *Cineaste* 23(3) (1998): 8–12.

Hansen, Peter H. "The Dancing Lamas of Everest: Cinema, Orientalism, and Anglo-Tibetan Relations in the 1920s." *American Historical Review* 101(3) (1996): 712–47.

Lu, Sheldon H. "Representing the Chinese Nation-State in Filmic Discourse." In *East of West: Cross-Cultural Performance and the Staging of Difference*, edited by Claire Sponsler and Xiaomei Chen, 111–24. New York: Palgrave, 2000.

Norbu, Jamyang. "Dances with Yaks." *Cinemaya: The Asian Film Quarterly* 43 (1999): 48–49.

———. "Tibet in Film, Fiction and Fantasy of the West." *Tibetan Review* 33(1) (January 1998): 18–23.

Schell, Orville. *Virtual Tibet: Searching for Shangri-La from the Himalayas to Hollywood.* New York: Metropolitan Books, 2000.

Lamerica (1994) Gianni Amelio; France/Italy; Italian and Albanian with English subtitles; Color; 116 m; New Yorker Films (DVD, VHS); Albania, early 1990s.

In post-Communist Albania, a disreputable Italian businessman promises industry and jobs to desperate citizens. *Lamerica* is a bleak picture of grinding poverty, violence, a devastated infrastructure, people longing to migrate, and Western Europeans eager to exploit the situation.

Caparrós-Lera, J.M. "*Lamerica.*" *Film-Historia* 6(1) (1996): 67–68.
Cardullo, Bert. "Lands of the Free." *Hudson Review* 49(4) (1997): 637–44.
Crowdus, Gary, and Richard Porton. "Beyond Neorealism: Preserving a Cinema of Social Conscience." *Cineaste* 21(4) (1995): 6–13.
Iordanova, Dina. "Balkan Film Representations since 1989: The Quest for Admissibility." *Historical Journal of Film, Radio & Television* 18(2) (1998): 263–80.

The Land / al-Ard (1969) Youssef Chahine; Egypt; Arabic with English subtitles; Black and White; 130 m; Facets (VHS); Egypt, 1933.

An adaptation of the novel by Abdel Rahman al-Sharqawi, *The Land* depicts a fictional Egyptian farm village that endures the oppression and corruption of the ruling class and the government of Isma'il Sidqi. The main character, Abu Swaylim, is a small farmer who fought in World War I and participated in the Revolution of 1919. He struggles to regenerate community ties of solidarity when the village opposes the land expropriation necessary to accommodate government plans for a new road.

Downs, Susannah. "Egyptian Earth between the Pen and the Camera: Youssef Chahine's Adaptation of 'Abd Al-Rahman Al-Sharqawi's *Al-Ard.*" *Alif: Journal of Comparative Poetics* 15 (1995): 153–77.
Fawal, Ibrahim. "*Al-Ard (The Earth*, 1969)." In *Youssef Chahine: The Many Worlds of an Egyptian Director*, 72–80. London: BFI, 2001.

Land and Freedom (1995) Ken Loach; United Kingdom/Spain/Germany/Italy; English and Spanish with English subtitles; Color; 109 m; Polygram (VHS); Spain, 1930s.

Land and Freedom, ostensibly about an Englishman's participation in the Spanish Civil War, carries viewers between present and past, asking that distant events acquire meaning for subsequent generations. As the granddaughter of David Carr interrogates the meaning of the contents of his old suitcase after his death, she represents a contemporary audience for whom the events of the Spanish war are relatively unknown.

The suitcase's artifacts—a red silk scarf, pictures of an unknown woman, clippings from *The Evening Standard* and *The Daily Worker*—are the detritus of Carr's personal history, and the collective history of the European left in Spain. Reports of *Land and Freedom*'s popularity in Spain upon its release suggest that Loach's desire to teach subsequent generations about the war has been to an extent fulfilled.

See also: *Libertarias*

Cardullo, Bert. "Lands of the Free." *Hudson Review* 49(4) (1997): 637–44.
Porton, Richard. *Film and the Anarchist Imagination*. New York: Verso, 1999.
———. "Review of Land and Freedom." *Cineaste* 22(1) (1996): 32–34.

————. "The Revolution Betrayed: An Interview with Ken Loach." *Cineaste* 22(1) (1996): 30–31.

Ryan, Susan, and Richard Porton. "The Politics of Everyday Life: An Interview with Ken Loach." *Cineaste* 24(1) (1998): 22–25.

Land in Anguish / Terra em transe (1967) Glauber Rocha; Brazil; Portuguese with English subtitles; Black and White; 112 m; Facets (VHS); Brazil, 1500/1960s.

A 1964 coup d'état in Brazil saw the beginnings of a long period of extreme right-wing presidents. It also launched what is described as the second phase of the Brazilian *Cinema Novo*. Instead of preoccupation with the conditions of rural people or neorealist aesthetics, filmmakers like Glauber Rocha began to assess the Left's failures. Rocha's challenging allegorical film presents 1960s Brazil as the realization of sixteenth-century conquistadors. The fictional Republic of El Dorado provides the setting for the unsettling and satirical story of Paulo, a poet and journalist, who deliberates over the choice of two candidates in a presidential election.

Armes, Roy. "Glauber Rocha." In *Third World Film Making and the West*, 255–68. Berkeley, CA: University of California Press, 1987.

Stam, Robert. "*Land in Anguish*." In *Brazilian Cinema*, 149–61. Rutherford, NJ: Associated University Press, 1982.

Stam, Robert. *Tropical Multiculturalism: A Comparative History of Race in Brazilian Cinema and Culture*. Durham, NC: Duke University Press, 2004.

The Last Emperor (1987) Bernardo Bertolucci; France/Italy/United Kingdom; English, Mandarin, and Japanese with English subtitles; Color; 160 m (Theatrical), 218 m (Director's Cut); Artisan Entertainment (DVD, VHS); China, 1908–1959.

From the perspective of a historian, *The Last Emperor* is a fascinating exploration of how past lives are constructed in personal memory and national myth, whether on the page or screen. The title character, China's Qing Emperor Pu Yi (1906–1967), tells his Scottish tutor: "They are always telling me what to say." The young Pu Yi, so controlled by his handlers in the Forbidden City, cannot make his own history. In scenes that flash forward to the deposed emperor's detention in 1950 at a Communist "reeducation" center, he is as constrained as ever. His task is to fill the empty white pages of a book with the story of his life, but the center's governor warns: Pu Yi's "salvation" will be determined by the "attitude" he takes in writing his life.

Extended flashbacks of Pu Yi's life are positioned as his own recollections of events and experiences. He accedes to the throne as a 3-year-old. When the royal family is deposed, it is allowed to retain its titular power within the confines of the royal palace of the Forbidden City during the early years of China's Republican era (1911–1949). The film then focuses on the waning days of the Qing court, the royal family's expulsion from the palace in 1924, and Pu Yi's titular role as emperor of the Japanese-controlled Manchukuo.

Berry, Chris. "*The Last Emperor*: Opulent, Empty." *Beijing Review* 31 (1988): 36–37.

Burgoyne, Robert. "The Stages of History." In *Bertolucci's The Last Emperor: Multiple Takes*, edited by Bruce H. Sklarew, Bonnie S. Kaufman, Ellen Handler Spitz and Diane Borden, 223–33. Detroit: Wayne State University Press, 1998.

Chow, Rey. "Seeing Modern China: Toward a Theory of Ethnic Spectatorship." In *Woman and Chinese Modernity: The Politics of Reading between West and East*, 3–33. Minneapolis, MN: University of Minnesota Press, 1991.

Fairbank, John King. "Born Too Late." In *Bertolucci's The Last Emperor: Multiple Takes*, edited by Bruce H. Sklarew, Bonnie S. Kaufman, Ellen Handler Spitz, and Diane Borden, 203–11. Detroit: Wayne State University Press, 1998.

Sklarew, Bruce H., and Ellen Handler Spitz. "Interview with Bernardo Bertolucci." In *Bertolucci's The Last Emperor: Multiple Takes*, edited by Bruce H. Sklarew, Bonnie S. Kaufman, Ellen Handler Spitz, and Diane Borden, 37–54. Detroit: Wayne State University Press, 1998.

Zaller, Robert. "After the Revolution." In *Bertolucci's The Last Emperor: Multiple Takes*, edited by Bruce H. Sklarew, Bonnie S. Kaufman, Ellen Handler Spitz, and Diane Borden, 235–50. Detroit: Wayne State University Press, 1998.

The Last Supper / *La Última cena* (1974) Tomás Gutiérrez Alea; Cuba; Spanish with English subtitles; Color; 120 m; Facets (VHS); Cuba, 18th century.

Based on a documented anecdote of the event, *The Last Supper* is set at a Havana sugar plantation during Holy Week, where a dinner for twelve slaves takes place. Their host, the plantation owner, self-righteously lectures his "apostles" and a slave revolt follows later in the week.

See also: *Burn!*; *Quilombo*

Davis, Natalie Zemon. "Ceremony and Revolt: *Burn!* and *The Last Supper*." In *Slaves on Screen: Film and Historical Vision*, 41–68. Toronto: Vintage Canada, 2000.

Mraz, John. "Recasting Cuban Slavery: *The Other Francisco* and *The Last Supper*." In *Based on a True Story: Latin American History at the Movies*, edited by Donald F. Stevens, 103–22. Wilmington, DE: Scholarly Resources, 1997.

Lawrence of Arabia (1962) David Lean; United Kingdom; English; Color; 227 m; Columbia/TriStar (DVD, VHS); Middle East, 1916–1918.

Lawrence of Arabia is purported by screenwriter Robert Bolt to be based on the autobiography of T.E. Lawrence, *The Seven Pillars of Wisdom*. Bolt has devised a story around a series of flashbacks, beginning with Lawrence's 1935 death in a motorcycle accident in England, and his London funeral. Cutting to a scene of British military headquarters in Cairo in 1916, the film commences its introduction to the British lieutenant's work as a liaison officer for the British army, accepting a job as an observer with Arab Prince Feisal and his forces, and eventually participating in the Arab Revolt against the Ottoman Empire.

There is little evidence from the film itself that its scenes, characterization, and historical interpretation conform very closely to *Seven Pillars*—itself fictionalized—or to documented fact. This is a film that is undeniably of enormous visual, dramatic, and thematic interest and power. It is also undeniable that *Lawrence of Arabia* is fictionalized enough as to resemble only loosely the historical persons and events it engages as its subjects. Lawrence was hardly a prewar pacifist, and his egomania in the film has been strongly protested as ahistorical. While there really was a Sherif Ali ibn Kharish, the Sherif Ali of the film is a fictional character—a composite of the many Arab leaders with whom T.E. Lawrence associated—and the real Sherif Ali was not present at the events in which his namesake is placed in the film. The somewhat strained relationship between Feisal and Lawrence in the film obscures their much closer working relationship.

Lawrence is depicted as a dupe in a cynical British, and Arab, manipulation—each for its own political and wartime gains—but the evidence suggests that Lawrence had his own, real misgivings about his role in the Arab Revolt.

What can one say about the enduring popular admiration for the film *Lawrence of Arabia* in the face of universal disapprobation of historians about its misleading and error-filled treatment of history? One response comes from filmmaker Oliver Stone—himself a practitioner of historical films—who says, "*Lawrence of Arabia*, which I saw as a young boy, was torn apart by the reviewers, who called it a camel opera. People said much of it never happened, that Lawrence was never at the massacre of the Turks. But watching that film made me want to go back and read *The Seven Pillars of Wisdom* because the movie excited my interest. . . . Movies are just the first draft. They raise questions and inspire students to find out more." Another response is found in the analysis of Christina B. Kennedy, who privileges the "myth of heroism" constructed in the film, and its resonance for modern audiences: "Certainly the film and the character of T.E. Lawrence are illusory in many respects, but they provide a myth that offers a model of heroic behavior that touches our awareness of the human condition." These two suggestions of the impact of *Lawrence of Arabia* capture wonderfully the desire of audiences to find out about the past, and the irresistible drive to have the past give meaning to the present.

Bohne, Luciana. "Leaning toward the Past: Pressures of Vision and Narrative in *Lawrence of Arabia*." *Film Critic* 15(1) (Fall 1990): 2–16.

Brecher, Frank W. "*Lawrence of Arabia* as History." *Film & History: An Interdisciplinary Journal of Film and Television Studies* 19(4) (1989): 92–94.

Caton, Steven C. *Lawrence of Arabia: A Film's Anthropology*. Berkeley, CA: University of California Press, 1999.

n/a. "A Conversation between Mark Carnes and Oliver Stone." In *Past Imperfect: History According to the Movies*, edited by Mark C. Carnes, 305–12. New York: Henry Holt, 1995.

Raw, Laurence. "T.E. Lawrence, the Turks, and the Arab Revolt in the Cinema: Anglo-American and Turkish Representations." *Literature/Film Quarterly* 33(4) (2005): 252–61.

Richards, Jeffrey, and Jeffrey Hulbert. "Censorship in Action: The Case of *Lawrence of Arabia*." *Journal of Contemporary History* 19(1) (January 1984): 153–70.

Weintraub, Stanley. "*Lawrence of Arabia*." *Film Quarterly* 17(3) (Spring 1964): 51–54.

The Leopard / Il Gattopardo (1963) Luchino Visconti; Italy/France; original Italian-language version, with English subtitles and Italian dubbing of Burt Lancaster (183 m); original English-language dubbed version for American release (161 m); Color; Criterion Collection (DVD); Sicily, 1860–1862.

The Leopard is at once a character study, a spectacle, a family saga, and a political and social history. Luchino Visconti has adapted Giuseppe di Lampedusa's 1958 novel into a rich study of a moment in Italian history. Consistent with his creation of multi-layered films that are appreciated by different audiences for different reasons, a plot description of *The Leopard* likely fails to convey the many things the film is about. The fictional character of Sicilian Don Fabrizio faces the eclipse of feudal aristocratic society with the advent of the *Risorgimento*, or "resurgence" of a unified Italy. As we are introduced to Don Fabrizio and his family at their estate, Garibaldi and his forces have made their 1860 landing at Marsala. By film's end, the year is 1862, and Fabrizio declines his nomination for senator of the government of newly unified Italy.

This is a gorgeous, meditative, romantic, rational, and engaging film that is epic in its themes and aesthetic scale, and yet at the same time accomplishes a deeply personal and focused study of a single man. While the events one might associate with a film about the Risorgimento are present—the Battle of Palermo, and the October 1860 plebiscite make their appearance—they exist on the periphery of the film's narrative, which instead fixes its gaze on the character of Don Fabrizio. He is at once dignified in his resignation to the advent of a new era, and at the same time inexorably drawn into complicity with the new middle class regime and its desire to extinguish the populist republicanism of the Garibaldians. As he says, "I am a member of the old ruling class, hopelessly linked to the past regime and tied to it by chains of decency if not affection. I belong to an unfortunate generation straddling two worlds, and ill at ease in both. And what is more, I am utterly without illusions." Such are his lack of illusions that Don Fabrizio accepts the marriage of his nephew Tancredi to Angelica, daughter of Don Calogero, after protracted negotiations about the wealth Angelica will bring with her to the House of Salina.

The Leopard ends with a scene of Don Fabrizio, kneeling alone in a dawn courtyard, wishing on a star. As a carriage carrying Tancredi, Angelica, and Calogero is seen departing from the scene of a fabulous ball that portends the end of an era, shots are heard. Don Fabrizio knows that the execution of the revolutionaries seals the direction of the nation. Traveling away from him are those passengers of the carriage, symbols of the new alliance of the bourgeoisie and aristocracy.

Landy, Marcia. "The Operatic as History: Two Risorgimento Narratives." In *Cinematic Uses of the Past*, edited by Marcia Landy, 107–50. Minneapolis, MN: University of Minnesota Press, 1996.

Marcus, Millicent. "Visconti's *Leopard*: The Politics of Adaptation." In *Filmmaking by the Book: Italian Cinema and Literary Adaptation*, 45–66. Baltimore: Johns Hopkins University Press, 1993.

Sorlin, Pierre. "*The Italian Risorgimento.*" In *The Film in History: Restaging the Past*, 116–40. Totowa, NJ: Barnes and Noble, 1980.

Sorlin, Pierre. "*The Leopard.*" *History Today* 45(9) (September 1995): 46–51.

Let There Be Peace / Daresalam (2000) Issa Serge Coelo; France/Burkina Faso/Chad; French and Arabic with English subtitles; Color; 105 m; California Newsreel (DVD; VHS); Chad, 1970s.

Daresalam personalizes the experience of civil strife in Africa by telling the story of two friends who participate in the civil war in Chad, a three-decades long conflict that began in the 1970s. This first feature by director Issa Serge Coelo depicts the actions of the FRAP (*Front Revolutionnaire du Peuple*) in Chad at the same time as suggesting the universal experience of ordinary people affected by historical events beyond their control.

The personal costs of this prolonged and unresolved conflict are the essential theme of the story. The first third of the film shows the arbitrary power of the police over villagers whose quality of life is intimately tied to the success of the harvest, the price of millet, and the land tax rates. When inhabitants of the rural village of Rass ask for postponement of the national loan tax so that it does not coincide with land tax payments, the visiting Minister of the Interior chastises their lack of duty. With protest comes a brutal police massacre, a shocking event that seems so premature in its fury that the viewer is left to come to terms with the reality of government oppression for this peaceful and relatively prosperous village.

Daresalam refuses to idealize or vilify combatants, instead providing a nuanced look at the great personal losses of the civil war in Chad. If any responsibility is to be placed in the origins or outcome of the war, Coelo targets three long-term factors: French colonialism, religious divisions, and human weakness.

Elley, Derek. "*Daresalam.*" *Variety* 382 (March 12/18, 2001): 39.

Letters from Marusia / Actas de Marusia (1975) Miguel Littín; Mexico; Spanish; Color; 110 m; Oxxo Films (VHS); Chile, 1907.

The village of Marusia was the site of a massacre by the Chilean army when saltpeter miners refused to end their strike against British mine owners. The film is not subtle in its condemnation of the exploitation of the workers by the state, the capitalists, and the military; critic Walter Goodman calls it "agitprop ascendant." *Letters from Marusia*'s allegorical relationship to the 1973 coup in Chile (from which director Littín had fled) is also notable.

See also: *Song of Chile*

Goodman, Walter. "Film: Littín's *Marusia.*" *The New York Times* 134 (July 11, 1985): C22.
Schwartz, Ronald. "*Actas De Marusia* (*Letters from Marusia*)." In *Latin American Films, 1932–1994: A Critical Filmography*, 23. Jefferson, NC: McFarland, 1997.

Libertarias / Freedomfighters (1996) Vicente Aranda; Spain/Italy/Belgium; Spanish with English subtitles; Color; 125 m; Venevision International (DVD); Spain, 1936–39.

At the beginning of the Spanish Civil War a nun and a few prostitutes are rescued from a brothel by the female anarchist group *Mujeres Libres* (Free Women). The film follows their subsequent indoctrination and participation in the ill-fated rebel movement.

Aranda, Vicente, and María Asunción Gómez. "A Nostalgic Reinvention of History: *Libertarias* (1996)." *Film-Historia* 9(3) (1999): 253–64.

Life of Oharu / Saikaku Ichidai Onna (1952) Kenji Mizoguchi; Japan; Japanese with English subtitles; Black and White; 136 m; Facets (DVD, VHS); Japan, 17th century.

In flashback, 50-year-old Oharu, prostitute and former lady-in-waiting at the imperial court, considers her life. This is an unrelentingly grim story, based on a seventeenth-century novel, that shows the consequences of Oharu's refusal to conform to the expectations of women in her feudal society.

Bordwell, David. "Mizoguchi, or Modulation." In *Figures Traced in Light: On Cinematic Staging*, 83–139. Berkeley, CA: University of California Press, 2005.
Le Fanu, Mark. "The Great Triptych." In *Mizoguchi and Japan*, 49–67. London: BFI, 2005.
Kinoshita, Chika. "Choreography of Desire: Analysing Kinuyo Tanaka's Acting in Mizoguchi's Films." *Screening the Past* 13 (December 2001), http://www.latrobe.edu.au/screeningthepast/firstrelease/fr1201/ckfr13a.htm (accessed May 30, 2006).

Lin Zexu (1959) Zheng Junli; China; Mandarin with English subtitles; Color; 103 m; no current; China, 1838–1841.

Zheng Junli's *Lin Zexu* memorializes the commissioner appointed by the Chinese emperor in 1838 to stop Chinese imports of British opium. The film begins with a voiceover explaining that by 1838, the almost century-long British practice of importing opium into China was taking a terrible economic and social toll: "Silver poured out of China, almost bankrupting her. The number of addicts grew. The people were angered. The ruling class was divided." Enter the story of Lin Zexu from his appointment to his forced exile in 1841. This biopic is not interested in portraying any aspect of Lin's private life; our subject is nothing but a public figure.

In keeping with its production during the first decade of the consolidation of the Communist People's Republic of China, the film anoints "the people" as heroes as much as its biographical subject. Not only is Commissioner Lin a man of courage, smarts, and determination, he is responsive and sympathetic to the common people who inhabit the trading city of Guangzhou. Viewers are asked to esteem this trait in Lin above all others, thereby acknowledging the central importance of their actions and place in achieving a new (Communist) China by 1949.

In contrast to the heroic underclass, the ranks of imperial Chinese officialdom are portrayed in *Lin Zexu* as highly corrupt and duplicitous. Their complicity with the foreigners—whose actions are portrayed as nothing less than attempting complete subjugation of the empire—is a sign of the irretrievable decay of the imperial system. As one official says about the potential success of Lin in ending the opium trade, "Our profits will go to the wind!" Even the emperor loses patience with his appointee when, by 1839, he tires of hearing Lin's criticism of the collusion of imperial officials with the British to protect the trade.

Using vivid characters, a storyline filled with clever twists and turns, and rousing battle scenes, *Lin Zexu* is a vivid introduction to a Maoist-era interpretation of the first Opium War. The voiceover at film's end proclaims, "The opium of the aggressor failed to stupefy the Chinese people. It roused them to action. This is how the Chinese people began their struggle...." Accompanying this message is the image of a mass of ordinary Chinese who have gathered on a hill overlooking Guangzhou harbor in May of 1841, where they have forced British troops to retreat. The voiceover, victorious smiles, and military banners signal Chinese unity in victory. This final scene ignores events to come, which culminated in British military victory and China's signing of the Treaty of Nanjing.

Lin Zexu places the Opium War of 1839–1842 as the first stage in the war to end foreign aggression in China, and to end imperial rule. It positions Lin and the characters of two exploited boat ferriers as pioneers of the nationalist and socialist cause.

See also: *The Opium War*

Karl, Rebecca E. "The Burdens of History: *Lin Zexu* (1959) and *The Opium War* (1997)." In *Whither China? Intellectual Politics in Contemporary China*, edited by Xudong Zhang, 229–62. Durham, NC: Duke University Press, 2001.

Xiao, Zhiwei. "Nationalism in Chinese Popular Culture: A Case Study of *The Opium War*." In *Exploring Nationalisms of China: Themes and Conflicts*, edited by C.X. George Wei and Xiaoyuan Liu, 41–54. Westport, CT: Greenwood Press, 2002.

The Lion's Den / La boca del lobo (1988) Francisco J. Lombardi; Peru/Spain; Spanish with English subtitles; Color; 122 m; Facets (VHS); Peru, 1980s.

In 1987 the town of Chuspi in the Peruvian Andes was the site of a Peruvian army massacre of forty-seven Amerindian peasants suspected of affiliation with the "Shining Path" terrorist group. *The Lion's Den* turns its lens on the military unit whose mission is to garrison the town. The conscience of the fictional character Luna, a young soldier who aspires to the officer corps, is increasingly challenged by demands that he obey Lieutenant Roca, his uncompromising commander. Luna eventually refuses to participate in the violence Roca and his increasingly brutal fellow soldiers inflict on villagers. *The Lion's Den* offers little explanation of the political, social, and economic conditions that prevail for the peasants, or their relationship to the guerillas. But the tension created by the film effectively suggests the atmosphere of dread, violence, and persecution experienced by locals, and the implication of everyday Peruvians in government policy against Shining Path.

See also: *The Principal Enemy*

Schwartz, Ronald. "*La Boca Del Lobo (The Lion's Den)*." In *Latin American Films, 1932–1994: A Critical Filmography*, 47. Jefferson, NC: McFarland, 1997.

Lucía (1969) Humberto Solás; Cuba; Spanish with English subtitles; Black and White; 160 m; New Yorker Films (theatrical); Cuba 1895, 1933, 1960.

Three Cuban women who share the name *Lucía* but who inhabit different time periods and social classes are the vehicle through which is conveyed an epic and stylistically diverse reconstruction of Cuban history. In each period Lucía inhabits—as an aristocrat during the war against Spain in 1895, as a member of the bourgeoisie at Machado's overthrow in 1933, and as a peasant in post-revolution 1960—she represents the history of women's, and Cuba's, struggle for liberation.

Fraunhar, Alison. "*Mulata Cubana*: The Problematics of National Allegory." In *Latin American Cinema: Essays on Modernity, Gender and National Identity*, edited by Lisa Shaw and Stephanie Dennison, 160–79. Jefferson, NC: McFarland, 2005.

Mraz, John. "*Lucía*: Visual Style and Historical Portrayal." *Jump Cut: A Review of Contemporary Media* 19 (December 1978): 21–27.

Myerson, Michael. "About *Lucía*." In *Memories of Underdevelopment: Three Revolutionary Films of Cuba*, 111–21. New York: Grossman, 1973.

Rose, Peter W. "The Politics of the Trilogy Form: *Lucía*, the *Oresteia*, and *the Godfather*." *Film-Historia* 5(2–3): 93–116.

Weinstein, Barbara. "*Lucía*: Inventing Women's History on Film." In *Based on a True Story: Latin American History at the Movies*, edited by Donald F. Stevens, 123–42. Wilmington, DE: Scholarly Resources, 1997.

Lumumba (2000) Raoul Peck; France/Belgium/Germany/Haiti; French and Lingala with English subtitles; Color; 115 m; Zeitgeist Films (DVD, VHS); Congo, 1959–1961.

Patrice Lumumba was the first prime minister of the newly independent Republic of Congo, whose term ended with his execution after only a few months in office. Lumumba was a gifted orator, and in this film version of his political life, Lumumba continues to speak, this time from the dead. In the introductory scene, his voiceover recalls the night he and two others were murdered. The graphic depiction of two Belgian policemen—fortified by drink—cutting up and dissolving the bodies in acid, is accompanied by Lumumba's voice, posthumously entreating his wife: "You won't tell the children everything."

Lumumba is an interesting biopic because its (deceased) subject "writes" and voices his own story. Director Raoul Peck, best known for his 1991 documentary treatment of the same subject (*Lumumba: Death of a Prophet*) acknowledges that Lumumba's fate is well known, and therefore constructs the narrative around the question of who was responsible for his death. The film's investigation begins with Lumumba's arrival in 1950s Belgian-colonial Stanleyville. He achieves the co-leadership of the MNC (*Mouvement National Congolais*) and ultimately the position of prime minister of the National Unity government of independent Congo in 1960. Lumumba's handling of the secession of Katanga province, disagreements with President Kasavubu, and the challenge of military head—and former ally—Colonel Joseph-Désiré Mobutu suggest his increasing isolation in the power plays among civil, military, and international interests following Congo's decolonization. The film ends with Lumumba's execution in January 1961 by a Congolese firing squad, witnessed by Katanga leader Moise Tshombe, in a remote forest. Lumumba's voiceover defends his actions and assures his wife that "History will have its say one day."

The history that Peck constructs is evidently an attempt to refute the official Congolese explanation of Lumumba's death. The claim that Lumumba was rightfully under arrest for treason, and shot in an attempted escape, has been given little credence for decades. But the story has been in a sense freed with the deposing of Lumumba's successor, Mobutu Sese Seko, in 1997. Peck's version of Lumumba's story has garnered supporters and detractors. The lynchpin of evaluation is whether the emphasis on Mobutu's collusion with the American Central Intelligence Agency to murder Lumumba is rightfully placed, or whether the film dangerously ignores too much of the story's context, especially that of the region's internal conflicts, and the Cold War dimensions of the involvement of the United Nations after Katanga's secession.

These arguments about *Lumumba*'s history lesson reflect the extremely difficult process of selection and emphasis that informs any effort at historical interpretation. Peck here uses a very interesting blend of visual and verbal cues to bolster the veracity of his narrative. Many images in the film carefully reproduce photographs and newsreel footage from the era, and the screenplay incorporates where possible the recorded words of the protagonist and others. In other instances, narrative emphases support a more emotional interpretation of his subject, especially Lumumba's depiction as a devoted husband and father.

The virtues of *Lumumba* are its creation of a suspenseful atmosphere, vivid characters, its posthumous structuring of voice, and its attention to the visual details of the era (the westernized appearance of late-1950s urban Stanleyville might surprise some viewers). Amy Abugo Ongiri says Peck "is doing far more than simply recreating Lumumba's story and Congolese history for a generation and a wider audience that may or may not be familiar with it." She defends the film's importance because it "celebrates the innocence" of the early postcolonial era "at the same time that it laments its loss." It is difficult to refute this claim; *Lumumba* very movingly envisions the contrast between idealism and politics.

But if "history" is really to "have its say," then positioning Lumumba's story as a symbolic, generalizing tale does a disservice to the particulars of the case. The Belgian and American presence in postcolonial Congo is vaguely treated with scenes of anonymous officials gliding away in limousines. *Lumumba* tells us little about its title character's ideology apart from his anticolonialism and encouragement of tribal and political unity; there is no explanation of why, for example, the CIA pronounced him a Communist. While viewers of *Lumumba* are moved to contemplate universal lessons here, they also leave the theater with hazy understanding of some of the particulars of Patrice Lumumba's story.

Briley, Ron. "Review of *Lumumba*." *Cineaste* 27(1) (2001): 37–39.

Kyle, Keith. "Review of *Lumumba*." *International Affairs* 78(3) (2002): 595–604.

Ongiri, Amy Abugo. "Review of *Lumumba*." *American Historical Review* 107(2) (2002): 675–76.

Watson, Julia. "Raoul Peck's *Lumumba*: A Film for Our Times." *Research in African Literatures* 33(2) (2002): 230–35.

Luther: Genius, Rebel, Liberator (2003) Eric Till; Germany; English; Color; 113 m; MGM (DVD; VHS); Germany, 1519–1525.

Aside from a brief scene dramatizing the decision of Martin Luther to become a monk, this biopic of the German religious reformer concentrates on the years 1517 through 1525. In describing these event-filled years in under two hours, *Luther* compresses events enough to make gargantuan cinematic leaps across time that to an extent confuse cause and effect. But these years are arguably the most potent in their dramatic potential, and are understandably milked for their entertainment value. The hell-and-brimstone sermons of indulgence-selling Friar Tetzel caricature Catholic practices; villainous Pope Leo X responds to Luther's *95 Theses* with an excommunication order; and Luther's appearance before Emperor Charles V at the Diet of Worms shows him to be the nonconformist biopics induce us to expect. His experience as an "outlaw" of the Holy Roman Empire makes Luther enough of an action hero to counter the scenes of his spiritual anguish, and the spectacle of peasants burning things adds some plebian weight to the more abstract debates about faith and salvation that take place among theologians.

While no doubt one might have liked to have been a fly on the wall of the historical meeting of Luther and Elector Frederick of Saxony, contrary to the scene of such a meeting staged in *Luther*, the two never met. But this error could be forgiven, or seem less glaring, if the characterization of Luther, and the explanation of events, were handled in a less histrionic, and more explanatory, manner. The truth of Luther's revelations about God's love, about the selling of indulgences, or about his conscience in the face of the authority of church and empire is posited in the film as, simply, self-evident. As such, *Luther* interprets history as the unfolding of the will of God.

See also: *Kundun*; *The Message: The Story of Islam*

Hendrix, Scott. "Reflections of a Frustrated Film Consultant." *Sixteenth Century Journal* 35(3) (September 1, 2004): 811–14

Hillerbrand, Hans. "Protestant Heroics." *Christian Century* 120(22) (2003): 42–44.

Ozment, Steven. "Review of *Luther*." *American Historical Review* 109(5) (December 2004): 1662–63.

MacArthur's Children /Setouchi shonen yakyudan (1984) Masahiro Shinoda; Japan; Japanese with English subtitles; Color, Black and White; 125 m; Universal Studios Home Entertainment (VHS); Japan, 1945.

In this fiction film based on a novel by Yu Aku, a fishing village on the Japanese island of Awaji is a microcosm of the era of Japan's postwar American occupation. *MacArthur's Children* shows history through the eyes of a child, an orphan of the fifth grade named Ryuta, whose personal experiences intersect with the political milieu. Films like *Goodbye, Children, The Blue Kite,* and *Come and See* are successful in negotiating the theme of childhood innocence lost without being cloying or resorting to empty sentiment. *MacArthur's Children* has the same basic ingredients of childhood experience of historical upheaval, and handles them well, but with less imagination, resonance, and cohesion. The film is an effective introduction to some of the social implications of the occupation period. A former admiral faces a war crimes trial and his daughter suffers a hatred for the Americans. School textbook references to the Emperor must be inked out. Uncertainty about the future is voiced by one of the boys, Saburo, who claims he'll be a gangster when he grows up because there is no more admiralty. These episodes create a collection of snapshots of the period that are more pleasant and touching than revealing.

See also: *Black Rain; Hiroshima, mon amour; Record of a Tenement Gentleman*

Ehrlich, Linda C. "Erasing and Refocusing: Two Films of the Occupation." In *The Confusion Era: Art and Culture of Japan During the Allied Occupation, 1945–1952,* edited by Mark Sandler, 39–52. Seattle: University of Washington Press, 1997.

Hitano, Kyoko. "An Interview with Masahiro Shinoda." *Cineaste* 14(3) (1986): 51.

Silberman, Robert, and Kyoka Hirano. "Review of *MacArthur's Children*." *Cineaste* 14(3) (1986): 50, 52.

The Madness of King George (1994) Nicolas Hytner; United Kingdom; English; Color; 107 m; MGM (DVD, VHS); Great Britain, 18th century.

George III, King of England, was reputed to have suffered throughout his life from a (possibly hereditary) mental illness. Screenwriter and playwright Alan Bennett is not much interested in a biographical treatment of the king and his troubles. Instead, George's "madness"—the film isolates one bout of the disease—becomes the pretext for exploring the theme of national (and self) identity in a time of historical transition.

One of the film's great successes is the endearing portrayal of George by Nigel Hawthorne, who conveys a sense of the figure's innate humanity and dignity despite his troubles. George can then be juxtaposed effectively with the ridiculous figures who surround him and seek to capitalize on his situation: the indolent and manically aspirant Prince of Wales, royal physicians, and Ministers Pitt and Fox.

The conventional drama of the film is played out as a recovered George races to Parliament to prove his fitness to rule before the passing of a bill granting Prince George the regency. Royal intrigues, bordering on the farcical, amuse and create an economical snapshot of the state of English politics: the American colonies have been lost, and parliamentary politics supersede royal authority but the popularity of the House of Commons tempers the republican leanings of the ministers. Voicing the uneasy status of English nationhood, the agitated George says, "I've had no peace of mind since we lost America."

This is an historical film that does not provide documentary markers of its exact setting or date. No intertitles announce in what period we find ourselves, although a postscript explains the modern diagnosis of George's ailment as porphyria. While the lack of explanation could be ascribed to director Hytner's and writer Bennett's assumption of their audience's knowledge of English history, the generic thrust of the lack of dating allows scope for its modern themes.

Fleming, Michael, and Roger Manvell. *Images of Madness: The Portrayal of Insanity in the Feature Film*. Rutherford, NJ: Fairleigh Dickinson University Press, 1985.

McKechnie, Kara. "Taking Liberties with the Monarch: The Royal Bio-Pic in the 1990s." In *British Historical Cinema: The History, Heritage, and Costume Film*, edited by Claire Monk and Amy Sargeant, 217–36. London: Routledge, 2002.

McKechnie, Kara. "Mrs. Brown's Mourning and Mr. King's Madness: Royal Crisis on Screen." In *Retrovisions: Reinventing the Past in Film and Fiction*, edited by Deborah Cartmell, I. Q. Hunter, and Imelda Whelehan, 102–19. London: Pluto Press, 2001.

O'Mealy, Joseph H. "Royal Family Values: The Americanization of Alan Bennett's *The Madness of George III*." *Literature/Film Quarterly* 27(2) (1999): 90–96.

Prasch, Thomas. "Review of *The Madness of King George*." *American Historical Review* 100(4) (October 1995): 1225–26.

The Making of the Mahatma (1996) Shyam Benegal; India/South Africa; English; Color; 144 m; Facets (DVD); South Africa, 1893–1914.

The Making of the Mahatma focuses on the 21 years that Mohandas K. Gandhi lived and worked as a barrister in South Africa. While the production values of this film might not rival Attenborough's more famous study, the film considers these South Africa years as formative in the formation of Gandhi's social and political conscience. *The Making of the Mahatma* clearly venerates Gandhi for his sense of justice and the development of his concept of *satyagraha*. Scenes devoted to his relationship with wife Kasturba suggest Gandhi's personal flaws as well. The film is based on South African sociologist Fatima Meer's book *Apprenticeship of a Mahatma*.

See also: *Gandhi*

Datta, Sangeeta. "Histories and Epics." In *Shyam Benegal*, 120–44. London: BFI, 2002.

The Makioka Sisters / Sasame Yuki (1983) Kon Ichikawa; Japan; Japanese with English subtitles; Color; 140 m; Facets (DVD); Japan, 1930s.

From its opening scene of rain audibly pouring on hills of luscious spring cherry blossoms, *The Makioka Sisters* promises to be a visually stunning recreation of 1930s Japan. Director Kon Ichikawa has taken Junichiro Tanazaki's acclaimed novel (originally titled *A Light Snowfall* and then *The Makioka Sisters* for foreign versions) and produced a quiet, respectful, and revealing interpretation of Japanese social mores and the strains and promise of modernization. The four sisters of the title achieve adulthood during a time when prewar Japan confronts unprecedented challenges in the face of social, economic, and political modernization. Their annual pilgrimage to view the Kyoto blossoms serves as a touchstone of change and continuity.

Desser, David. "Space and Narrative in *The Makioka Sisters*." In *Kon Ichikawa*, edited by James Quandt, 373–84. Waterloo: Wilfrid Laurier University Press, 2001.

Geist, Kathe. "Adapting *The Makioka Sisters*." In *Word and Image in Japanese Cinema*, edited by Carole Cavanaugh and Dennis Washburn, 108–25. Cambridge: Cambridge University Press, 1993.

Nornes, Markus. "Context and *The Makioka Sisters*." *East-West Film Journal* 5(2) (1991): 46–68.

The Man by the Shore / L' Homme sur les quais (1993) Raoul Peck; France/ Canada; French with English subtitles; Color; 106 m; KJM3 Entertainment Group (theatrical); Haiti, 1960s.

The central character of *The Man by the Shore* is a fictional 8-year-old Haitian girl named Sarah. She is growing up in 1960s Haiti, a country experiencing the increasingly authoritarian regime of François "Papa Doc" Duvalier. The story alternates between Sarah's experience in hiding with her siblings in the attic of her grandmother, and her memories of two years earlier, when she witnessed the torture of her father at the hands of a member of the *tontons macoutes*, Haiti's feared government-endorsed militia. Director Peck was born in Haiti; he fled the country with his family when he was a young boy.

Kauffmann, Stanley. "On Films: Mystery, Tyranny, Humbuggery." *The New Republic* 215 (July 8, 1996): 26–27.

Sealey, Wendy. "Exploring the Relationship Between Official Discourse and Popular Memory in Raoul Peck's *The Man by the Shore*." *Black Arts Quarterly* 4(1) (Winter/Spring 1999), http://www.stanford.edu/group/CBPA/BAQWinterSpring1999.pdf (accessed May 30, 2006).

Spaas, Lieve. "Haiti." In *The Francophone Film: A Struggle for Identity*, 124–25. Manchester: Manchester University Press, 2000.

Taylor, Clyde. "Autopsy of Terror." *Transition: An International Review* 6(1) (1996): 236–46.

A Man for All Seasons (1966) Fred Zinnemann; United Kingdom; English; Color; 120 m; Sony Pictures Home Entertainment (DVD, VHS); England, 1529–1535.

English playwright Robert Bolt has the screenplay of many historical films to his credit, including *The Mission*, *The Bounty*, *Doctor Zhivago*, and *Lawrence of Arabia*. He is a master of achieving verisimilitude for his historical characters and situations, largely through his appeal to romantic–heroic archetypes of men of conscience opposing obvious injustice. Whether an archetype that resonates for audiences is the same thing as a sound historical interpretation based on evidence is a matter of debate. This is true of historical biography, where arriving at an understanding of personal motives and agency, even where documentation abounds, is a very difficult enterprise, such as it tends to tread in the arena of inner psychology.

A Man for All Seasons, derived from Bolt's play, is about the refusal of Lord Chancellor Sir Thomas More to swear the 1534 Act of Supremacy that established Henry VIII as supreme head of the Church in England. Intelligent dialogue, effective staging, and memorable performances make this film excellent drama. But the More of the film is, according to his biographer Richard Marius, "an icon of purity and principle who provoked reverence and affection." This portrayal is out of step with the great body of evidence of his (less salutary, perhaps) "furious and cascading hatred of the Protestants."

See also: *Luther: Genius, Rebel, Liberator*

Asimow, Michael, and Paul Bergman, eds. "*A Man for All Seasons*." In *Reel Justice: The Courtroom Goes to the Movies*, 30–34. Kansas City, MI: Andrews McMeel, 1996.

Grindon, Leger. "Drama and Spectacle as Historical Explanation in the Historical Fiction Film." *Film & History: An Interdisciplinary Journal of Film and Television Studies* 17(4) (1987): 74–80.

Herman, Gerald H., and Wendy S. Wilson. "Unit 6: The Reformation. Teacher's Guide: *A Man for All Seasons*." In *World History on the Screen: Film and Video Resources*, 35–37. Portland, ME: Walch, 1990.

Marius, Richard. "*A Man for All Seasons*." In *Past Imperfect: History According to the Movies*, edited by Mark C. Carnes, 70–73. New York: Henry Holt, 1995.

Smith, Kevin. "Battling for Integrity." *Sight & Sound* 7 (November 1997): 61.

Super, Joel N. "Fred Zinnemann, *A Man for All Seasons*, and Documentary Fiction." In *The Films of Fred Zinnemann: Critical Perspectives*, edited by Arthur Nolletti Jr., 157–78. New York: Suny Press, 1999.

Man of Iron / Czlowiek z zelaza (1981) Andrzej Wajda; Poland; Polish with English subtitles; Color, Black and White; 153 m; MGM (DVD, VHS); Poland, 1968, 1970, and 1980.

"This should be shown over and over again to all workers in Poland. To rid them of any lingering illusions." So says the projectionist and struggling radio engineer who introduces journalist Winkel to the secret footage he possesses of the brutal army repression of a 1970 uprising of Polish shipyard workers. It is now 1980, and the workers are again active, having initiated a general strike and blockaded themselves in the buildings of the Gdansk yards. Introducing popular audiences to this (real) footage in the 1981 film *Man of Iron*, director Andrzej Wajda has fulfilled the projectionist's wish, asking that events of 1970 be claimed in national and individual memory to soberly inspire Poles to support the cause of Poland's Solidarity movement.

This mix of the actual and fictional is a hallmark of *Man of Iron*, a provocative blend that signifies to the viewer that Wajda is "documenting" the origins of Solidarity in Poland in a way that only imagination can achieve effectively. The opening intertitle asks audiences to accept that "The people in the film are all imaginary, but the situations are real, and use has been made of documentary material." In a further challenge to our comfort with the separation of fictional and documentary film, *Man of Iron* invites appearances by famously real Solidarity leader Lech Walesa. Walesa at times appears in Wajda's footage, milling among the striking workers, and at other times he appears in documentary footage. The most striking use of Walesa is his appearance as one of three witnesses to the marriage of the film's young fictional protagonist, Maciek Tomczyk, and his activist filmmaker lover, Agnieszka. His "blessing" of the union, captured in affectionate kisses of bride and groom, reinforces Wajda's paternal approval of their commitment to the political movement.

Man of Iron is a sequel to Andrzej Wajda's film *Man of Marble*, which first introduced Maciek's father Birkut. Wajda's interpretation of the history of the Solidarity movement is explained through several interesting fictional characters whose stories intersect across a decade of political tension. Former activist and now struggling alcoholic Winkel is the hub of the relationships. Hired to discredit Maciek, Winkel's investigations slowly lead him into an almost Kafkaesque world where youthful heroism is challenged by pragmatist politics and personal tragedy. Unraveling the personal history of Maciek—the man of iron "forged" in the travails of the workers' movement—awakens in Winkel his sense of justice. (As a female member of the Gdansk strike committee says to Winkel, "I know you're talented, but a little bit lost. . . .") By the end of the film, with Walesa announcing "we won!" Winkel resigns his job, symbolizing his decision to end his exploitation by the Communist authorities who have preyed on his fear and greed to expose the movement.

See also: *Man of Marble; Moonlighting*

Falkowska, Janina. *The Political Films of Andrzej Wajda: Dialogism in Man of Marble, Man of Iron,* and *Danton.* Oxford: Berghahn Books, 1996.

Lewis, Cliff, and Carroll Britch. "Light out of Poland: Wajda's *Man of Marble* and *Man of Iron.*" *Film & History: An Interdisciplinary Journal of Film and Television Studies* 12(4) (December 1982): 82–89.

Long, Kristi S. "*Man of Iron*: Representing and Shaping Historical Consciousness through Film—a Polish Case." *Journal of Popular Culture* 30(1) (1996): 163–71.

Turim, Maureen. "Remembering and Deconstructing: The Historical Flashback in *Man of Marble* and *Man of Iron.*" In *The Cinema of Andrzej Wajda: The Art of Irony and Defiance,* edited by John Orr and Elzbieta Ostrowska, 93–102. London: Wallflower Press, 2003.

Man of Marble / *Czlowiek z marmuru* (1977) Andrzej Wajda; Poland; Polish with English subtitles; Color, Black and White; 160 m; Facets (DVD); Poland, 1950s and 1970s.

In the 1970s a young Polish film student, Agnieszka, is making a film about the life of Birkut, a champion bricklayer of the 1950s who enjoyed national acclaim as a model worker. Multiple points of view emerge in the film as Agnieszka investigates Birkut's story by gathering evidence from interviews and by viewing state-produced film footage of his feats. The narrative is intercut with interviewee's own flashback scenes recalling Birkut's story. The result is a multi-layered film about the formation of truth and memory in an oppressive regime.

See also: *Man of Iron; Moonlighting*

Falkowska, Janina. *The Political Films of Andrzej Wajda: Dialogism in Man of Marble, Man of Iron,* and *Danton.* Oxford: Berghahn Books, 1996.

Lewis, Cliff, and Carroll Britch. "Light out of Poland: Wajda's *Man of Marble* and *Man of Iron.*" *Film & History: An Interdisciplinary Journal of Film and Television Studies* 12(4) (December 1982): 82–89.

Turim, Maureen. "Remembering and Deconstructing: The Historical Flashback in *Man of Marble* and *Man of Iron.*" In *The Cinema of Andrzej Wajda: The Art of Irony and Defiance,* edited by John Orr and Elzbieta Ostrowska, 93–102. London: Wallflower Press, 2003.

Mapantsula (1988) Oliver Schmitz; South Africa; Zulu, Sotho, Afrikaans and English with English subtitles; Color; 104 m; California Newsreel (VHS); South Africa, 1980s.

Panic is a "mapantsula," a streetwise resident of 1980s Soweto who commits petty crimes in Johannesburg and enjoys its nightlife. He does not have the blatantly heroic characteristics of Denzel Washington's Steven Biko (*Cry Freedom*) or Kevin Kline's Donald Woods (*A Dry White Season*). And he does not befriend and enlighten liberal white South Africans—as is the case in the two aforementioned treatments of the same era. Panic instead, in his last words in *Mapantsula*, utters the word "No" to his Afrikaans interrogator when asked to sign a statement indicting an activist acquaintance for inciting a riot and training with the resistance in Botswana. Panic's refusal to comply with the authoritarian apartheid regime is the culmination of a film that traces—through cutting between scenes of his jail and interrogation and those scenes devoted to explaining how he landed there—his slow route from resignation to defiance.

Mapantsula is a remarkable film. The sights and sounds of urban and township life in the apartheid era are presented less as the stuff of epic films and histrionics, than that of everyday life. The struggle of these South Africans does produce heroes and villains, but most often in the guise of ordinary petty crooks, union leaders, domestic workers, and the unemployed. Their suffering, anger, and determination lead to organized action. Rallies ask for accountability from their local community council about rental rates. Demonstrations elicit unplanned violence, police shootings, and roundups.

Panic loses his girlfriend Pat when he causes her firing from her job as a domestic (he swears at her white employer and breaks a window of the house). His quest to find his landlady's son—later discovered to have been killed in police custody—places him in closer and closer contact with an activist, a man that Panic admires and resents. Still attracted to the aimless amusements of the city he enjoys with his Soweto pals, Panic's disengagement from politics is profound. But when the police chase down Panic in their brutal response to a Soweto march, Panic must now share a jail cell with men who refuse to allow his indifference. His cooperation with the inspector—acting as an informant on the jailed group—does not save Panic from police beatings and verbal abuse in custody. As the inspector rationalizes, "They say they want one man, one vote. But that's not what they want. They want to kill us."

Mapantsula's conception of history is articulated in a scene when Panic visits a woman who reads bones to hear the ancestors speak. Panic cannot answer when she asks, "What can you tell me about our history?" This ignorance has obviously been an obstacle to Panic's political awareness. But the seer/oracle adds, "The past and future are for dreaming about. The present is for living in." Exhorting Panic that you "reap what you sow," she speaks to the danger of his inertia and resignation.

See also: *Cry Freedom*; *A Dry White Season*

Gugler, Josef. "*Mapantsula* (1988): Black Resistance to White Oppression." In *African Film: Re-Imagining a Continent*, 91–96. Bloomington: Indiana University Press, 2003.

Magogodi, Kgafela oa. "Sexuality, Power and the Black Body in *Mapantsula* and *Fools*." In *To Change Reels: Film and Film Culture in South Africa*, edited by Isabel Balseiro and Ntongela Masilela, 187–200. Detroit: Wayne State University Press, 2003.

Nixon, Rob. "Cry White Season: Anti-Apartheid Heroism and the American Screen." In *Homelands, Harlem and Hollywood: South African Culture and the World Beyond*, edited by Rob Nixon, 77–97. New York: Routledge, 1994.

Margaret's Museum (1995) Mort Ransen; Canada/United Kingdom; English; Color; 114 m; Lion's Gate Home Entertainment (VHS); Canada, late 1940s.

Margaret's Museum has generated a small, but rich, critical literature that shows significant disagreement over the aesthetic value of the film as well as its portrayal of the past. As the film could be described as Canada's version of workers' cinematic history, it has a place alongside such films as *Daens*, *Letters from Marusia*, *Germinal*, *The Adalen Riots*, or *Rebellion in Patagonia*.

Adapted from a 1995 novel by Sheldon Currie, the film takes place in Glace Bay, Nova Scotia in the late 1940s. Margaret MacNeil is a young woman who works as a cleaner in the local hospital, and whose family members have a long, and tragic, history working in the coal mine. The film is a romantic drama: Margaret and Neil Currie fall in love, and he breaks his agreement to her condition that he would never return to work at the mine. Margaret's mother, grandfather, uncle, and brother are characters in the subplot about the past dangers of the mine to the family. The invalid grandfather has lungs "full of dust," and Uncle Angus tries to prevent his nephew from wasting his life in mine work. Mother—like most of the women in the film—adopts a mixture of stoicism, anger, and bitter resignation to her lack of control over the fate of her loved ones. If they are men, they will be injured or die in the mine; if they are women, they will perpetuate through their reproduction of children this cycle of love and loss.

For those willing to be engaged by the film's scenery, predictable but well-acted characters, and predictable but well-plotted story, *Margaret's Museum* will be a thoughtful study of working class history in early postwar Canada. Particularly striking is the treatment of gender, wherein themes of powerlessness and empowerment cut across stereotypical divisions of the sexes. Scott Henderson argues that the film also effectively undercuts expectations that arise from stereotypes of (Canadian) East Coast society, inscribed in the opening aerial shots of the coastal landscape, and in the familiar character-types of a coal mining town. A more negative critical reading of the film argues that *Margaret's Museum*'s (covert) preoccupation with the real Westray Mine explosion of 1992 causes it to conflate the history of twentieth century capital and labor. For historian David Frank, Glace Bay here "stand[s] outside history. . . ."

Frank, David. "The Social Landscape of *Margaret's Museum*." *Canadian Dimension* 32(4) (July/August 1998): 41–43.

Gittings, Christopher E. "*Margaret's Museum*." In *Canadian National Cinema: Ideology, Difference and Representation*, 135–41. London: Routledge, 2002.

Golfman, Noreen. "Mining *Margaret's Museum*." *Canadian Forum* 74(848) (April 1, 1996): 28–31.

Hannant, Larry. "Film Reviews." *Canadian Historical Review* 78(4) (December 1997): 695–708.

Henderson, Scott. "Mort Ransen: *Margaret's Museum*." In *Where Are the Voices Coming from? Canadian Culture and the Legacies of History*, edited by Coral Ann Howells, 179–90. Amsterdam: Rodopi, 2004.

Muise, D.A. "Who Owns History Anyway? Reinventing Atlantic Canada for Pleasure and Profit." *Acadiensis* 27(2) (1998): 124–34.

Parpart, Lee. "Pit(iful) Male Bodies: Colonial Masculinity, Class and Folk Innocence in *Margaret's Museum*." *Canadian Journal of Film Studies* 8(1) (Spring 1999): 63–86.

Marianne and Juliane / Die bleierne Zeit (1981) Margarethe von Trotta; West Germany; German with English subtitles; Color; 106 m; New Yorker Films (VHS); West Germany, 1970s.

This fictionalized film draws from the real-life stories of two German sisters, Christiane Ensslin, a left-wing feminist journalist, and Gudrun Ensslin, a terrorist with the Baader-Meinhof group. The setting is West Germany in the 1970s. The character of Marianne is captured in 1972 after spending three years on the run for participation with other Baader-Meinhof members in the bombing of a department store. Juliane becomes obsessed with finding out the truth of her sister's 1977 death in prison (officially recorded as a suicide). Flashbacks describe the sisters' postwar childhood in the household of a stern Christian father.

Marianne and Juliane studies a strained, competitive, and loving sibling relationship. Juliane's need to keep her distance from Marianne is impossible to fulfill. Marianne's radicalism is dangerous, but her needs—for a home for her son Felix, for brief harbor from the authorities, for a visitor in prison—draw Juliane. She defends her own reform feminism, but her sister's death creates a heightened sense of the lies and corruption of the political system. Juliane's investigation also alienates her from her boyfriend, who sees the "lifetime" ahead of them as lost: "You're ruining ten years of our lives," he pleads.

This history of Marianne and Juliane's private lifetime, as it were, is linked in many ways with the social and political history of both postwar and Nazi Germany. Nazi terror, suggests director von Trotta, was unabated because of well-meaning Germans akin to the character of the boyfriend, whose resignation is an obstacle to justice. The dilemmas of Germans on the Left in the late 1960s are symbolized in the apparent futility of Marianne's actions, and the equally impotent quality of Juliane's journalistic activism. As an editor responds to Juliane's submission of a story about her sister: "You know the rules of journalism. If it is not current, it is useless—it can only be used in book form as a historical subject."

Byg, Barton. "German History and Cinematic Convention Harmonized in Margarethe Von Trotta's *Marianne und Juliane*." In *Gender and German Cinema: Feminist Interventions, Vol. II: German Film History/German History on Film*, edited by Sandra Frieden, Richard W. McCormick, Vibeke R. Petersen, and Laurie Melissa Vogelsang, 259–89. Providence, RI: Berg, 1993.

DiCaprio, Lisa. "*Marianne and Juliane/The German Sisters*: Baader-Meinhof Fictionalized." *Jump Cut: A Review of Contemporary Media* 29 (1984): 56–59.

Linville, Susan E. "Retrieving History: Margarethe Von Trotta's *Marianne and Juliane*." *PMLA* 106(3) (May 1991): 446–58.

Meyer, Eliane. "The Fictionalisation of Terrorism in West German Cinema." In *100 Years of European Cinema: Entertainment or Ideology?* edited by Diana Holmes and Alison Smith, 120–33. Manchester: Manchester University Press, 2000.

Seiter, Ellen. "The Political Is Personal: Margarethe Von Trotta's *Marianne und Juliane*." In *Films for Women*, edited by Charlotte Brunsdon, 109–16. London: BFI, 1986.

Sklar, Robert, and Adrienne Harris. "Review of *Marianne and Juliane*." *Cineaste* 12(3) (1983): 41–44.

La Marseillaise (1938) Jean Renoir; France; French with English subtitles; Black and White; 130 m; Nostalgia Family Video (VHS); France, 1789–1792.

La Marseillaise is a spirited film, following three volunteer "patriots" from Marseilles—a toll clerk, a mason, and a peasant—as they leave behind their provincial interests and merge with the greater cause of the French Revolution. The film begins in July 1789, with a noble bringing news of the "storming" of the Paris Bastille to French King Louis XVI. Louis, enjoying a post-hunt feast, asks, "Is it a revolt?" "No, sire, it is a revolution," answers the messenger. Between that scene and the film's concluding image—French troops sing *La Marseillaise* as they march off to battle in the aftermath of the August 1792 attack on the Tuileries Palace—the film lives up to its promise that its subject is nothing as irrational as revolt.

Director Jean Renoir argues the motivating force for those peasants, artisans, and other ordinary "citizens" who participate in the revolution is its philosophical basis—liberté, fraternité, egalité—and its promise to be made manifest in social equality and national unity. This cinematic master narrative of the formation of modern French national identity conveniently ends before ideological divisions within the revolutionary movement create messy conflicts like the September Massacres, debate over the fate of the king, or the "Terror."

As an example of the French Revolution interpreted as an act of populism and nationalism, *La Marseillaise* is highly recommended. But it is difficult to read the film exclusively as an interpretation of the eighteenth century's liberal challenge to the *ancien régime*. Produced and released in the interwar era, the film was a rallying device for contemporary French citizens, whose Third Republic was challenged by domestic ideological divisions as well as the threat of war with National Socialist Germany.

See also: *Danton*; *Napoléon*; *The Night at Varennes*; *Ridicule*

Bann, Stephen. "The Odd Man Out: Historical Narrative and the Cinematic Image." In *The Inventions of History: Essays on the Representation of the Past*, 171–99. Manchester: Manchester University Press, 1999.

Burley, Peter. "A Farrago of Nonsense?: The French Revolution in the Cinema." *History Today* 39(5) (May 1989): 51–56.

Grindon, Leger. "History and the Historians in *La Marseillaise*." *Film History* 4(3) (1990): 227–35.

———. "Hollywood History and the French Revolution: From *The Bastille* to *The Black Book*." *Velvet Light Trap: A Critical Journal of Film & Television* 28 (Fall 1991): 32–49.

Hanley, Sarah. "European History in Text and Film: Community and Identity in France, 1550–1945." *French Historical Studies* 25 (Winter 2002): 3–10.

Harison, Casey. "The French Revolution on Film: American and French Perspectives." *The History Teacher* 38(3) (May 2005): 299–324.

Max Havelaar (1976) Fons Rademakers; Indonesia/Netherlands; Dutch and Malay with English subtitles; Color; 170 m; no current; Indonesia, 19th century.

Based on the 1859 autobiographical novel of Multatuli, this is the story of a Dutch administrator in colonial Java whose sympathies with local villagers lead him to challenge the practices of the Dutch East Indies government.

See also: *November 1828*; *Tjoet Nja' Dhien*

Covino, M. "*Max Havelaar*." *Film Quarterly* 33(2) (1979): 46–48.

Sen, Krishna. "Filming 'History' under the New Order." In *Histories and Stories: Cinema in New Order Indonesia*, 49–59. Australia: Centre of Southeast Asian Studies, Monash University, 1988.

Sen, Krishna. "Narrating the Nation for a Military State." In *Indonesian Cinema: Framing the New Order*, 79–104. London: Zed Books, 1994.

Stam, R. "*Max Havelaar*." *Cineaste* 9(3) (1979): 47–8.

May & August / Wuyue Bayue (2002) Raymond To Kwok-Wai; Hong Kong; Mandarin with English subtitles; Color; 87 m; Tai Seng (VHS); China, 1937.

May & August is stylistically and narratively a very conventional film. An account of one fictional family victimized by the Japanese during the imperial army's murderous takeover of Nanjing in December 1937, the film hinges on the sympathetic characters of two little sisters who suffer the death of their parents (their mother is raped, representing the thousands of victims who historically suffered that crime) and then must fend for themselves while evading the Japanese. Finding shelter at the Red Cross safety zone, and then with an uncle and family, the girls eventually lead a contingent of orphans back to the edge of the city where they offer a mass vocal goodbye to their mothers. *May & August*'s approach to history is to represent the fear, terror, and abandonment suffered by the Chinese in Nanjing by asking for audiences to be engaged with the fate of a few innocent characters. The Japanese soldiers are faceless, omnipresent, and undifferentiated. Any context for the invasion, the relative lack of Chinese resistance, or the excesses of the Japanese actions, is largely ignored.

Berry, Michael. "Cinematic Representations of the Rape of Nanking." In *Japanese War Crimes: The Search for Justice*, edited by Peter Li, 203–25. New Brunswick, NJ: Transaction Books, 2003.

Mephisto (1981) István Szabó; West Germany/Hungary/Austria; German with English subtitles; Color; 144 m; Facets (DVD); Hamburg and Berlin, 1930s.

Mephisto is about a fictional German stage actor, Hendrik Höfgen, whose egotism and opportunism lead him to ingratiate himself with the Nazis despite his attacks of conscience. The performance of Klaus Maria Brandauer as Höfgen is especially successful in evincing this very human and very compromising character, who only realizes the monstrous proportions of his guilt in supporting the regime by the end of the film. *Mephisto* is adapted from the novel by Klaus Mann, whose Höfgen was based on real-life German actor Gustav Gründgens.

See also: *The Damned*

Christensen, Peter Glenn. "Collaboration in István Szábo's *Mephisto*." *Film Criticism* 12(3) (Spring 1988): 20–32.

Hughes, John W. "*Mephisto*: István Szabó and 'the Gestapo of Suspicion.'" *Film Quarterly* 35(4) (Summer 1982): 13–18.

Reimer, Robert C., and Carol J. Reimer. "*Mephisto*." In *Nazi-Retro Film: How German Narrative Cinema Remembers the Past*, 31–35. New York: Twayne, 1992.

Warchol, Tomasz. "Patterns of Central European Experience in István Szabó's Trilogy and *Sunshine*." *Social Identities* 7(4) (2001): 659–75.

The Message: The Story of Islam / Mohammed: Messenger of God / Al-Risala (1977) Moustapha Akkad; Syria; Arabic version (198 m) and English version (178 m); Color; Arab Film Distribution (DVD); Mecca and Medina, 7th century.

This film about the birth of Islam is essentially the story of Mohammed, its historical prophet, and the development of his following. While the film depicts major events in his life, Mohammed is never depicted in character, image, or word—consistent with the tenets of Islam. The film dramatizes Mohammed's vision of the angel Gabriel, his criticism of the idolatry in Mecca, the rallying of his followers, his and their exile to Medina, and their eventual return to Mecca for battle. Intended to educate, and appeal to Muslim, non-Muslim, and secular audiences alike, *The Message* is produced in the vein of a big-budget epic. Its dialogue and sequencing are effective, but unimaginative, and, like some other religious biopics, it does not question Mohammed's ideas and actions as anything but revelations from God.

See also: *Luther: Genius, Rebel, Liberator*; *Kundun*

Bakker, Freek L. "The Image of Muhammad in *The Message*, the First and Only Feature Film About the Prophet of Islam." *Islam and Christian-Muslim Relations* 17(1) (January 2006): 77–92.

Fraser, C. Gerald. "*Mohammad* Director Says Film Is Meant to Inform Non-Moslems." *The New York Times* 126 (March 11, 1977): A13.

Shohat, Ella. "Sacred Word, Profane Image: Theologies of Adaptation." In *A Companion to Literature and Film*, edited by Robert Stam and Alessandra Raengo, 23–45. Malden, MA: Blackwell, 2004.

Mishima: A Life in Four Chapters (1985) Paul Schraeder; United States; English and Japanese with English subtitles; Color, Black and White; 121 m; Warner Home Video (DVD, VHS); Japan, 1920s–1970.

This structurally unconventional biopic approaches the life and work of Japanese writer Mishima Yukio (1925–1970) by enacting scenes of his life, and creating theatrically-styled enactments of his work. In doing so, multiple versions of the man are constructed. *Mishima* is very effective in capturing the tensions between militarism and pacifism, tradition and westernization, in postwar Japan.

See also: *José Rizal*

Jaehne, Karen. "Schrader's *Mishima*: An Interview." *Film Quarterly* 39(3) (Spring 1986): 11–17.

Wilson, J.H. "Sources for a Neglected Masterpiece: Paul Schrader's *Mishima*." *Biography: An Interdisciplinary Quarterly* 20(3) (1997): 265–83.

The Mission (1986) Roland Joffé; United Kingdom; English; Color; 126 m; Warner Home Video (DVD, VHS); South America, 1750–1754.

The geographical setting of *The Mission* is the Spanish and Portuguese colonial possessions in the region of present-day Uruguay, northern Argentina, and southern Brazil. The Jesuit mission of San Carlos, which is central to the film, was one of a group historically known as the "Territory of the Seven Missions," located on the east side of the Uruguay River, falling within Spanish colonial territory. Here the Jesuits lived with the Guarani, who traditionally lived in widely scattered groups in Paraguay and Argentina.

Like Joffé's *The Killing Fields*, *The Mission* creates a compelling drama about the friendship of two men in the midst of political conflict. Father Gabriel is an English priest, founder of the Jesuit mission "above the falls" in Spanish territory. Mendoza is a Spanish "mercenary"/slave trader, who after killing his brother repents and devotes his new life to training for the Jesuit order under the tutelage of Father Gabriel. But the devotion of these men to the protection and conversion of the Guarani is challenged when in 1750 the Treaty of Madrid—negotiated by the Portuguese and Spanish—decides the Portuguese will assume control of the territory in which the missions reside.

As the film shows, the fate of the Jesuit mission and the Guarani was hotly debated, and a representative of the Pope assigned to make an assessment. When "His Eminence" receives word that the Portuguese will expel all Jesuits from Portugal if they do not evacuate the mission, he accepts that church policy—and European politics—demands compliance. In 1754 the Jesuits and Guarani refused to leave San Carlos, and openly rebelled against the Portuguese troops sent to expel them. The film shows in effect (an almost) total massacre of the mission inhabitants, including Father Gabriel.

The Mission's pretext is an examination of the historical conflict of church, state, colonists, and indigenous peoples in eighteenth-century colonial Latin America. But the film's interests lie in contemporary—not historic—issues of justice, resistance, pacifism, faith, and brotherhood. Father Gabriel resists the idea, presented by Mendoza and some of the other priests, that armed resistance to the mission's dissolution is the best option. "If might is right," he says, "then love has no place in the world." The cinematic exploitation of a historical event for the benefit of exploring universal themes such as that could be described as innocent. In the case of *The Mission*, though, this presentism conditions a rewriting of the past that is at best ahistorical and at worst dangerously misleading. In the film, some of the Jesuits decide to arm, train, and participate with the Guarani in the mission's defense. In truth, the Jesuits relinquished their mission, and it was the Guarani alone who mounted their defense.

As Saeger says, "Movie Indians need Jesuit help." In order to support the film's concern with its Western martyr's dilemmas, the Guarani of *The Mission* are infantilized, made voiceless, assigned as primitive, and in desperate need of paternalism to help them against their colonial masters.

See also: *Black Robe*; *Cabeza de Vaca*; *Jericho*

Berrigan, Daniel S.J. *The Mission: A Film Journal*. San Francisco: Harper and Row, 1986.

Ganson, Barbara. "'Like Children under Wise Parental Sway': Passive Portrayals of the Guaraní Indians in European Literature and *The Mission*." *Colonial Latin American Historical Review* 3(4) (1994): 399–422.

Marcos, Fernando Sánchez. "A Historical Reading of Roland Joffé's *The Mission*." *Film-Historia* 3(3) (1993): 411–16.

Mota Santos, Paula. "Good Indians and Bad Indians: The European Perspective of Native Americans as Depicted in *The Mission* and *Black Robe*." In *Native American Women in Literature and Culture*, edited by Susan Castillo and Victor M.P. Da Rosa, 185–90. Porto, Portugal: Fernando Pessoa University Press, 1997.

Schofield Saeger, James. "*The Mission* and Historical Missions: Film and the Writing of History." In *Based on a True Story: Latin American History at the Movies*, edited by Donald F. Stevens, 63–84. Wilmington, DE: Scholarly Resources, 1997.

Stone, Cynthia Leigh. "The Filming of Colonial Spanish America." *Colonial Latin American Historical Review* 5(2) (1996): 315–20.

Moonlighting (1982) Jerzy Skolimowski; United Kingdom/West Germany; English and Polish; Color; 97 m; Universal Home Video (VHS); London, 1981.

Storytelling's memorable contribution to learning about the past is beautifully exemplified in this deceptively simple tale of four Polish men renovating a London apartment in 1981. Nowak and three other men arrive in England under the pretense of a buying spree. A customs officer warns that they cannot work for pay, and that they are limited to a month's stay. The only English speaker of the group, Nowak tells the officer that he is not a member of Solidarity; his voiceover tells viewers, "That was the only true answer I gave." In fact, the workers are in the employ of their Polish factory boss, who will pay them in Polish *zlotys*, for their remodeling of his foreign-owned flat. Skolimowski places his Polish characters in physical, linguistic, and cultural isolation in the middle of Thatcherite London. A grey, grim, and humorless place, the disparity between the rich and the poor and the banality of the consumer society is no less noticeable for the greater desperation of its East bloc visitors.

The film follows the (sometimes humorous) labors of these men, their survival on a thin budget, and most importantly, their increasing physical isolation when Nowak learns about the military coup back home and the imposition of martial law. With all phone communication and airline travel to Poland suspended, and no more money from home, he decides to hide this knowledge from his comrades. Nowak's excursions to steal newspapers and watch television images in store windows provide him with information about political developments in Poland. He sees grainy news footage of tanks, and reads in *The Times* of workers shot at Katowice. His deception becomes more and more difficult to conceal, and Nowak becomes increasingly erratic and desperate in his behavior, stealing a neighbor's bicycle and food from the local grocery, burning letters from Poland, and eventually locking the workers in the flat.

Moonlighting has the peculiar ability to make the experience of workers of a twentieth-century communist state tangible without portraying their life there. Variously read as an allegory of Soviet authoritarianism (with Nowak as the oppressor), a condemnation of Western values, or a powerful character study, *Moonlighting* is an absorbing microcosmic look at four Polish men separated from loved ones and vulnerable to political events outside of their control.

See also: *Man of Iron; Man of Marble*

Combs, R. "Lost in Translation: *Moonlighting.*" *Sight & Sound* 51(4) (1982): 298–99.
Shivas, Mark. "'Au Clair de la lune' (Interview with Jerzy Skolimowski about *Moonlighting*)." *Monthly Film Bulletin* (September 1982): 188–89.
Yakir, Dan. "Polestar." *Film Comment* (November/December 18, 1982): 28–32.

The Music Room / Jalsaghar (1958) Satyajit Ray; India; Bengali with English subtitles; Black and White; 100 m; Sony Pictures Home Entertainment (VHS); Bengal, 1920s.

The main character of *The Music Room*, feudal lord Biswambhar Roy, is arrogant, obstinate, and demanding. He is also one of the most surprisingly sympathetic characters in the cinema, thanks to actor Chabi Biswas, who creates a moving portrait of a man who faces the eclipse of his wealth, status, and influence during the decline of traditional Bengali society.

Much of the story of *The Music Room* is told in extended flashback. The first scene introduces us to an aged Biswambhar, on the high terrace of his magnificent but increasingly decrepit house, alone but for the attentions of his servant Ananta, and refusing an invitation from the new *zaminder*, Mahim Ganguly. Upon hearing music of the *shehnai* (a pipe instrument) from neighboring Mahim estate, he is reminded of the same music accompanying his son's sacred thread ceremony years earlier, and the retrospective begins. *The Music Room* relates the consequences of Biswambhar's love of traditional music. His wife more ominously describes this love as his "obsession." Biswambhar refuses to acknowledge or address the mounting pressures on his finances in the face of flooding, his practice of charging minimal interest to the locals, and his status rivalry with the upstart Mahim, whose own wealth is derived from money-lending.

The Music Room is a beautiful film for a variety of reasons, including its performances, its cinematography, and its music. The film is also a sensitive evocation of Biswambhar's inhabitation of a kind of world outside of time, a world that he cannot defend against his own and his family's mortality, or the end of the feudal era in Indian history.

See also: *The Home and the World*

Cooper, Darius. "*Jalsaghar*: A Critical Evaluation Rendered through Rasa." In *The Cinema of Satyajit Ray: Between Tradition and Modernity*, 64–74. Cambridge: Cambridge University Press, 2000.

Dirks, Nicolas B. "The Sovereignty of History: Culture and Modernity in the Cinema of Satyajit Ray." In *Questions of Modernity*, edited by Timothy Mitchell, 148–65. Minneapolis, MN: University of Minnesota Press, 2000.

My Love Has Been Burning / Waga koi wa moenu (1949) Kenji Mizoguchi; Japan; Japanese with English subtitles; Black and White; 96 m; New Yorker Films (theatrical); Japan, 1880s.

Eiko Kageyama was a Japanese educator and feminist, who in 1883 founded a school for girls and in 1887 was tried for her participation in the "Osaka Incident," an attempt to support political independence for Korea. Her memoirs are the basis for the story of fictional character Eiko Hirayama, the subject of *My Love Has Been Burning*. Moving to Tokyo from her native Okayama, Hirayama eventually marries, then divorces, the leader of the fledgling Liberal Party. Her frustrations with the paternalism and gender inequalities in her society—and in the Left— are made personal when Hirayama discovers her husband's sexual exploitation of their servant.

See also: *Raden Ajeng Kartini; Rosa Luxemburg*

Le Fanu, Mark. "Respectable Women." In *Mizoguchi and Japan*, 129–46. London: BFI, 2005.

Freiberg, Freda. "Tales of Kageyama." *East-West Film Journal* 6(1) (January 1992): 94–110.

Leach, James. "Mizoguchi and Ideology: Two Films from the Forties." *Film Criticism* 8(1) (1983): 66–78.

Wood, Robin. "Three Films of Mizoguchi: Questions of Style and Identification." In *Sexual Politics and Narrative Film: Hollywood and Beyond*, 227–47. New York: Columbia University Press, 1998.

Napoléon / Abel Gance's Napoléon / Napoléon vu par Abel Gance (1927) Abel Gance; Sweden/Italy/France/Czechoslovakia/Germany; Silent with English intertitles; Black and White; 235 min; Universal Studios Home Entertainment (VHS); France, 18th century.

With the 1981 restoration of this 1927 silent cinema classic, modern audiences have the privilege of watching this technically pioneering film. In almost four hours running time, it stages events from Napoleon's youth in Corsica through to his command of the invasion of Italy in 1796. The scale and ambition of *Napoléon* rivals the reputation of the French Emperor himself; the film employs mobile camera work, very fast cutting, varying color tones, and nothing less than a 20-minute panoramic final scene projected on three screens.

See also: *Danton; Time Bandits; The Emperor's New Clothes; La Marseillaise*

Burley, Peter. "A Farrago of Nonsense?: The French Revolution in the Cinema." *History Today* 39(5) (May 1989): 51–56.

Harison, Casey. "The French Revolution on Film: American and French Perspectives." *The History Teacher* 38(3) (May 2005): 299–324.

Kaplan, Nelly. *Napoléon*. London: BFI, 1994.

King, Norman. "History and Actuality: Abel Gance's *Napoléon Vu Par Abel Gance* (1927)." In *French Film: Texts and Contexts*, edited by Susan Hayward and Ginette Vincendeau, 25–35. London: Routledge, 1990.

Pencak, William. "Neopoleonic Semiosis: *Napoléon Vu Par Abel Gance*." In *History, Signing In: Essays in History and Semiotics*, edited by William Pencak. New York: Peter Lang, 1993.

Stewart, Garrett. "Leaving History: Dickens, Gance, Blanchot." *Yale Journal of Criticism* 2(2) (Spring 1989): 145–90.

Nasser 56 / Nasser Sitawkhamseen (1996) Mohamed Fadel; Egypt; Arabic with English subtitles; Black and White; 142 m; Arab Film Distribution (VHS); Egypt, 1956.

This epic-scale reconstruction of the Suez Crisis of 1956 begins with President Gamal Abdel Nasser's speech declaring Egypt's nationalization of the French and British-controlled Suez Canal. "Today, Egypt's freedom is complete," announces Nasser to an enthusiastic crowd. Ships crowded with soldiers chanting, "Gamal! Gamal!" stand by. Nasser adds, "Yet we all know the struggle is not over."

While the foreshadowing is blunt, *Nasser 56* is for the most part a nuanced and interesting reconstruction of the events of 1956 from the perspective of the actions of Nasser. To a significant extent this is a character study of the charismatic Nasser, told from an Egyptian nationalist point of view. The portrait that emerges, through scenes of his political activities as well as his private family life, is that of a visionary Nasser, bold in the cause of Egyptian sovereignty and nationalism, but also careful, calculating, rational and consultative. He tells advisors that in decisions over the Suez, "We'll depend on good thinking and justice." Nasser is also modest in his personal needs, refusing his children their request for a swimming pool.

The film didactically explains to viewers unfamiliar with Egyptian history or international relations of the 1950s some of the issues of the era. One scene in particular establishes the Egyptian perspective on its historical relations with foreign powers. Nasser, alone with his dilemmas over the possibility of war arising from Egypt's claims on the Canal, uses his office as a late-night screening room, playing a newsreel history. A voiceover accompanying the footage explains the origins of the "unjust" treaty in 1854 between Said Pasha and Ferdinand de Lesseps that created the Suez Canal Company and offered to Egypt the "burden" of the death of 120,000 men during their labor in its construction.

As much as it is an interpretation of the origins and impact of the Suez crisis, *Nasser 56* is also compelling drama. Suspenseful conditions of timing, strategy, diplomacy, and secrecy are enacted as we follow Nasser's approach to nationalization. At a covert meeting in Yugoslavia, he seeks support from Indian Prime Minister Nehru, who cautions him that there will be meager international support for his actions.

The military engagement of Egyptian, Israeli, British, and French forces brings further domestic conflict, as the potential of Nasser's strategy to fail draws out the aspirations of some military officers and traditional Pashas to see Nasser off the political stage. The film draws to an end with Nasser's decision that the best political and military strategy is retreat of the Egyptian army to the west side of the Canal, without surrender of its control. He conveys this decision at a speech at a mosque, where once again—to the acclaim of ordinary Egyptians—the president's public words establish the historical record and thereby the interpretation viewers are served.

See also: *Saladin*

Gordon, Joel. "Film, Fame and Public Memory: Egyptian Biopics from Mustafa Kamil to *Nasser 56*." *International Journal of Middle East Studies* 31(1) (1999): 61–79.

———. "*Nasser 56*/Cairo 96: Reimaging Egypt's Lost Community." In *Mass Mediations: New Approaches to Popular Culture in the Middle East and Beyond*, edited by Walter Armbrust, 161–81. Berkeley, CA: University of California Press, 2000.

The Nasty Girl / Das schreckliche Mädchen (1990) Michael Verhoeven; West Germany; German with English subtitles; Color; 92 m; HBO Home Video (VHS); Germany, 1970s and 1980s.

The Nasty Girl uses a broadly satirical style to tell the story of a young girl who lives in the fictional Bavarian town of Pfilzing. Competition in national essay contests leads Sonja to investigate the townspeople's behavior during the Third Reich. The film is based on events in the life of Anja Elisabeth Rosmus, born in 1960 in Passau, Germany. Director Verhoeven also made a 45 minute documentary on Rosmus for German television.

Several prominent distancing effects are used by Verhoeven in the film, including switches in the film stock's color, Sonja's direct addresses to the film audience, and frequently stylized sets. As Robert and Carol Reimer suggest, "The stylized scenes dealing with historical truth are so different from the other naturalistic narrative scenes that they are, in a sense, indexed and put aside as part of a specific theme. Parentheses are put around them in this way, and they are lifted out of the narrative for special consideration and reflection."

Grundmann, Roy. "*The Nasty Girl*." *Cineaste* 18(2) (1991): 49–51.

Kang, Min Soo. "Review of *Das Schreckliche Maedchen*." *American Historical Review* 96(4) (1991): 1132–34.

Reimer, Robert C., and Carol J. Reimer. "*The Nasty Girl*." In *Nazi-Retro Film: How German Narrative Cinema Remembers the Past*, 51–53. New York: Twayne, 1992.

The Navigator: A Medieval Odyssey (1988) Vincent Ward; Australia/New Zealand; English; Color; 90 m; Facets (DVD); England, 1348, and a contemporary unspecified Western city.

The Navigator's plot revolves around a small group of fourteenth-century Cumbrians who are on a quest to save their village from the Black Death. The film literally brings its characters—and history—into the present when the villagers find themselves in a modern city. (Viewers might recognize Auckland, New Zealand.) A vision of the young boy, Griffin, has led them to attempt the erection of a great cross on a modern steeple, thereby assuaging the ravages of the plague. Upon their return to the village they realize their travels were "just a dream," but Griffin insists that if they believe his story, it will be efficacious—they will be safe from the plague.

This is a highly entertaining film that is atmospheric and suspenseful. For a historian interested in the way that popular movies interrogate the past, there are at least two aspects of *The Navigator* worth noting. First, at least until the protagonist Griffin and crew arrive in modern times, a striking—and bleak—portrayal of their medieval lives suggests the film is firmly ensconced in the "historical film" vein and is "about" the middle ages. But the story's escape across time allows the film to indulge the issue with which it is much preoccupied: faith, and personal agency, in a time of crisis. In other words this is a presentist rather than historical film. Arthur Lindley's claim applies well to *The Navigator*: ". . . it seems to me that the medieval past, in film at least, is *always* pretext. It may be pretext for revisiting ourselves as children or in simplified and stylized forms, but the subject is always ourselves."

Second, *The Navigator* invites discussion of somewhat uncomfortable questions about the conceptual underpinnings of history and historiography. The villagers in 1348 equate dreams with reality, belief with safety, and stories with truth. As we watch them violate our modern norms of what is possible in the physical world—they make an act made in the future resound on the past—we are challenged to consider the extent to which our modern interpretation of the past is governed by invented time–space "realities."

See also: *Time Bandits*; *The Seventh Seal*

Biddick, Kathleen. "Review of *The Navigator: A Medieval Odyssey*." *American Historical Review* 97(4) (October 1992): 1152–53.

Driver, Martha W. "Writing About Medieval Movies: Authenticity and History." *Film & History: An Interdisciplinary Journal of Film and Television Studies* 29(1–2) (1999): 5–7.

Lindley, Arthur. "The Ahistoricism of Medieval Film." *Screening the Past* 3 (May 29, 1998), http://www.latrobe.edu.au/screeningthepast/firstrelease/fir598/ALfr3a.htm (accessed May 30, 2006).

Perry, Nicholas. "Antipodean Camp." In *Hyperreality and Global Culture*, 4–23. London: Routledge, 1998.

Williams, David John. "Looking at the Middle Ages in the Cinema: An Overview." *Film & History: An Interdisciplinary Journal of Film and Television Studies* 29(1–2) (1999): 8–19.

Newsfront (1978) Phillip Noyce; Australia; English; Color, Black and White; 110 m; Facets (DVD); Australia, 1940s and 1950s.

Newsfront is a reminiscence of the post–World War II era in Australia, told through the story of a fictional Cinetone newsreel cameraman named Len McGuire—a character reputedly based on filmmaker Ken G. Hall. With its innovative intercutting of historical newsreel footage from the era with dramatizations of Cinetone editors, narrators, and producers creating the newsreels, the film presents an engaging blend of fictionalized and archival evidence that underscores the historical relevance of this feature film. The microcosm of McGuire's personal and professional drama unfolds in a broader social, political, and technological context that is never far away, thanks to the interaction of these two mediums.

Some might dismiss *Newsfront* as light nostalgia, as it does seem to separate the 1940s and 1950s from the present as a "bygone" era. Black-and-white footage of swimming competitions, a rabbit catch, the conquest of Everest, and the Redex Round Australia car race provide the sense of an optimistic, but distant, past. The film pays homage to the contributions of newsreel companies like Cinetone and Newsco to journalism and public affairs in the postwar era: original newsreel footage of the defeat of Labor Prime Minister Ben Chifley in 1949, the anti-Communist referendum of 1951, and the catastrophic floods of 1954 is included.

Newsfront potentially yields a nuanced interpretation of Australian history and cinematic efforts to portray the past. In an early scene, director Philip Noyce alludes to the anguished process of selection, emphasis, and omission that historians, filmmakers, and others entrusted with the reconstruction of the past experience. A Cinetone editor warns his fellow editor to "go easy" in the cutting process. "That's world history you're kicking on the floor," he says. His confident colleague replies, "It's no loss. None of them are." One of the main historical themes of *Newsfront* is how individuals and societies confront the inexorable passage of time and the change that this often involves. Len McGuire is an effective focus for this study. At once assured and traditional—a Catholic, a family man, and a loyal employee at Cinetone—he nevertheless uneasily confronts the disintegration of his marriage, dissolving gender roles, his brother's desire for new opportunities in the United States, the advent of television news, and the anti-Communist position of the Menzies government.

As Annette Van den Bosch says, "The established values of the Australia depicted in the opening sequence are exposed as contradictions." Certainly McGuire feels these contradictions. Ultimately, *Newsfront* performs an important feat for nostalgia, making it a meaningful starting point, rather than a simplistic endpoint, for the viewer's understanding of postwar Australia and the exigencies of history.

See also: *Aya*; *'Breaker' Morant*; *Gallipoli*

Rayner, Jonathan. "*Newsfront*: The Nation on Record." In *Contemporary Australian Cinema: An Introduction*, 84–86. Manchester: Manchester University Press, 2000.

Van den Bosch, Annette. "Australian History and Its Reconstruction in Australian Film." In *The First Australian History and Film Conference Papers*, edited by Anne Hutton, 244–65. New South Wales, Australia: Australia Film and Television School, 1982.

The Night / al-Lail / al-Leil (1992) Mohamad Malas; Syria; Arabic with English subtitles; Color; 116 m; no current; Syria, 1930s and 1940s.

This is an autobiographical film where personal, family, and national history intersect. Director Malas creates an alter ego who is piecing together the history of his dead father, a Palestinian who joined the 1936 Arab Revolt and volunteered in the 1948 Arab–Israeli war. The setting of much of the story is the town of Quneitra, Syria (Golan Heights), in the 1930s and 1940s. Growing up in this period, the young boy/young Malas witnesses the effects on his family and society of French and British colonialism, Syrian independence, and the founding of Israel—including the arrival of Palestinian refugees to his town. Malas must reconcile himself to memories of his father's erratic behavior and frequent absences, as well as to his mother's interpretations of the family history.

See also: *The Dupes*; *Exodus*; *The House on Chelouche Street*

Blecher, Robert. "History as Social Critique in Syrian Film: Muhammad Malas' *al-Lail* and Ryad Chaia's *al-Lajat*." *Middle East Report* 204 (July–September 1997): 44–46.

Dehni, Salah. "Malas' *Al Leil*." *Cinemaya: The Asian Film Quarterly* 19 (Spring 1993): 67.

Holden, Stephen. "*The Night*: A Memoir of Growing up in Syria." *The New York Times* 143 (October 4, 1993): C15.

Night and Fog in Japan / Nihon no yoru to kiri (1960) Nagisa Oshima; Japan; Japanese with English subtitles; Color; 107 m; Facets (DVD); Japan, 1950s and 1960s.

The 1960 ratification of the renewal of the U.S.-Japanese Security Treaty looms over this study of Japanese student activism, and the failure of the Japanese Left to challenge the militarization of the country and U.S. influence. The marriage ceremony of Reiko and Nozawa, a couple who met during their participation in protests against the treaty, reunites former student activists. Reunion descends into confrontation, as the students revisit their activism and argue about its failure. Oshima uses very long takes and a minimalist *mise en scène*; these give *Night and Fog in Japan* a theatrical, staged quality that places emphasis on the film's dialogue.

Desser, David. "Night and Fog in Japan: Ideology and Narrativity." In *Eros Plus Massacre: An Introduction to the Japanese New Wave Cinema*, 13–38. Bloomington: Indiana University Press, 1988.

Polan, Dana. "Politics as Process in Three Films by Nagisa Oshima." *Film Criticism* 11(1/2) (1987): 66–74.

Turim, Maureen. "Cruel Stories of Youth and Politics." In *The Films of Oshima Nagisa: Images of a Japanese Iconoclast*, 27–60. Berkeley, CA: University of California Press, 1998.

The Night at Varennes / La nuit de Varennes (1982) Ettore Scola; France/Italy; French and Italian with English subtitles; Color; 133 m; Sony Pictures Home Entertainment (VHS); France, 1791.

It is 1791 in Paris and the writer, prolific lover, and lesser noble Rétif de la Bretonne is visiting a brothel when he hears rumors that Louis XVI and other members of the Bourbon royal family have fled the city. Soon, Rétif, Thomas Paine, a countess, two male servants, a student, an opera singer, and an assortment of other characters are traveling together in a public coach. Casanova also makes the scene, often traveling separately. Rétif is chasing his hunch that the countess—Marie Antoinette's lady-in-waiting—is in league with the royals' escape plot, and he suspects they are ahead of them in another coach. The pretext for this (invented) congregation of characters is set. This is not a plebeian bunch: coach-mates engage in intellectual discussion, with much of the dialogue loaded with cultural, especially literary, references. But there is also sufficient witty repartee, gossip, and flirtation to suggest the travelers' interest in the political issues of the day has its limits. There is an air of almost cheerful inevitability about the outcome of the revolution that infuses *The Night at Varennes*. The film is refreshingly unburdened—as are its characters—by the need for a suspenseful attitude to events. Rétif and his friends are at a watershed moment in history, and they are determined to enjoy the ride.

See also: *Danton; La Marseillaise; Napoléon*

Burley, Peter. "A Farrago of Nonsense?: The French Revolution in the Cinema." *History Today* 39(5) (May 1989): 51–56.

Harison, Casey. "The French Revolution on Film: American and French Perspectives." *The History Teacher* 38(3) (May 2005): 299–324.

Landes, Joan B. "Women and Revolution." In *Women and the Public Sphere in the Age of the French Revolution*, 93–151. Ithaca, NY: Cornell University Press, 1988.

Testa, Carlo. "Global Trends, Local Crises (1973–82)." In *Italian Cinema and Modern European Literatures: 1945–2000*, 79–114. Westport, CT: Praeger, 2002.

The Night of Counting the Years / The Mummy / El-mumia / Al-mummia
(1969) Shadi Abdel Salam; Egypt; Arabic with English subtitles; Color; 102 m; New Yorker Films (theatrical); Egypt, 1881.

When their father dies, two boys are initiated into the secret of the source of their family's wealth: raiding a local pharaonic tomb for profit. Based on true events, the moral dilemma posed by this information leads to conflicts between the family, Egyptian antiquities dealers, and French Egyptologists.

Shafik, Viola. *Arab Cinema: History and Cultural Identity*. Cairo: American University in Cairo Press, 1998.

Shohat, Ella. "Gender and Culture of Empire: Toward a Feminist Ethnography of the Cinema." In *Visions of the East: Orientalism in Film*, edited by Matthew Bernstein and Gaylyn Studlar, 19–66. New Brunswick, NJ: Rutgers University Press, 1997.

Taylor, John Russell. "Shadi Abdelsalam/*The Night of Counting the Years*." *Sight & Sound* 40 (1971): 17.

The Night of the Pencils / La noche de los lápices
(1986) Héctor Olivera; Argentina; Spanish with English subtitles; Color; 105 m; Latin American Video Archives (VHS); Argentina, 1976.

The period of Argentina's military dictatorship (1976–1983) produced what is known as the "Dirty War," when thousands of citizens suspected by the regime to have threatening ties to the Left were imprisoned, executed, or simply disappeared. The trauma of this period began to be explored on film in the late 1980s, as Argentinians slowly came to terms with their recent history.

Héctor Olivera's *The Night of the Pencils* succeeds to some extent in revisiting the period of the Dirty War by telling the documented story of six high school students who were its victims. The first half of the film relates the participation of these La Plata youth in protests demanding free bus passes. Brief scenes of their home life—with some emphasis on that of the main female protagonist, Claudia—show family members adopting different ideological positions and coping strategies in the face of the military regime. Generational differences are exposed, and these create some of the early narrative tension in the film. From such a seemingly innocuous cause as that of bus fees, comes the most unbearable consequences: a nighttime raid of their homes in September 1976 produces the students for their arrest and incarceration, without charge, in prison.

The second half of *The Night of the Pencils* concentrates on the harrowing prison experience of the students. Here the political context of events is subordinate to a study of human nature, or human survival, in captivity. This segment is extremely effective in conveying, without histrionics, the complex coping strategies, social relationships, and human weakness of prisoners in the presence of fear, isolation, deprivation, interrogation, and brutality. By the film's conclusion, we learn that one student is freed, and the remaining captives join the list of the disappeared.

See also: *Canoa; The Official Story; Red Dawn*

Greenbaum, Richard. "*Night of the Pencils*." *Films in Review* 38 (1987): 607–8.

Ranalletti, Mario. "La Construccion Del Relato De La Historia Argentina En El Cine, 1983-1989." *Film-Historia* 9(1) (1999): 3–15.

Schwartz, Ronald. "*La Noche De Los Lápices* (*The Night of the Pencils*)." In *Latin American Films, 1932–1994: A Critical Filmography*, 181–82. Jefferson, NC: McFarland, 1997.

Night of the Shooting Stars / La notte di San Lorenzo (1982) Paolo Taviani and Vittorio Taviani; Italy; Italian with English subtitles; Color; 105 m; Facets (DVD); Italy, 1944.

A church in the Tuscan village of San Miniato was the scene of a massacre on July 1944, when retreating members of the German army sought reprisal for the Italian partisan shooting of a German soldier. Villagers, entreated by the local bishop to seek refuge in the church from the expected German destruction of their homes, uneasily gathered there, only to be killed in a bomb attack. Brothers Paolo and Vittorio Taviani, natives of the village, first explored the event in their 1954 documentary *San Miniato, July 1944*. The Night of the Shooting Stars sees the filmmakers return to the story, this time in a fascinating, highly fictionalized film that considers the ambiguities of Italian resistance, wartime experience, and historical memory.

See also: *1900*

Kael, Pauline. "*The Night of the Shooting Stars*." The New Yorker (February 7, 1983):117–20.

Landy, M. "Neorealism, Politics, and Language in the Films of the Tavianis." *Annali-d'Italianistica* 6 (1988): 236–51.

Liehm, Mira. "Under the Sign of Violence." In *Passion and Defiance: Film in Italy from 1942 to the Present*, 307–18. Berkeley, CA: University of California Press, 1986.

Marcus, Millicent. "The Taviani Brothers' *Night of the Shooting Stars*: Ambivalent Tribute to Neorealism." In *Italian Film in the Light of Neorealism*, 360–90. Princeton, NJ: Princeton University Press, 1987.

Sorlin, Pierre. "*The Night of the Shooting Stars*: Fascism, Resistance, and the Liberation of Italy." In *Revisioning History: Film and the Construction of a New Past*, edited by Robert A. Rosenstone, 77–87. Princeton, NJ: Princeton University Press, 1995.

November 1828 (1979) Teguh Karya; Indonesia; Indonesian and Dutch with English subtitles; Color; 140 m; Between Three Worlds Video (VHS); Dutch colonial Java, 1828.

Set in the period of the Java War (1825–1830), *November 1828* is one of the first Indonesian films to achieve critical attention outside of the country. A valuable example of an Indonesian interpretation of its colonial history, the film combines enough historical explanation to satisfy Western audiences with little background knowledge of the era.

The scene is set with a lengthy intertitle that explains the failure of Dutch forces to capture Javanese leader Prince Diponegoro and to extend their control. Action commences with the arrival of a Dutch garrison in the village of Bageleh. Furious at the rebel's evasion, Dutch commander Captain de Bork vows to extract intelligence from those who are hiding him. Sentot Prawirodirjo, a lieutenant of Diponegoro, organizes an attack on the Dutch occupiers, using a visiting "dance troupe" as his cover for an advance of Javanese soldiers. Aided by villagers and Sentot's arriving reinforcements, the Javanese subject the Dutch fortress to a brutal assault, and are victorious, reclaiming their village.

The film embodies the best of popular Indonesian cinema: dramatic action, narrative intrigues, vivid characters, a requisite love story, and some lively humor are all present. As such it provides an entertaining framework for its historical subject and the nationalistic themes important to director Teguh Karya.

See also: *Max Havelaar; Tjoet Nja' Dhien*

Hanan, David. "Film and Cultural Difference: *November 1828.*" In *Histories and Stories: Cinema in New Order Indonesia*, edited by Krishna Sen, 25–47. Australia: Centre of Southeast Asian Studies, Monash University, 1988.

Sen, Krishna. "Filming 'History' under the New Order." In *Histories and Stories: Cinema in New Order Indonesia*, 49–59. Australia: Centre of Southeast Asian Studies, Monash University, 1988.

Sen, Krishna. "Narrating the Nation for a Military State." In *Indonesian Cinema: Framing the New Order*, 79–104. London: Zed Books, 1994.

October (Ten Days That Shook the World) / Oktyabr (1927) Grigori Aleksandrov and Sergei M. Eisenstein; Soviet Union; Silent with English intertitles; Black and White; 103 m; Facets (DVD), Kultur Films (VHS); Russia, 1917.

October, inspired by John Reed's *Ten Days That Shook the World*, is an ideological film that dramatizes events of the Russian Revolution, beginning with the February overthrow of the Romanov dynasty and ending with the Bolshevik seizure of power. The film differs from other cinematic accounts of the Russian revolution produced in the 1920s, in that Lenin and the Bolshevik party are central to the story, rather than the heroic, but common and anonymous, Russians. The film shows the Bolshevik leader's arrival at the Finland Station in April 1917, and his October directive that the Winter Palace be targeted. Thus Lenin's decisive role—and decisiveness—in the revolution is emphasized, and contrasted with that of more cautious comrades. Russian Provisional Government leader Kerensky is also juxtaposed with Lenin. Indecisive, uncharismatic, and passive, Kerensky represents the continuities with the Tsarist regime.

See also: *The Battleship Potemkin; The End of St. Petersburg; Rasputin*

Corney, Frederick C. *Telling October: Memory and the Making of the Bolshevik Revolution.* Ithaca, NY: Cornell University Press, 2004.

Lövgren, Håkan. "Eisenstein's *October*: On the Cinematic Allegorization of History." In *Eisenstein at 100: A Reconsideration*, edited by Al La Valley and Barry P. Scherr, 77–88. New Brunswick, NJ: Rutgers University Press, 2001.

The Official Story / La historia oficial (1985) Luis Puenzo; Argentina; Spanish with English subtitles; Color; 112 m; Facets (DVD); Argentina, 1983.

The Official Story's main character is Alicia Marnet de Ibañez, a history professor, mother of adopted daughter Gaby, and wife of Roberto, a businessman. She lives a comfortable middle class life in Buenos Aires, and appears somewhat discomfited at a dinner party when the talk turns to politics. She agrees she is "not very modern" about such matters, which in this period of the apogee of the military dictatorship (1976–1983) suggests she tries to remain unpolitical.

Alicia tells her students that "History is the memory of the peoples." The intersection of her own story with the "official" history of Argentina will only occur as the film progresses, and in effect only through her at first involuntary, and then increasingly deliberate research. An old school friend, Anna, returns after having left the country in 1976, with stories of a mutual friend, Clara, now in Caracas. Clara was tortured and raped by soldiers because of her connection to a politically suspect boyfriend. Alicia's shock and outrage registers the beginning of the end of her isolation and political apathy. Her historical education becomes much more personal as she begins to suspect that her daughter might have been stolen from a family of *los desaparecidos* ("those who disappeared")—the thousands of Argentinians who were victims of paramilitary death squads for their political unreliability. She comes to know the Mothers of the Plaza de Mayo, those who return to the site of the presidential palace day after day and silently reproach the dictatorship for its victimization of their families.

While the film does not resolve the details of Gaby's parentage, in an angry and violent scene between Alicia and Roberto, Roberto admits knowledge of the baby's origins from a "missing" mother. This revelation is the last in Alicia's increasing misgivings about Roberto; the financial benefits accrued from Roberto's relationship to the regime have already been troubling her, and she announces she is leaving the marriage.

Alicia's research reveals a painful history of Argentinians' experience in the years of the dictatorship. The counter-discourse to the "official story" is founded on the testimony—Alicia calls it "memory"—of the victims she learns about. But Alicia's own story is at first shaped by her sense of innocence; isolated from and generally ignorant of the experience of families of the disappeared, she does not feel responsible for the actions of the regime. But over the course of the film, she realizes her own history with Roberto and Gaby has made her complicit all along, a citizen upholding the "official" story.

See also: *Night of the Pencils*; *Waterland*

Schwartz, Ronald. "*La Historia Oficial (The Official Story)*." In *Latin American Films, 1932–1994: A Critical Filmography*, 114–15. Jefferson, NC: McFarland, 1997.

Szuchman, Mark D. "Depicting the Past in Argentine Films: Family Drama and Historical Debate in *Miss Mary* and *The Official Story*." In *Based on a True Story: Latin American History at the Movies*, edited by Donald F. Stevens, 173–200. Wilmington, DE: Scholarly Resources, 1997.

The Opium War / Yapian zhanzheng (1997) Xie Jin; Japan/China; Mandarin with English subtitles; Color; 150 m; Facets (DVD); China, 1839–1842.

Directed by one of China's most eminent and popular filmmakers, Xie Jin, and planned to premiere on the occasion of the British handover of Hong Kong to China in 1997, *The Opium War* is a lavish and action-packed recounting of the 1839–1942 war between Britain and China. The film follows a fairly predictable narrative of events, from the arrival in Guangzhou of the official envoy Lin Zexu with his imperial mandate to end the illegal foreign trade in opium, to Emperor Daoguang's eventual capitulation to the force of British arms. Along the way, the stock characters that will complete a reasonably representative picture of this history make an appearance: there are corrupt Chinese middlemen, poor Chinese addicts, indecisive Chinese officials, and exploitative British traders and politicians, including Captain Charles Elliott, the British Superintendent of Commerce in Guangzhou. The character of He Shanzhi acts as a sort of sidekick to Lin; the son of a Chinese opium seller, he turns tables on foreign exploitation by using his English language skills in the service of Chinese diplomacy.

For all its well-produced convention, however, the film's interpretation of this war that "opened" China to a series of "unequal treaties" with foreign powers is worth considering. *The Opium War*'s Chinese nationalist perspective on the period suggests some ambivalency about the weaknesses of Chinese authorities. Generally characterized as foolishly arrogant, ignorant, and isolated, officials like Qi Shan are poorly equipped to mitigate the impact of the more vigorous—even progressive—British economic, military, and diplomatic incursion.

See also: *Lin Zexu*

Karl, Rebecca E. "The Burdens of History: *Lin Zexu* (1959) and *The Opium War* (1997)." In *Whither China? Intellectual Politics in Contemporary China*, edited by Xudong Zhang, 229–62. Durham, NC: Duke University Press, 2001.

Li, Cheuk-to. "*Yapian Zhanzheng (The Opium War).*" *Cinemaya: The Asian Film Quarterly* (October/December 1997): 30–31.

Washitani, Hana. "*The Opium War* and the Cinema Wars: A Hollywood in the Greater East Asian Co-Prosperity Sphere." *Inter-Asia Cultural Studies* 4(1) (April 2003): 63–76.

Xiao, Zhiwei. "Nationalism in Chinese Popular Culture: A Case Study of *The Opium War*." In *Exploring Nationalisms of China: Themes and Conflicts*, edited by C.X. George Wei and Xiaoyuan Liu, 41–54. Westport, CT: Greenwood Press, 2002.

———. "The Opium War in the Movies: History, Politics and Propaganda." *Asian Cinema: a Publication of the Asian Cinema Studies Society* 11(1) (Spring/Summer 2000): 68–83.

Les Ordres (1974) Michel Brault; Canada; French with English subtitles; Color, Black and White; 109 m; Quebec, Canada, 1970.

There is a quiet scene in Michel Brault's *Les Ordres* that is resonant with tension, and it evokes the incalculable number of times an event of similar strains has played out in history. The police have arrived at Richard Lavoie's small Quebec apartment as he is diapering his baby son. "We've got company, kid," says Lavoie wryly, as he submits resignedly to being taken into custody. A roundup of suspected terrorists has been enabled by Canada's War Measures Act. But Lavoie has no one to watch his two young children, and the police impatiently agree to wait for his wife Ginette to rush home from her waitressing job to assume the care of their children so that her husband can go to jail. Lavoie waits in the back of a police car as his children watch innocently from a terrace. The police pace in the narrow street. Ginette's taxi arrives; she is barely out the door when the car carrying Lavoie roars off. Brault's story of a parent's need to secure the care of his children in the midst of a crisis is an extremely powerful invocation of historical experience. (The experience is replayed in a similar scene when a mother must get her eldest daughter to quickly enlist the neighbor to watch her girls before she is whisked off by the police.)

Les Ordres announces, "This film is based on the true stories of the victims of the War Measures Act." Professing to be based on interviews with fifty of the "450 citizens imprisoned" (all later released without charges) after the invocation of the War Measures Act, *Les Ordres* eschews the reenactment of events familiarly associated with what is known as Canada's "October Crisis," such as the kidnapping of Quebec cabinet minister Pierre Laporte and British diplomat James Cross by members of the *Front de libération du Québec*. Instead Brault introduces us to characters and their detainment experiences. All of them are bewildered and frightened because they are not informed of what charges are pending (some experience incarceration without charge from 6 to 16 days), and because some are subject to cruelty (Lavoie endures a mock execution).

Brault provocatively asks audiences to consider the experience of a few of the hundreds of ordinary Quebeckers subject to the suspension of civil rights in October 1970. And Brault's political message is resoundingly clear: when the violation of civil freedoms is met with silence there are dangerous consequences. A voiceover at the film's conclusion says: "What happened to us is nothing really. But we must realize it shows something's rotten somewhere. We musn't let the sickness spread." *Les Ordres* also suggests its stories have verisimilitude to the experiences recounted by interviewees; we can trust scenes because Brault is willing to expose the fictional construction of this film. Speaking directly to the camera, the actors who play the film's characters—a union activist, his wife, a social worker, a doctor, and an unemployed Lavoie—introduce themselves, as in "My name is Jean Lapointe and I play the role of Clermont Boudreau."

Clandfield, David. "Perils of the Unsaid in Michel Brault's Film *Les Ordres.*" *University of Toronto Quarterly* 63(4) (Summer 1994): http://128.100.205.43/access/jour.ihtml?lp=product/utq/634/634_clandfield.htm (accessed May 30, 2006).

Gittings, Christopher E. *"Les Ordres."* In *Canadian National Cinema: Ideology, Difference and Representation*, 182–85. London: Routledge, 2002.

The Organizer / I Compagni (1963) Mario Monicelli; Italy/France/Yugoslavia; Italian with English subtitles; Black and White; 126 m; Hen's Tooth Video (VHS); Turin, Italy, late 19th century.

Mario Monicelli is the prolific king of socially conscious Italian comedy films. *The Organizer* bears his interest in the stories of ordinary Italians and their often hapless encounters with injustice and authority. In this case, textile workers in 1890s Turin attempt to negotiate with employers over long hours and frequent and uncompensated injuries. But timid, lacking in confidence, and uneducated, their delegation is unsuccessful; even a planned work stoppage goes awry when they botch a plan to blow the whistle an hour early at day's end. Those who attend school after work can barely stay awake to hear their teacher's lofty claims about their future power as an educated proletariat.

The teacher is harboring the "Professor," a labor organizer whose skill at rousing the workers to action, while discouraging intemperance, leads to a positive vote to strike. "This fight began with Spartacus!" he cries. Seeking a 13-hour workday, the workers over the course of the 30-day strike are increasingly divided over tactics in the face of scab replacements at the factory, bare cupboards, and the tragic intervention of the army.

Some characters and scenes in *The Organizer* elicit genuine laughs; the film also constructs a serious analysis of the aspirations of the workers. The strike is a failure: workers return to work having been completely defeated in their quest for reduced hours. But one of the Professor's protégés flees to another city, no doubt to continue the workers' battle.

See also: *Daens*; *Germinal*

Landy, Marcia. "Gramsci and Italian Cinema." In *Italian Film*, 149–80. Cambridge: Cambridge University Press, 2000.

Young, D. "Poverty, Misery, War and Other Comic Material: An Interview with Mario Monicelli." *Cineaste* 29(4) (2004): 36–40.

Zaniello, Tom. *"The Organizer."* In *Working Stiffs, Union Maids, Reds, and Riffraff: An Organized Guide to Films About Labor*, 187–89. Ithaca, NY: ILR Press/Cornell University Press, 1996.

Orlando (1992) Sally Potter; United Kingdom; English; Color; 93 m; Facets (DVD); England, Central Asia, Central Europe, 16th–20th centuries.

Orlando is a Virginia Woolf novel, here adapted as a piece of mainstream art cinema by director Sally Potter. Told with stunning period details and an episodic structure, this is the story of the aristocratic courtier Orlando, who without much aging, and with a switch of genders mid-point, lives and travels across four centuries. One interesting reading of *Orlando* from the perspective of the study of historical films is to consider its subversion of the costume drama, especially released as it was after a decade of popular—and much less stylistically and thematically adventurous—films such as *A Room with a View*, *Maurice*, and *Howard's End*.

See also: *The Navigator: A Medieval Odyssey*; *Time Bandits*

Ferriss, Suzanne, and Kathleen Waites. "Unclothing Gender: The Postmodern Sensibility in Sally Potter's *Orlando*." *Literature/Film Quarterly* 27(2) (1999): 110–15.

Garrett, Roberta. "Costume Drama and Counter Memory: Sally Potter's *Orlando*." In *Postmodern Subjects/Postmodern Texts*, edited by Steven Earnshaw, 89–99. Amsterdam: Rodopi, 1995.

Gibson, Pamela Church. "Fewer Weddings and More Funerals: Changes in the Heritage Film." In *British Cinema of the 90s*, edited by Robert Murphy, 115–24. London: BFI, 2000.

Levine, Michael L. "*Orlando* on Screen: Three Hundred Years of Nothing Happening." *Virginia Woolf Miscellany* 42(3) (1994): 3–4.

Pidduck, Julianne. "Travels with Sally Potter's *Orlando*: Gender, Narrative, Movement." *Screen* 38 (1997): 172–89.

Pan Tadeusz / The Last Foray in Lithuania (1999) Andrzej Wajda; Poland/France; Polish with English subtitles; Color; 157 m; Facets (DVD; VHS); Lithuania, 1811–1812.

A popular, if not critical, success in Poland, *Pan Tadeusz* is an expansive tale of two petty noble Polish families in Russian-controlled Lithuania whose historic feud comes to a dénouement at the moment of Napoleon's invasion. The film is based on the 1834 epic poem of Adam Mickiewicz, the nineteenth-century Polish patriot in French exile.

Di Bartolomeo, Lisa. " 'Ojczyzno Moja': Adapting *Pan Tadeusz*." In *The Cinema of Andrzej Wajda: The Art of Irony and Defiance*, edited by John Orr and Elzbieta Ostrowska, 172–89. London: Wallflower Press, 2003.

Kalinowska, Izabela. "Changing Meanings of Home and Exile: From *Ashes and Diamonds* to *Pan Tadeusz*." In *The Cinema of Andrzej Wajda: The Art of Irony and Defiance*, edited by John Orr and Elzbieta Ostrowska, 64–75. London: Wallflower Press, 2003.

Mazierska, Ewa. "In the Land of Noble Knights and Mute Princesses: Polish Heritage Cinema." *Historical Journal of Film, Radio & Television* 21(2) (June 1, 2001): 167–82.

The Passion of Joan of Arc / La Passion de Jeanne d'Arc (1928) Carl Theodor Dreyer; France; Silent with French intertitles and English subtitles; Black and White; 82 m; Criterion (DVD), Home Vision Entertainment (VHS); France, 1431.

Separating myth from history in the case of Jeanne d'Arc is a dubious enterprise. This fifteenth-century French girl, and Catholic saint, has become the object and symbol of various religious, nationalist, and feminist causes and "lessons" over the centuries. Her portrayal on screen has no less delivered interpretations of Joan that are shaped by the preoccupations of their time. Dreyer's stunning cinematic description of her trial and execution is sometimes described as the best "Joan film," largely because of its visual, structural, and thematic execution and the astonishing—mostly wordless—performance of Maria Falconetti as Joan.

The production, reception, and restoration history of *The Passion of Joan of Arc* is a story in itself; this is instead a brief survey of the film's interpretation of the historical figure. It's important to acknowledge the scope of the film; this is not a biopic of Joan but a film that concentrates solely on the event of her 1431 Rouen heresy trial, conducted by the Bishop of Beauvais, to whom Joan had been "relinquished" by the English army. Dreyer was interested in creating a filmic "reality" of an almost documentary quality for this subject. Dialogue was drawn directly from the transcripts of the trial, no makeup was applied to the actors, and there was no accompanying score. At the same time, Dreyer's realist aesthetic embraced a highly stylized approach, found in austere sets, an extreme reliance on close-ups, and even anachronism.

The opening scroll of *The Passion of Joan of Arc*, intercut with hands flipping through an aged document, emphasizes the film's documentary basis and introduces the Joan of the film: "Reading it [the trial record], we discover the real Joan ... not in armor, but simple and human ... a young woman who died for her country ... and we are witness to an amazing drama: a young, pious woman confronted by a group of orthodox theologians and powerful judges." Dreyer's history is not the spectacle of Joan commanding an army, nor the reconstruction of Joan's motives, the actions of King Charles VII, or the Catholic Church. Instead, this is the evocation of a particular woman's particular historical experience, what Tony Pipolo calls "an almost primal rendering of her literal situation. . . ."

See also: *Day of Wrath*

Aberth, J. "Movies and the Maid: Joan of Arc Films." In *A Knight at the Movies: Medieval History on Film*, 257–98. London: Routledge, 2003.

Benson, Edward. "Oh, What a Lovely War! Joan of Arc on Screen." In *The Medieval Hero on Screen: Representations from Beowulf to Buffy*, edited by Martha W. Driver and Sid Ray, 217–36. Jefferson, NC: McFarland, 2004.

Harty, Kevin. "Jeanne Au Cinéma." In *Fresh Verdicts on Joan of Arc*, edited by Bonnie Wheeler and Charles T. Wood, 237–264. New York: Garland, 1996.

Lerner, Gerda. "Joan of Arc: Three Films." In *Past Imperfect: History According to the Movies*, edited by Mark C. Carnes, 54–55. New York: Henry Holt, 1995.

Margolis, Nadia. *Joan of Arc in History, Literature and Film: A Select, Annotated Bibliography*. New York: Garland, 1990.

Oudart, Jean-Pierre. "An Active Fear (*The Passion of Joan of Arc*)." In *Cahiers Du Cinéma: Vol. 4, 1973–1978: History, Ideology, Cultural Struggle: An Anthology from Cahiers Du Cinéma Nos. 248–292, September 1973-September 1978*, edited by David Wilson and Bérénice Reynaud, 309–12. London: Routledge, 2000.

Pipolo, Tony. "Joan of Arc: The Cinema's Immortal Maid." *Cineaste* 25(4) (Fall 2000): 16–27.

Rosenstone, Robert A. "The Reel Joan of Arc: Reflections on the Theory and Practice of the Historical Film." *The Public Historian* 25(3) (Summer 2003): 61–77.

Yervasi, Carina. "The Faces of Joan: Cinematic Representations of Joan of Arc." *Film & History: An Interdisciplinary Journal of Film and Television Studies* 29(3–4) (1999): 8–19.

Paths of Glory (1957) Stanley Kubrick; United States; English; Black and White; 86 m; Facets (DVD); France, World War I.

Drawn from an event of the First World War, *Paths of Glory* begins in 1916 at the western front. An attack on the German position at Ant Hill—ordered by divisional General Mireau despite misgivings about the strongly fortified target, and the morale and fitness of his soldiers—is a disaster. Mireau, enraged as he watches the second attack wave from the trenches fail to materialize, orders his battery commander to fire on his own troops, claiming they are "mutinying." Captain Rousseau refuses. In a bid to cover up the criminality of his own order, Mireau orders the court-martial of two privates and a corporal on the charge of cowardice. Colonel Dax, a field commander and lawyer in civilian life, who reluctantly commanded the attack, is assigned to defend the men, and the film follows the trial and its outcome.

As Tom Wicker suggests, many movies about the Great War are "*war* movies more nearly than *Great War* movies." *Paths of Glory* is a wonderful film for many reasons, including the intensity of the plotting, the unromantic framing of the battle scene, and the memorable characterizations. Whether the First World War is its subject, though, is a matter of debate. This is certainly an antiwar film, and it is also a film that argues the decadence and logical demise of the European aristocracy. The physical and moral isolation of the French officers from their soldiers, for example, is emphasized in the pristine conditions of their uniforms, the comforts of their headquarters at Schleissheim Castle, and their (mis)use of the justice system to protect their privileges.

See also: *'Breaker' Morant*; *Stalingrad*

Asimow, Michael, and Paul Bergman, eds. "*Paths of Glory.*" In *Reel Justice: The Courtroom Goes to the Movies*, 78–80. Kansas City, MI: Andrews McMeel, 1996.

Bier, Jesse. "Cobb and Kubrick: Author and Auteur." *Virginia Quarterly Review* 61(3) (Summer 1985): 453–71.

Falsetto, Mario. "*Paths of Glory.*" In *Stanley Kubrick: A Narrative and Stylistic Analysis, New and Expanded Second Edition*, 38–41. Westport, CT: Praeger, 2001.

Kelly, Andrew. "The Brutality of Military Incompetence: *Paths of Glory* (1957)." *Historical Journal of Film, Radio and Television* 13(2) (June 1993): 215–27.

Wicker, Tom. "World War I: Five Films." In *Past Imperfect: History According to the Movies*, edited by Mark C. Carnes, 186–91. New York: Henry Holt, 1995.

Pelle the Conqueror (1988) Bille August; Sweden; Swedish and Danish with English subtitles; Color; 160 m; Anchor Bay Entertainment (DVD; VHS); Denmark, 1860s.

The new land to which Lassefar and his son Pelle are journeying is a place "where children play all day long," says Lassefar. The dreams of migrant children, and the promises of their parents, might well have encouraged the decision to leave home. As this story of Swedish migrants working on a farming estate in Denmark in the 1860s shows, the experience might consist of prolonged physical and emotional hardship more than child's play.

Pelle the Conqueror is adapted from the first of a four-volume semi-autobiographical novel by Martin Anderson Nexø. The film adopts a quiet, but event-filled, approach to Lassefar and Pelle's years at Stone Farm on Bornholm Island. Pelle graduates from cowherd to barn manager, and acts as runner for estate owner Kongstrup's lonely wife. Lassefar, reminded often that he is too old for much, fusses over Pelle's needs and endures the indignity of his low status as a general laborer on the farm.

The film remains steadily focused on the world of these characters and on important sub-characters like Erik, another hired hand whose dream of sailing to America fuels Pelle's later escape. In this cinematic social history, little of the context is overtly explained. Instead, the powerful use of inference constructs a picture of labor relations, social manners, and the social inferiority of Swedes in nineteenth-century Denmark.

Pelle the Conqueror is also a very poignant story of a father whose gamble in Denmark seems to be amounting to little, and who does what a father might do in this situation. He tries to make the best for his son's future, giving him advice, his boots, and heartbreaking leave to try again, without him, in America.

Cardullo, Bert. "Boys' Life." *Hudson Review* 42(2) (1989): 290–98.

Kauffmann, Stanley. "An End and a Beginning." *The New Republic* 200 (January 23, 1989): 26–27.

Lebowitz, Naomi. "Magic Socialism and the Ghost of *Pelle Erobreren*." *Scandinavian Studies* 76(3) (Fall 2004): 341–368.

Simon, John. "Plum Danish." *National Review* May 5, 1989: 54–58.

Perfumed Nightmare / Mababangong bangungot (1977) Kidlat Tahimik; Philippines; English and Tagalog with English subtitles; Color; 93 m; Facets (DVD; VHS); Philippines, Paris, Germany, 1970s.

Not a conventional narrative film, *Perfumed Nightmare* erases the distinction between director, screenwriter, camera operator, character, and actor by adopting Kidlat Tahimik's singular voice. With Tahimik appearing in voiceover, in body, and as disembodied voice in scenes with others, this is both a character study and a memoir about a young Filipino man's relationship to his Americanized culture. He is the president of the Wernher von Braun fan club, and is infatuated with American technology and Voice of America radio broadcasts. His disillusionment with the West is fuelled when Tahimik accepts a job in Paris, refilling bubble-gum machines for an American-owned business.

Aitken, Stuart C., and Leo E. Zonn. "Third Cinema: Geography and Practice." In *Place, Power, Situation, and Spectacle: A Geography of Film*, 37–43. Lanham, MD: Rowman & Littlefield, 1994.

Dixon, Deborah, and Leo E. Zonn. "Confronting the Geopolitical Aesthetic: Fredric Jameson, *The Perfumed Nightmare* and the Perilous Place of Third Cinema." *Geopolitics* 10(2) (Summer 2005): 290–315.

Jameson, Fredric. *The Geopolitical Aesthetic: Cinema and Space in the World System*. Bloomington: Indiana University Press, 1992.

Metz, A.M. "Technology and National Identity in Kidlat Tahimik's *Perfumed Nightmare*." *Ariel* 28(3) (1997): 119–42.

Sison, Antonio D. "*Perfumed Nightmare*: Religion and the Philippine Postcolonial Struggle in Third Cinema." In *Representing Religion in World Cinema: Filmmaking, Mythmaking, Culture Making*, edited by S. Brent Plate, 181–96. New York: Palgrave MacMillan, 2003.

The Pianist (2002) Roman Polanski; France/Germany/United Kingdom/Poland; English, German, and Russian with English subtitles; Color; 150 m; Universal Studios Home Entertainment (DVD, VHS); Warsaw, Poland, 1939–1945.

Polish pianist Wladyslaw Szpilman's 1945 memoir *Death of a City* is the basis of this story of his 1941 deportation to the Warsaw Ghetto, his escape, and his hiding in the city. From his vantage point Szpilman witnesses the 1943 Warsaw Ghetto uprising, as well as the general Warsaw uprising of 1944. While some of the scenarios and themes visited in *The Pianist* have been addressed in other films about the period, its recreation of the at times almost banal world of Szpilman's everyday survival is outstanding. As often as not he is alone, in hiding in a small apartment, improvising ways of looking out at the city or finding food through his supports in the Polish underground. Director Polanski boldly allows the film to gaze on this often very isolated figure, whose heroism is in survival more than bravery. Less interesting is the film's impenetrable realist mode, which leaves little room for explicit questions about the construction of personal experience in Szpilman's memoirs.

See also: *Border Street; Korczak; Schindler's List*

Badt, Karin. "Art after Auschwitz?" *Tikkun* 18(3) (May/June 2003): 93–94.

Landsberg, Alison. "America, the Holocaust, and the Mass Culture of Memory: The 'Object' of Remembering." In *Prosthetic Memory: The Transformation of American Remembrance in the Age of Mass Culture*, 111–40. New York: Columbia University Press, 2004.

Portuges, Catherine. "Review of *The Pianist.*" *American Historical Review* 108(2) (April 2003): 622.

Quart, Leonard. "*The Pianist.*" *Cineaste* 28(3) (Summer 2003): 2–43.

Stein, Alexander. "Music and Trauma in Polanski's *The Pianist* (2002)." *International Journal of Psychoanalysis* 85(3) (June 1, 2004): 755–65.

Yacowar, Maurice. "Survivors." *Queen's Quarterly* 110(1) (Spring 2003): 43–50.

Pioneers of Freedom / Para perintis kemerdekaan (1980) Asrul Sani; Indonesia; Indonesian with English subtitles; Color; 121 m; Between Three Worlds Video (VHS); West Sumatra, Indonesia, 1920s.

Halimah is a Sumatran woman of the 1920s. Her husband calls her a "disobedient wife" and even has the judgment of the local *Kadi* (Islamic judge) in his favor. But Halimah lives in an era of the waning authority of the Dutch, and Indonesian nationalism and modernization divide the local Muslim clergy. *Pioneers of Freedom* uses Halimah's search for a revised Islamic interpretation of her wifely duties as a pretext for Asrul Sani's close study of the social, religious, and political mores of a small cross-section of Indonesian society in the 1920s.

The Principal Enemy / El enemigo principal (1972) Jorge Sanjinés; Bolivia/Peru; Quechua with English subtitles; Black and White; 100 m; no current; Peru, 1965.

Hector Béjar, the leader of the insurgent *Ejército de Liberación Nacional* (National Liberation Army), wrote the prison memoir *Peru 1965: Notes on a Guerrilla Experience* from which *The Principal Enemy* derives its story. Indian villagers in the mountains of Peru seek justice from the local court when a landlord murders a peasant in a dispute over a stolen bull. When peasant witnesses are imprisoned, a revolt is planned and coordinated with the leadership of a small band of guerillas. When "the principal enemy "—the imperialists, here embodied in a U.S. colonel—commands a government military counter-attack, the revolt is quelled.

See also: *Blood of the Condor; The Courage of the People/The Night of San Juan; The Lion's Den*

Alexander, William. "Jorge Sanjinés and Tomás Gutiérrez Alea: Class, Film Language and Popular Cinema." *Jump Cut: A Review of Contemporary Media* 30 (March 1985): 45–48.

Campbell, Leon G., and Carlos E. Cortes. "Film as a Revolutionary Weapon: A Jorge Sanjinés Retrospective." *The History Teacher* 12(3) (May 1979): 383–402.

Wallis, Victor. "*The Principal Enemy*: Fighting Imperialism in The Andes." *Jump Cut: A Review of Contemporary Media* 12/13 (December 30, 1976): 8.

The Private Life of Henry VIII (1933) Alexander Korda; United Kingdom; English; Black and White; 97 m; Facets (DVD, VHS); England, 1530s and 1540s.

Debatably more costume drama than historical film, *The Private Life of Henry VIII* has the Tudor king marrying his third wife, Jane Seymour, on the same day as the execution of second wife Anne Boleyn. Erroneous as this sequencing may be (Seymour and Henry wed some 10 days later), it suggests director Alexander Korda's compression of events to accommodate his ambition for the film: to revisit all of Henry's marriages (save his first, to Catherine of Aragon), and to create an entertaining and memorable characterization of a king who, in his private world, had a huge—and generally amiable—appetite for women, food, and life. This "coarse and uncomplicated tyrant," as the *Monthly Film Bulletin* called Charles Laughton's Henry VIII, seems largely removed from the public affairs of state. That the film was hugely successful at the cinema, and Laughton's portrayal has indelibly etched an almost archetypal image of Henry in the popular mind, makes *The Private Life of Henry VIII* important historically, even if it has never received the appellation of being much "historical" itself.

See also: *Anne of the Thousand Days*; *A Man for All Seasons*

n/a. "*The Private Life of Henry VIII* (1933)." *Monthly Film Bulletin* 13(1) (July 1946): 94–95; http://www.screenonline.org.uk/media/mfb/1002684/index.html (accessed May 30, 2006).

Crafton, Donald. "The Portrait as Protagonist: *The Private Life of Henry VIII*." *Iris* 14/15 (Autumn 1992): 25–43.

Dalrymple, Ian. "Alexander Korda." *Quarterly Review of Film and Video* 11(3) (Spring 1957): 294–309.

Street, Sarah. "Stepping Westward: The Distribution of British Feature Films in America, and the Case of *The Private Life of Henry VIII*." In *British Cinema: Past and Present*, edited by Andrew Higson and Justine Ashby, 51–62. London: Routledge, 2000.

The Promised Land / La tierra prometida (1973) Miguel Littín; Chile; Spanish with English subtitles; Color; 80 m; Tricontinental Film Center (theatrical); Chile, 1930–1932.

For a very brief period in 1932, Chile's unstable political and economic conditions led to the establishment of a socialist republic under Colonel Marmaduke Grove. In this context, a group of peasants led by José Durán, who had already settled and cultivated the lands of absentee owners, were emboldened to extend their claims. But with the takeover of power by Arturo Alessandri, and the landowners wishing to evict the settlers, the peasants must defend their ownership against the army, and are massacred in the process. This is a widescreen Eastmancolor epic, an ambitious attempt at political commentary using allegory, symbolism, music, and myth to reconstruct the event.

See also: *Chronicle of the Years of Embers*; *Letters from Marusia*; *Rebellion in Patagonia*

Barnard, Timothy, and Peter Rist. "*La Tierra Prometida.*" In *South American Cinema: A Critical Filmography, 1915–1994*, edited by Timothy Barnard and Peter Rist, 226–29. New York: Garland, 1999.

Schwartz, Ronald. "*La Tierra Prometida (The Promised Land).*" In *Latin American Films, 1932–1994: A Critical Filmography*, 243–45. Jefferson, NC: McFarland, 1997.

Toubiana, Serge, and Pascal Bonitzer. "*The Promised Land.*" In *Cahiers Du Cinéma: Vol. 4, 1973–1978: History, Ideology, Cultural Struggle: An Anthology from Cahiers Du Cinéma Nos. 248–292, September 1973-September 1978*, edited by David Wilson and Bérénice Reynaud, 244–51. London: Routledge, 2000.

Promised Land / *Ziemia obiecana* (1974) Andrzej Wajda; Poland; Polish and German with English subtitles; Color; 178 m; Facets (DVD; VHS); Lodz, Poland, late 19th century.

This is a spirited and robust epic about capital and labor in industrializing Poland at the end of the nineteenth century, based on the novel by Wladyslaw Reymont. *Promised Land* is built around the story of three men (a German and two Poles, one Jewish and one Christian) who are partners in building a new factory. Characters represent almost every stock type of the era, including sexually exploited country girls who work in a textile factory, frustrated white-collar clerks, and unethical factory owners. But these archetypes fit with, rather than jar, the grandiose tone and structure of the film. *Promised Land* captures well the aggrandizing actions of Central Europe's aristocrats as they become by virtue of their lending and investments, factory ownership, or their children's ventures, businessmen forever linked to the successful, if uncultured, bourgeoisie. It is equally resonant in its portrayal of often strained ethnic interrelationships in the city of Lodz. Eventually, predicts one of its citizens, "The ragmen will all go to hell, but Lodz will remain."

Fox, Frank. "*Promised Land (Ziemia Obiecana).*" *Film Heritage* 11(4) (1976): 27–31.

Nurczyńska-Fedelska, Ewelina. "Andrzej Wajda's Vision of *The Promised Land.*" In *The Cinema of Andrzej Wajda: The Art of Irony and Defiance*, edited by John Orr and Elzbieta Ostrowska, 160–71. London: Wallflower Press, 2003.

The Puppetmaster / *Hsimeng rensheng* (1993) Hou Hsiao-hsien; Taiwan; Mandarin, Taiwanese, and Japanese with English subtitles; Color; 142 m; Facets (DVD; VHS); Taiwan, 1909–1945.

The memories of real-life Taiwanese puppet master Li Tien-lu's experiences of the Japanese occupation of Taiwan are explored in his own storytelling and an actor's portrayal. *The Puppetmaster* is a fascinating extended meditation on time, memory, and history.

See also: *City of Sadness; Good Men, Good Women; A Time to Live and a Time to Die*

Lu, Tonglin. "From a Voiceless Father to a Father's Voice: Hou Xiaoxian: *A Time to Live and a Time to Die; City of Sadness; The Puppetmaster.*" In *Confronting Modernity in the Cinemas of Taiwan and Mainland China*, 95–115. Cambridge: Cambridge University Press, 2002.

Yip, June Chun. "Remembering and Forgetting Part II: Hou Hsiao-hsien's Taiwan Trilogy." In *Envisioning Taiwan: Fiction, Cinema, and the Nation in the Cultural Imaginary*, 85–130. Durham, NC: Duke University Press, 2004.

Quilombo (1984) Carlos Diegues; Brazil/France; Portuguese with English subtitles; Color; 114 m; New Yorker Films (DVD; VHS); Palmares, Brazil, 1650–1695.

One manifestation of black resistance to slavery in Brazil was the establishment by Bantu runaway slaves of a self-governing community known as Quilombo dos Palmares, which lasted much of the seventeenth century. This film reconstructs three distinct episodes in the history of Palmares: the flight of slaves from a sugar plantation, the thriving economic and social life of their new community and the members' internal fights, and their defense against the Portuguese. With extravagant color, music, and characterization, *Quilombo* is unabashed in its admiration for the community, including its charismatic founder and chieftain, Ganga Zumba. *Quilombo* is the sequential follow-up to Diegues' *Ganga Zumba*, which concentrated on the origins of the Palmares community.

See also: *Burn!*; *The Last Supper*

Fusco, Coco. "Choosing between Legend and History: An Interview with Carlos Diegues." *Cineaste* 15(1) (1986): 12–14.

Schwartz, Ronald. "*Quilombo*." In *Latin American Films, 1932–1994: A Critical Filmography*, 207–08. Jefferson, NC: McFarland, 1997.

Stam, Robert, and Ismael Xavier. "Transformation of National Allegory: Brazilian Cinema from Dictatorship to Redemocratization." In *Resisting Images: Essays on Cinema and History*, edited by Robert Sklar and Charles Musser, 279–307. Philadelphia, PA: Temple University Press, 1990.

Welch, Cliff. "Review of *Quilombo*." *American Historical Review* 97(4) (October 1992): 1162–64.

Raden Ajeng Kartini / R. A. Kartini (1983) Sjuman Djaya; Indonesia; Indonesian, Javanese and Dutch with English subtitles; Color; 165 m; Between Three Worlds Video (VHS); North Central Java, 1879–1904.

This is a biopic of the Javanese feminist who pioneered primary education for native girls at the turn of the century, and whose life choices challenged traditional expectations of gender roles in marriage. The film offers a sound introduction to the political and social conditions in colonial Java. Kartini's noble and reformist father is appointed a regent, and must implement, though reluctantly, a Dutch policy that favors the cultivation of cash crops over that of local rice production. His lament that Java is an "oppressed and bitter land ... that needs fighters for freedom and independence" foreshadows his children's later commitment to social reform and political independence. Peasant poverty and unrest are also disclosed in brief scenes. "Tini" is portrayed in heroic fashion; even her husband, whose sexual relations with household servants results in her admonition, becomes a contrite and adoring admirer by the end of the film.

See also: *My Love Has Been Burning*

Coté, Joost. "Raden Ajeng Kartini: The Experience and Politics of Colonial Education." In *Gender, Colonialism and Education: The Politics of Experience*, edited by Joyce Goodman and Jane Martin, 199–224. London: Frank Cass, 2002.

Heider, Karl G. "Models for Modernization." In *Indonesian Cinema: National Culture on Screen*, 71–98. Honolulu, HI: University of Hawaii Press, 1991.

Ramparts of Clay / Remparts d'argile (1971) Jean-Louis Bertucelli; France/Algeria; Arabic and French with English subtitles; Color; 87 m; Facets (VHS); Tunisia, 1962.

Sociologist Jean Duvignaud's study *Change at Shebika: Report from a North African Village* (1970) is the basis for this fictionalized story of a village in newly-independent Tunisia. The year is 1962, and the village is the scene of a strike when male salt miners are not paid their promised wage. Assistance is provided by the local women, including a young girl who is learning to read and whose actions against the army demand she relinquish her traditional roles.

See also: *Silences of the Palace*

Geertz, Clifford. "In Search of North Africa." *New York Review of Books* (April 22, 1971): 20–24.

Gendzier, Irene. "*Ramparts of Clay* by Jean-Louis Bertucelli." *American Anthropologist* 76(3) (September 1974): 692–93.

Landy, Marcia, and Stanley Shostak. "Politics and Ethnography: *Ramparts of Clay*." *Film Criticism* 8(2) (1984): 14–26.

Maxwell, Richard. "The Reality Effect of Third World Cinema: Ethnography in *Ceddo* and *Ramparts of Clay*." *Cresset* 43(3) (January 1980): 21–22.

Rashomon (1950) Akira Kurosawa; Japan; Japanese with English subtitles; Black and White; 90 m; Facets (DVD; VHS); Japan, 12th century.

Rashomon is loosely based on two short stories of Ryunosuke Akutagawa. Under a ruined gate in twelfth-century Kyoto. Over the course of the film, four people—the woodcutter, a bandit, a rape victim, and the dead man (through a medium)—each offer testimony about their relationship to the scene, and flashbacks reenact these perspectives. As each account differs significantly from the others, the audiences' desire for, or expectation of, a resolution to the mystery grows.

Rashomon offers no definitive answer to the cause of the man's death, nor to the motives for the characters' accounts. Instead the film's elliptical approach points viewers toward a consideration of the subjective truth of each account, and the falseness of our expectation of objective testimony. The implications of this theme to the historical dimensions of *Rashomon* are very interesting. The late Heian period was a time of often violent transition, with the increasing challenge to the central government by regional military and political powers creating anarchic conditions that might provide context for the rape and murder in the film. But its setting in medieval Japan might be considered more a pretext for assigning characteristics to Kurosawa's own age than a considered investigation of the past itself. In this regard, much has been made of the film's argument of the continuity of "feudalism" into the modern era. That the film does not have as its *raison d'être* the explanation of a historical era does not, however, negate its value to the study of history: *Rashomon* considers the essential trait of historical "event"—experience—and then discloses its relationship to the fashioning of historical "interpretation" through memory, investigation, testimony, documentation, and reconstruction. *Rashomon*'s refusal to assign to a single witness or interpreter preferential assignment as the truth-teller is a departure from most films that engage the past.

See also: *Gate of Hell; Hiroshima, mon amour; Taira Clan Saga*

Jones, Elizabeth. "Locating Truth in Film, 1940-1980." *Post Script: Essays in Film and the Humanities* 6(1) (Fall 1986): 53–65.

McDonald, Keiko I. "The Dialectic of Light and Darkness in Kurosawa's *Rashomon*." In *Cinema East: A Critical Study of Major Japanese Films*, 23–35. Rutherford, NJ: Farleigh Dickenson University Press, 1983.

Richie, Donald, ed. *Focus on Rashomon.* Garden City, NY: Anchor, 1972.

Sato, Tadao. "Tradition in a Time of Transition." *Cinemaya: The Asian Film Quarterly* 42 (Winter 1998): 28–34.

Rasputin / Agony / Agoniya (1977) Elem Klimov; Soviet Union; Russian with English subtitles; Color; 104 m; Facets (DVD, VHS); Russia, 1915–1916.

Rasputin is a delirious, expressionistic interpretation of the Siberian monk Rasputin and his influence on the Romanov family. Here Klimov emphasizes the charisma, sensuality, and ego of Rasputin, and the weakness and irrationality of his followers, including Tsarina Alexandra. The portrait of the corruption of the imperial government exempts Tsar Nicholas II, who is presented as a sympathetic character, agonized by the course of the war and his own impotence as Russian leader in the face of foreign and domestic pressures.

Dunlop, John B. "Elem Klimov's *Agony.*" In *The Red Screen: Politics, Society, Art in Soviet Cinema*, edited by Anna Lawton, 243–6. London: Routledge, 1992.

Menashe, Louis. "*Rasputin.*" *Film Quarterly* 40 (1986): 17–21.

Rebellion in Patagonia / La Patagonia rebelde (1974) Héctor Olivera; Argentina; Spanish with English subtitles; Color; 110 m; Facets (DVD); Argentina, 1920s.

Rebellion in Patagonia was released during the third presidency of Juan Perón, whose return from exile provided a (brief) respite from military rule. The film quite closely follows Osvaldo Bayer's history of the same name, recreating a 1920s general strike (and army slaughter) of agricultural workers—mostly sheep farmers—organized by anarcho-syndicalists in the remote southern region of Argentina. Told in flashback, from the point when the massacre's sole survivor assassinates Colonel Zavala of the army command, the film indicts President Hipólito Yrigoyen and foreign pressures for action against strikers, who are viewed as jeopardizing Russian, Spanish, American, British, and other foreign-owned economic interests in the region. *Rebellion in Patagonia* also turns its eye to the politics within the fractured Left.

See also: *A Funny, Dirty Little War; The Traitors*

Barnard, Timothy, and Peter Rist. "*La Patagonia Rebelde.*" In *South American Cinema: A Critical Filmography, 1915–1994*, edited by Timothy Barnard and Peter Rist, 55–56. New York: Garland, 1999.

Porton, Richard. "Anarcho-Syndicalism in Fiction and Documentary Cinema." In *Film and the Anarchist Imagination*, 119–30. New York: Verso, 1999.

Schwartz, Ronald. "*La Patagonia Rebelde* (*Rebellion in Patagonia* or *Uprising in Patagonia*)." In *Latin American Films, 1932–1994: A Critical Filmography*, 193–94. Jefferson, NC: McFarland, 1997.

West, Dennis. "Review of *Rebellion in Patagonia.*" *Cineaste* 10(1) (Winter 1979–80): 50–52.

Record of a Tenement Gentleman / Nagaya shinshiroku (1947) Yasujiro Ozu; Japan; Japanese with English subtitles; Black and White; 72 m; Facets (VHS); Tokyo, post-World War II.

This is a warm and funny fictional story about the inhabitants of a small Japanese town and their dilemma about what to do with a boy found wandering the streets.

In the guise of an unpretentious story, a social history of ordinary Japanese in the immediate post-World War II period emerges, showing the plight of both children and adults who are impoverished, underfed, and suffering the loss of family.

See also: *MacArthur's Children*

Fowler, Edward. "Piss and Run: Or How Ozu Does a Number on SCAP." In *Word and Image in Japanese Cinema*, edited by Carole Cavanaugh and Dennis Washburn, 273–92. Cambridge: Cambridge University Press, 1993.

The Red and the White / Csillagosok, katonák (1967) Miklós Jancsó; Hungary; Hungarian and Russian with English subtitles; Black and White; 92 m; Kino (DVD, VHS); Ukraine, 1919.

As with many historical films, describing *The Red and the White* as "about" an event in the Russian Civil War (1918–1921) ignores thematic dimensions of the film that cannot be categorized as "historical." Here, director Miklós Jancsó represents the engagement of Bolshevik (Red) and anti-Communist (White) forces at an abandoned monastery and a riverfront hospital in 1919 Ukraine in a manner that eschews the epic style of careful chronicling of seminal events in a heroic narrative.

The film's very long takes and its extreme long shots often create humans—individual or massed—as aesthetic ornaments on the landscape. The men and women of *The Red and the White* are not just organized by director Jancsó to create a desired visual composition. The subjects are being arranged, and rearranged, over and over again in the course of the narrative, by those in command, whether their captors or their captains. The often forced movement of people places them into categories of their historical fate: some to be executed, some to be released, some to march in an expedition, some to face an opposing—likely horse-mounted—army. This sorting that is reiterated in the visual and narrative qualities of the film reinforces *The Red and the White*'s tendency to reduce the ideological polarities of the two sides represented in the title; neither the Bolsheviks and their Hungarian volunteers, nor the counter-revolutionaries, are clearly differentiated. The film also often disregards explicit plot explanation, leaving viewers to concentrate less on the details of the story's direction, than on the quality of events.

See also: *The Chekist*; *Le Coup de Grâce*

Czigány, Lóránt. "Jancsó Country: Miklós Jancsó and the Hungarian New Cinema." *Film Quarterly* 26(1) (Autumn 1972): 44–50.
Horton, Andrew. "The Aura of History: The Depiction of the Year 1919 in the Films of Miklós Jancsó." *Kinoeye: New Perspectives on European Film* 3(3) (February 17, 2003), http://www.kinoeye.org/03/03/horton03.php (accessed May 30, 2006).
Rothschild, Wayne, and Amy Lawrence. "The Masses Are Not a Subject: Eisenstein and Jancsó." *Spectator: The University of California Journal of Film and Television Criticism* 7(2) (1987): 1–5.

Red Dawn / Rojo amanecer (1989) Jorge Fons; Mexico; Spanish; Color; 96 m; Mexcinema Video Corp (VHS); Mexico City, October 1968.

In reconstructing the massacre of protesting university students at Tlatelolco plaza, *Red Dawn* is confined chronologically to a single day in October, 1968, and spatially to the apartment of a fictional Mexico City family. At first observing events from their window and rooftop, family members are increasingly drawn into events. They try to assist and hide a wounded student, but the police soon burst in on their home—a space that increasingly comes to represent the lost illusions of middle-class Mexicans.

See also: *Canoa*; *The Night of the Pencils*

Foster, David William. "*Rojo Amenecer.*" In *Mexico City in Contemporary Mexican Cinema*, 2–12. Austin: University of Texas Press, 2002.

Red River Valley / Honghe gu (1996) Feng Xiaoning; China; Mandarin and English with English subtitles; Color; 115 m; Facets (DVD); Tibet, turn of the 20th century to 1904.

With gorgeous panoramic shots of Tibet, this is a rousing action–adventure–romance set in the context of British attempts to occupy Tibet in the early twentieth century. Its somewhat predictable and histrionic storyline follows a young Han woman named Snow Dawa, who in 1900 is rescued from a religious sacrifice by a dashing Tibetan herdsman. Snow Dawa later rescues British travelers Major Rockland and his interpreter Mr. Jones, and these foreigners come to represent two sides of the "other" in Tibet. Rockland is the conqueror, Jones the sympathetic "stranger in a strange land" who exchanges with his hosts information about his culture, in return for learning about theirs. A love triangle of Snow Dawa, her rescuer, and the beautiful daughter of a local chief complicates matters, but the lovers set aside their (especially class) differences with the advent of the British invasion, in order to put up heroic resistance.

A Shanghai Film Studios production, the introduction to this DVD version of *Red River Valley* credits the film's origins in popular novelist and travel author Peter Fleming's 1961 book *Bayonets to Lhasa: The First Full Account of the British Invasion of Tibet in 1904*. The Sino–British provenance is evident in the film. On the Chinese side, the film's interpretation of Tibet's history falls squarely in line with the position of the People's Republic that the historical people of Tibet were subject to the tyranny of a feudal theocracy, that the attempt at British occupation violated China's sovereignty, and that Tibetan culture is still valued and respected within the Chinese-nationalist fold. The influence of Fleming gives an "authentic" voice to the British characters, and one which is critical of the outcome of the historical 1903–04 Tibet expedition led by British Colonel Younghusband.

See also: *Kundun*; *Seven Years in Tibet*

Buckley, Michael. "Red River Valley." In *Travelers' Tales Tibet: True Stories*, edited by James O'Reilly and Larry Habegger, 173–83. Berkeley, CA: Publishers Group West, 2003.

Jihong, Wan, and Richard Kraus. "Hollywood and China as Adversaries and Allies." *Pacific Affairs* 75(3) (Fall 2002): 419–34.

Lu, Sheldon H. "Narratives of the Nation-State." In *The Cinema of Hong Kong: History, Arts, Identity*, edited by Poshek Fu and David Desser, 273–76. New York: Cambridge University Press, 2000.

Lu, Sheldon H. "Representing the Chinese Nation-State in Filmic Discourse." In *East of West: Cross-Cultural Performance and the Staging of Difference*, edited by Claire Sponsler and Xiaomei Chen, 111–24. New York: Palgrave, 2000.

Repentance / Pokayaniye / Pokaianie (1986) Tengiz Abuladze; Soviet Union; Georgian and Russian with English subtitles; Color; 153 m; Facets (DVD; VHS); Soviet Union, 1930s.

At various times wry, chilling, surreal, and theatrical, *Repentance* is a fascinating film. While its fictional story is not entirely linear, it follows this outline: The mayor of a small Georgian town, Varlam Aravidze, has died and been buried, but the corpse keeps turning up. When the police arrest Keti for interfering with the body, she argues that the historical deeds of this man—some of which terrorized her family—musn't be forgotten. Keti's trial becomes the pretext for flashbacks to this history. While not all analysts accept the thesis, *Repentance* is often interpreted as an allegorical condemnation by Georgian director Tengiz Abuladze of the Stalinist era.

See also: *The Inner Circle*

Christensen, Julie. "Tengiz Abuladze's *Repentance* and the Georgian Nationalist Cause." *Slavic Review* 50(1) (Spring 1991): 163–75.

Christensen, Peter Glenn. "Tengiz Abuladze's *Repentance*: Despair in the Age of Perestroika." *Soviet and East-European Drama, Theater and Film* 8(2–3) (December 1988): 64–72.

Youngblood, Denise J. "*Repentance*: Stalinist Terror and the Realism of Surrealism." In *Revisioning History: Film and the Construction of a New Past*, edited by Robert A. Rosenstone, 139–54. Princeton, NJ: Princeton University Press, 1995.

———. "Review of *Repentance*." *American Historical Review* 95(4) (October 1990): 1133–36.

Woll, Josephine, and Denise J. Youngblood. *Repentance: The Film Companion*. London: I.B. Tauris, 2001.

The Return of Martin Guerre / Le retour de Martin Guerre (1982) Daniel Vigne; France; French with English subtitles; Color; 122 m; Fox Lorber (DVD; VHS); France, 1530s–1560s.

The story of a sixteenth-century man whose claim of identity as peasant Martin Guerre of the village of Artigat is tested by villagers, family members, and ultimately a French court, has been told in many popular tales since its occurrence. Daniel Vigne's *The Return of Martin Guerre* is a modern film version, adding to the plays, operas, and popular and scholarly books that have engaged the story. This particular film has received much attention from historians, principally because historian Natalie Zemon Davis worked as a consultant on the film, and then after the experience produced her own, mildly provocative, academic history of the same title, claiming, "I was prompted to dig deeper into the case, to make historical sense of it . . . I felt I had my own historical laboratory [the film set] generating not proofs, but historical possibilities." The cinematic *Return of Martin Guerre* has thus prompted an uncommonly rich field of literature about the film, and frequent screening of the film in undergraduate history classrooms.

To comprehensively synthesize the vibrant debate about the veracity of the story itself, Vigne's interpretation, and Davis' own book version would be a task hardly less than that the Toulouse judges faced when the clever Arnaud du Tilh insisted on his identity as Martin. *The Return of Martin Guerre* focuses on the Guerre family, who live in the village of Artigat, Languedoc province, in the sixteenth century. The film begins with the marriage of Bertrande de Rols and Martin Guerre in 1538. (The historical record of the couple includes a number of "retellings" of their story through the ages, including *Arrest Memorable* in 1561, written by Jean de Coras, a judge in the trial of Martin at Toulouse.) Eight years after Martin departs from his life in Artigat, his whereabouts unknown, a man arrives to claim he is Martin returned. Resuming (or beginning) a romantically and likely sexually satisfying relationship, the couple enjoy several years of happiness before suspicions arise about the true identity of the returned "Martin."

One major departure of Davis' book from the film's narrative of events illustrates the compression demanded by a feature length film, and highlights interpretive differences between Davis and the filmmakers. Davis describes two trials of "Martin." The first took place at the local court of Rieux, where he is charged with taking someone else's name and person, the penalty being anything from a fine to death. Pierre Guerre, the accuser, brings "Martin" to these charges by falsifying Bertrande's signature. Then Bertrande decides to appear to "go along" with Pierre. Hoping/believing the Rieux case will be lost by Pierre, she "covers" herself by coaching "Martin" covertly and publicly supporting Pierre. As Davis says, "The couple had to be prepared to counter his [Pierre's] arguments, and now they probably worked out the strategy they would eventually follow during the trials...." "Martin" is found guilty of the crime, sentenced to beheading, and appeals to the Parlement of Toulouse. In this second trial, Bertrande and "Martin" connive to present Bertrande as a woman who was coerced into a lie by Pierre. Davis interprets Bertrande's actions as a "double game," ascribing to Bertrande an agency and decisive role in the defense of her personal interests in the case (the child born to "Martin" and Bertrande would be declared illegitimate should "Martin" be convicted). The film version of the case, however, does not show Bertrande accusing "Martin." Instead, her romantic devotion motivates her to stand by him until irrefutable evidence of his imposture arrives.

Aufderheide, Pat. "Interview with Natalie Davis." *Radical History Review* 28–30 (1984): 136–39.

Benson, Ed. "The Look of the Past: *Le Retour De Martin Guerre*." *Radical History Review* 28–30 (1984): 125–35.

———. "Martin Guerre, the Historian and the Filmmakers: An Interview with Natalie Zemon Davis." *Film & History: An Interdisciplinary Journal of Film and Television Studies* 13(3) (1983): 49–65.

Davis, Natalie Zemon. "'Any Resemblance to Persons Living or Dead': Film and the Challenge of Authenticity." *The Yale Review* 76(4) (1987): 457–82.

———. "Movie or Monograph? A Historian/Filmmaker's Perspective." *The Public Historian* 25(3) (2003): 45–48.

———. *The Return of Martin Guerre*. Cambridge, MA: Harvard University Press, 1983.

Guneratne, Anthony Rajah. "Cinehistory and the Puzzling Case of Martin Guerre." *Film & History: An Interdisciplinary Journal of Film and Television Studies* 21(1) (1991): 2–19.

Voeltz, Richard A. "*The Return of Martin Guerre*: Teaching History in Images, History in Words." *Teaching History: A Journal of Methods* 2 (Fall 1993): 68–72.

Ridicule (1996) Patrice Leconte; France; French with English subtitles; Color; 102 m; Miramax Home Entertainment (DVD, VHS); France, 1783.

Ridicule is as much French "heritage" cinema as historical film. At every turn, its depiction of the setting of Versailles, its courtiers, and its system of social and political gamesmanship is grandiose and appealing as spectacle. Huge wigs, sumptuous costumes, inflated egos, insatiable social appetites, and ridiculous obstacles to success all reference for viewers a kind of sensory memory of the excesses of the court of Louis XVI honed by exposure to everything from film versions of *The Three Musketeers* to biopics. This palimpsestic experience of *Ridicule* (perhaps dangerously) reassures the audience of *Ridicule*'s authenticity. However, there is a strong possibility that the film's superbly constructed "formula" of wit, drama, and romance allows viewers to recognize *Ridicule* as a modern construction of the past, and therefore recognize its preoccupations are as current as they are historical. Playfully engaging viewers from beginning to end, director Patrice Leconte has managed to not only "ridicule" the *ancien régime*, but by implication our own sense of its inferiority.

Ridicule's plot revolves around the attempts of a lesser noble to secure royal patronage for his scheme to drain the disease-ridden waters of the Dombes marshes near Lyon. Ponceludon is a symbol of our modern ideal, "historically" emergent in the eighteenth century. He is humane and by implication democratic—sympathetic to the peasants of the Dombes—humble, scientific, and not particularly monarchist in his politics. Ponceludon will experience challenges to these virtues as he becomes more and more entwined in the intrigues of Louis' court as he seeks a rare audience with the king to present his engineering plan. A lascivious and powerful Abbé and his lover Madame de Blayac, and various bureaucrats, all scheme to make Ponceludon's quest their ticket to social superiority at Versailles. Their most potent weapon is command of wit, which can cruelly level the most virtuous of men.

Representing a touchstone for his "real" self is the comely Mathilde, daughter of the Marquis de Bellegarde, who becomes Ponceludon's guide to the intricacies of court etiquette and especially its games of wit. Mathilde is Ponceludon's equal, or female mirror image. She is independent, researching diving apparatus and pollination, interested in marriage to an ancient suitor only for financial ends. Her rationalism extends to the claim that love is an illusion, but we suspect that at least that will fall to the effects of romance and compatibility with Ponceludon—love and friendship being sentiments our modern values allow to coexist with reason. Mathilde's marriage of convenience and her eventual partnership with Ponceludon could be read as a victory for feminism—as she alone dictated her choices—or as its defeat to bourgeois and patriarchal convention.

As the story unfolds—at an irreverent and witty clip—one cannot help but be endeared to the portrait of the *ancien régime* that emerges. As a brief and tangible case study of the transition from the early modern to modern era, *Ridicule* is a pleasant history lesson.

See also: *La Marseillaise; The Rise of Louis XIV; Vatel*

Adams, Christine. "Review of *Ridicule*." *Film & History: An Interdisciplinary Journal of Film and Television Studies* 34(1) (2004): 73–74.

Humbert, Brigitte E. "Patrice Leconte's *Ridicule*: Women in the Political Sphere: Transforming Memory into Modernity?" *Studies in French Cinema* 3(3) (2003): 137–47.

Kwass, Michael, and Laura Mason. "Review of *Ridicule*." *American Historical Review* 102(3) (1997): 936–7.

Rosello, Mireille. "Dissident Voices before the Revolution: *Ridicule*." In *French Cinema in the 1990s: Continuity and Difference*, edited by Phil Powrie, 81–91. Oxford: Oxford University Press, 1999.

The Rise of Louis XIV / The Rise to Power of Louis XIV / La prise de pouvoir par Louis XIV (1966) Roberto Rossellini; France; French with English subtitles; Color; 100 m; Facets (DVD with no subtitles), Hen's Tooth Video (VHS); France, 17th century.

Martin Walsh has suggested "... it is probably not too much to say that *Louis XIV* is one of the most extraordinary meditations on the nature and power of spectacle that the cinema has yet produced." Indeed, this treatment of Louis—hardly fitting the term "biopic" as it narrows its attention to the rituals of court, not a developmental character arc over the space of a life—creates a filmic spectacle that supports director Rossellini's argument that the French king constructed and secured his power by the regulation of images and social relationships. The film tells us virtually nothing about Louis' personality; image and Louis are indivisible, as is his person and the State. And while the film begins with the camera following doctors to the royal palace to attend to the dying Mazarin, after it reaches the court, it never leaves, drawing the audience into the hope of an audience with the king as did his impotent and domesticated courtiers.

In *The Rise of Louis XIV* the enactment of royal spectacle and ritual—in Louis' meal, his waking, or his prayers—is inextricably linked to both the film's aesthetic and its interpretive discourse on the contrivances that were the root of the king's power. Whether or not today's historians are satisfied that this thesis is borne in the evidence, King Louis' image-making still exercises its spell centuries later.

See also: *Ridicule*; *Vatel*

Burke, Peter. "Rossellini's *Louis XIV*." In *Eyewitnessing: The Uses of Images as Historical Evidence*, 162–64. Ithaca, NY: Cornell University Press, 2001.

Grindon, Leger. "Drama and Spectacle as Historical Explanation in the Historical Fiction Film." *Film & History: An Interdisciplinary Journal of Film and Television Studies* 17(4) (1987): 74–80.

Walsh, Martin. "*Rome, Open City*; *The Rise to Power of Louis XIV*: Re-Evaluating Rossellini." *Jump Cut: A Review of Contemporary Media* 15 (1977): 13–15.

A River Called Titas / Titash ekti nadir naam (1973) Ritwik Ghatak; India; Bengali with English subtitles; Black and White; 151 m; Facets (DVD); East Bengal, 1930s.

This is a cinematic elegy for the changes wrought by the partition of Bengal in 1947, telling the story of a fishing village in East Bengal in the 1930s. The culture and society of those who live on the banks of the Titas River are threatened by a kidnapping and environmental catastrophe.

See also: *The Tree of Wooden Clogs*

Raghavendra, M.K. "The River as History." *Deep Focus* 8(1/2) (1998): 87–90.

Rosa Luxemburg (1986) Margarethe von Trotta; Czechoslovakia/West Germany; German and Polish with English subtitles; Color; 122 m; New Yorker Films (VHS); Poland and Germany, 1900–1919.

Director Margarethe von Trotta's biopic of "Red Rosa," the Polish-born Marxist theoretician and leading member of the German social democratic movement, adheres to many of the genre's conventions. It treats its subject with sentimentality and veneration (some critics have called the film "hagiography"), it lingers over personal conflict and public drama and reduces the complexity of intellectual or political contexts. Nevertheless *Rosa Luxemburg* is an instructive glimpse into numerous features of the social, political, and intellectual milieu of imperial Germany. The film also provides an effective introduction to Western audiences of a major female figure of Europe's age of socialist revolution.

Using a narrative structure infused with numerous flashbacks, *Rosa Luxemburg* focuses on the title character's adult private and public life. Several periods of her imprisonment provide the narrative and symbolic centerpoint; von Trotta's screenplay was inspired by her reading of the just-published prison letters of Luxemburg.

The private self of the publicly "Red" Rosa is fairly bluntly suggested in numerous scenes. Luxemburg and friend Luise Kautsky enjoy a lakeside excursion, indulging in nothing more serious than giggly confessions. Rosa's affection for her cat Mimi, niece, and younger lover Kostja Zetkin present her as peace-loving, sensitive, and, indeed, feminine. Luxemburg's turbulent love affair with Polish revolutionary Leo Jogiches indicates her longing for the conventions of a bourgeois life—husband, home, and children. These longings challenge Leo's fidelity, and her own revolutionary mission. In a classic exposition of the tension between individual and collective values, Leo says, "Rosa, you have to choose: mother or revolutionary. . . . Your task is to give birth to ideas, not children."

The public Luxemburg is a woman of intellect, action, and, reflecting a trope of biographical films, unwavering conviction. Her actions in this sphere are accounted for in the film in scenes of Luxemburg at the podium delivering passionate speeches, engaged in inter-Party debates around a dinner table, and in her composition of articles for various socialist newspapers. *Rosa Luxemburg* is to a great extent a film about words, not unfitting for a biography of an intellectual. In addition to her speeches and journalistic writing, Luxemburg frequently recites excerpts from her letters and diaries in voiceovers. This emphasis on Luxemburg's words also has opened the film up to critics who charge that some of the figure's most important ideas are ignored, most notably her criticism of Lenin's theory of the revolutionary vanguard. Richard Porton calls Luxemburg "one of the revolutionary left's most anomalous figures," but the film's public Luxemburg is more one-dimensional. We see little of "a Marxist who refused to capitulate to Leninism, a militant woman who evinced little interest in feminism, a Jew who was rarely preoccupied with anti-Semitism, and a Pole who was severely critical of her compatriots' characteristic nationalism."

A number of leading figures of German social democracy are represented in the film, and their conflicts with Luxemburg reflect the tensions and disagreements that historically existed in the movement at the turn of the century: August Bebel, leader of the SPD to 1913; Karl Kautsky, a leading ideologue and reformist within the SPD; his wife Luise Kautsky; Clara Zetkin, head of the SPD's women's division; and Karl Liebknecht, co-leader with Rosa Luxemburg of the factional Spartacus Union and later briefly leader of the Communist Party (established January 1, 1919), until his assassination in the same month. A ballroom scene wherein SPD members ring in the New Year and Century even shows Rosa refusing to dance with "silly Edouard," the pioneer of German evolutionary socialism Edouard Bernstein.

The final scenes of the film—interposed with original film footage—show Liebknecht bravely committed to a workers' revolution, and Luxemburg worriedly cautious about the readiness of the postwar masses. Luxemburg's and Liebknecht's personal and ideological resolution poignantly takes place not in the violent and chaotic streets of 1919 Berlin, but in a quiet parlor, Liebknecht assenting to play on the piano *Moonlight Sonata* for his friend and comrade. Soon after, members of the German military shoot captive Luxemburg, dumping her body in a canal.

The film hearkens the loss at the moment of Luxemburg's death of Germany's postwar opportunity to recapture its enlightened roots. If the young Republican government had embraced, rather than (by collusion with the German military establishment) brutally repressed its more radical socialists, the new Germany might have had a more promising start. Von Trotta implies—not unlike other (oft-debated) interpreters of Germany's interwar period—that the Third Reich found dangerously fertile ground in the foundations of the Republic. Certainly in offering such an interpretation of this period of German history von Trotta, born in 1942, betrays just as much of her own generation's sensibilities as her historical sense. As Renate Hehr suggests, *Rosa Luxemburg* "is a swan song for a utopia that is identical with the vision of the future held by the '68ers and the woman's movement."

See also: *Fever*

Diggins, John Patrick. "*Rosa Luxemburg*." In *Past Imperfect: History According to the Movies*, edited by Mark C. Carnes, 196–99. New York: Henry Holt, 1995.

Hehr, Renate. *Margarethe Von Trotta: Filmmaking as Liberation*. Stuttgart: Edition Axel Menges, 2000.

Kuhn, Anna. "A Heroine for Our Time: Margarethe Von Trotta's *Rosa Luxemburg*." In *Gender and German Cinema: Feminist Interventions, Vol. II: German Film History/German History on Film*, edited by Sandra Frieden, Richard W. McCormick, Vibeke R. Petersen, and Laurie Melissa Vogelsang, 163–84. Providence, RI: Berg, 1993.

Porton, Richard. "*Rosa Luxemburg*." *Film Quarterly*(2) (1989): 39–42.

Rosenstrasse (2003) Margarethe von Trotta; Germany/Netherlands; German with English subtitles; Color; 136 m; Facets (DVD); Berlin, 1943, and contemporary New York.

Rosenstrasse presents an excellent case study of the debate that can be engendered by history on film. The film is an imaginative reconstruction of the 1943 protest of Berlin women whose German Jewish husbands were incarcerated and bound for deportation to camps. Released in the Internet age, *Rosenstrasse* was the subject of an on-line forum for the members of *H-German*, a list-serv whose subscribers include many active and leading scholars of modern German history. The scholarly discussion of the film and the event upon which it was based is a rich trove of information and competing insights that illustrates some of the ways cinematic history is analysed by historians.

Several themes emerge in the literature about the film. The first is the challenge of rationalizing the fact that *Rosenstrasse* invents characters and events, despite claims in an opening intertitle that "The events that unfolded on Rosenstrasse in Berlin from February 27 till March 6, 1943, are a historical fact." In an interview conducted for *Cineaste*, von Trotta refers to a number of autobiographical and oral sources—unrelated to the Rosenstrasse event specifically, but which are connected to the subjects of intermarriage and resistance in the era—that inspired some of *Rosenstrasse*'s characters and scenarios. For the director, the invention of aristocratic Lena's sexual liaison with Goebbels (suggested as securing the Nazi order for the husbands' release) is justified, because it symbolizes the isolation of the protestors from the elite who are "behaving as if there were no war." Some argue the Lena–Goebbels contrivance reduces the historic collective action of the protesting wives to a level of insignificance that is indefensible. Von Trotta's rationale is accepted by some, perhaps reluctantly, as the price of bringing the experience of intermarried Germans and the German women's protest to public attention.

See also: *The White Rose*

Boettcher, Susan, Christopher Fischer, David Imhoof, and Paul Steege. "H-German Forum: *Rosenstrasse*." http://www.h-net.org/~german/discuss/Rosenstrasse/Rosenstrasse_index.htm (accessed May 30, 2006).

Sklar, Robert. "Invaded by Memories of Germany's Past: An Interview with Margarethe Von Trotta." *Cineaste* 29(2) (Spring 2004): 10–12.

The Round-Up / Szegénylegények (1965) Miklós Jancsó; Hungary; Hungarian with English subtitles; Black and White; 90 m; Facets (VHS); Hungary, 1868.

Among those Hungarians rounded up by the Austro-Hungarian Army in 1868 are partisans of the Hungarian independence movement that reaches back to the revolution of 1848. The closed and oppressive environment of the detention prison is the scene of the guards' interrogation and coercion of the peasants to expose the revolutionaries in their midst.

Rucinski, Krzysztof. "Two Men against History: A Comparative Analysis of Films by Miklós Jancsó and Andrzej Wajda." *Kinoeye: New Perspectives on European Film* 3(3) (February 17, 2003), http://www.kinoeye.org/03/03/rucinski03.php (accessed May 30, 2006).

Russian Ark / Russkiy kovcheg (2002) Aleksandr Sokurov; Russia/Germany; Russian with English subtitles; Color; 96 m; Wellspring (DVD, VHS); St. Petersburg, Russia, 18th and 19th centuries.

The technical feat of sustaining a single take of 87 minutes—the entirety of *Russian Ark*—is only one of the marvels of this film shot on location at the Hermitage Museum in St. Petersburg. As the camera follows an unnamed noble (based on Frenchman Marquis de Custine, who visited and wrote about Russia in the 1830s) through the building, the offscreen voice of a filmmaker engages him in discussion of two centuries of history, triggered by the scenes enacted in each room encountered.

Russian Ark is rich with allusions to Russian cultural, philosophical, and political history. Two aspects of its engagement of the past are notable. First, the film captures forcefully the historical unease between Russia and "Europe" over Russia's identity and place in the world: is Russia a backward cousin of Western Europe, a fundamentally "Oriental" society, or a thoroughly and magnificently European civilization? Second, *Russian Ark* demands of its audience an uninterrupted gaze. There are no editing breaks in this extended take, thus challenging the audience to reconsider their relationship to historical and cinematic time.

See also: *The Navigator: A Medieval Odyssey*; *Orlando*; *Time Bandits*; *The Travelling Players*

Gillespie, David, and Elena Smirnova. "Alexander Sokurov and the Russian Soul." *Studies in European Cinema* 1(1) (2004): 57–65.

Harte, Tim. "A Visit to the Museum: Aleksandr Sokurov's *Russian Ark* and the Framing of the Eternal." *Slavic Review* 64(1) (Spring 2005): 42–58.

Macnab, Geoffrey. "Palace in Wonderland." *Sight & Sound* 12(8) (August 2002): 20–23.

Ravetto-Biagioli, Kriss. "Floating on the Borders of Europe: Sokurov's *Russian Ark*." *Film Quarterly* 59(1) (Fall 2005): 18–26.

Saladin / Al-Nasir Salah al-Din (1963) Youssef Chahine; Egypt; Arabic with English subtitles; Color; 145 m; Facets (VHS); Palestine, 1187–1192.

Often described as the first epic of the Egyptian cinema, *Saladin* is a widescreen spectacle about the Arab hero who commanded an army in the successful defense of Jerusalem against the forces of English King Richard I (the "Lion-Hearted"), French King Phillip II, and Holy Roman Emperor Frederick I during the period of the Third Crusade (1189–1192). This heroic-nationalist melodrama is a wonderful example of the interpretation of the Crusades from the Arab perspective.

At the film's outset, Saladin, the Sultan of Egypt and Syria, proclaims his dream "is to see the Arab people united under one flag. Only then can we liberate Jerusalem from its captors." Chahine's *Saladin* is a thinly disguised representation of modern Egyptian President Nasser, who in the aftermath of the nationalization of the Suez canal and signing of the nonalignment pact, was the symbol of hope of much of the Arab (and "Third") world for the resolution of colonial and Arab-Israeli conflict. Saladin is as benevolent as he is brave, a pious Muslim, and devoted to the Arab struggle. In several scenes, he professes tolerance for Christians and offers them concessions such as their leave to worship in Jerusalem, or the cessation of fighting on Christmas. By film's end, his defeated Christian enemies have been humbled by Saladin's own humility. King Richard philosophically observes to Saladin that of the thousands of corpses he passed on his way to negotiate with Saladin, he couldn't tell the Muslims from the Christians. The love story subplot of a Christian Arab soldier named Isa and Louise de Lusignan, a captive crusader knight of the Hospitallers, reinforces the film's argument that, while Jerusalem rightly belongs to the Arabs, the brotherhood of all "men" is possible as well.

See also: *Lawrence of Arabia*; *Nasser 56*

Aberth, John. "God (and the Studio) Wills It!: Crusade Films." In *A Knight at the Movies: Medieval History on Film*, 63–147. London: Routledge, 2003.

Fawal, Ibrahim. "*Al-Nasir Salah Al-Din (Saladin, 1963)*." In *Youssef Chahine: The Many Worlds of an Egyptian Director*, 158–63. London: BFI, 2001.

Halim, Hala. "The Signs of Saladin: A Modern Cinematic Rendition of Medieval Heroism." *Alif: Journal of Comparative Poetics* 12 (January 1992): 78–94.

Shafik, Viola. *Arab Cinema: History and Cultural Identity*. Cairo: American University in Cairo Press, 1998.

Sambizanga (1972) Sarah Maldoror; Angola/Congo; Portuguese with English subtitles; Color; 102 m; New Yorker Films (theatrical); Angola, early 1960s.

Sambizanga is based on the novel *The Real Life of Domingos Xavier* (1961), and some of the events of the film are reputed by author and political prisoner José Luandino Vieira to be true to his own experiences. Vieira was arrested in 1959 by the Portuguese secret police at a dam construction site in Luanda, Angola, suspected of association with the MPLA (Popular Movement for the Liberation of Angola). Using amateur actors, director Sarah Maldoror tells the fictional story of Domingos' torture and death in prison, the efforts of the MPLA underground on his behalf, and his wife Maria's quest to find out where he is incarcerated. *Sambizanga*'s focus on Maria has led to praise for the film's validation of women's role in the independence struggle; it has also garnered criticism for its too-romantic hue. Nevertheless, the film, while offering a passionate indictment of colonial brutality and repression, creates a fairly nuanced portrait of various characters, all of whom have a stake in the imprisonment of Domingos. Maria, Portuguese colonials, pro-Angolan Portuguese immigrants, members of the MPLA underground, and Angolan officials in the colonial administration represent the racial, class, and political roots of the colonial struggle. The film's title identifies the Luandan neighborhood from which the MPLA launched its first attacks on Angolan prisons in 1961, signaling the beginnings of the militant independence movement.

Gugler, Josef. "African Writing Projected onto the Screen: *Sambizanga, Xala,* and *Kongi's Harvest.*" *African Studies Review* 42(1) (April 1999): 79–104.
———. "*Sambizanga* (1972): The Martyr, His Family, and the Movement." In *African Film: Re-Imagining a Continent,* 51–56. Bloomington: Indiana University Press, 2003.
Moorman, Marissa. "Of Westerns, Women, and War: Re-Situating Angolan Cinema and the Nation." *Research in African Literatures* 32(3) (Fall 2001): 103–22.

Sansho the Bailiff / Sanshô dayû (1954) Kenji Mizoguchi; Japan; Japanese with English subtitles; Black and White; 120 m; Home Vision Entertainment (VHS); Japan, 11th century.

At once grounded in a realist portrayal of its eleventh-century milieu, and at the same time invoking its roots in Japanese legend, *Sansho the Bailiff* is a deeply humanist film that champions equality and compassion. It also provides a memorable introduction to the society of Heian-era Japan.

The story begins with the journey of a mother, her son, and her daughter to reunite with the family patriarch, a former governor who has been exiled for his unwillingness to commit more peasants to military service. Victimized by unscrupulous boatmen, the woman and children are separated. Tamaki remains for years a captive of a bailiff on Sado island, forced into prostitution. Son Zushio and daughter Anju are bought by the cruel Sansho, a bailiff whose extreme labor exploitation of the children and many other captives is unremitting.

One of the most interesting aspects of *Sansho the Bailiff*'s approach to history is its emphasis on the power of memory to transform lived experience. Much of the film is grim: Zushio, Anju, Tamaki, and many supporting characters suffer unmitigated oppression. They are branded if they try to escape Sansho, must perform long hours of labor in rice cultivation, spinning or weaving, and are condemned to providing sexual services for the nobles. There is little hope for escape. Yet the film intercuts the story of their exploitation with flashbacks to the period when the family was still united. These scenes find the characters using touchstones like songs, an heirloom, or the breaking of a branch of a tree, to rediscover their father's departing words: "Without mercy a man is like a beast. Be sympathetic to others. . . ."

Cavanaugh, Carole. "*Sanshô Dayû* and the Overthrow of History." In *Sanshô Dayû,* edited by Dudley Andrew and Carole Cavanaugh, 11–40. London: BFI, 2000.
Chion, Michel. "The Siren's Song." In *The Voice in Cinema,* 109–22. New York: Columbia University Press, 1999.
Ehrlich, Linda C. "The Name of the Child: Cinema as Social Critique." *Film Criticism* 14(2) (Winter 1989–90): 12–23.
Le Fanu, Mark. "The Great Triptych." In *Mizoguchi and Japan,* 49–67. London: BFI, 2005.

Sarraounia (1986) Med Hondo; Burkina Faso/Mauritania/France; Diola, Peul, and French with English subtitles; Color; 121 m; Spia Media (theatrical); Niger region, West Africa, late 19th century.

Based on the novel by Abdoulaye Mamani, *Sarraounia* is about the historical—and legendary—queen of the Aznas of Central Africa. Depicted as an expert archer, as well as a sorceress, Sarraounia leads the resistance against a French expedition launched from the French Sudan in 1898.

Armes, Roy, and Lizbeth Malkmus. *Arab and African Film Making*. London: Zed Books, 1991.

Petty, Sheila. "Black African Feminist Film-Making?" In *African Experiences of Cinema*, edited by Imruh Bakari and Mbye B. Cham, 185–93. London: BFI, 1996.

Pfaff, Françoise. "*Sarraounia*: An Epic of Resistance; Interview with Med Hondo." In *With Open Eyes: Women and African Cinema*, edited by Kenneth W. Harrow, 151–58. Amsterdam: Rodopi, 1997.

Tandina, Ousmane. "*Sarraounia*, an Epic?" *Research in African Literatures* 24(2) (Summer 1993): 28–50.

Spaas, Lieve. "Mauritania." In *The Francophone Film: A Struggle for Identity*, 209–14. Manchester: Manchester University Press, 2000.

Schindler's List (1993) Steven Spielberg; United States; English, Hebrew, German and Polish; Black and White with color segments; 194 m; Universal Studios Home Video (DVD, VHS); Poland and Czechoslovakia, 1939–1945.

Schindler's List is an icon of Holocaust films for popular audiences and is a primary imagistic and explanatory source for their understanding of Holocaust history. Analyzing the film is laden with difficulties arising from that status, as well as from the conceptual and political minefield that constitutes the terrain of discussion of Holocaust representation. Less pessimistically, *Schindler's List* is a wonderful study for analysts of historical films, because so many considered voices have weighed in on the subject, producing a wealth of literature on the film's relationship to history.

Director Spielberg, drawing his story from the novel by Thomas Keneally (which itself is based on documented events), has used many cinematic devices to reinforce the truth claims of his film, two examples being a black-and-white palette and a scene at the film's end in which some of the real-life survivors from Schindler's list make an appearance. The film also accomplishes the admirable feat of creating indelible scenes and images of the central events of the Holocaust, including the destruction of the Kraków ghetto, the terror and brutality in the labor camp at Plaszó, selection for deportation, and death in the Auschwitz gas chambers. At once teaching "what happened," and affirming audiences' sense of what "must have been," these images insist on their realism.

At the same time, there are other traits of the film that insist on the universality, not historical particularity, of some aspects of the story. Historical filmmakers are very often uninterested in close dissection of cause, instead tending toward making meaning of the past for their audiences. That meaning is often discovered in claims about universal traits of human behavior, which might point the way to humanity's potential for redemption from the most terrible of (historical) human action. Thus *Schindler's List*'s interest in the transformation of Oskar Schindler. Schindler is a (Czech-born) German businessman whose desire for profit leads him indirectly to a saving role for the Jews; it is their value to him in business transaction that first links him to their fate. Only later, as Eley and Grossman describe, "Schindler's moral agency is released...." The voracious and flawed Schindler, supported by a cohort, Jewish accountant Stern, performs an act of goodness.

Schindler's List has come to represent the history of the Holocaust, but the film itself, and Spielberg, do not claim this is the master narrative of the event. Although foregrounding the narrative of a powerful German businessman rescuing people victimized by a rationalized, and irrational, killing regime, the film is primarily about witnessing, testimony, the preservation of Holocaust memory, and the memorialization of its victims and survivors.

See also: *Border Street*; *Korczak*; *The Pianist*; *The Shop on Main Street*; *Sunshine*; *Transport from Paradise*

Bartov, Omer. "Spielberg's Oskar: Hollywood Tries Evil." In *Spielberg's Holocaust: Critical Perspectives on Schindler's List*, edited by Yosefa Loshitzky, 41–60. Bloomington: Indiana University Press, 1997.

Eley, Geoff, and Atina Grossmann. "Watching *Schindler's List*: Not the Last Word." *New German Critique* 71 (Spring/Summer 1997): 41–63.

Elsaesser, Thomas. "Subject Positions, Speaking Positions: From *Holocaust, Our Hitler,* and *Heimat* to *Shoah* and *Schindler's List*." In *The Persistence of History: Cinema, Television, and the Modern Event*, edited by Vivian Sobchack, 145–83. New York: Routledge, 1996.

Gilman, Sander L. " 'Smart Jews': From *The Caine Mutiny* to *Schindler's List* and Beyond." In *Screening the Past: Film and the Representation of History*, edited by Tony Barta, 63–81. Westport, CT: Praeger, 1998.

Goldstein, Phyllis. "Teaching *Schindler's List*." *Social Education* 6 (October 1995): 362–64.

Hansen, Miriam Bratu. "*Schindler's List* Is Not *Shoah*: The Second Commandment, Popular Modernism, and Public Memory." In *The Historical Film: History and Memory in Media*, edited by Marcia Landy, 201–17. Piscataway, NJ: Rutgers University Press, 2001.

Hartman, Geoffrey. "The Cinema Animal: On Spielberg's *Schindler's List*." *Salmagundi* (106–107) (Spring/Summer 1995): 127–43.

Manchel, Frank. "Mishegoss: *Schindler's List*, Holocaust Representation and Film History." *Historical Journal of Film, Radio and Television* (August 1998): 431–37.

———. "A Reel Witness: Steven Spielberg's Representation of the Holocaust in *Schindler's List*." *Journal of Modern History* 67 (March 1995): 83–100.

Rapaport, Lynn. "Hollywood's Holocaust: *Schindler's List* and the Construction of Memory." *Film & History: An Interdisciplinary Journal of Film and Television Studies* 32(1) (2002): 55–65.

Wildt, Michael. "The Invented and the Real: Historiographical Notes on *Schindler's List*." *History Workshop Journal* 41 (Spring 1996): 240–49.

Zelizer, Barbie. "Every Once in a While: *Schindler's List* and the Shaping of History." In *Spielberg's Holocaust: Critical Perspectives on Schindler's List*, edited by Yosefa Loshitzky, 18–40. Bloomington: Indiana University Press, 1997.

The Sealed Soil / Khak-e Sar Behmorh (1977) Marva Nabili; Iran; Farsi with English subtitles; Color; 90 m; World Artists Home Video (VHS); Iran, 1970s.

The rural family of an eighteen-year-old woman is challenged by her nonconformity to Islamic orthodoxy when she refuses to marry. Highly stylized in form, the film criticizes the oppression in prerevolutionary Iranian society from the perspective of the young woman's story.

Akrami, Jamsheed. "*The Sealed Soil* (1977)." In *Film and Politics in the Third World*, edited by John Downing, 143. New York: Praeger, 1987.

Seven Years in Tibet (1997) Jean-Jacques Annaud; United States; English, German, Mandarin, and Tibetan with English subtitles; Color; 139 m; Columbia/Tristar (DVD, VHS); Austria, India, and Tibet, 1935–1959.
   See *Kundun*.

The Seventh Seal / Det sjunde inseglet (1957) Ingmar Bergman; Sweden; Swedish with English subtitles; Black and White; 92 m; Criterion (DVD); Sweden, 14th century.
   This art cinema masterpiece revolves around the story of a philosophical medieval knight, Block, returning to Sweden with his squire, Jons. Block has lost his faith during the Crusades, and hopes to win a reprieve from Death if he can defeat him in a chess game. The ravages of the plague in Sweden provide a context for the urgency with which Block pursues answers to his questions about the reality of God. The searing images of the *The Seventh Seal*—which encompass the harsh, the grotesque, and the humorous—and its existential themes, have become archetypes of the meaning of the middle ages. This transposition of philosophical to historical meaning, concretized in a historical setting, is a common feature of medieval movies. As Lindley observes of *The Seventh Seal*, "we are looking at a version of the Middle Ages that has been carefully lifted out of historical sequence in order to serve as a mirror and an alienating device for viewing the mid-century present and/or the timeless present of parable."
   See also: *Kristin Lavransdatter*; *The Navigator: A Medieval Odyssey*

Aberth, John. "Welcome to the Apocalypse: Black Death Films." In *A Knight at the Movies: Medieval History on Film*, 197–255. London: Routledge, 2003.

Bragg, Melvyn. *The Seventh Seal*. London: BFI, 1993.

Lindley, Arthur. "The Ahistoricism of Medieval Film." *Screening the Past* 3 (May 29, 1998), http://www.latrobe.edu.au/screeningthepast/firstrelease/fir598/ALfr3a.htm (accessed May 30, 2006).

Pressler, Michael. "The Idea Fused in the Fact: Bergman and *The Seventh Seal*." *Literature/Film Quarterly* 13(2) (1985): 95–101.

Williams, David John. "Looking at the Middle Ages in the Cinema: An Overview." *Film & History: An Interdisciplinary Journal of Film and Television Studies* 29(1–2) (1999): 8–19.

Woods, William F. "Authenticating Realism in the Medieval Film." In *The Medieval Hero on Screen: Representations from Beowulf to Buffy*, edited by Martha W. Driver and Sid Ray, 38–51. Jefferson, NC: McFarland, 2004.

The Shop on Main Street / Obchod na korze (1965) Ján Kadár and Elmar Klos; Czechoslovakia; Slovak, Czech, and German with English subtitles; Black and White; 128 m; Facets (DVD; VHS); Slovak Republic, 1941–1942.
   This is the tragicomic tale of a naive Slovakian carpenter named Tono whose Nazi brother-in-law bestows upon him the rights as "temporary administrator" of a Jewish widow's sewing supplies shop. Tono agrees to an elaborate ruse, concocted by her local protectors from the town's Jewish community, that will shield Mrs. Lautmann from the knowledge that her shop is effectively no longer hers. Developing a friendship with the aged proprietress, Tono must confront his

weakness and indecision when the Nazis begin to enact their plans to deport the town's Jews.

See also: *The Boat Is Full; Border Street*

Saperstein, Jeffrey. "'All Men Are Jews': Tragic Transcendence in Kadar's *The Shop on Main Street." Literature/Film Quarterly* 19(4) (1991): 247–51.

The Siberiade / Sibiriada (1979) Andrei Konchalovsky; Soviet Union; Russian with English subtitles; Color; 206 m; Ruscico (DVD), Kino (VHS); Siberia, 1909 to the 1960s.

The Solomins and the Ustyuzhanins are families from the small, isolated village Elan in Western Siberia. The families—one aristocratic, the other peasant—enjoy a long-standing feud, somewhat theatrically try to avoid intermarriage, and become embroiled in a murder. Three generations of the Solomins and Ustyuzhanins are the centerpiece of *Siberiade*, an epic historical film in several respects. Its story spans much of the twentieth century, combines the historical and mythic in grand proportions, has vivid and memorable characters, and supports "big" themes like nature vs. technology and the state vs. the individual. Above all, the epic scale of this boisterous and ambitious film is found in the landscape of Siberia, a place whose vast forests, dramatic change of seasons, and impenetrability can overwhelm the human and intimate scale of a village.

Time in *Siberiade* is marked by several devices. The most obvious markers are intertitles that rely upon familiar historical periodization, to which are attached a specific character's experience. Thus while we begin with "Early Twentieth Century," more intimate titles such as "Anastasia: The Twenties" or "Alexei, son of Nikolai, the 1950s" soon appear. The passage of time is also carved out of the taiga, as clearing for a road to civilization is accomplished, first through the manual labor of "Pa" Ustyuzhanin and later the work of machines. In all cases, time in *Siberiade* is something that seems inevitably to change the natural and human landscape. And the change is beholden to human activity, whether the conquest of the forest, or of the oil riches beneath the land, or the loss of life in the wars, or the ambitions of politicians and technocrats.

Siberiade also, perhaps reassuringly, provides evidence of timelessness in human experience. The most overt example is in the sustained treatment of the spirits that embody the fir trees that "weep" for their dead sisters, and the "Devil's Patch," swamplands that in one memorable scene devour a caterpillar tractor. Another example is the man who lives in time, but is also known as "Eternal Grandad" and makes appearances after his death to interact with the living. Even the village itself survives the explosion of an oil rig by the film's end. There is also a kind of cheerfulness, a spirited and raucous celebration of life in the tone of *Siberiade*, that provides a wonderful counterpoint to the apparently destructive effects of modernization.

The tensions of timelessness and time are perhaps best captured in the relationship of villagers to events that constitute the grand narrative of Russian history. Revolution, war, and the building of the socialist state are all in one way central events for these Siberians: Taya vows to wait her whole life until Alexei returns from the war against the Nazis, and Filka, now a Deputy with the Supreme Soviet, must bring news home that a planned dam/reservoir system will flood the (yet unchanged) village.

Early in the film, an escaped convict, devoted to revolution, is evading the authorities by hiding in the village. When he is finally apprehended, he reassures Kolya, the young member of the Ustyuzhanins: "Someday things will be great. Be patient. . . ." If one wishes to interpret this as a hopeful, not ironic, claim of the film, then *Siberiade*'s story of the twentieth century is only the fledgling episode of an even grander narrative of time and generational experience.

See also: *The Family* (Scola); *Heimat*; *Sunshine*

Dunlop, John B. "Andrei Mikhalkov-Konchalovsky's *Siberiade*." In *The Red Screen: Politics, Society, Art in Soviet Cinema*, edited by Anna Lawton, 235–38. London: Routledge, 1992.

Jaehne, Karen. "Rehabilitating the Superfluous Man: Films in the Life of Nikita Mikhalkov." *Film Quarterly* 34(4) (1981): 14–20.

Johnson, Vida T. "The Nature-Technology Conflict in Soviet Film: A Comparison of *Siberiade* and *Farewell*." *Studies in Comparative Communism* 21 (Fall/Winter 1988): 341–47.

Menashe, Louis. "Buttons, Buttons, Who's Got the Workers? A Note on the (Missing) Working Class in Late and Post-Soviet Russian Cinema." *International Labor and Working-Class History* 59 (Spring 2001): 52–59.

Youngblood, Denise J. "The Cosmopolitan and the Patriot: The Brothers Mikhalkov-Konchalovsky and Russian Cinema." *Historical Journal of Film, Radio and Television* 23(1) (2003): 27–42.

Silences of the Palace / Saimt el qusur (1994) Moufida Tlatli; France/Tunisia; Arabic and French with English subtitles; Color; 127 m; Capitol Entertainment (VHS); Tunisia, early 1950s.

Silences of the Palace takes us into the cloistered, isolated world of the women who reside in Tunisia's Bey compounds in the twilight of the French colonial period. The film is remarkable for its evocation of the fellowship these women of the kitchen forge in the face of their subordination, fear, and almost complete lack of control. The film's portrait of the experience of householders is fractured, painted from the memories of the character of a young woman who had left the confines some 10 years earlier and has returned on the occasion of her father's death. A series of extended flashbacks are triggered by her encounter with the people and landmarks of the estate. Viewers are privy to news of the impending political change—with its social implications—sweeping Tunisia outside compound walls. Radio broadcasts and occasional outside forays of a male member of the household staff allow filtered information for village women and film viewers alike.

See also: *Ramparts of Clay*

Armes, Roy. "A New Future Begins: *Silences of the Palace* (1994)." In *Postcolonial Images: Studies in North African Film*, 159–68. Bloomington: Indiana University Press, 2005.

Valassopoulos, Anastasia. "*The Silences of the Palace* and the Anxiety of Musical Creation." In *Movie Music, the Film Reader*, edited by Kay Dickinson, 99–108. London: Routledge, 2003.

A Single Spark / Jeon tae-il (1996) Park Kwang-su; South Korea; Korean with English subtitles; Color, Black and White; 93 m; Tai Seng (VHS); South Korea, 1960s and 1970s.

In this damning interpretation of social and political oppression, a fictional journalist named Kim Yong-su is writing a book about the life and death of real Korean labor activist Jeon Tae Il, but must hide from the authorities to complete his unauthorized research. Using black-and-white flashbacks to dramatize Jeon Tae Il's story of the late 1960s, and color flashbacks to Kim's investigations in 1975, the film suggests Kim's increasing identification with Jeon's story and the blurring of the lines of their experience.

Joo, Jinsook, Han Ju Kwak, and Eungjun Min. "*A Single Spark* (1995): Resistance as Memory." In *Korean Film: History, Resistance, and Democratic Imagination*, 124–31. Westport, CT: Praeger, 2003.

Kim, Kyung Hyun. "Post-Trauma and Historical Remembrance in Recent South Korean Cinema: Reading Park Kwang-Su's *A Single Spark* (1955) and Chang Son-U's *A Petal*." *Cinema Journal* 41(4) (Summer 2002): 95–115.

Park, Seung Hyun. "The Memory of Labor Oppression in Korean Cinema: The Death of a Young Worker in *Single Spark* (1995)." *Asian Cinema: a Publication of the Asian Cinema Studies Society* 11(2) (2000): 10–23.

Soleil O (1970) Med Hondo; Mauritania/France; French with English subtitles; Color; 105 m; New Yorker Films (theatrical); Africa and France, historical and contemporary.

Soleil O is about the experience of African immigrants in France, ostensibly conveyed through the story of one man. Stitched loosely together with voiceover narrative, the film serves up a collage of images, scenes, and camera perspectives—some of which enter a symbolic dream state—to convey a story of unemployment, racial discrimination, poverty, and forced transience.

Cottenet-Hage, Madeleine. "*Soleil O* and the Cinema of Med Hondo." In *Cinema, Colonialism, Postcolonialism: Perspectives from the French and Francophone World*, edited by Dina Sherzer, 173–87. Austin: University of Texas Press, 1996.

Pfaff, Françoise. "Films of Med Hondo: An African Filmmaker in Paris." *Jump Cut: A Review of Contemporary Media* 31 (March 1986): 44–6.

Song of Chile / Cantata de Chile (1976) Humberto Solás; Cuba; Spanish with English subtitles; Color; 119 m; Tricontinental Film Center (theatrical); Chile, 16th–20th centuries.

Song of Chile is a highly stylized, nonlinear and nonnarrative film. It engages the 1907 Iquique Massacre of striking nitrate miners as its starting point for a commentary on the history of Chile since the sixteenth-century Araucanian uprising against Spanish rule.

See also: *Letters from Marusia*

Burton, Julianne, and Marta Alvear. "Interview with Humberto Solás: 'Every Point of Arrival Is a Point of Departure'." *Jump Cut: A Review of Contemporary Media* 19 (December 1978): 32–33.

Schwartz, Ronald. "*Cantata De Chile (Song of Chile)*." In *Latin American Films, 1932–1994: A Critical Filmography*, 56–57. Jefferson, NC: McFarland, 1997.

Sorceress / Le Moine et la sorcière (1987) Suzanne Schiffman; France; French with English subtitles; Color; 97 m; Mystic Fire Video (VHS); France, 13th century.

Sorceress is particularly useful for students of medieval history who are interested in the historical coexistence of folk belief and institutionalized (Roman) Christianity, as well as the tensions between peasant culture and patriarchal and aristocratic society. Screenwriter Pamela Berger, an art historian, has drawn here from the account of one of the first Christian Inquisitors, a thirteenth-century Dominican friar named Etienne de Bourbon, who actively worked to fulfill Pope Gregory IX's order of the 1230s to extinguish the Albigensian heresy.

After an opening scene that enacts the origins of a small French village's patron saint, Guinefort, Etienne arrives, seeking out religious heretics. The local curé, who describes the determined friar as having "the eyes of a bat," says, "My people are as pious as they are poor. You'll find nothing here." The curé, we come to realize, also defends peasants' cultural practices, for example allowing such "pagan" rituals as a spring fertility rite to incorporate the icon of St. Christopher. Villagers, busy clearing land for cultivation, are similarly disinterested in Etienne's quest. They are instead seeking ways to defend what they consider their rights to land and water sources increasingly monopolized by the local noble. One woman denounces the Count to Etienne, suggesting his flooding of a nearby field in order to stock fish constitutes heresy. The friar protests that the noble can do what he wants with his land; he's not a heretic. The peasant woman disagrees; her concept of heresy is the violation of rights embodied in humans' belonging to the natural world: "He can't steal our right to sow the seed," she says. "Like the rain or the sun, it can't be taken." The French medieval peasants' animism, and their socioeconomic status, finds them out of step with the development of institutionalized Christianity, and the property rights of the elite. When Etienne meets Elda, the local "forest woman" who is adept at natural healing practices, he believes he has found his heretic. The triumvirate theme of historical female, class, and religious oppression is now ready to play out in the events of the film.

Sorceress doesn't tend to develop empathetic characters to draw audiences into the fate of Elda, or Etienne. It is more a drama of ideas, with events, and much dialogue, that buttress these. But these ideas about peasant and elite culture in the thirteenth century are clearly delineated, and evocatively suggested in the carefully authenticated *mise en scène*.

Feminism, patriarchy, loss of connection to nature—these appear in *Sorceress* as historical, but also timeless, concerns. Inescapably, as it seems for historical films, it is twentieth-century preoccupations that shape those voiced for the past. As Ed Benson states so succinctly: "The modern practice of history hides a contradiction between the urgency of our search for a usable past on the one hand and its irreducible alterity on the other." *Sorceress'* contradictions are fascinating for anyone interested in medieval commoners—and those modern artists and academics who are trying to understand them. Even our wise curé knew the lessons, however, would be ultimately impenetrable. Describing what he expected of Etienne's final report, he says: "Well ordered. Divided into parts . . . and parts within parts. . . . And when men read it, they'll never know what really happened."

See also: *Kristin Lavransdatter*; *The Navigator: A Medieval Odyssey*; *The Return of Martin Guerre*

Anderson, K. "Review of *Le Moine Et La Sorcière*." *American Historical Review* 94 (October 1989): 1037–39.

Benson, Ed. "Culture Wars Medieval and Modern in *Le Moine Et La Sorcière*." *Film & History: An Interdisciplinary Journal of Film and Television Studies* 29(1–2) (1999): 56–70.

Jackson, Lynne, and Susan Jhirad. "*Sorceress*: Interview with Pamela Berger." *Cineaste* 16(4) (1988): 45.

The Sparrow / Al-Usfur (1972) Youssef Chahine; Egypt/Algeria; Arabic with English subtitles; Color; 105 m; Facets (VHS); Egypt, 1967.

Banned by the Sadat government, *The Sparrow* is about the Six Day War of 1967. While the film is set during the conflict, there are no battle scenes. Instead, the Voice of the Arabs radio broadcasts narrate—and in some cases fabricate—the course of events, in the background. In the foreground, several interrelated stories of its listeners, ordinary Egyptians at the time of the crisis, highlight the argument that behind the veneer of national exuberance was a reality exposed with Egypt's losses: poverty, powerlessness, corruption, a lack of freedom, and stalled reforms.

Fawal, Ibrahim. "*Al-Usfur (The Sparrow, 1973)*." In *Youssef Chahine: The Many Worlds of an Egyptian Director*, 96–107. London: BFI, 2001.
Shafik, Viola. *Arab Cinema: History and Cultural Identity*. Cairo: American University in Cairo Press, 1998.

Spices / Mirch Masala (1985) Ketan Mehta; United Kingdom/India; Hindi with English subtitles; Color; 128 m; Facets (VHS); India, 1940s.

Spices has a memorable plot that probes historical relations of power in colonial India without the presence of a single British character. Its setting is a picturesque western Indian seaside community whose main economic activity is the cultivation of red chili peppers and their refinement and sale as hot chili powder. The social setting and village characters are well drawn, if simplistic. The comfortably wealthy chief enjoys the bed of his mistress more than his wife. The schoolteacher, a Gandhi follower, is the subject of gentle derision from the idle and gossipy village men. The local spice factory owner is anxious to make his profits.

The central character, Sonbai, is a married and childless woman whose ecstatic husband has just received a job with the railway and has gone to establish their new life beyond the village. She represents the shifting norms of social life and customs in the village. Sonbai's nemesis—indeed the village's—is the local *Subedar*, the Indian tax collector whose work for the British colonial administration makes him the beneficiary of status, wealth, and power. Sonbai is willing to defend her traditional honor against the *Subedar*'s sexual advances, and in doing so, draws female coworkers at the spice factory into an assertion of their independence from the dictates of patriarchal and colonial authority.

See also: *Distant Thunder; Emitai; The Home and the World*

Das Dasgupta, Shamita. "Feminist Consciousness in Woman-Centered Hindi Films." *Journal of Popular Culture* 30(1) (Summer 1996): 173–89.
Singer, Wendy. "Review of *Mirch Masala*." *American Historical Review* 97(4) (1992): 1148–50.

Spinning Wheel / Mulleya Mulleya (1984) Lee Doo-yong; South Korea; Korean; Color; 100 m; no current; Korea, 15th century.

Spinning Wheel is an almost unrelentingly violent film. The setting is fifteenth-century Korea, in the period of the Chosun Dynasty (1392–1910). The fictional protagonist, Gil-rye, enters into the noble Kim family through a posthumous marriage to their son. Forced into an extended period of mourning as is her duty, Gil-rye suffers terrible subjugation and violence, including rape. The film had a polarized reception, with some critics objecting to its sensationalist and exploitative approach, and others praising its honest depiction of Confucian patriarchy.

Wilson, Rob. "Filming 'New Seoul': Melodramatic Constructions of the Subject in *Spinning Wheel* and *First Son*." *East-West Film Journal* 5(1) (1991): 107–17.

Wilson, Rob. "Melodramas of Korean National Identity: From *Mandala* to *Black Republic*." In *Colonialism and Nationalism in Asian Cinema*, edited by Wimal Dissanayake, 90–104. Bloomington: Indiana University Press, 1994.

St. Michael Had a Rooster / San Michele aveva un gallo (1971) Paolo and Vittorio Taviani; Italy; Italian with English subtitles; Color; 87 m; Facets (DVD); Fox Lorber (VHS); Italy, 1870.

Allegorical in style, *St. Michael* invents the character of Giulio Manieri, a somewhat hapless anarchist whose gesture of redistributing the grain stores of a small Italian village among the peasants is not met with the support he expects. After his release from prison Manieri's disillusionment grows when he discovers his former comrades have become indifferent to revolutionary action.

See also: *The Organizer*

Liehm, Mira. "Under the Sign of Violence." In *Passion and Defiance: Film in Italy from 1942 to the Present*, 307–18. Berkeley, CA: University of California Press, 1986.

Testa, Carlo. "Democratization and Conflict (1963-1973)." In *Italian Cinema and Modern European Literatures 1945–2000*, 47–78. Greenwood, CT: Praeger, 2002.

Stalingrad (1993) Joseph Vilsmaier; Germany/Sweden; German and Russian with English subtitles; Color; 134 m; Fox Lorber (DVD, VHS); Soviet Union, 1942–1943.

The final image of Joseph Vilsmaier's film shows two German soldiers huddled together on a snowy Russian plain, dead from cold, exhaustion, wounds, and hunger. The main characters, disillusioned Lieutenant Witzland and the ironic Reiser, were the last alive of a group of ten featured in this story of a German battalion's experience in Stalingrad in 1942–1943. Viewer's hopes for a possibly triumphant ending for at least one member of the group are dashed with the deaths of both Witzland and Reiser in a bid to escape surrender to the Russians. This categorical conclusion suggests *Stalingrad*'s theme of the completely unredeeming nature of the German invasion of Russia, and its complete victimization of common German soldiers.

Critical debate about whether *Stalingrad* is about that Second World War event, or about the futility of war in general, is consistent with historical feature films' tendency to address both particular and universal subjects at the same time. Suffice it to say that Vilsmaier's work, released in newly unified Germany on the occasion of the fiftieth anniversary of the battle for Stalingrad, is characterized by some very familiar attributes of many modern war films. These include emphasis on a band of "ordinary" men whose camaraderie distinguishes their experience, tensions between the officer corps and the infantry over behavior and strategy, extreme physical and psychological hardship, and the increasingly anarchic character of individual behavior as the command structure breaks down.

But if one accepts that *Stalingrad* reconstructs a specific event in military history, then Vilsmaier's interpretation goes as follows: The invasion of Russia was poorly conceived and executed. Ordinary soldiers and many members of the officer corps were not ideological Nazis, but nevertheless worked to fulfill their patriotic duty or the requirements of their work as soldiers. This argument of the normalcy of ordinary soldiers is extended to the presentation of their lives in Nazi Germany before the war. With letters arriving from loved ones at home, the bunkered battalion members reminisce about their favorite pastimes back home, none of which refer to the Nazi movement at all.

See also: *Enemy at the Gates*

Graffy, Julian. "Review of *Stalingrad*." *Sight & Sound* 4 (May 1994): 55–56.

Menashe, Louis. "*Stalingrad*." *Cineaste* 23(2) (1997): 50–51.

Ward, James J. "Remembering World War II: The Differing Reception Histories of Steven Spielberg's *Saving Private Ryan* and Joseph Vilsmaier's *Stalingrad*." *Film & History: An Interdisciplinary Journal of Film and Television Studies* CD-ROM Annual (2000).

The Story of Qiu Ju / Qiu Ju daguansi (1992) Zhang Yimou; China/Hong Kong; Mandarin with English subtitles; Color; 110 m; Facets (DVD), Columbia/Tristar (VHS); China, 1980s.

The Story of Qiu Ju is about a Chinese peasant woman's search for justice on behalf of her husband. The film follows the pregnant Qiu Ju in her fight through several levels of bureaucracy when husband Wan Qinglai is insulted and kicked by village chief Wang. Adapted from Chen Yuanbin's novel *The Wan Family's Lawsuit*, this is a deceptively simply tale with a memorable protagonist. The film introduces many dimensions of Chinese society in the post-Mao era, including the relationship between city and country, gender roles and family structure, the standard of living, and the role of the Public Security Bureau in everyday life.

Anagnost, Ann S. "Chili Pepper Politics." In *National Past-Times: Narrative, Representation, and Power in Modern China*, 138–60. Durham, NC: Duke University Press, 1997.

Silbergeld, Jerome. "A Farewell to Arts: Allegory Goes to the Movies (*Farewell My Concubine* and *The Story of Qiu Ju*)." In *China into Film: Frames of Reference in Contemporary Chinese Cinema*, 96–131. London: Reaktion Books, 1999.

Young, John Dragon. "Review of *The Story of Qiu Ju*." *American Historical Review* 98(4) (October 1993): 1158–61.

The Story of Women / Une affaire de Femmes (1988) Claude Chabrol; France; French with English subtitles; Color; 108 m; New Yorker Video (DVD, VHS); Vichy France, WWII.

Based loosely on the life of the last woman guillotined in France, Marie Louise Giraud, this is the story of a working-class wife and mother in Vichy France who performs abortions and provides rooms for prostitutes. Intensely tired and unhappy as she cares for her two young children during her husband's absence at a prison camp, Marie reports, "I've been a slave since I was fourteen." The remarkable performance of Isabelle Huppert as the inscrutable Marie reinforces the film's lack of pretense or melodrama.

Scullion, Rosemarie. "Family Fictions and Reproductive Realities in Vichy France: Claude Chabrol's *Une Affaire De Femmes*." In *Identity Papers: Contested Nationhood in Twentieth-Century France*, edited by Steven Ungar and Tom Conley, 156–77. Minneapolis, MN: University of Minnesota Press, 1996.

The Sun-Seekers / Sonnensucher (1958/1972) Konrad Wolf; East Germany; German and Russian with English subtitles; Black and White; 110 m; DEFA Film Library (DVD); East Germany, 1950s.

Completed in 1958 but only later released in the Honecker regime of the GDR in 1972, *The Sun-Seekers* is an excellent start for those interested in discovering aspects of the Eastern bloc experience in the early Cold War. Workers and managers at the Wismut uranium mine are a colorful crew of men and women, including former POWs and Nazis, Soviet-trained technocrats, and those doing prison labor. The film's protagonist, a young woman named Lutz, has effectively arrived at Wismut through her escape from abuse and poverty back home. Working-class camaraderie, sexual exploitation, and tensions between Soviets and Germans are explored in this episodic narrative that ultimately exalts the heroism and progressiveness of the workers. As the opening scroll of the 1972 release version says, "And who recalls today how socialism started for us? . . . This is how we began, and how we became."

See also: *The Gleiwitz Case*

Coulson, Anthony S. "Paths of Discovery: The Films of Konrad Wolf." In *DEFA: East German Cinema, 1946–1992*, edited by Seán Allan and John Sandford, 164–82. New York: Berghahn, 1999.

Silberman, Marc. "Remembering History: The Filmmaker Konrad Wolf." *New German Critique* 49 (Winter 1990): 163–91.

Sunshine / A napfény íze (1999) István Szabó; Germany/Canada/Hungary/Austria; English; Color, Black and White; 180 m; Paramount Home Entertainment (DVD, VHS); Hungary, late 19th century to 1989.

"Politics has made a mess of our lives. But still, life was beautiful," says an elderly Valerie Sors in the aftermath of the 1956 Hungarian Uprising and decades of upheaval experienced by herself, her family, and her country.

Sunshine narrates the story of the (eventful) lives of three generations of Valerie's Jewish-Hungarian Sonnenschein family. The private lives of its main characters are somewhat breathlessly established in set pieces of harmonious or troubled family dinners or love relationships. Valerie alone survives each era and is the constant touchstone of the nineteenth-century roots of the family. Ignaz, Adam, and Ivan are the successive, descendent male Sonnenscheins who represent family fortunes in each generation.

Sunshine presents historical experience as only partly determined by individuals' choices or calculations. Powerful forces of ideology, often joined in an unholy alliance with personal aggrandizement, inflict almost random harm. The film condemns several evils for which prosperous, liberal Hungarian Jews were the crucible: the conservative elitism of the Austro-Hungarian empire, the fanaticism of fascism, and the paranoia of communism. The film condemns those who "turned ideals into crimes"; morality must supersede politics.

Valerie concludes that the purpose of life is "Life itself. That we are here. A long time ago we were happy." Yet director Szabó is interested in the redemptive power of moral behavior more than survival. In each of the film's historical eras, the three main male protagonists—all memorably portrayed by Ralph Fiennes—face terrible ethical dilemmas, and sometimes adopt compromising positions in the face of these. Ignaz assimilates by changing his name to Sors (Hungarian for "fate"). Adam converts to Catholicism to smooth his admittance to the national fencing team. In 1956, Ivan quits the police and joins the uprising against Soviet domination. In 1989 he is finally free. Readopting the Sonnenschein name, he can reap the rewards of his opposition to oppression.

This family epic adopts a generalized explanation for the nature of the political regimes governing Hungary for a century, but *Sunshine* excels in relating through effective performances and a cumulative narrative the historical experience of one family.

See also: *The Family* (Scola); *Heimat*; *Siberiade*

Portuges, Catherine. "Review of *Sunshine*." *American Historical Review* 105(2) (April 2000): 656–67.

Suleiman, Susan Rubin. "Central Europe, Jewish Family History, and *Sunshine*." In *Comparative Central European Culture*, edited by Steven Tötösy de Zepetnek, 169–88. West Lafayette, IN: Purdue University Press, 2002.

———. "Jewish Assimilation in Hungary, the Holocaust, and Epic Film: Reflections on István Szabó's *Sunshine*." *Yale Journal of Criticism* 14(1) (2001): 233–52.

Warchol, Tomasz. "Patterns of Central European Experience in István Szabó's Trilogy and *Sunshine*." *Social Identities* 7(4) (2001): 659–75.

Swing Kids (1993) Thomas Carter; United States; English; Color; 112 m; Buena Vista Home Entertainment (DVD, VHS), Hollywood Pictures (VHS); Germany, 1930s.

Swing Kids is set in National Socialist Germany, and revolves around the friendship of Peter, Thomas, and Arvid, members of the underground "swing" movement. Tensions arise as the boys develop individual responses to Nazi expectations of youth conformity, including membership in the Hitler Youth.

One can only imagine the earnest—or cynical—discovery by the creators of *Swing Kids* that the story of the "swing" movement in the Third Reich would be the perfect subject for a popular film. What could be more appealing than a story set in the archetypically oppressive Third Reich, where generic themes of complicity and resistance, or friendship and loyalty, could be played out in the context of romance and suspense? To top it all off, grand spectacle in the form of energetic swing dance scenes in a grand old Hamburg hall would surely appeal.

Swing Kids mines these elements to create a kind of textbook study of Hollywood film conventions. In the process, the film devises a grossly simplistic argument about the antidote to totalitarianism: stand up for what's right. As Arvid, who will soon martyr himself to his principles in a suicide, says, ". . . anytime you go along with them it just makes it easier for them." It is doubtful that *Swing Kids* directs Arvid's statement at analysis of how the Nazis maintained their control of Germany in the 1930s. Like so many popular historical films, its message is an ideological one designed for the audiences of today.

See also: *Europa, Europa*

Schulte-Sasse, Linda. "Introduction." In *Entertaining the Third Reich: Illusions of Wholeness in Nazi Cinema*, 1–16. Durham, NC: Duke University Press, 1996.

Taira Clan Saga / Tales of the Taira Clan / Shin Heike monogatari (1955) Kenji Mizoguchi; Japan; Japanese with English subtitles; Color; 108 m; Facets (DVD; VHS); Japan, 12th century.

This Mizoguchi film, set in 1137, is based on the historical novel by Eiji Yoshikawa, *The Heike Story* (which itself is drawn from the anonymous chronicle known as *Heike monogatari*.) The film revolves around Kiyomori, of the Taira clan of swordsmen. He is loyal to the Cloistered Emperor Toba and must either reconcile himself to, or defeat, the influence of the Hiei monks of the court, as well as his father Tadamori's submissive stance to the courtiers. This is a character study, and a portrait of the politics of an era when the samurai were on the cusp of achieving dominance in the social and political hierarchy of Japan.

See also: *Gate of Hell; Rashomon*

Le Fanu, Mark. "Visions of History." In *Mizoguchi and Japan*, 97–127. London: BFI, 2005.

The Terrorist (1998) Santosh Sivan; India; Tamil with English subtitles; Color; 95 m; Facets (DVD; VHS); India, 1990s.

We first encounter the character of a fictional Tamil girl who is recruited as a terrorist and assigned the task of assassinating a high-ranking Indian politician, in a guerilla camp in the jungle. Expertly dispatching a traitor with a machine gun, she then stares straight into the camera and says, "Malli. Nineteen years old. Thirty successful operations completed."

Words are spare in *The Terrorist*; the beautiful images produced by cinematographer-turned director Santosh Sivan, especially close-ups of Malli's face, often substitute for dialogue. But Malli's introduction frames much of the point of the film. Malli is defined by her actions, and little explanation of how she has come to be an assassin is provided, either overtly or elliptically. Her duty to the cause of Tamil independence from Sri Lanka is paramount and once that is established *The Terrorist* concentrates on studying the psychological impact of the imminence of death for Malli, the suicide bomber.

See also: *The Battle of Algiers; Marianne and Juliane; Welcome to Canada*

Morton, Stephen. "The Unhappy Marriage of "Third World" Women's Movements and Orientalism." In *After Orientalism: Critical Entanglements, Productive Looks*, edited by Inge E. Boer, 165–81. Amsterdam: Rodopi, 2003.

Rao, Maithili. "*The Terrorist.*" *Cinemaya: The Asian Film Quarterly* 42 (Winter 1998): 22–23.

Willis, Holly. "*The Terrorist.*" *American Cinematographer* 80 (April 1999): 111–13.

Teutonic Knights / Knights of the Teutonic Order / Krzyżazy (1960) Aleksander Ford; Poland; Polish with English subtitles; Color; 166 m; Second Run, UK (DVD); Poland, 15th century.

This epic war spectacle chronicles the Battle of Grunwald, where in 1410 the army of the Germanic Teutonic Knights was defeated by the allied Kingdom of Poland and Grand Duchy of Lithuania. *Teutonic Knights* is based on the popular 1900 novel by Henryk Sienkiewicz.

See also: *Alexander Nevsky*

Aberth, John. "God (and the Studio) Wills It!: Crusade Films." In *A Knight at the Movies: Medieval History on Film*, 63–147. London: Routledge, 2003.

Those Whom Death Refused / Mortu Nega (1988) Flora Gomes; Guinea-Bissau; Criolo with English subtitles; Color; 85 m; California Newsreel (VHS); Guinea-Bissau, 1973–1975.

During an adult literacy class in a small village in postcolonial Guinea-Bissau, the lesson is on the word "struggle." The teacher asks his students—all of whom endured in one way or another the now concluded 10-year independence fight against colonial Portugal—"is the struggle over?" One woman answers that the struggle to feed her family in the midst of a terrible drought and the effects of wartime disruption of the harvest continues. For Sako, a former member of the guerilla forces, who now suffers from a serious foot wound caused by a landmine, the answer comes with a wry and knowing smile: "No," he says.

The theme of the challenges of postindependence reconstruction and reconciliation is paramount in Flora Gomes' beautiful story of Diminga and Sako, a married couple who are adjusting to the return to their village home, and civilian life, after years of living as guerillas. The film begins in the very late stages of the war against the "colonial criminals." It is January 1973, only weeks before the assassination of Amílcar Cabral, leader of the movement against colonial rule in Portuguese New Guinea. Scenes of the long and dangerous trek of a group transporting arms to a guerilla base camp begin the film. At the camp, rebels learn by radio of Cabral's death. The significance of the decisive Battle of Komo is symbolized in the scene of Diminga and other women feeling free to spread their laundry to dry in the sun, no longer worried that Portuguese helicopters will discover the bright colors of the fabric as a sign of rebel activity.

Soon, Diminga returns to her home village, and now, despite an absence of 10 years, she must resume cultivation of her field and a normal civilian life. But this postwar and postcolonial adjustment will be fraught with struggle. Despite the socialist ruling party's attempts to institute central planning, the development of a black market for state-supplied rice, oil, and soap causes tensions among villagers. A drought poses a serious threat of famine. Even some old comrades of Sako's, enjoying desk jobs for the government in Bissau, refuse to become involved in his serious medical problems. When Sako—seeking treatment at the hospital in Bissau—asks Diminga to find help, she finds his now-bureaucrat friend refuses to acknowledge to Diminga any memory of the man he fought beside for years.

Gomes' reconstruction of 1970s Guinea-Bissau history emphasizes the centrality of women to the history of the period. Women like Diminga joined the guerillas, in the process seeing their children die in the dangerous conditions. Women like Diminga also remained in family villages, struggling to raise children, grow crops, and defend their property—all in the absence of village men who were away fighting. By film's end, Diminga and other village women decide that the ongoing problems with drought and corruption demand the invocation of a traditional rite. Their organization of this ceremony of ancestors is an example of the power of their collective action, and the catalyst for their greater unity, as well as rainfall. *Those Whom Death Refused* ends on this hopeful note, children of the village joyously welcoming the rain as they had earlier greeted the end of the war.

See also: *Flame*

Dhada, Mustafah. "Review of *Mortu Nega*." *Visual Anthropology Review* 14(2) (Fall/Winter 1998–1999): 109–11.

Ukadike, N. Frank. "In Guinea-Bissau, Cinema Trickles Down: An Interview with Flora Gomes." *Research in African Literatures* 26(3) (1995): 179–85.

The Tiger from Tjampa / Harimau Tjampa (1953) D. Djayakusuma; Indonesia; Indonesian with English subtitles; Black and White; 97 m; Between Three Worlds Video (VHS); West Sumatra, Indonesia, 1930s.

"What suffering life is!" sings an (unseen) male chorus in *The Tiger from Tjampa*. Set in West Sumatra in the 1930s, the film follows the character of Lukman, a young man who studies the traditional self-defense form called *pencak silat* with a master of the art. Lukman wants to avenge the death of his father by confronting the man who is responsible, Datuk Langit. Datuk is himself adept at *pencak silat*. He is also an avaricious and insensitive head of the local government, whose unwillingness to forgive or reduce rice tax payments earns him the hatred of many locals.

While *The Tiger from Tjampa* is told, in entertaining fashion, as a ballad-like fable, it has also been lauded as an impeccable depiction of many aspects of the traditional culture and society of the Minangkabau people of West Sumatra.

Van der Heide, William. *Malaysian Cinema, Asian Film: Border Crossings and National Cultures*. Amsterdam: Amsterdam University Press, 2002.

Time Bandits (1981) Terry Gilliam; United Kingdom; English; Color; 110 m; Criterion (DVD), Anchor Bay Entertainment (VHS); Napoleonic Italy, Medieval England, Ancient Greece, and others.

A young English boy is reluctant assistant to a band of time-traveling robbers whose special map allows them to steal from the likes of Napoleon and Agamemnon. This wonderful comedy-fantasy engages and parodies stereotypes of Western historical and mythic figures.

See also: *The Navigator: A Medieval Odyssey*

Von Gunden, Kenneth. "*Time Bandits*: Child as Hero." In *Flights of Fancy: The Great Fantasy Films*, 186–99. Jefferson, NC: McFarland, 1989.

A Time to Live and a Time to Die / Tongnian wangshi (1985) Hou Hsiao-hsien; Taiwan; Taiwanese and Mandarin with English subtitles; Color; 138 m; Facets (DVD); Taiwan, 1940s and 1950s.

Three generations of a Chinese family move to Taiwan from the Chinese mainland in 1949 and grapple with their dislocation, transience, and generational differences. Political events of the 1940s and 1950s are in the background of this subtle story told through the experiences of the child and adolescent character, Ah-hsiao.

See also: *City of Sadness; Good Men, Good Women; The Puppetmaster; Sunshine*

Lu, Tonglin. "From a Voiceless Father to a Father's Voice: Hou Xiaoxian: *A Time to Live and a Time to Die; City of Sadness; The Puppetmaster*." In *Confronting Modernity in the Cinemas of Taiwan and Mainland China*, 95–115. Cambridge: Cambridge University Press, 2002.

Tjoet Nja' Dhien (1988) Eros Djarot; Indonesia; Indonesian, Acehnese, and Dutch with English subtitles; Color; 105 m; Between Three Worlds Video (DVD, VHS); Aceh, Sumatra, 1896–1905.

Set in the period of the Aceh War of 1873–1904, *Tjoet Nja' Dhien* has many of the best qualities of popular narrative cinema. It has beautiful and compelling images that depict battles between Dutch and Acehnese, marching throngs of armed peasants, and the green and mist-covered mountains of Aceh. The film also has a brave, smart, pious, and loving heroine—the real-life Acehnese guerilla leader Tjoet Nja' Dhien. Other characters include loyal followers such as "Poet," a man who will act as observer and historian for posterity. Dutch colonialists are the villains in the film, but are differentiated enough to be credible. For example, while Dutch army commanders and soldiers commit barbarous and cruel acts in their pursuit of Tjoet Nja' Dhien, there are characters who conspire with the Acehnese by supplying arms, just as some of the Acehnese act as informers for the Dutch. Even Poet introduces a measured view of the Dutch, despite having observed the horrors of the Dutch massacre of the Acehnese in 1904. While he condemns the Dutch for their actions, he argues that the "poor soldiers" are only the "tools" of war. These dimensions of *Tjoet Nja' Dhien* make the film a very accessible introduction to an Indonesian perspective of its anticolonial history.

Tjoet Nja' Dhien characterizes the fight of the Acehnese to preserve their independence from the Dutch as determined in the face of almost overwhelming odds, and righteous in terms of the Islamic faith. The film also interprets colonizers as primarily motivated by the profits they enjoy from their exploitation of Indonesia. This juxtaposition of faith and greed, while tempered by the presence of traitors to the cause on both sides, is reinforced by the characterization of Tjoet Nja' Dhien. Never wavering from her conviction that the Dutch are "infidels," and her condemnation of how the Dutch have "soiled the land," she preaches unity to her followers. The film ends with her capture, and a concluding intertitle—"the Acehnese continued to fight"—suggests that the ultimate legacy of Dhien's actions was the liberation of Indonesia.

See also: *Flame*; *Max Havelaar*; *November 1828*; *Those Whom Death Refused*

n/a. "Study Guide for Eros Djarot's Film *Tjoet Nja' Dhien* (Indonesia, 1988)." In *Tjoet Nja' Dhien* (DVD and VHS, Between Three Worlds Video), TjoetGuideFinal.pdf. Melbourne, Australia: Monash Asia Institute, Monash University.
Stratton, David. "*Tjoet Nja'dhien.*" *Variety* 355 (May 17/23, 1989): 33.

The Traitors / Los traidores

The Traitors / Los traidores (1973) Raymundo Gleyzer; Argentina; Spanish with English subtitles; Color; 113 m; Cinema Guild (theatrical); Argentina, 1950s and 1970s.

Alternating between Argentine labor history of the 1950s and 1973, *The Traitors* is an ambitious condemnation of the weakness of the Perónist regime's support for workers, and the collusion of corrupt union officials with the authoritarian government. Director Raymundo Gleyzer constructs a fast-paced, complicated, and engaging story that revolves around the contrived "disappearance" of a national union leader named Roberto Barrera, who successfully plots a fake kidnapping in order to garner sympathy and a win in union elections. His deteriorating principles are traced by scenes of his participation with his father and brother in 1950s labor activism.

See also: *A Funny, Dirty Little War*

Burton, Julianne. "The Traitors." *Film Quarterly* 30(1) (1976): 57–9.
Monteon, Michael. "The Traitors." *The History Teacher* 12(2) (February 1979): 288–90.

Transport from Paradise / Transport z ráje

Transport from Paradise / Transport z ráje (1962) Zbynek Brynych; Czechoslovakia; Czech and German with English subtitles; Black and White; 94 m; Facets (VHS); Czechoslovakia, 1944.

The pre-title sequence of *Transport from Paradise* is brilliant in its ironic invocation of Nazi propaganda about Theresienstadt, the Bohemian fortress town of Terezin fashioned as a model ghetto-camp for European Jews. With Nazi filmmakers arriving in the camp to execute officials' "brilliant idea" to make a "Jewish" film that will disprove "their hands are stained with blood," a well-dressed woman disembarks from the latest train to arrive at the camp. "I am so glad to be in Theresienstadt at last," she offers the cameras. Following instructions by the film's director (a Jewish inmate), other prisoners—in a variety of European languages—woodenly utter lines like "I am fine here in Terezin. I have everything I need."

Drawing from Theresienstadt survivor Arnošt Lustig's short story collection *Night and Hope*, director Zbynek Brynych slowly unreels—in the course of a day in its life—what lies beneath the façade of Theresienstadt's paradise of "self-government." As Camp Commandant von Holler explains to visiting SS General Knecht, the Judenrat "even draw[s] up the transport list; we only state the number."

This study of a single day in Theresienstadt in 1944 is a self-contained representation of a complex set of relationships, and the desperate lived experience of Jews concentrated therein. The film's shift from an ironic treatment of the Nazi propaganda about Theresienstadt (a film *Hitler Presents a Town to the Jews* was in fact produced on Goebbels' orders), to an emotionally devastating portrait of inmates presenting themselves for train deportation to Auschwitz-Birkenau (and certain death), reinforces the disjunction between contrived appearances and reality. But the reality of Jewish experience depicted in the film extends beyond the separation of inmates and the imminent death of those who will arrive at Birkenau. This is a film about victimization, but also complicity, agency, and allegiances in the face of Nazi terror, and as such, poses unsettling questions.

The character of Ignaz Marmulstaub, the new Deputy Chair of the Jewish council, represents the dilemmas of Jews either thrust into, or volunteering for, representative positions in the ghettos. Alone but for a Nazi guard in the room, he must fill the latest quota for transport, and is, in bureaucratic fashion, looking over lists, tallying and retallying. He knows well his soon-to-be-deported Chair, Löwenbach, has acknowledged to the Nazis that "There is gas where the transport is going." (Löwenbach will at the scene of the roundup try to exact a moral victory: "I know ... gas ... crematoria ... but I also know you'll lose the war.") In contrast to the tepid compliance of the deputy, the camp has subversives who gather intelligence about the advance of Soviet troops, operate a printing press, and try to elude ruthless German guards.

The scene of the roll call for the transport reiterates the chillingly bureaucratic dimensions of the Holocaust. Marmulstaub's assistant is at a desk in a large field-like space. As he calls each name, the deportee runs to present himself or herself before the Oberstürmfuhrer. As inmates run this grassy gauntlet, and then return to the lineup, a persistent voice among them calls for more and more attention: "Like sheep. Never again. Never again. Never again." This profound but objectively feeble protest is soon lost in the embarkation for Birkenau. Marmulstaub silently watches the train leave, and German officers order champagne.

See also: *Schindler's List*

Liebman, Stuart and Leonard Quart. "Homevideo: Czech Films of the Holocaust." *Cineaste* 22(1) (April 1996):49–51.

Margry, Karel. "'Theresienstadt' (1944–1945): The Nazi Propaganda Film Depicting the Concentration Camp as Paradise." *Historical Journal of Film, Radio and Television* 12(2) (1992): 145–62.

The Travelling Players / O Thiassos (1975) Theo Angelopoulos; Greece; Greek with English subtitles; Color; 230 m; Facets (VHS); Greece 1939–1952.

Actors performing the folk tale "Golfo the Shepherdess" in Greece are named after characters from ancient Greek myth: Agamemnon, Clytemnestra, and Aegisthus. The stories of the actors' own experiences of Greek political history beginning in the 1930s at times interrupts the play's performance, with characters' mythological relationships transposed onto the present. *The Travelling Players*, produced during the end of Greece's military dictatorship (1967–1974), has been interpreted as disguising its critique of reactionary politics behind Aeschylus' trilogy. Perhaps more dimensional than an allegory, though, the film creates a dialectical relationship between the ancient and modern eras of history.

See also: *Ulysses' Gaze*

Georgakas, Dan. "Angelopoulos, Greek History and *The Travelling Players*." In *The Last Modernist: The Films of Theo Angelopoulos*, edited by Andrew Horton, 27–42. Westport, CT: Praeger, 1997.

Horton, Andrew. "Theodor Angelopoulos and the New Greek Cinema." *Film Criticism* 11(1/2) (1987): 84–94.

Mitchell, Tony. "Animating Dead Space and Dead Time." *Sight & Sound* 50(1) (1981): 29–33.

Pappas, Peter. "Culture, History and Cinema: A Review of *The Travelling Players*." *Cineaste* 7(4) (1977): 36–9.

Tarr, Susan, and Hans Proppe. "*The Travelling Players*: A Modern Greek Masterpiece." *Jump Cut: A Review of Contemporary Media* 10/11 (Summer 1976): 5–6.

The Tree of Wooden Clogs / L'albero degli zoccoli (1978) Ermanno Olmi; Italy/France; Italian with English subtitles; Color; 186 m; Facets (DVD); Italy, early 20th century.

The Tree of Wooden Clogs is set in turn-of-the century Bergamo, Italy, and focuses on several very poor peasant families who live together at a farmstead. The film is not much driven by plot. One of its central "events" is the destruction of a boy's wooden clogs; his father cuts down a landlord's tree to replace the clogs and eventually this act leads to terrible consequences for the family. Lyrical and realist in tone and style, the film has been highly praised for its ability to convey the timelessness of Italian rural society, and yet also suggest the emerging social, economic, and political changes that will alter that society irrevocably. Amateur actors—peasants who reside in the region and speak the local dialect—were used for the film, a common practice for director Olmi. Filming the actors in real time, he then used the editing process to shape their actions into his fictional story.

See also: *1900*; *St. Michael Had a Rooster*

Hirshfield, Claire. "*The Tree of Wooden Clogs*." *Film & History: An Interdisciplinary Journal of Film and Television Studies* 11(1) (1981): 18–20.

Landy, Marcia. "Gramsci and Italian Cinema." In *Italian Film*, 149–80. Cambridge: Cambridge University Press, 2000.

Liehm, Mira. "Under the Sign of Violence." In *Passion and Defiance: Film in Italy from 1942 to the Present*, 307–18. Berkeley, CA: University of California Press, 1986.

Trek of Life / Yol (1982) Şerif Gören; Turkey; Turkish with English subtitles; Color; 114 m; Columbia/Tristar (VHS); Turkey, 1980s.

The journey motif is ubiquitous in historical films. Physical travel across landscape, or travel across various psychological states, places characters in a relationship to history that denotes change or continuity over time. In *Trek of Life*, some prisoners at the Turkish island of Imrali are granted a week's leave. The journeys they undertake are framed by the fact of their mandated return, and this eclipse of their freedom haunts the experience of their travel. These are not sentimental voyages; the prisoners' travels attune them to the drastically changed circumstances of their families since their absence, thus undercutting the static quality of time/history found in the milieu of prison.

Trek of Life plots events of the week by intercutting the travels of five of the men released on leave. Omer will travel to his family's village in Kurdistan, and discover that his fantasies of its pastoral life have been shattered by a raid by the Turkish military. Seyit must find his wife at her parents' home in a mountain village, to where she and their son have been banished by his family because she had resorted to prostitution. The other men face similar disillusionment and strained family relations.

Yilmaz Güney's screenplay is inspired by his own prison experiences (he escaped and fled to France in 1981). This is an exceptionally well-told story that in its plotting, images, and characterization manages to construct a week's leave as a microcosm of the experience of Turks and Kurds living in a modern militaristic political regime. Ironically, while the men experience imprisonment, so are the "free" subjects of the Turkish regime subject to stifling gender roles, ethnic divisions, and political oppression. Seyit, wracked with pain for his role in his wife's death, weeps in the train that carries him back to Imrali.

Grenier, Richard. "All Turkish, No Delight." *Commentary* 75 (January 1983): 59–63.
Naficy, Hamid. "Chronotopes of Imagined Homeland/Homeland as Prison: Close-Up: Yilmaz Güney." In *An Accented Cinema: Exilic and Diasporic Filmmaking*, 181–87. Princeton, NJ: Princeton University Press, 2001.
Rayns, Tony. "From Isolation." *Sight & Sound* 52(2) (Autumn 1983): 88–93.

Ulysses' Gaze / To Vlemma tou Odyssea (1995) Theo Angelopoulos; Greece/France/Italy; Greek and English with English subtitles; Color, Black and White; 173 m; Fox Lorber (DVD, VHS); Balkans, 20th century.

The character of "A." has returned to Greece after 35 years, having enjoyed a successful filmmaking career in the United States. While his latest film premieres in his Greek hometown to much excitement, A. seems much more affected by another agenda: his search for the reputedly lost three reels of film produced by Greek brothers Yannakis and Miltos Manakis. The (real-life) Manakis brothers were early twentieth-century pioneers of Balkan cinema.

Ulysses' Gaze engages three layers of filmmaking—and historical—experience. Director Angelopoulos tells the story of director A. who is trying to reconstruct the story of the filmmaking Manakis brothers. That the historical research (and eventual storytelling) is as much about the researcher as his subject becomes an important theme as the film unwinds.

The experiences of A. and the Manakis' are deeply intertwined with the complexities of twentieth-century Balkan history. A. is physically journeying over much of the region, reflecting the brothers' own far-flung filmmaking journeys. In both cases, whether it is 1914, 1938, or 1994, the filmmakers' stories and storytelling are bound up with war, deprivation, loss of home and family, and the changing face of political authority. As A. says, ". . . how many borders must we cross to reach home?"

Ulysses' Gaze is a beautiful and stimulating film in many ways, offering a narratively and thematically complex meditation on the region's twentieth-century strife and on the meaning and reliability of sight, story, and memory. One scene in particular is so affecting in its evocation of family and national history that it captures wonderfully the potential of dramatic film to find new ways of telling about the past. In this scene—typical of others in the film that conflate time by placing noncontemporaneous characters together—A. travels with his mother to a family gathering in their home in Romania. It is New Year's Eve, the advent of 1945, and (the incongruously adult) A. reunites with beloved uncles, grandparents, and siblings in a sumptuous home. His father arrives home to much jubilation—it is now 1946—and a reunion with A. With a piano, and a chorus of *Auld Lang Syne*, those gathered enjoy a dance. Soon, the dance carries them almost seamlessly through time; the song remains the same, but it is now "Happy 1948" and two men arrive to arrest uncle. When the dance resumes after talk of migrating to Greece, the maid interrupts that "The People's Confiscation Committee" has arrived. With household belongings and the piano taken away, the date is now 1950. The family gathers for "one last family picture" and A. takes up his spot, now appearing as his boyhood self. Angelopoulos' collapse—in a single take—of five years of history into a single scene in a family drawing room, is so cogent and affecting, that it powerfully fixes the role of art in the study of history.

See also: *Ararat; A King and His Movie; The Travelling Players*

Horton, Andrew. "*Ulysses' Gaze.*" *Cineaste* 22(1) (1996): 43–45.

Iordanova, Dina. *Cinema of Flames: Balkan Film, Culture and the Media*. London: BFI, 2001.

Jameson, Fredric. "Theo Angelopoulos: The Past as History, the Future as Form." In *The Last Modernist: The Films of Theo Angelopoulos*, edited by Andrew Horton, 78–95. Westport, CT: Praeger, 1997.

Portuges, Catherine. "Review of *Ulysses' Gaze.*" *American Historical Review* 101(4) (1996): 1158–59.

Rutherford, Anne. "Precarious Boundaries: Affect, *Mise En Scène* and the Senses in Theodorus Angelopoulos' Balkans Epic." In *Art and the Performance of Memory: Sounds and Gestures of Recollection*, edited by Richard Candida-Smith, 63–84. London: Routledge, 2002.

Under the Domim Tree / Etz Hadomim Tafus (1994) Eli Cohen; Israel; Hebrew with English subtitles; Color; 102 m; Fox Lorber (VHS), Sisu Entertainment (DVD); Israel, 1953.

Based on the memoirs of Gilma Almagor, this is the story of European Jewish children who have survived the Holocaust and are housed at one of the many "youth villages" established in Israel. *Under the Domim Tree* is a devastating look at the relations of a family of adolescents who are deeply traumatized by their experiences.

See also: *Exodus; The Wooden Gun*

Bartov, Omer. "Review of *Anne Frank Remembered* and *Under the Domim Tree*." *American Historical Review* 101(4) (1996): 1154–56.

Insdorf, Annette. "Dysfunction as Distortion: The Holocaust Survivor on Screen and Stage." In *Indelible Shadows: Film and the Holocaust*, 3rd ed., 293–299. New York: Cambridge University Press, 2003.

Underground / Bila jednom jedna zemlja (1995) Emir Kusturica; France/Yugoslavia/Germany/Hungary; Serbo-Croatian, German and French with English subtitles; Color; 167 m; New Yorker Films (DVD, VHS); Yugoslavia, World War II to 1990s.

This highly stylized black comedy is a damning interpretation of Yugoslavian history from World War II to the Bosnian War. In early 1940's Belgrade, two friends engineer a profitable underground arsenal. For 50 years they maintain the fiction that the war isn't over, deceiving sheltered workers into continuing production for the anti-Nazi resistance.

See also: *Before the Rain*

Iordanova, Dina. *Kusturica*. London: BFI, 2002.

———. "Kusturica's *Underground* (1995): Historical Allegory or Propaganda?" *Historical Journal of Film, Radio and Television* 19(1) (1999): 69–86.

Keene, Judith. "The Filmmaker as Historian, Above and Below Ground: Emir Kusturica and the Narratives of Yugoslav History." *Rethinking History* 5(2) (July 2001): 233–53.

The Uprising / La Insurrección (1980) Peter Lilienthal; West Germany/Nicaragua; Spanish with English subtitles; Color; Facets (VHS); 96 m; Nicaragua, 1979.

German-born and Latin American-raised Lilienthal adopts an invented storyline about one family's experience in Léon during the final stages of civil war that in 1979 led to the overthrow of Nicaragua's dictator, Anastasio Somoza, by the Sandinista Liberation Front (FSLN). Young Agustín is persuaded by his family and priest to desert the National Guard, and is ultimately killed in a confrontation with his former captain, Flores.

The Uprising has a documentary quality. Filmed just four months following the end of the war, it uses mostly amateur actors, including former soldiers of the FSLN. Foregoing any sustained explanation of the economic, social, or political context of events, the film instead uses a melodramatic story to celebrate the courage of ordinary Nicaraguans in support of the leftist cause.

Halverson, Rachel J., and Ana María Rodríguez-Vivaldi. "*La Insurrección/Der Aufstand*: Cultural Synergy, Film, and Revolution." In *The Lion and the Eagle: Interdisciplinary Essays on German-Spanish Relations over the Centuries*, edited by Thomas Wolber, Cameron M. Hewitt and Conrad Kent, 442–56. New York: Berghahn, 2000.

Schwartz, Ronald. "*The Uprising*." In *Latin American Films, 1932–1994: A Critical Filmography*, 258–59. Jefferson, NC: McFarland, 1997.

Siegel, Joanna. "*The Uprising* (1982): History through Film." *Film & History: An Interdisciplinary Journal of Film and Television Studies* 13(1) (1983): 12–16.

Utopia / Saaraba (1988) Amadou Saalum Seck; Senegal/Germany; Wolof and French with English subtitles; Color; 86 m; California Newsreel (VHS); Senegal, 1980s.

Tamsin is a young man arriving back in Senegal after 18 years in Paris. He discovers corruption and disillusionment underneath the thriving appearance of modern Dakar. The way of life in his village is threatened by the local politician's promises of a sewage system and salt factory. At the same time, Tamsin's love interest Lissa is out of his reach, betrothed in accordance with tradition, to another man. *Utopia* is a modest and effective drama about the tensions produced by modernization in Senegalese society.

See also: *The Blue Eyes of Yonta; Hyenas; Identity Pieces; Soleil O; Those Whom Death Refused*

Ellerson, Beti. "The Female Body as Symbol of Change and Dichotomy: Conflicting Paradigms in the Representation of Women in African Film." In *With Open Eyes: Women and African Cinema*, edited by Kenneth W. Harrow, 30–41. Amsterdam: Rodopi, 1997.

Gadjigo, Samba. "Africa through African Eyes." *Research in African Literatures* 23(4) (1992): 97–105.

Pitman, Randy. "*Saaraba (Utopia)/Wend Kuuni (God's Gift)/Yeelen (Brightness)*." *Library Journal* 116(9) (May 15, 1991): 125.

Utu (1982) Geoff Murphy; New Zealand; English; Color; 122 m; Facets (VHS); New Zealand, 1870s.

Te Wheke is a Māori man who witnesses a brutal British colonial army raid and burning of his village in 1870. Te Wheke is also a Māori scout for that army, who after deserting, enacts "Utu" (a rite of settlement, or "justice") by murdering *Pakeha* (white settlers), and attempting the murder of a British officer. He is eventually captured and tried in a military tribunal for these crimes, and sentenced to execution. Adopting a structure that intercuts scenes of Te Wheke confronting his captors, and flashbacks to the events he describes, *Utu* interestingly describes its history through its protagonist. And this protagonist is both victim and criminal, albeit a criminal who argues for the justice of his crimes.

Utu is based on the short story *A Bush Court Martial* by James Cowan, which is about the trial of the real figure Wi Heretaunga during the Māori Wars. Much attention has been given to the film's appropriation of the American western film genre, some describing this as a subversion of colonial master nàrratives. It is difficult to decide whether the film cynically exploits Māori culture and history in order to tell an entertaining (and violent) "outlaw" story, or whether giving Te Wheke command of the storytelling creates a film that explains his actions from the perspective of his experience and culture. Te Wheke, our victim, warrior, and storyteller, frames himself as the wronged, but graphic scenes of his crimes might elicit little sympathy from viewers. This paradox lies at the heart of *Utu*'s fascinating, and troubling, discussion of race in nineteenth-century New Zealand.

See also: *The Chant of Jimmie Blacksmith*

Harris, Kenneth Marc. "American Film Genres and Non-American Films: A Case Study of *Utu*." *Cinema Journal* 29(2) (1990): 36–59.

Mitchell, Tony. "*Utu*: A New Zealand Revenge Tragedy." *Film Criticism* 8(3) (1984): 47–53.

Orr, Bridget. "Birth of a Nation?: From *Utu* to *The Piano*." In *Piano Lessons: Approaches to the Piano*, edited by Felicity Coombs, 148–62. Sydney: John Libbey, 1999.

Perkins, Reid. "Imag(in)ing Our Colonial Past: Colonial New Zealand on Film from *The Birth of New Zealand* to *The Piano*, Part II." *Illusions* 26 (Winter 1997): 17–21.

Vatel (2000) Roland Joffé; France; French with English subtitles; Color; 103 m; Buena Vista Home Entertainment (DVD, VHS); France, 1671.

This highly embellished story of a visit by French King Louis XIV to the Duc de Condé's Chantilly estate in 1671 centers on the role of real-life chef François Vatel. Vatel's burden is nothing less than the fate of France. He must impress the king with his food and gala spectacles in order to secure a military office for his boss in the pending French war with the Netherlands. *Vatel* is a trifle of a story but is a memorable spectacle of the excesses of the era.

See also: *Ridicule*

Shapiro, Stephen. "Roland Joffé's *Vatel*: Refashioning the History of the Ancien Régime." In *EMF: Studies in Early Modern France Vol. 10: Modern Interpretations of the Early Modern*, edited by Anne L. Birberick and Russell Ganim, 77–88. Charlottesville VA: Rookwood Press, 2005.

The Vikings (1958) Richard Fleischer; United States; English; Color; 114 m; MGM Home Entertainment (DVD, VHS); Northumbria, Great Britain, 9th century.

In "The Role of Feature Films in the Teaching of History" Terence Gwynne and Ian Willis comment: "As a purely personal judgement we feel *The Vikings* ... has never been excelled as a splendidly *bad* historical feature film." This is such an intriguing statement, and *The Vikings* such a well-known reference point for audiences of popular historical films, that the film, whether bad, or splendidly so, deserves critical attention.

The plot of *The Vikings*, based on the novel by Edison Marshall, borrows from an amalgam of Norse saga, Arthurian legend, monastic chronicle, imagination, and pre-revisionist historical scholarship. Einar is the son of Viking king Ragnar; he is unaware that the English slave Eric is his half-brother and an heir to the kingdom of Northumbria. Viking conquest, English deceit, and rivalry for the love of Princess Morgana are all gloriously complicated by Eric's secret identity.

Enjoying a healthy production budget, *The Vikings* pays close attention to those material period details that are sometimes mistaken for "authenticity" in medieval feature films. These include a replica of a Viking village in Norway. There is little doubt that the result of this attention is a cinematic spectacle that was highly enjoyable for 1950s film audiences. Behind the surface of such details lie the more troublesome layers of stereotyping and presentism that are so typical of films set in the Middle Ages. One example would be the film's emphasis on the brothers' devotion to the Norse god Odin, avoiding disclosure of the pantheism of the Vikings and the importance of Thor therein. Aberth argues that *The Vikings'* filmmakers do so to "elide the difference between Christianity and Viking paganism."

Aberth, John. "Lights, Camera, Pillage!: Viking Films." In *A Knight at the Movies: Medieval History on Film*, 29–61. London: Routledge, 2003.

Douglas, Kurt. *The Ragman's Son*. New York: Simon & Schuster, 1988.

Driver, Martha W. "What's Accuracy Got to Do with It?: Historicity and Authenticity in Medieval Film." In *The Medieval Hero on Screen: Representations from Beowulf to Buffy*, edited by Martha W. Driver and Sid Ray, 19–22. Jefferson, NC: McFarland, 2004.

Fleischer, Richard. *Just Tell Me When to Cry: A Memoir*. New York: Carol & Graf, 1993.

Gwynn, Terence, and Ian Willis. "The Role of Feature Films in the Teaching of History." *Teaching History: A Journal of Methods* 3 (1974): 204–8.

Viva Zapata! (1952) Elia Kazan; United States; English; Black and White; 113 m; Twentieth Century Fox Home Video (VHS); Mexico, late 19th and early 20th centuries.

This highly romanticized version of the life of Mexican revolutionary Emiliano Zapata begins with his birth in 1879, and focuses on his leadership of the Liberation Army of the South and his alliance with Pancho Villa against the regime of Porfirio Diaz beginning in 1910.

Biskind, Peter, and Dan Georgakas, "An Exchange on *Viva Zapata.*" *Cineaste* 7(2) (Spring 1976): 10–17.
Porton, Richard. *Film and the Anarchist Imagination.* New York: Verso, 1999.
Underwood, Paul. "An American Cold Warrior: *Viva Zapata!*" In *American History/American Film: Interpreting the Hollywood Image,* edited by John O'Connor and Martin Jackson, 183–201. New York: Ungar, 1979.
———. "The Image of Mexican Heroes in American Films." *Film-Historia* 2(3) (1992): 221–44.
Zaniello, Tom. "*Viva Zapata!*" In *Working Stiffs, Union Maids, Reds, and Riffraff: An Organized Guide to Films About Labor,* 265–67. Ithaca, NY: ILR Press/Cornell University Press, 1996.

The Wannsee Conference / Die Wannseekonferenz (1984) Heinz Schirk; West Germany; German with English subtitles; Color; 87 m; Home Vision Entertainment (VHS); Germany, 1942.

Heinz Schirk's film reconstructs, with a mixture of invention and documented fact, the "Wannsee Conference," a brief meeting of high-ranking Nazi state and party officials at a private residence in suburban Berlin in January 1942. Its purpose was discussion of the mechanics of achieving a "Final Solution"—the mass murder of European Jews—as well as the establishment of Reinhard Heydrich and the SS as the supreme authority in its implementation. A summary of the Wannsee meeting written by participant Adolf Eichmann is known as the *Protokoll.* This surviving document provides the general outline of the proceedings from which the film extrapolates. Some of the film's dialogue and situations have been invented, because Eichmann's summary is not detailed in this regard. Statements about the Wannsee meeting given by Eichmann during his trial in Israel in the early 1960s have also been considered in producing the screenplay.

Hilberg, Raul. "Is It History, or Is It Drama?" *The New York Times* 137 (December 13, 1987): 14 + [2 p] sec 2.
Reimer, Robert C., and Carol J. Reimer. "*The Wannsee Conference.*" In *Nazi-Retro Film: How German Narrative Cinema Remembers the Past,* 137–39. New York: Twayne, 1992.

Waterland (1992) Stephen Gyllenhaal; United Kingdom; English; Color; 95 m; Facets (DVD); England, 1911–1940s, and Pittsburgh, 1970s.

High school history teacher Tom Crick spends a lot of class time recounting his adolescent experiences. His students are only too happy to substitute the study of the French Revolution for the terrors of Crick's tragic past in the fenlands of

England some 30 years earlier. When his principal, citing a decline in enrollment, announces "a little merger" of history and social studies, Crick protests that his course has not suffered the decline. The principal explains why: "You're not teaching the curriculum. You're telling these children stories."

The inextricable relationship of history to storytelling is the central motif of the film, refuting the principal's notion that storytelling is something quite separate from the teaching of history. "Once upon a time, children," Crick begins, invoking a sense of the fairy tale quality of narration, "there was a history teacher." As Crick explains about his teen years during the Blitz, he offers, "You might say things were approaching a bit of a climax."

The plot of *Waterland* involves the journey of Crick and his students to find meaning in their study of the past. Crick and his students want to discover the relationship of their personal stories to the apparently "real" history that is mandated in the curriculum. At the beginning of the film, one student suggests she likes history, "even if it has no point." Another student, a boy named Price, states: "The only thing interesting I see about history is that it's about to end." By the end of the film, Crick's personal story—full of family secrets that are painfully exposed—has intersected with, and added meaning to, the grand narrative of world war. At his final assembly, Crick again chooses storytelling—his "disease"—to explain why he studies history. After experiencing the devastation of postwar Germany, he says, "the only way I could cope with what I was seeing was to think of it as history—as part of a story—and not just those bits of meat. And that's what we've been doing; telling stories, children."

There are grounds for criticizing the film. For example, there is little explanation for Crick's arrival in Pittsburgh, and the presentation of his wife as having a mystical—and implied irrational—relationship to the world reinforces a gendered presentation of characters that began with the depiction of Crick's female students. Most troubling narratively is *Waterland*'s struggle to maintain the relationship of the contemporary and the historical components of the story. Crick "literally" leads his students back in time to explore the life of his ancestral village in 1911 and the family estate in 1922. The class is even released for an hour into a drunken crowd of townsfolk celebrating the coronation of George V. But following a scene in which Crick and Price look around the attic of his boyhood home, the film abandons this imaginative collapsing of time and place. Crick hears the sound of the approach of his brother's motorcycle, signaling the end of a date with Crick's beloved Mary. Price asks, "Already?" Crick replies, "It's hard to keep track of time." Soon, students are back in class listening to Crick, but these scenes are subsumed by the increasing focus on portraying Crick's past, and his current relations with wife Mary. While there is an inherent logic in the plot's increasing absorption in Crick's own story, it awkwardly discards the time-travel device.

These flaws do not diminish the utility of *Waterland*, which generates wonderful ideas for students of history about how to "keep track" of time and its relationship to our present.

Brewer, John, and Stella Tillyard. "History and Telling Stories: Graham Swift's *Waterland*." *History Today* 35(1) (January 1985): 49–51.
Laura Mason, "Review of *Waterland*," *American Historical Review* 98(4) (October 1993): 1171–1172.

Welcome to Canada (1989) John M. Smith; Canada; English; Color; 86 m; National Film Board of Canada (VHS); Newfoundland, Canada, 1986.

Based on a broadly similar incident, this is the story of eight Tamil refugees who are discovered adrift on an inflatable raft by Newfoundland fishers. Striking a naturalistic tone, this is a quiet and effective study of cross-cultural interaction in the late twentieth century. Perhaps less successfully, scenes juxtapose Canadian life with glimpses of the militarization and terrorism in Sri Lankan society. Director John M. Smith creates a subtly moving study of the isolated and generous villagers and their discovery of common ground with these foreigners from Sri Lanka, a place which for most is only vaguely identifiable with their old habit of drinking Ceylon tea. As the local priest admonishes the police constable to whom he is reporting about the refugees' country of origin: "You've never heard of it? My God, where'd you do your studies?" *Welcome to Canada* is also a political film, arguing for a humane and generous Canadian refugee and immigration policy.

See also: *Boat People*; *The Boat Is Full*; *The Dupes*; *Journey of Hope*; *Kedma*

Welcome, Mr. Marshall! / Bienvenido, Mr. Marshall! (1953) Luis García Berlanga; Spain; Spanish; Black and White; 95 m; Video Mercury Films (VHS); Spain, post-WWII.

In this neorealist satirical comedy, a backwater Castilian village prepares to host two Marshall Plan officials. The extreme and comical efforts of these Spanish villagers to compete for a share of post-World War II aid provide a light-hearted and revealing microcosm of the history of Europe's reconstruction.

Caparrós-Lera, José M., and Llorenç Esteve. "Berlanga's *Bienvenido Mr. Marshall* (1952) and *Calabuch* (1956): A Historical Approach." *Film-Historia* 1(3) (1991): 185–203.
Pavlović, Tatjana. "The Traumatized Body." In *Despotic Bodies and Transgressive Bodies: Spanish Culture from Francisco Franco to Jesús Franco*, 49–70. Albany, NY: Suny Press, 2003.

The White Rose / Die Weiße Rose (1982) Michael Verhoeven; West Germany; German with English subtitles; Color; 123 m; Facets (VHS); Germany, WWII.

"White Rose" was a small, short-lived resistance group based in Munich, Bavaria, in 1942–3. Its members included Munich University students Hans Scholl and his sister Sophie, and philosophy/musicology Professor Kurt Huber. Verhoeven's film version of their story is the first in his trio of films about the experience and effects of the Third Reich (*The Nasty Girl*, 1990; *My Mother's Courage*, 1995). *The White Rose* is partly based on the memoirs of eldest sister Inge Aicher-Scholl and extant letters of Hans and Sophie Scholl. Verhoeven invents much of the romantic subplot of the story, but has been faithful to the basic chronology of events.

The film eschews a lengthy narrative of the pre-resistance lives of the group's members. Instead, the film places viewers at a Munich train station in May 1942, where Sophie Scholl has arrived to join brother Hans at the university. She soon discovers the truth about Hans' activities when she realizes he is the author of an anti-Nazi flyer found in a university hallway. Events follow in rapid succession, culminating in the execution of Hans and Sophie in February 1943. The story describes the Gestapo arrest of the Scholls' father, Sophie's participation in White Rose activities (despite the protective opposition of Hans and the other male members), Sophie's sabotage lessons during summer "work service" in a munitions factory, the army medical service of Hans on the Eastern Front (where he observes a mass shooting), and the increasingly risky activities of members and the increasingly close scrutiny of the Gestapo.

The concentration and quick development of the narrative in *The White Rose* has a peculiar—and intended—effect on the viewer. That Sophie could journey from "innocence" to execution in such a short time underlies the brutality of the regime as well as the heroism and tragedy of the resisters. Even suspenseful scenes are not drawn out; Verhoeven refuses such indulgence.

This is a film in which questions of importance to historians of the Nazi era are answered only implicitly. The motivations of the resisters are assessed in indirect ways. For example, there is little extended rhetorical condemnation of the regime, and only brief allusion to the Scholls' liberal family background, the humane and rational basis of German philosophy, and the effect of witnessing brutality and mass murder. The film portrays the group's reasoning as generally self-evident.

Verhoeven's exploration of the history of the White Rose is more drama and chronicle than analysis. *The White Rose* is a kind of eulogy for these victims, and a lament for the loss of their innocence.

See also: *A Generation*; *. . .And Give My Love to the Swallows*; *Rosenstrasse*

Reimer, Robert C., and Carol J. Reimer. "The White Rose." In *Nazi-Retro Film: How German Narrative Cinema Remembers the Past*, 86–92. New York: Twayne, 1992.

Rubenstein, L. "*The White Rose.*" *Cineaste* 11(4) (1983): 60.

Winstanley (1975) Kevin Brownlow and Andrew Mollo; United Kingdom; English; Black and White; 95 m; Milestone (DVD, VHS); England, 1649–1650.

Gerrard Winstanley was an English Protestant radical. The film examines the period from 1649–1650 when he and a small band of followers, known as "Diggers," maintained a commune at St. George's Hill, Surrey. Advocating that need should determine the sharing of common property, the group defends its right to occupy lands owned by Sir Francis Drake against Lord General Fairfax, commander of the New Model Army, and a local Parson whose wife joins Winstanley and the commune.

Winstanley is based on the novel *Comrade Jacob* by David Caute, additionally drawing from the extant pamphlet writings of Winstanley, such as his *The New Law of Righteousness*. The film has achieved the difficult feat of creating a moving story out of distant and peculiar events, without resorting to obvious devices of cinematic emotional manipulation, or to the comfortable and familiar. As such, true to directors Kevin Brownlow's and Andrew Mollo's aim, the film has an authenticity that transcends the material aspects of costume, landscape, rotten teeth, or regional dialect. At the same time, it is difficult to ignore parallels between the independent filmmakers and their motley crew of unprofessional cast and crew creatively working over a period of some 10 years and under severe budget restraints, and the Diggers' own communal ventures.

See also: *Cromwell*

Porton, R. "*Winstanley.*" *Cineaste* 25(4) (2000): 51.

Rubenstein, Lenny. "Winstanley and the Historical Film." *Cineaste* 10(4) (Fall 1980): 22–25.

Tibbetts, J.C. "Between the Map and the Painted Landscape: Kevin Brownlow's Historical Films: *It Happened Here* (1965) and *Winstanley* (1975)." *Historical Journal of Film, Radio and Television* 20(2) (June 2000): 227–51.

Tibbetts, J.C. "'Winstanley'; or, Kevin Brownlow Camps out on St. George's Hill." *Literature/Film Quarterly* 31(4) (2003): 312–18.

The Wooden Gun / Roveh Huliot (1979) Ilan Moshenson; Israel; Hebrew with English subtitles; Color; 91 m; Facets (DVD; VHS); Tel Aviv, 1950s.

The Wooden Gun's main character is Yoni Schreiber, a 10-year-old boy living in 1950s Tel Aviv. A first-generation *Sabra* (Israeli-born), Yoni has a mother who survived the Holocaust, and a father the Arab-Israeli War. The story is about Yoni's participation in a gang rivalry—where the youth use wooden guns and in effect model the militarism of their parents—and his important discoveries about the Holocaust.

See also: *Exodus; Under the Domim Tree*

Insdorf, Annette. "Dysfunction as Distortion: The Holocaust Survivor on Screen and Stage." In *Indelible Shadows: Film and the Holocaust*, 3rd ed., 293–299. New York: Cambridge University Press, 2003.

Quart, B.K. "The Wooden Gun." *Cineaste* 11(4) (1982): 51–2.

The Year of Living Dangerously (1982) Peter Weir; Australia; English; Color; 117 m; MGM (DVD, VHS); Indonesia, 1965.

Some analysts argue that the subtexts of Peter Weir's film version of C.J. Koch's novel of the same name are rich, comprising such characteristics as intercultural sensitivity, or self-reflexive criticism of Western ideology and modes of representation. Not denying the openness of the film to sophisticated analysis, as a "historical film," *The Year of Living Dangerously* is a disappointment. Set in Indonesia in the revolutionary year of 1965, the film manages to explain little to audiences about the military coup that year that caused the demise of the charismatic and authoritarian regime of Sukarno. Instead, as the film's promotional literature suggests, the real dramatic tension and interest lies in "A love caught in the fire of revolution." A few first scenes establish the politically and economically unstable environment of Sukarno's Indonesia. These are observed by a novice foreign correspondent, journalist Guy Hamilton of the Australian Broadcasting Corporation, and his "insider" photographer of Australian–Chinese descent, Billy Kwan. Screen time is then more and more consumed with the burgeoning romance of Hamilton and Jill Bryant of the British Embassy. The love story is played out in sweltering heat, tropical downpours, and the threat of reprisals by the aspirant Communist PKI over Hamilton's investigation into arms shipments from China. But one too many films showing love in dangerous times might render one's patience with *The Year of Living Dangerously* thin.

See also: *Circle of Deceit*

Farnsworth, Rodney. "An Australian Cultural Synthesis: Wayang, the Hollywood Romance, and *The Year of Living Dangerously*." *Film Quarterly* 24(4) (1996): 348–59.

MacBean, James Roy. "Watching the Third World Watchers: The Visual, the Verbal, the Personal and the Political in *Under Fire* and *The Year of Living Dangerously*." *Film Quarterly* 37(3) (1984): 1–13.

Maes-Jelinek, Hena. "History and the Mythology of Confrontation in *The Year of Living Dangerously*." *Kunapipi* 8 (1986): 27–35.

Orr, John. "Peter Weir's Version: *The Year of Living Dangerously*." In *Cinema and Fiction: New Modes of Adapting, 1950–1990*, edited by John Orr, 54–65. Edinburgh, UK: Edinburgh University Press, 1992.

Rayner, Jonathan, ed. *The Films of Peter Weir*. 2nd ed. New York: Continuum, 2003.

Spring, Lori. "The Other Dream: *The Year of Living Dangerously*." *CineAction* 3/4 (Winter 1986): 58–71.

Yeelen / Brightness (1987) Souleymane Cissé; Mali/Burkina Faso/France/West Germany; French and Bambara with English subtitles; Color; 105 m; Kino (DVD, VHS); Mali, 13th century and mythic.

This is a rare cinematic glimpse of the history of the culture and society of the Malian Empire of the thirteenth century. The foundation of *Yeelen*'s history is oral mythology of the Bambara, whose civilization was one of the most sophisticated in African history. Thanks to a careful explanatory intertitle at the outset of the film, Western viewers are given a primer on the symbolic items that will play a central role in *Yeelen*'s narrative: the vulture, wooden horse, curved scepter, and magic pylon all guide the initiate into the Kore, the seventh and final stage of the quest for "Komo," or divine knowledge.

The film manages to ground the mythological treatment of a Bambara creation story in a temporal historical setting and narrative that is visually stunning, has vivid characters, and maintains dramatic intensity. The result is a historical world that is at once apprehensible and meaningful for Western audiences, and yet which challenges their culturally conditioned concepts of the relationship of time and space, the natural and the supernatural.

Yeelen's storyline follows a family conflict that is at once both specific and archetypal. A young man (Nianankoro) and his mother have for 10 years been eluding his father, Soma. Soma must protect the Komo, which has for centuries empowered his family. But Nianankoro's mission is to destroy the Komo, whose misuse by his estranged father threatens the society. With Soma in pursuit of his son and the powerful ancestral fetishes that protect him and his mother, Nianankoro travels to his uncle, with whom he can safeguard the fetishes. Uncle, a seer, urges Nianankoro to finally defeat Soma in order to save the world from a great, impending disaster. The father–son conflict is dwarfed in their final confrontation by the immense power of magic to restore the order of good and justice in the world.

See also: *Atanarjuat*; *God's Gift*; *Keïta! The Heritage of the Griot*

Andrew, Dudley. "The Roots of the Nomadic: Gilles Deleuze and the Cinema of West Africa." In *The Brain Is the Screen: Deleuze and the Philosophy of Cinema*, edited by Gregory Flaxman, 215–49. Minneapolis, MN: University of Minnesota Press, 2000.

Downing, John D.H. "Post-Tricolor African Cinema: Toward a Richer Vision." In *Cinema, Colonialism, Postcolonialism: Perspectives from the French and Francophone World*, edited by Dina Sherzer, 188–228. Austin: University of Texas Press, 1996.

MacRae, Suzanne H. "*Yeelen*: A Political Fable of the Komo Blacksmith/Sorcerers." *Research in African Literatures* 26(3) (Fall 1995): 57–66.

Oyekunle, Segun. "A Review of Souleymane Cissé's Film *Yeelen*." *Présence Africaine* 148 (1988): 183–84.

Ukadike, N. Frank. "Souleymane Cissé (Mali)." In *Questioning African Cinema: Conversations with Filmmakers*, 19–28. Minneapolis, MN: University of Minnesota Press, 2002.

Yellow Earth / Huang tudi (1984) Chen Kaige; China; Mandarin with English subtitles; Color; 89 m; Fox Lorber (VHS); China, 1939.

Yellow Earth is a highly symbolic film that depicts traditional China on the verge of revolutionary change. The film is set in Northern Shaanxi Province in 1939, which the Guomindang (China's national government) had acknowledged was part of a northern Communist region—a nod to the GMD-CCP "Unified Front" against Japan. Little in the way of revolutionary change is evident in the agricultural community that a member of the Communist 8th Route Army, Gu Qing, visits in order to collect folk songs. A traditional wedding procession of a young bride, laborious work in the home and fields, and the gender division of labor are all aspects of the society he comes to know. His friendship with the children of his host, a peasant widower, provides the context for a highly ambiguous portrait of the success of the People's Liberation Army in drawing the people into "struggle" against their feudal society.

Berry, Chris, and Mary Ann Farquhar. "Post-Socialist Strategies: An Analysis of *Yellow Earth* and *Black Cannon Incident*." In *Cinematic Landscape: Observations on the Visual Arts and Cinema of China and Japan*, edited by Linda C. Ehrlich and David Desser, 81–116. Austin: University of Texas Press, 1994.

Farquhar, Mary Ann. "The Hidden Gender in *Yellow Earth*." *Screen* 33 (Summer 1992): 154–64.

Kendall, Timothy. "*Yellow Earth* and Ethnographic Knowledge: The Interpretation of Culture/the Culture of Interpretation." *Journal of Media & Cultural Studies* 14(2) (July 2000): 215–30.

Kennedy, Harlan. "*Yellow Earth*." *Film Comment* 21 (November/December 1985): 75.

Lu, Tonglin. "Continuity and Subversion: Chen Kaige: *Yellow Earth*; *Big Parade*; *King of the Children*." In *Confronting Modernity in the Cinemas of Taiwan and Mainland China*, 25–57. Cambridge: Cambridge University Press, 2002.

Silbergeld, Jerome. "Drowning on Dry Land: *Yellow Earth* and the Traditionalism of the 'Avant-Garde.'" In *China into Film: Frames of Reference in Contemporary Chinese Cinema*, 15–52. London: Reaktion Books, 1999.

Yau, Esther C.M. "*Yellow Earth*: Western Analysis and a Non-Western Text." *Film Quarterly* 41 (Winter 1987/88): 22–33.

Zulu (1964) Cy Endfield; United Kingdom; English; Color; 138 m; MGM (DVD, VHS); Southern Africa, 1879.

Zulu's "reenactment" of the 1879 Battle of Rorke's Drift in Natal province—the location of a British field hospital and supply depot—dramatically pits a small British company against a Zulu corps of approximately four thousand men. With the structuring of action that could be as much at home in the genre of an American western, this is a film that celebrates (British) rogues who, just in time, use their wit and bravery to try and save the day. At least in terms of the British defeat at Rorke's Drift, they save British honor; even the victorious Zulus salute their worthy opponents.

At first appearance *Zulu* is a conventional—and very entertaining—"Empire" film of the 1960s. But the film, a popular if not critical success, has an attendant literature that suggests its openness to competing interpretation. Some analysts praise the movie for its limited but well-meaning attempt to portray Zulu culture; others see a racist depiction of the Zulus and the event. Some views of *Zulu* are so polarized about the overall meaning of the film that some argue the film is an apologia for imperialism, and others that it condemns the practice.

See also: *55 Days at Peking; 'Breaker' Morant; Khartoum*

Hall, Sheldon. "Monkey Feathers: Defending *Zulu.*" In *British Historical Cinema: The History, Heritage, and Costume Film*, edited by Claire Monk and Amy Sargeant, 110–28. London: Routledge, 2002.

Ivens, Phil. "Debating the Politics of *Zulu.*" *Cineaste* 26(2) (2001): 59.

Nicholson, Kathryn. "Misinterpreting *Zulu.*" *Cineaste* 26(2) (2001): 59–60.

Schleh, Eugene P.A. "Zulu." *Film & History: An Interdisciplinary Journal of Film and Television Studies* 11(1) (1981): 16–17.

Sharrett, Christopher. "*Zulu*, or the Limits of Liberalism." *Cineaste* 25(4) (2000): 28–33.

Cross References to Films

A NOTE ON CROSS REFERENCING

The following Thematic, Geographical, and Period Cross Reference sections allow the appearance of the same film in different categories. For example, *The Great White Man of Lambaréné* (a film about Albert Schweitzer in pre- and postcolonial Gabon) appears in two thematic categories: "Crossing Cultures" and "History as Biography." The film makes an appearance in both "Europe" and "Africa" in the regional lists.

The language and geographical definitions adopted to describe major regions of the world have long been subject to debate. Periodization is similarly open to academic interpretation. The regional and period categories used here reflect, for better or worse, a conceptual division of the world that still widely prevails in the West, and to an extent mirror those found in university and secondary school textbooks in the United States and Canada.[1]

Categorization of films by theme follows those described in detail in "Themes in World History on Screen."

Production data recorded for each film is as follows: *Title/Original Title* (Year); Director; Setting.

FILMS CROSS REFERENCED BY THEME

History as Biography

1492: Conquest of Paradise (1992); Ridley Scott; Spain and the Caribbean, 1492–1501.

Aguirre, the Wrath of God/Aguirre, der Zorn Göttes (1972); Werner Herzog; Amazon River, 1560–1561.

Alexander Nevsky/Aleksandr Nevsky (1938); Sergei M. Eisenstein and Dmitri Vasilyev; Russia, 13th century.

. . . And Give My Love to the Swallows/. . . a pozdravuji vlastovky (1972); Jaromil Jires; Czechoslovakia, World War II.

Anna Göldin, the Last Witch/Anna Göldin, letzte Hexe (1991); Gertrud Pinkus; Switzerland, 18th century.

Anne of the Thousand Days (1969); Charles Jarrott; England, 1527–1536.

Berlin Jerusalem/Berlin-Yerushalaim (1989); Amos Gitai; Berlin and Palestine, 1904–1945.

Bethune:The Making of a Hero/Dr. Bethune (1990); Phillip Borsos; Canada and China, 1920s and 1930s.

Braveheart (1995); Mel Gibson; Scotland, 1280–1314.

Cabeza de Vaca (1991); Nicolás Echevarría; Colonial Mexico, 1520s and 1530s.

Camila (1995); María Luisa Bemberg; Argentina, 1840s.

The Chant of Jimmie Blacksmith (1978); Fred Schepisi; Australia, turn of the 20th century.

Cromwell (1970); Ken Hughes; Great Britain, 1640–1653.

Cry Freedom (1987); Richard Attenborough; South Africa, 1970s.

Daens (1993); Stijn Coninx; Flanders, Belgium, 1890s to 1907.

Danton (1983); Andrzej Wajda; France, 1793–1794.

Dersu Uzala (1975); Akira Kurosawa; Eastern Siberia, 1902–1910.

Elizabeth (1998); Shekhar Kapur; England, 1558–c. 1563.

Europa, Europa/Hitlerjunge Salomon (1990); Agnieszka Holland; Germany, Soviet Union, and Poland, 1938–1945.

Gandhi (1982); Richard Attenborough; India and South Africa, 1893–1948.

The Great White Man of Lambaréné/Le grand blanc de Lambaréné (1995); Bassek Ba Kobhio; Gabon, 1944–1965.

I, The Worst of All/Yo, la peor de todas (1990); María Luisa Bemberg; Mexico, 17th century.

Ivan the Terrible, Part One/Ivan Groznyj I (1945); Sergei M. Eisenstein; Russia, 1547–1564.

Ivan the Terrible, Part Two/The Boyars' Plot/Ivan Groznyj II: Boyarsky zagovor (1958); Sergei M. Eisenstein and M. Filimonova; Russia, 1560s.

Jericho/Jericó (1991); Luis Alberto Lamata; Amazon region, 16th century.

José Rizal (1998); Marilou Diaz-Abaya; Philippines, late 19th century.

Korczak (1990); Andrzej Wajda; Warsaw, Poland, 1930s and 1940s.

Kundun (1997); Martin Scorsese; Tibet, 1930s–1950s.

The Last Emperor (1987); Bernardo Bertolucci; China, 1908–1959.

Lawrence of Arabia (1962); David Lean; Middle East, 1916–1918.

Lin Zexu (1959); Zheng Junli; China, 1838–1841.

Lumumba (2000); Raoul Peck; Congo, 1959–1961.

Luther: Genius, Rebel, Liberator (2003); Eric Till; Germany, 1519–1525.

The Madness of King George (1994); Nicolas Hytner; Great Britain, 18th century.

The Making of the Mahatma (1996); Shyam Benegal; South Africa, 1893–1914.

A Man For All Seasons (1966); Fred Zinnemann; England, 16th century.

The Message: The Story of Islam/Al-Risala (1977); Moustapha Akkad; Mecca and Medina, 7th century.

Mishima: A Life in Four Chapters (1985); Paul Schraeder; Japan, 1920s–1970.

My Love Has Been Burning/Waga koi wa moenu (1949); Kenji Mizoguchi; Japan, 1880s.

Napoléon/Abel Gance's Napoléon/Napoléon vu par Abel Gance (1927); Abel Gance; France, 18th century.

Nasser 56/Nasser Sitawkhamseen (1996); Mohamed Fadel; Egypt, 1956.

The Passion of Joan of Arc/La Passion de Jeanne d'Arc (1928); Carl Theodor Dreyer; France, 1431.

The Pianist (2002); Roman Polanski; Warsaw, Poland, 1939–1945.

The Private Life of Henry VIII (1933); Alexander Korda; England, 1530s and 1540s.

The Puppetmaster/Hsimeng rensheng (1993); Hou Hsiao-hsien; Taiwan, 1909–1945.

Raden Ajeng Kartini/R. A. Kartini(1983); Sjuman Djaya; North Central Java, 1879–1904.

Rasputin/Agony/Agoniya (1977); Elem Klimov; Russia, 1915–1916.

The Rise of Louis XIV/La prise de pouvoir par Louis XIV (1966); Roberto Rossellini; France, 17th century.

Rosa Luxemburg (1986); Margarethe von Trotta; Poland and Germany, 1900–1919.

Saladin/Al-Nasir Salah al-Din (1963); Youssef Chahine; Palestine, 1187–1192.

Sarraounia (1986); Med Hondo; Niger region, West Africa, late 19th century.

Seven Years in Tibet (1997); Jean-Jacques Annaud; Austria, India, and Tibet, 1935–1959.

A Single Spark/Jeon tae-il (1996); Park Kwang-su; South Korea, 1960s and 1970s.

Tjoet Nja' Dhien (1988); Eros Djarot; Aceh, Sumatra, 1896–1905.

Vatel (2000); Roland Joffé; France, 1671.

Viva Zapata! (1952); Elia Kazan; Mexico, late 19th and early 20th centuries.

The White Rose/Die Weiße Rose (1982); Michael Verhoeven; Germany, WWII.

Crossing Cultures: Conquest, Exchange, Diaspora

55 Days at Peking (1963); Nicholas Ray; China, 1900.

1492: Conquest of Paradise (1992); Ridley Scott; Spain and the Caribbean, 1492–1501.

Adanggaman (2000); Roger Gnoan M'Bala; West Africa, 17th century.

Adieu Bonaparte/Wadaan ya Bonaparte/Al-Wada' ya Bonaparte (1985); Youssef Chahine; Egypt, 1798–1799.

Aguirre, the Wrath of God/Aguirre, der Zorn Göttes (1972); Werner Herzog; Amazon River, 1560–1561.

Alsino and the Condor/Alsino y el cóndor (1982); Miguel Littín; Nicaragua, late 1970s.

Ararat (2002); Atom Egoyan; Canada, present day, and Armenia, 1915–1918.

At Play in the Fields of the Lord (1991); Hector Babenco; Brazil, contemporary.

Aya (1990); Solrun Hoaas; Australia, 1950s–1970s.

The Battle of Algiers/La bataille d'Alger (1966); Gillo Pontecorvo; Algeria, 1954–1957.

Berlin Jerusalem/Berlin-Yerushalaim (1989); Amos Gitai; Berlin and Palestine, 1904–1945.

Bethune: The Making of a Hero/Dr. Bethune (1990); Phillip Borsos; Canada and China, 1920s and 1930s.

Beyond Rangoon (1995); John Boorman; Burma, 1988.

Black and White In Color/Noirs et blancs en couleur/La Victoire en chantant (1976); Jean-Jacques Annaud; fictional French African colony, World War I.

Black Robe (1991); Bruce Beresford; New France (Canada), 1634.

Blood of the Condor/Yawar Mallku (1969); Jorge Sanjinés; Bolivia, 1960s.

Boat People/Tou bun no hoi (1982); Ann Hui; South Vietnam, late 1970s.

'Breaker' Morant (1979); Bruce Beresford; South Africa, 1901.

Burn!/¡Queimada! (1969); Gillo Pontecorvo; fictional Caribbean island, mid-19th century.

Cabeza de Vaca (1991); Nicolás Echevarría; Colonial Mexico, 1520s and 1530s.

The Camp at Thiaroye/Camp de Thiaroye (1987); Ousmane Sembène and Thierno Faty Sow; Senegal, end of WWII.

Ceddo/The People (1977); Ousmane Sembène; West Africa, conflating the 17th–19th centuries.

The Chant of Jimmie Blacksmith (1978); Fred Schepisi; Australia, turn of the 20th century.

The Chess Players/Shatranj ke Khilari (1977); Satyajit Ray; India, 1850s.

Chronicle of the Years of Embers/Chronique des années de braise/Waqaii Sanawat Al-Jamr (1975); Mohammed Lakhdar-Hamina; Algeria, 1939–1954.

Cry Freedom (1987); Richard Attenborough; South Africa, 1970s.

Dersu Uzala (1975); Akira Kurosawa; Eastern Siberia, 1902–1910.

Diên Biên Phu (1992); Pierre Schoendoerffer; Vietnam, 1950s.

A Dry White Season (1989); Euzhan Palcy; South Africa, 1976–1977.

Earth (1998); Deepa Mehta; Lahore, Punjab, 1947.

Emitai/God of Thunder (1971); Ousmane Sembène; West Africa, early 1940s.

Empire of the Sun (1987); Steven Spielberg; China, 1941–1945.

Exodus (1960); Otto Preminger; Cyprus and Palestine, 1947–1948.

Fall of Otrar/Gibel Otrara (1990); Ardak Amirkulov; Central Asia, 13th century.

The First Charge of the Machete/La primera carga al machete (1969); Manuel Octavio Gómez; Cuba, 1868.

Gaijín: A Brazilian Odyssey/Gaijín, Caminhos da Liberdade (1980); Tizuka Yamasaki; Japan and Brazil, early 20th century.

Gandhi (1982); Richard Attenborough; India and South Africa, 1893–1948.

Gone, Gone Forever Gone/Gate, gate paragate (1996); Hô Quang Minh; Vietnam, 1940s–1980s.

The Great White Man of Lambaréné/Le grand blanc de Lambaréné (1995); Bassek Ba Kobhio; Gabon, 1944–1965.

Hamsin/Eastern Wind (1982); Daniel Wachsmann; Israel, 1982.

Hot Winds/Garam Hava/Garm Hawa (1973); M.S. Sathyu; India, late 1940s.

How Tasty Was My Little Frenchman/Como era gostoso o meu francês (1971); Nelson Pereira dos Santos; Brazil, 16th century.

The Human Condition: No Greater Love/Ningen no joken I (1958); Masaki Kobayashi; Manchuria, 1943.

The Human Condition: Road to Eternity/Ningen No Joken II (1959); Masaki Kobayashi; Manchuria, 1944–1945.

The Human Condition: A Soldier's Prayer/Ningen No Joken III (1961); Masaki Kobayashi; Siberia and Manchuria, 1945.

Identity Pieces/Pièces d'identités (1998); Mweze Ngangura; Belgium and Congo, contemporary.

Indochine (1992); Régis Wargnier; Indochina, 1930–1954.

Jericho/Jericó (1991); Luis Alberto Lamata; Amazon region, 16th century.

José Rizal (1998); Marilou Diaz-Abaya; Philippines, late 19th century.

Journey of Hope/Reise der Hoffnung (1990); Xavier Koller; Turkey and Switzerland, 1980s.

Junoon (1978); Shyam Benegal; India, 1857–1858.

Kadarwati/The Five Faces of Kadarwati/Kadarwati, wanita dengan lima nama (1983); Sophan Sophiaan; Java and Singapore, 1942–1945.

Kedma (2002); Amos Gitai; Palestine, 1948.

Khartoum (1966); Basil Dearden and Eliot Elisofon; Sudan, late 19th century.

The Killing Fields (1984); Roland Joffé; Cambodia and New York, 1970s.

A King and His Movie/La película del Rey (1986); Carlos Sorin; Argentina, 1860s and 1980s.

The Kitchen Toto (1987); Harry Hook; Kenya, 1950s.

Kundun (1997); Martin Scorsese; Tibet, 1930s–1950s.

Land in Anguish/Terra em transe (1967); Glauber Rocha; Brazil, 1500/1960s.

The Last Supper/La Última cena (1974); Tomás Gutiérrez Alea; Cuba, 18th century.

Lawrence of Arabia (1962); David Lean; Middle East, 1916–1918.

Lin Zexu (1959); Zheng Junli; China, 1838–1841.

Lucía (1969); Humberto Solás; Cuba 1895, 1933, 1960.

Lumumba (2000); Raoul Peck; Congo, 1959–1961.

MacArthur's Children/Setouchi shonen yakyudan (1984); Masahiro Shinoda; Japan, 1945.

The Making of the Mahatma (1996); Shyam Benegal; South Africa, 1893–1914.

Max Havelaar (1976); Fons Rademakers; Indonesia, 19th century.

The Mission (1986); Roland Joffé; South America, 1750–1754.

Moonlighting (1982); Jerzy Skolimowski; London, 1981.

The Night of Counting the Years/The Mummy/El-mumia/Al-mummia (1969) Shadi Abdel Salam; Egypt, 1881.

November 1828 (1979); Teguh Karya; Dutch colonial Java, 1828.

The Opium War/Yapian zhanzheng (1997); Xie Jin; China, 1839–1842.

Orlando (1992); Sally Potter; England, Central Asia, Central Europe, 16th–20th centuries.

Pelle the Conqueror (1988); Bille August; Denmark, 1860s.

Perfumed Nightmare/Mababangong bangungot (1977); Kidlat Tahimik; Philippines, 1970s.

The Principal Enemy/El enemigo principal (1972); Jorge Sanjinés; Peru, 1965.

Quilombo (1984); Carlos Diegues; Palmares, Brazil, 1650–1695.

Raden Ajeng Kartini/R. A. Kartini (1983); Sjuman Djaya; North Central Java, 1879–1904.

Red River Valley/Honghe gu (1996); Feng Xiaoning; Tibet, turn of the 20th century to 1904.

Saladin/Al-Nasir Salah al-Din (1963); Youssef Chahine; Palestine, 1187–1192.

Sambizanga (1972); Sarah Maldoror; Angola, early 1960s.

Sarraounia (1986); Med Hondo; Niger region, West Africa, late 19th century.

Seven Years in Tibet (1997); Jean-Jacques Annaud; Austria, India, and Tibet, 1935–1959.

Soleil O (1970); Med Hondo; Africa and France, historical and contemporary.

Song of Chile/Cantata de Chile (1976); Humberto Solás; Chile, 16th–20th centuries.

Spices/Mirch Masala (1985); Ketan Mehta; India, 1940s.

Tjoet Nja' Dhien (1988); Eros Djarot; Aceh, Sumatra, 1896–1905.

Trek of Life/Yol (1982); Şerif Gören; Turkey, 1980s.

Utu (1982); Geoff Murphy; New Zealand, 1870s.

Welcome to Canada (1989); John M. Smith; Newfoundland, Canada, 1986.

Welcome, Mr. Marshall!/¡Bienvenido, Mr. Marshall! (1953); Luis García Berlanga; Spain, post-WWII.

The Year of Living Dangerously (1982); Peter Weir; Indonesia, 1965.

Zulu (1964); Cy Endfield; Southern Africa, 1879.

Civil, International, and Sectarian Conflict

55 Days at Peking (1963); Nicholas Ray; China, 1900.

1900/Novecento (1976); Bernardo Bertolucci; Italy, 1900–1945.

The Adalen Riots/Ådalen '31 (1969); Bo Widerberg; Sweden, 1931.

Adieu Bonaparte/Wadaan ya Bonaparte/Al-Wada' ya Bonaparte (1985); Youssef Chahine; Egypt, 1798–1799.

Alexander Nevsky/Aleksandr Nevsky (1938); Sergei M. Eisenstein and Dmitri Vasilyev; Russia, 13th century.

Alsino and the Condor/Alsino y el cóndor (1982); Miguel Littín; Nicaragua, late 1970s.

. . . And Give My Love to the Swallows/. . . a pozdravuji vlastovky (1972); Jaromil Jires; Czechoslovakia, World War II.

Anne of the Thousand Days (1969); Charles Jarrott; England, 1527–1536.

Ararat (2002); Atom Egoyan; Canada, present day, and Armenia, 1915–1918.

Ashes and Diamonds/Popiol i diament (1958); Andrzej Wajda; Poland, 1945.

Ballad of a Soldier/Ballada o soldate (1959); Grigori Chukhrai; Soviet Union, World War II.

The Battle of Algiers/La bataille d'Alger (1966); Gillo Pontecorvo; Algeria, 1954–1957.

The Battle of Canudos/Guerra de Canudos (1997); Sergio Rezende; Brazil, 1890s.

The Battleship Potemkin/Bronenosets 'Potyomkin' (1925); Sergei M. Eisenstein; Russia, 1905.

Before the Rain/Pred dozhdot (1994); Milcho Manchevski; Macedonia and London, early 1990s.

Berlin Jerusalem/Berlin-Yerushalaim (1989); Amos Gitai; Berlin and Palestine, 1904–1945.

Bethune: The Making of a Hero/Dr. Bethune (1990); Phillip Borsos; Canada and China, 1920s and 1930s.

Beyond Rangoon (1995); John Boorman; Burma, 1988.

Bitter Sea/Amargo mar (1984); Antonio Eguino; Bolivia, 1879.

Black Cannon Incident/Heipao shijian (1986); Huang Jianxin; China, 1980s.

Black Rain/Kuroi Ame (1989); Shohei Imamura; Japan, 1945 and 1950.

Blood of the Condor/Yawar Mallku (1969); Jorge Sanjinés; Bolivia, 1960s.

Bloody Sunday (2002); Peter Greengrass; Northern Ireland, January 1972.

The Blue Kite/Lan feng zheng (1993); Tian Zhuangzhuang; China, 1953 to 1967.

The Boat/Das Boot (1981); Wolfgang Petersen; North Atlantic Ocean, 1942.

The Boat Is Full/Das Boot ist voll (1981); Markus Imhoof; Switzerland, WWII.

Boat People/Tou bun no hoi (1982); Ann Hui; South Vietnam, late 1970s.

Border Street/Ulica graniczna (1949); Aleksander Ford; Warsaw, Poland, 1939–1943.

Boycott/Baycot (1985); Mohsen Makhmalbaf; Iran, 1970s.

Braveheart (1995); Mel Gibson; Scotland, 1280–1314.

'Breaker' Morant (1979); Bruce Beresford; South Africa, 1901.

The Burmese Harp/Biruma no tategoto (1956); Kon Ichikawa; Burma, end of WWII.

Camila (1995); María Luisa Bemberg; Argentina, 1840s.

Canal/Kanal (1957); Andrzej Wajda; Poland, 1944.

Canoa (1976); Felipe Cazals; Mexico, 1968.

The Captivating Star of Happiness/Zvezda plenitelnogo schastya (1975); Vladimir Motyl; Russia, 1820s.

Ceddo/The People (1977); Ousmane Sembène; West Africa, conflating the 17th–19th centuries.

The Chekist (1992); Alexandr Rogozhkin; Soviet Union, c. 1918–1922.

Chronicle of the Years of Embers/Chronique des années de braise/Waqaii Sanawat Al-Jamr (1975); Mohammed Lakhdar-Hamina; Algeria, 1939–1954.

Circle of Deceit/Die Fälschung (1981); Volker Schlöndorff; Lebanon, late 1970s.

City of Sadness/Beiqing chengshi (1989); Hou Hsiao-hsien; Taiwan, 1945–1949.

The Cloud-Capped Star/Meghe dhaka tara (1960); Ritwik Ghatak; Calcutta, late 1950s.

Colonel Wolodyjowski/Pan Wolodyjowski (1969); Jerzy Hoffman; Poland, 1668.

Come and See/Idi i smotri (1985); Elem Klimov; Byelorussia, WWII.

Le Coup de Grâce/Der Fangschuß (1976); Volker Schlöndorff; Latvia, 1919.

The Courage of the People/The Night of San Juan/El coraje del pueblo/La Noche de San Juan (1971); Jorge Sanjinés; Bolivia, 1942–1967.

Cromwell (1970); Ken Hughes; Great Britain, 1640–1653.

Crows and Sparrows/Wuya yu maque (1949); Zheng Junli; Shanghai, China, 1948–1949.

Cry Freedom (1987); Richard Attenborough; South Africa, 1970s.

Daens (1993); Stijn Coninx; Flanders, Belgium, 1890s to 1907.

The Damned/La Caduta degli dei (1969); Luchino Visconti; Germany, 1933–1934.

Danton (1983); Andrzej Wajda; France, 1793–1794.

Day of Wrath/Vredens Dag (1943); Carl Theodor Dreyer; Denmark, 1623.

Diên Biên Phu (1992); Pierre Schoendoerffer; Vietnam, 1950s.

A Dry White Season (1989); Euzhan Palcy; South Africa, 1976–1977.

Earth (1998); Deepa Mehta; Lahore, Punjab, 1947.

Empire of the Sun (1987); Steven Spielberg; China, 1941–1945.

The End of St. Petersburg/Konets Sankt-Peterburga (1927); Vsevolod Pudovkin; Russia, WWI.

Enemy at the Gates (2001); Jean-Jacques Annaud; Soviet Union, 1942.

Europa, Europa /Hitlerjunge Salomon (1990); Agnieszka Holland; Germany, Soviet Union, and Poland, 1938–1945.

Exodus (1960); Otto Preminger; Cyprus and Palestine, 1947–1948.

Fall of Otrar/Gibel Otrara (1990); Ardak Amirkulov; Central Asia, 13th century.

Farewell My Concubine/Ba wang bie ji (1993); Chen Kaige; China, 1920s–1970s.

Fever/Goraczka (1981); Agnieszka Holland; Poland, 1905.

Fires on the Plain/Nobi (1959); Kon Ichikawa; Philippines, 1945.

The First Charge of the Machete/La primera carga al machete (1969); Manuel Octavio Gómez; Cuba, 1868.

Flame (1996); Ingrid Sinclair; Rhodesia/Zimbabwe, 1970s.

A Funny, Dirty Little War/No habrá más penas ni olvido (1983); Héctor Olivera; Argentina, 1970s.

Gallipoli (1981); Peter Weir; Australia, Egypt and Dardanelles, Ottoman Empire, 1914–1915.

Gandhi (1982); Richard Attenborough; India and South Africa, 1893–1948.

The Garden of the Finzi-Continis/Il Giardino dei Finzi-Contini (1970); Vittorio De Sica; Italy, 1938–1943.

Gate of Hell/Jigoku mon (1953); Teinosuke Kinugasa; Japan, 12th century.

A Generation/Pokolenie (1954); Andrzej Wajda; Warsaw, Poland, 1942.

Germany, Pale Mother/Deutschland, bleiche Mutter (1980); Helma Sanders-Brahms; Germany, 1930s and 1940s.

Germinal (1993); Claude Berri; France, 1860s.

The Gleiwitz Case/Der fall Gleiwitz (1961); Gerhard Klein; Poland, 1939.

Gone, Gone Forever Gone/Gate, gate paragate (1996); Hô Quang Minh; Vietnam, 1940s–1980s.

Good Men, Good Women/Haonan haonu (1995); Hou Hsiao-hsien; Taiwan and China, 1940s and 1990s.

Goodbye, Children/Au revoir les enfants (1987); Louis Malle; France, 1944.

Hamsin/Eastern Wind (1982); Daniel Wachsmann; Israel, 1982.

Hill 24 Doesn't Answer/Giv'a 24 Eina Ona (1955); Thorold Dickinson; Palestine, 1947.

The Home and the World/Ghare-Baire (1984); Satyajit Ray; Bengal, 1907–1908.

Hot Winds/Garam Hava/Garm Hawa (1973); M.S. Sathyu; India, late 1940s.

The House on Chelouche Street/Ha-Bayit Berechov Chelouche / Habayit B'Rechov Chelouche (1973); Moshé Mizrahi; Tel Aviv, 1946–1948.

The Human Condition: No Greater Love/Ningen no joken I (1958); Masaki Kobayashi; Manchuria, 1943.

The Human Condition: Road to Eternity/Ningen No Joken II (1959); Masaki Kobayashi; Manchuria, 1944–1945.

The Human Condition: A Soldier's Prayer/Ningen No Joken III (1961); Masaki Kobayashi; Siberia and Manchuria, 1945.

In the Heat of the Sun/Yangguang canlan de rizi (1994); Jiang Wen; China, 1970s.

Indochine (1992); Régis Wargnier; Indochina, 1930–1954.

The Inner Circle/Blizhniy krug (1991); Andrei Konchalovsky; Soviet Union, 1939–1953.

It's Raining on Santiago/Il pleut sur Santiago (1976); Helvio Soto; Chile 1970–1973.

Ivan the Terrible, Part One/Ivan Groznyj I (1945); Sergei M. Eisenstein; Russia, 1547–1564.

Ivan the Terrible, Part Two/The Boyars' Plot/Ivan Groznyj II: Boyarsky zagovor (1958); Sergei M. Eisenstein and M. Filimonova; Russia, 1560s.

José Rizal (1998); Marilou Diaz-Abaya; Philippines, late 19th century.

Journey to the Sun/Günese yolculuk (1999); Yesim Ustaoglu; Turkey, contemporary.

Judgment at Nuremberg (1961); Stanley Kramer; West Germany, 1948.

Kadarwati/The Five Faces of Kadarwati/Kadarwati, wanita dengan lima nama (1983); Sophan Sophiaan; Java and Singapore, 1942–1945.

Kafr Kassem (1974); Borhane Alaouie; Israel, 1956.

Kameradschaft (1931); G.W. Pabst; German–French border, 1919.

Kedma (2002); Amos Gitai; Palestine, 1948.

The Killing Fields (1984); Roland Joffé; Cambodia and New York, 1970s.

King of the Children/Haizi wang (1987); Chen Kaige; China, 1970s.

Kippur (2000); Amos Gitai; Israel, 1973.

The Kitchen Toto (1987); Harry Hook; Kenya, 1950s.

Korczak (1990); Andrzej Wajda; Warsaw, Poland, 1930s and 1940s.

Kundun (1997); Martin Scorsese; Tibet, 1930s–50s.

The Land/al-Ard (1969); Youssef Chahine; Egypt, 1933.

Land and Freedom (1995); Ken Loach; Spain, 1930s.

The Last Emperor (1987); Bernardo Bertolucci; China, 1908–1959.

The Leopard/Il Gattopardo (1963); Luchino Visconti; Sicily, 1860–1862.

Let There Be Peace/Daresalam (2000); Issa Serge Coelo; Chad, 1970s.

Letters from Marusia/Actas de Marusia (1975); Miguel Littín; Chile, 1907.

Libertarias/Freedomfighters (1996); Vicente Aranda; Spain, 1936–1939.

Lin Zexu (1959); Zheng Junli; China, 1838–1841.

The Lion's Den/La boca del lobo (1988); Francisco J. Lombardi; Peru, 1980s.

Lucía (1969); Humberto Solás; Cuba 1895, 1933, 1960.

Lumumba (2000); Raoul Peck; Congo, 1959–1961.

Luther: Genius, Rebel, Liberator (2003); Eric Till; Germany, 1519–1525.

MacArthur's Children/Setouchi shonen yakyudan (1984); Masahiro Shinoda; Japan, 1945.

The Man By the Shore/L' Homme sur les quais (1993); Raoul Peck; Haiti, 1960s.

A Man For All Seasons (1966); Fred Zinnemann; England, 16th century.

Man of Iron/Czlowiek z zelaza (1981); Andrzej Wajda; Poland, 1968, 1970, and 1980.

Man of Marble/Czlowiek z marmuru (1977); Andrzej Wajda; Poland, 1950s and 1970s.

Mapantsula (1988); Oliver Schmitz; South Africa, 1980s.

Marianne and Juliane/Die bleierne Zeit (1981); Margarethe von Trotta; West Germany, 1970s.

La Marseillaise (1938); Jean Renoir; France, 1789–1792.

May & August/Wuyue Bayue (2002); Raymond To Kwok-Wai; China, 1937.

Mephisto (1981); István Szabó; Hamburg and Berlin, 1930s.

The Message: The Story of Islam/Al-Risala (1977); Moustapha Akkad; Mecca and Medina, 7th century.

Moonlighting (1982); Jerzy Skolimowski; London, 1981.

Napoléon/Abel Gance's Napoléon/Napoléon vu par Abel Gance (1927); Abel Gance; France, 18th century.

Nasser 56/Nasser Sitawkhamseen (1996); Mohamed Fadel; Egypt, 1956.

The Nasty Girl/Das schreckliche Mädchen (1990); Michael Verhoeven; Germany, 1970s and 1980s.

The Night/al-Lail/al-Leil (1992); Mohamad Malas; Syria, 1930s and 1940s.

Night and Fog in Japan/Nihon no yoru to kiri (1960); Nagisa Oshima; Japan, 1950s and 1960s.

The Night of the Pencils/La noche de los lápices (1986); Héctor Olivera; Argentina, 1976.

Night of the Shooting Stars/La notte di San Lorenzo (1982); Paolo Taviani and Vittorio Taviani; Italy, 1944.

October (Ten Days That Shook the World)/Oktyabr (1927); Grigori Aleksandrov and Sergei M. Eisenstein; Russia, 1917.

The Official Story/La historia oficial (1985); Luis Puenzo; Argentina, 1983.

The Opium War/Yapian zhanzheng (1997); Xie Jin; China, 1839–1842.

Les Ordres (1974); Michel Brault; Quebec, Canada, 1970.

The Organizer/I Compagni (1963); Mario Monicelli; Turin, Italy, late 19th century.

Pan Tadeusz/The Last Foray in Lithuania (1999); Andrzej Wajda; Lithuania, 1811–1812.

The Passion of Joan of Arc/La Passion de Jeanne d'Arc (1928); Carl Theodor Dreyer; France, 1431.

Paths of Glory (1957); Stanley Kubrick; France, WW1.

The Pianist (2002); Roman Polanski; Warsaw, Poland, 1939–1945.

Pioneers of Freedom/Para Perintis Kemerdekaan (1980); Asrul Sani; West Sumatra, Indonesia, 1920s.

The Principal Enemy/El enemigo principal (1972); Jorge Sanjinés; Peru, 1965.

The Promised Land/La tierra prometida (1973); Miguel Littín; Chile 1930–1932.

Promised Land/Ziemia obiecana (1974); Andrzej Wajda; Lodz, Poland, late 19th century.

Quilombo (1984); Carlos Diegues; Palmares, Brazil, 1650–1695.

Raden Ajeng Kartini/R. A. Kartini (1983); Sjuman Djaya; North Central Java, 1879–1904.

Ramparts of Clay/Remparts d'argile (1971); Jean-Louis Bertucelli; Tunisia, 1962.

Ran (1985); Akira Kurosawa; Japan, 16th century.

Rasputin/Agony/Agoniya (1977); Elem Klimov; Russia, 1915–1916.

Rebellion in Patagonia/La Patagonia rebelde (1974); Héctor Olivera; Argentina, 1920s.

The Red and the White/Csillagosok, katonák (1967); Miklós Jancsó; Ukraine, 1919.

Red Dawn/Rojo amanecer (1989); Jorge Fons; Mexico City, 1968.

Repentance/Pokayaniye/Pokaianie (1986); Tengiz Abuladze; Soviet Union, 1930s.

Rosa Luxemburg (1986); Margarethe von Trotta; Poland and Germany, 1900–1919.

Rosenstrasse (2003); Margarethe von Trotta; Berlin, 1943 and contemporary New York.

The Round-Up/Szegénylegények (1965); Miklós Jancsó; Hungary, mid-19th century.

Sambizanga (1972); Sarah Maldoror; Angola, early 1960s.

Schindler's List (1993); Steven Spielberg; Poland and Czechoslovakia, 1939–1945.

The Shop on Main Street/Obchod na korze (1965); Ján Kadár and Elmar Klos; Slovak Republic, 1941–1942.

The Sibiriade/Sibiriada (1979); Andrei Konchalovsky; Siberia, 1909 to the 1960s.

A Single Spark/Jeon tae-il (1996); Park Kwang-su; South Korea, 1960s and 1970s.

Song of Chile/Cantata de Chile (1976); Humberto Solás; Chile, 16th–20th centuries.

The Sparrow/Al-Usfur (1972); Youssef Chahine; Egypt, 1967.

Spices/Mirch Masala (1985); Ketan Mehta; India, 1940s.

St. Michael Had a Rooster/San Michele aveva un gallo (1971); Paolo and Vittorio Taviani; Italy, 1870.

Stalingrad (1993); Joseph Vilsmaier; Soviet Union, 1942–1943.

The Sun-Seekers/Sonnensucher (1958/1972); Konrad Wolf; East Germany, 1950s.

Sunshine/A napfény íze (1999); István Szabó; Hungary, late 19th century to 1989.

Swing Kids (1993); Thomas Carter; Germany, 1930s.

Taira Clan Saga/Tales of the Taira Clan/Shin Heike monogatari (1955); Kenji Mizoguchi; Japan, 12th century.

The Terrorist (1998); Santosh Sivan; India, 1990s.

Teutonic Knights/Knights of the Teutonic Order/Krzyżazy (1960); Aleksander Ford; Poland, 15th century.

Those Whom Death Refused/Mortu Nega (1988); Flora Gomes; Guinea-Bissau, 1973–1975.

A Time to Live and a Time to Die/Tongnian wangshi (1985); Hou Hsiao-hsien; Taiwan, 1940s and 1950s.

Tjoet Nja' Dhien (1988); Eros Djarot; Aceh, Sumatra, 1896–1905.

The Traitors/Los traidores (1972); Raymundo Gleyzer; Argentina, 1950s and 1970s.

Transport from Paradise/Transport z ráje (1962); Zbynek Brynych; Czechoslovakia, 1944.

The Travelling Players/O Thiassos (1975); Theo Angelopoulos; Greece 1939–1952.

Ulysses' Gaze/To Vlemma tou Odyssea (1995); Theo Angelopoulos; Balkans, 20th century.

Under the Domim Tree/Etz Hadomim Tafus (1994); Eli Cohen; Israel, 1953.

Underground/Bila jednom jedna zemlja (1995); Emir Kusturica; Yugoslavia, World War II to 1990s.

The Uprising/La Insurrección (1980); Peter Lilienthal; Nicaragua, 1979.

Utu (1982); Geoff Murphy; New Zealand, 1870s.

Vatel (2000); Roland Joffé; France, 1671.

The Vikings (1958); Richard Fleischer; Northumbria, Great Britain, 9th century.

Viva Zapata! (1952); Elia Kazan; Mexico, late 19th and early 20th centuries.
The Wannsee Conference/Die Wannseekonferenz (1984); Heinz Schirk; Germany, 1942.
The White Rose/Die Weiße Rose (1982); Michael Verhoeven; Germany, WWII.
Winstanley (1975); Kevin Brownlow and Andrew Mollo; England, 1649–1650.
The Wooden Gun/Roveh Huliot (1979); Ilan Moshenson; Tel Aviv, 1950s.
The Year of Living Dangerously (1982); Peter Weir; Indonesia, 1965.
Yellow Earth/Huang tudi (1984); Chen Kaige; China, 1939.

Society: Modernization and Tradition

1900 /Novecento (1976); Bernardo Bertolucci; Italy, 1900–1945.
The Adalen Riots/Ådalen '31 (1969); Bo Widerberg; Sweden, 1931.
Anna Göldin, the Last Witch/Anna Göldin, letzte Hexe (1991); Gertrud Pinkus; Switzerland, 18th century.
Atanarjuat: The Fast Runner (2001); Zacharias Kunuk; (Canadian) Arctic, unspecified legendary times.
Aya (1990); Solrun Hoaas; Australia, 1950s–1970s.
Barren Lives/Vidas secas (1963); Nelson Pereira dos Santos; Brazil, 1940s.
Black Cannon Incident/Heipao shijian (1986); Huang Jianxin; China, 1980s.
The Blue Eyes of Yonta/Udju azul di Yonta (1992); Flora Gomes; Guinea-Bissau, 1980s.
City of Sadness/Beiqing chengshi (1989); Hou Hsiao-hsien; Taiwan, 1945–1949.
The Cloud-Capped Star/Meghe dhaka tara (1960); Ritwik Ghatak; Calcutta, late 1950s.
Colonel Chabert/Le Colonel Chabert (1994); Yves Angelo; Battle of Eylau, 1807 and post-Napoleonic France.
Crows and Sparrows/Wuya yu maque (1949); Zheng Junli; Shanghai, China, 1948–1949.
Daens (1993); Stijn Coninx; Flanders, Belgium, 1890s to 1907.
The Damned/La Caduta degli dei (1969); Luchino Visconti; Germany, 1933–1934.
A Dance for Heroes/Finzan (1990); Cheick Oumar Sissoko; Mali, contemporary.
Day of Wrath/Vredens Dag (1943); Carl Theodor Dreyer; Denmark, 1623.
Distant Thunder/Ashani Sanket (1973); Satyajit Ray; Bengal, 1943.
Drylanders (1962); Don Haldane; Saskatchewan, Canada, 1907–1938.
The Dupes/al-Makhdu'un (1972); Tewfik Saleh; Iraq, 1950s.
Earth/Zemlya (1930); Alexander Dovzhenko; Ukraine, 1929.
Effi Briest (1974); Rainer Werner Fassbinder; Germany, 19th century.
Eijanaika (1981); Shohei Imamura; Japan, 1860s.
The End of St. Petersburg/Konets Sankt-Peterburga (1927); Vsevolod Pudovkin; Russia, WWI.
The Family/La Famiglia (1987); Ettore Scola; Rome, Italy, 1906–1986.
Family/Jia (1957); Chen Xihe and Ye Ming; China, 1916–1920.
Floating Life (1996); Clara Law; Hong Kong, Australia, Germany, 1990s.
Germany, Pale Mother/Deutschland, bleiche Mutter (1980); Helma Sanders-Brahms; Germany, 1930s and 1940s.
Germinal (1993); Claude Berri; France, 1860s.
Girls in Uniform/Mädchen in Uniform (1931); Leontine Sagan; Prussia, Germany, 1913.
Gone, Gone Forever Gone/Gate, gate paragate (1996); Hô Quang Minh; Vietnam, 1940s–1980s.
Harvest 3000 Years/Mirt sost shi amit (1976); Haile Gerima; Ethiopia, 1970s.
Heimat/Heimat: Eine deutsche Chronik (1984); Edgar Reitz; Germany, 1918–1982.
The Home and the World/Ghare-Baire (1984); Satyajit Ray; Bengal, 1907–1908.
Hyenas/Hyènes (1992); Djibril Diop Mambety; Senegal, contemporary.

I, Pierre Rivière, Having Slaughtered My Mother, My Sister and My Brother .../Moi, Pierre Rivière, ayant égorgé ma mère, ma soeur et mon frère ... (1974); René Allio; France, 1835.

Journey of Hope/Reise der Hoffnung (1990); Xavier Koller; Turkey and Switzerland, 1980s.

The Joyless Street/Die freudlose Gasse (1925); G.W. Pabst; Vienna, Austria, early 1920s.

Kristin Lavransdatter (1995); Liv Ullmann; Norway, 14th century.

Lamerica (1994); Gianni Amelio; Albania, early 1990s.

The Land/al-Ard (1969); Youssef Chahine; Egypt, 1933.

Letters from Marusia/Actas de Marusia (1975); Miguel Littín; Chile, 1907.

Life of Oharu/Saikaku Ichidai Onna (1952); Kenji Mizoguchi; Japan, 17th century.

MacArthur's Children/Setouchi shonen yakyudan (1984); Masahiro Shinoda; Japan, 1945.

The Makioka Sisters/Sasame Yuki (1983); Kon Ichikawa; Japan, 1930s.

Margaret's Museum (1995); Mort Ransen; Canada, late 1940s.

The Message: The Story of Islam/Al-Risala (1977); Moustapha Akkad; Mecca and Medina, 7th century.

The Music Room/Jalsaghar (1958); Satyajit Ray; Bengal, 1920s.

My Love Has Been Burning/Waga koi wa moenu (1949); Kenji Mizoguchi; Japan, 1880s.

The Navigator: A Medieval Odyssey (1988); Vincent Ward; England, 1348, and contemporary unspecified Western city.

Newsfront (1978); Phillip Noyce; Australia, 1940s and 1950s.

The Night/al-Lail/al-Leil (1992); Mohamad Malas; Syria, 1930s and 1940s.

The Organizer/I Compagni (1963); Mario Monicelli; Turin, Italy, late 19th century.

Orlando (1992); Sally Potter; England, Central Asia, Central Europe, 16th–20th centuries.

Pelle the Conqueror (1988); Bille August; Denmark, 1860s.

Pioneers of Freedom/Para Perintis Kemerdekaan (1980); Asrul Sani; West Sumatra, Indonesia, 1920s.

The Promised Land/La tierra prometida (1973); Miguel Littín; Chile 1930–1932.

Promised Land/Ziemia obiecana (1974); Andrzej Wajda; Lodz, Poland, late 19th century.

Raden Ajeng Kartini/R. A. Kartini (1983); Sjuman Djaya; North Central Java, 1879–1904.

Ramparts of Clay/Remparts d'argile (1971); Jean-Louis Bertucelli; Tunisia, 1962.

Rebellion in Patagonia/La Patagonia rebelde (1974); Héctor Olivera; Argentina, 1920s.

Record of a Tenement Gentleman/Nagaya shinshiroku (1947); Yasujiro Ozu; Tokyo, post-World War II.

The Return of Martin Guerre/Le retour de Martin Guerre (1982); Daniel Vigne; France, 1530s–1560s.

Ridicule (1996); Patrice Leconte; France, 1783.

A River Called Titas/Titash ekti nadir naam (1973); Ritwik Ghatak; East Bengal, 1930s.

Sansho the Bailiff/Sanshô dayû (1954); Kenji Mizoguchi; Japan, 11th century.

The Sealed Soil/Khak-e Sar Behmorh (1977); Marva Nabili; Iran, 1970s.

The Seventh Seal/Det sjunde inseglet (1957); Ingmar Bergman; Sweden, 14th century.

The Sibiriade/Sibiriada (1979); Andrei Konchalovsky; Siberia, 1909 to the 1960s.

Silences of the Palace/Saimt el qusur (1994); Moufida Tlatli; Tunisia, early 1950s.

Sorceress/Le Moine et la sorcière (1987); Suzanne Schiffman; France, 13th century.

Spinning Wheel/Mulleya Mulleya (1984); Lee Doo-yong; Korea, 15th century.

St. Michael Had a Rooster/San Michele aveva un gallo (1971); Paolo and Vittorio Taviani; Italy, 1870.

The Story of Qiu Ju/Qiu Ju daguansi (1992); Zhang Yimou; China, 1980s.

The Story of Women/Une affaire de Femmes (1988); Claude Chabrol; Vichy France, WWII.

The Sun-Seekers/Sonnensucher (1958/1972); Konrad Wolf; East Germany, 1950s.

Sunshine/A napfény íze (1999); István Szabó; Hungary, late 19th century to 1989.

Those Whom Death Refused/Mortu Nega (1988); Flora Gomes; Guinea-Bissau, 1973–1975.

The Tiger from Tjampa/Harimau Tjampa (1953); D. Djayakusuma; West Sumatra, Indonesia, 1930s.

A Time to Live and a Time to Die/Tongnian wangshi (1985); Hou Hsiao-hsien; Taiwan, 1940s and 1950s.

The Tree of Wooden Clogs/L'albero degli zoccoli (1978); Ermanno Olmi; Italy, early 20th century.

Utopia/Saaraba (1988); Amadou Saalum Seck; Senegal, 1980s.

Welcome to Canada (1989); John M. Smith; Newfoundland, Canada, 1986.

God's Gift/Wend Kuuni (1982); Gaston Kaboré; Mossi village, Africa, mythic.

Winstanley (1975); Kevin Brownlow and Andrew Mollo; England, 1649–1650.

The Wooden Gun/Roveh Huliot (1979); Ilan Moshenson; Tel Aviv, 1950s.

Yellow Earth/Huang tudi (1984); Chen Kaige; China, 1939.

Redefining Historical Narrative: Reflexivity, Myth, Memory, Satire

Aguirre, the Wrath of God/Aguirre, der Zorn Göttes (1972); Werner Herzog; Amazon River, 1560–1561.

Ararat (2002); Atom Egoyan; Canada, present day, and Armenia, 1915–1918.

Atanarjuat: The Fast Runner (2001); Zacharias Kunuk; (Canadian) Arctic, unspecified legendary times.

The Ball/Le bal (1982); Ettore Scola; France, 1930s–1980s.

Before the Rain/Pred dozhdot (1994); Milcho Manchevski; Macedonia and London, early 1990s.

Berlin Jerusalem/Berlin-Yerushalaim (1989); Amos Gitai; Berlin and Palestine, 1904–1945.

Black and White In Color/Noirs et blancs en couleur/La Victoire en chantant (1976); Jean-Jacques Annaud; fictional French African colony, World War I.

Chac the Rain God /Chac: Dios de la lluvia (1974); Rolando Klein; Mexico, unspecified/mythic.

Eijanaika (1981); Shohei Imamura; Japan, 1860s.

The Emperor's New Clothes (2001); Alan Taylor; France, early 19th century.

The First Charge of the Machete/La primera carga al machete (1969); Manuel Octavio Gómez; Cuba, 1868.

God's Gift/Wend Kuuni (1982); Gaston Kaboré; Mossi village, Africa, mythic.

Good Men, Good Women/Haonan haonu (1995); Hou Hsiao-hsien; Taiwan and China, 1940s and 1990s.

Heimat/Heimat: Eine deutsche Chronik (1984); Edgar Reitz; Germany, 1918–1982.

Hiroshima, My Love/Hiroshima, mon amour (1959); Alain Resnais; Japan, 1959.

How Tasty Was My Little Frenchman/Como era gostoso o meu francês (1971); Nelson Pereira dos Santos; Brazil, 16th century.

I, Pierre Rivière, Having Slaughtered My Mother, My Sister and My Brother .../Moi, Pierre Rivière, ayant égorgé ma mère, ma soeur et mon frère ... (1974); René Allio; France, 1835.

It Happened Here (1966); Kevin Brownlow and Andrew Mollo; England, 1944.

Keïta! The Heritage of the Griot/Keita! L'héritage du griot (1994); Dani Kouyaté; Mali, mythic, 13th and 20th centuries.

A King and His Movie/La película del Rey (1986); Carlos Sorin; Argentina, 1860s and 1980s.

Land in Anguish/Terra em transe (1967); Glauber Rocha; Brazil, 1500/1960s.

Lucía (1969); Humberto Solás; Cuba 1895, 1933, 1960.

Mishima: A Life in Four Chapters (1985); Paul Schraeder; Japan, 1920s–1970.

The Nasty Girl/Das schreckliche Mädchen (1990); Michael Verhoeven; Germany, 1970s and 1980s.

The Navigator: A Medieval Odyssey (1988); Vincent Ward; England, 1348, and contemporary unspecified Western city.

The Night at Varennes/La nuit de Varennes (1982); Ettore Scola; France, 1791.

Les Ordres (1974); Michel Brault; Quebec, Canada, 1970.

Orlando (1992); Sally Potter; England, Central Asia, Central Europe, 16th–20th centuries.

Perfumed Nightmare/Mababangong bangungot (1977); Kidlat Tahimik; Philippines, 1970s.

The Puppetmaster/Hsimeng rensheng (1993); Hou Hsiao-hsien; Taiwan, 1909–1945.

Rashomon (1950); Akira Kurosawa; Japan, 12th century.

Rasputin/Agony/Agoniya (1977); Elem Klimov; Russia, 1915–1916.

Repentance/Pokayaniye/Pokaianie (1986); Tengiz Abuladze; Soviet Union, 1930s.

Russian Ark/Russkiy kovcheg (2002); Aleksandr Sokurov; St. Petersburg, Russia, 18th and 19th centuries.

Soleil O (1970); Med Hondo; Africa and France, historical and contemporary.

Time Bandits (1981); Terry Gilliam; Napoleonic Italy, medieval England, ancient Greece, and others.

The Travelling Players/O Thiassos (1975); Theo Angelopoulos; Greece 1939–1952.

Ulysses' Gaze/To Vlemma tou Odyssea (1995); Theo Angelopoulos; Balkans, 20th century.

Underground/Bila jednom jedna zemlja (1995); Emir Kusturica; Yugoslavia, World War II to 1990s.

Waterland (1992); Stephen Gyllenhaal; England, 1911–1940s and Pittsburgh, 1970s.

Welcome, Mr. Marshall!!/¡Bienvenido, Mr. Marshall! (1953); Luis García Berlanga; Spain, post-WWII.

Yeelen/Brightness (1987); Souleymane Cissé; Mali, 13th century and mythic.

FILMS CROSS REFERENCED BY GEOGRAPHIC AREA

South, East, and Central Asia

55 Days at Peking (1963); Nicholas Ray; China, 1900.

Aya (1990); Solrun Hoaas; Australia, 1950s–1970s.

Bethune: The Making of a Hero/Dr. Bethune (1990); Phillip Borsos; Canada and China, 1920s and 1930s.

Beyond Rangoon (1995); John Boorman; Burma, 1988.

Black Cannon Incident/Heipao shijian (1986); Huang Jianxin; China, 1980s.

Black Rain/Kuroi Ame (1989); Shohei Imamura; Japan, 1945 and 1950.

The Blue Kite/Lan feng zheng (1993); Tian Zhuangzhuang; China, 1953 to 1967.

Boat People/Tou bun no hoi (1982); Ann Hui; South Vietnam, late 1970s.

The Burmese Harp/Biruma no tategoto (1956); Kon Ichikawa; Burma, end of WWII.

The Chess Players/Shatranj ke Khilari (1977); Satyajit Ray; India, 1850s.

City of Sadness/Beiqing chengshi (1989); Hou Hsiao-hsien; Taiwan, 1945–1949.

The Cloud-Capped Star/Meghe dhaka tara (1960); Ritwik Ghatak; Calcutta, late 1950s.

Crows and Sparrows/Wuya yu maque (1949); Zheng Junli; Shanghai, China, 1948–1949.

Dersu Uzala (1975); Akira Kurosawa; Eastern Siberia, 1902–1910.

Diên Biên Phu (1992); Pierre Schoendoerffer; Vietnam, 1950s.

Distant Thunder/Ashani Sanket (1973); Satyajit Ray; Bengal, 1943.

Earth (1998); Deepa Mehta; Lahore, Punjab, 1947.

Eijanaika (1981); Shohei Imamura; Japan, 1860s.

Empire of the Sun (1987); Steven Spielberg; China, 1941–1945.

Fall of Otrar/Gibel Otrara (1990); Ardak Amirkulov; Central Asia, 13th century.

Family/Jia (1957); Chen Xihe and Ye Ming; China, 1916–1920.

Farewell My Concubine/Ba wang bie ji (1993); Chen Kaige; China, 1920s–1970s.

Fires on the Plain/Nobi (1959); Kon Ichikawa; Philippines, 1945.

Floating Life (1996); Clara Law; Hong Kong, Australia, Germany, 1990s.

Gandhi (1982); Richard Attenborough; India and South Africa, 1893–1948.

Gate of Hell/Jigoku mon (1953); Teinosuke Kinugasa; Japan, 12th century.

Gone, Gone Forever Gone/Gate, gate paragate (1996); Hô Quang Minh; Vietnam, 1940s–1980s.

Good Men, Good Women/Haonan haonu (1995); Hou Hsiao-hsien; Taiwan and China, 1940s and 1990s.

Hiroshima, My Love/Hiroshima, mon amour (1959); Alain Resnais; Japan, 1959.

The Home and the World/Ghare-Baire (1984); Satyajit Ray; Bengal, 1907–1908.

Hot Winds/Garam Hava/Garm Hawa (1973); M.S. Sathyu; India, late 1940s.

The Human Condition: No Greater Love/Ningen no joken I (1958); Masaki Kobayashi; Manchuria, 1943.

The Human Condition: Road to Eternity/Ningen No Joken II (1959); Masaki Kobayashi; Manchuria, 1944–1945.

The Human Condition: A Soldier's Prayer/Ningen No Joken III (1961); Masaki Kobayashi; Siberia and Manchuria, 1945.

In the Heat of the Sun/Yangguang canlan de rizi (1994); Jiang Wen; China, 1970s.

Indochine (1992); Régis Wargnier; Indochina, 1930–1954.

José Rizal (1998); Marilou Diaz-Abaya; Philippines, late 19th century.

Junoon (1978); Shyam Benegal; India, 1857–1858.

Kadarwati/The Five Faces of Kadarwati/Kadarwati, wanita dengan lima nama (1983); Sophan Sophiaan; Java and Singapore, 1942–1945.

The Killing Fields (1984); Roland Joffé; Cambodia and New York, 1970s.

King of the Children/Haizi wang (1987); Chen Kaige; China, 1970s.

Kundun (1997); Martin Scorsese; Tibet, 1930s–1950s.

The Last Emperor (1987); Bernardo Bertolucci; China, 1908–1959.

Life of Oharu/Saikaku Ichidai Onna (1952); Kenji Mizoguchi; Japan, 17th century.

Lin Zexu (1959); Zheng Junli; China, 1838–1841.

MacArthur's Children/Setouchi shonen yakyudan (1984); Masahiro Shinoda; Japan, 1945.

The Making of the Mahatma (1996); Shyam Benegal; South Africa, 1893–1914.

The Makioka Sisters/Sasame Yuki (1983); Kon Ichikawa; Japan, 1930s.

Max Havelaar (1976); Fons Rademakers; Indonesia, 19th century.

May & August/Wuyue Bayue (2002); Raymond To Kwok-Wai; China, 1937.

Mishima: A Life in Four Chapters (1985); Paul Schraeder; Japan, 1920s–1970.

The Music Room/Jalsaghar (1958); Satyajit Ray; Bengal, 1920s.

My Love Has Been Burning/Waga koi wa moenu (1949); Kenji Mizoguchi; Japan, 1880s.

Night and Fog in Japan/Nihon no yoru to kiri (1960); Nagisa Oshima; Japan, 1950s and 1960s.

November 1828 (1979); Teguh Karya; Dutch colonial Java, 1828.

The Opium War/Yapian zhanzheng (1997); Xie Jin; China, 1839–1842.

Orlando (1992); Sally Potter; England, Central Asia, Central Europe, 16th–20th centuries.

Perfumed Nightmare/Mababangong bangungot (1977); Kidlat Tahimik; Philippines, 1970s.

Pioneers of Freedom/Para Perintis Kemerdekaan (1980); Asrul Sani; West Sumatra, Indonesia, 1920s.

The Puppetmaster/Hsimeng rensheng (1993); Hou Hsiao-hsien; Taiwan, 1909–1945.

Raden Ajeng Kartini/R. A. Kartini (1983); Sjuman Djaya; North Central Java, 1879–1904.

Ran (1985); Akira Kurosawa; Japan, 16th century.

Rashomon (1950); Akira Kurosawa; Japan, 12th century.

Record of a Tenement Gentleman/Nagaya shinshiroku (1947); Yasujiro Ozu; Tokyo, post-World War II.

Red River Valley/Honghe gu (1996); Feng Xiaoning; Tibet, turn of the 20th century to 1904.

A River Called Titas/Titash ekti nadir naam (1973); Ritwik Ghatak; East Bengal, 1930s.

Sansho the Bailiff/Sanshô dayû (1954); Kenji Mizoguchi; Japan, 11th century.

Seven Years in Tibet (1997); Jean-Jacques Annaud; Austria, India and Tibet, 1935–1959.

A Single Spark/Jeon tae-il (1996); Park Kwang-su; South Korea, 1960s and 1970s.

Spices/Mirch Masala (1985); Ketan Mehta; India, 1940s.

Spinning Wheel/Mulleya Mulleya (1984); Lee Doo-yong; Korea, 15th century.

The Story of Qiu Ju/Qiu Ju daguansi (1992); Zhang Yimou; China, 1980s.

Taira Clan Saga/Tales of the Taira Clan/Shin Heike monogatari (1955); Kenji Mizoguchi; Japan, 12th century.

The Terrorist (1998); Santosh Sivan; India, 1990s.

The Tiger from Tjampa/Harimau Tjampa (1953); D. Djayakusuma; West Sumatra, Indonesia, 1930s.

A Time to Live and a Time to Die/Tongnian wangshi (1985); Hou Hsiao-hsien; Taiwan, 1940s and 1950s.

Tjoet Nja' Dhien (1988); Eros Djarot; Aceh, Sumatra, 1896–1905.

The Year of Living Dangerously (1982); Peter Weir; Indonesia, 1965.

Yellow Earth/Huang tudi (1984); Chen Kaige; China, 1939.

Canada, Australia, and New Zealand

Ararat (2002); Atom Egoyan; Canada, present day, and Armenia, 1915–1918.

Atanarjuat: The Fast Runner (2001); Zacharias Kunuk; (Canadian) Arctic, unspecified legendary times.

Aya (1990); Solrun Hoaas; Australia, 1950s–1970s.

Bethune: The Making of a Hero/Dr. Bethune (1990); Phillip Borsos; Canada and China, 1920s and 1930s.

Black Robe (1991); Bruce Beresford; New France (Canada), 1634.

'Breaker' Morant (1979); Bruce Beresford; South Africa, 1901.

The Chant of Jimmie Blacksmith (1978); Fred Schepisi; Australia, turn of the 20th century.

Drylanders (1962); Don Haldane; Saskatchewan, Canada, 1907–1938.

Floating Life (1996); Clara Law; Hong Kong, Australia, Germany, 1990s.

Gallipoli (1981); Peter Weir; Australia, Egypt, and Dardanelles, Ottoman Empire, 1914–1915.

Margaret's Museum (1995); Mort Ransen; Canada, late 1940s.

The Navigator: A Medieval Odyssey (1988); Vincent Ward; England, 1348, and contemporary unspecified Western city.

Newsfront (1978); Phillip Noyce; Australia, 1940s and 1950s.

Les Ordres (1974); Michel Brault; Quebec, Canada, 1970.

Utu (1982); Geoff Murphy; New Zealand, 1870s.

Welcome to Canada (1989); John M. Smith; Newfoundland, Canada, 1986.

Europe

55 Days at Peking (1963); Nicholas Ray; China, 1900.

1492: Conquest of Paradise (1992); Ridley Scott; Spain and the Caribbean, 1492–1501.

1900/Novecento (1976); Bernardo Bertolucci; Italy, 1900–1945.

The Adalen Riots/Ådalen '31 (1969); Bo Widerberg; Sweden, 1931.

Adieu Bonaparte/Wadaan ya Bonaparte/Al-Wada' ya Bonaparte (1985); Youssef Chahine; Egypt, 1798–1799.

Aguirre, the Wrath of God/Aguirre, der Zorn Göttes (1972); Werner Herzog; Amazon River, 1560–1561.

Alexander Nevsky/Aleksandr Nevsky (1938); Sergei M. Eisenstein and Dmitri Vasilyev; Russia, 13th century.

... And Give My Love to the Swallows/... a pozdravuji vlastovky (1972); Jaromil Jires; Czechoslovakia, World War II.

Anna Göldin, the Last Witch/Anna Göldin, letzte Hexe (1991); Gertrud Pinkus; Switzerland, 18th century.

Anne of the Thousand Days (1969); Charles Jarrott; England, 1527–1536.

Ararat (2002); Atom Egoyan; Canada, present day, and Armenia, 1915–1918.

Ashes and Diamonds/Popiól i diament (1958); Andrzej Wajda; Poland, 1945.

The Ball/Le bal (1982); Ettore Scola; France, 1930s–1980s.

Ballad of a Soldier/Ballada o soldate (1959); Grigori Chukhrai; Soviet Union, World War II.

The Battle of Algiers/La bataille d'Alger (1966); Gillo Pontecorvo; Algeria, 1954–1957.

The Battleship Potemkin/Bronenosets 'Potyomkin' (1925); Sergei M. Eisenstein; Russia, 1905.

Before the Rain/Pred dozhdot (1994); Milcho Manchevski; Macedonia and London, early 1990s.

Berlin Jerusalem/Berlin-Yerushalaim (1989); Amos Gitai; Berlin and Palestine, 1904–1945.

Black Robe (1991); Bruce Beresford; New France (Canada), 1634.

Black and White In Color/Noirs et blancs en couleur/La Victoire en chantant (1976); Jean-Jacques Annaud; fictional French African colony, World War I.

Bloody Sunday (2002); Peter Greengrass; Northern Ireland, January 1972.

The Boat/Das Boot (1981); Wolfgang Petersen; North Atlantic Ocean, 1942.

The Boat Is Full/Das Boot ist voll (1981); Markus Imhoof; Switzerland, WWII.

Border Street/Ulica graniczna (1949); Aleksander Ford; Warsaw, Poland, 1939–1943.

Braveheart (1995); Mel Gibson; Scotland, 1280–1314.

'Breaker' Morant (1979); Bruce Beresford; South Africa, 1901.

Burn!/¡Queimada! (1969); Gillo Pontecorvo; fictional Caribbean island, mid-19th century.

Cabeza de Vaca (1991); Nicolás Echevarría; Colonial Mexico, 1520s and 1530s.

The Camp at Thiaroye/Camp de Thiaroye (1987); Ousmane Sembène and Thierno Faty Sow; Senegal, end of WWII.

Canal/Kanal (1957); Andrzej Wajda; Poland, 1944.

The Captivating Star of Happiness/Zvezda plenitelnogo schastya (1975); Vladimir Motyl; Russia, 1820s.

The Chekist (1992); Alexandr Rogozhkin; Soviet Union, c. 1918–1922.

The Chess Players/Shatranj ke Khilari (1977); Satyajit Ray; India, 1850s.

Chronicle of the Years of Embers/Chronique des années de braise/Waqaii Sanawat Al-Jamr (1975); Mohammed Lakhdar-Hamina; Algeria, 1939–1954.

Colonel Chabert/Le Colonel Chabert (1994); Yves Angelo; Battle of Eylau, 1807 and post-Napoleonic France.

Colonel Wolodyjowski/Pan Wolodyjowski (1969); Jerzy Hoffman; Poland, 1668.

Come and See/Idi i smotri (1985); Elem Klimov; Byelorussia, WWII.

Le Coup de Grâce/Der Fangschuß (1976); Volker Schlöndorff; Latvia, 1919.

Cromwell (1970); Ken Hughes; Great Britain, 1640–1653.

Daens (1993); Stijn Coninx; Flanders, Belgium, 1890s–1907.

The Damned/La Caduta degli dei (1969); Luchino Visconti; Germany, 1933–1934.

Danton (1983); Andrzej Wajda; France, 1793–1794.

Day of Wrath/Vredens Dag (1943); Carl Theodor Dreyer; Denmark, 1623.

Dersu Uzala (1975); Akira Kurosawa; Eastern Siberia, 1902–1910.

Diên Biên Phu (1992); Pierre Schoendoerffer; Vietnam, 1950s.

Earth/Zemlya (1930); Alexander Dovzhenko; Ukraine, 1929.

Effi Briest (1974); Rainer Werner Fassbinder; Germany, 19th century.

Elizabeth (1998); Shekhar Kapur; England, 1558–c. 1563.

Emitai/God of Thunder (1971); Ousmane Sembène; West Africa, early 1940s.

The Emperor's New Clothes (2001); Alan Taylor; France, early 19th century.

Empire of the Sun (1987); Steven Spielberg; China, 1941–1945.

The End of St. Petersburg/Konets Sankt-Peterburga (1927); Vsevolod Pudovkin; Russia, WWI.

Enemy at the Gates (2001); Jean-Jacques Annaud; Soviet Union, 1942.

Europa, Europa/Hitlerjunge Salomon (1990); Agnieszka Holland; Germany, Soviet Union, and Poland, 1938–1945.

Exodus (1960); Otto Preminger; Cyprus and Palestine, 1947–1948.

Fall of Otrar/Gibel Otrara (1990); Ardak Amirkulov; Central Asia, 13th century.

The Family/La Famiglia (1987); Ettore Scola; Rome, Italy, 1906–1986.

Fever/Goraczka (1981); Agnieszka Holland; Poland, 1905.

The First Charge of the Machete/La primera carga al machete (1969); Manuel Octavio Gómez; Cuba, 1868.

Flame (1996); Ingrid Sinclair; Rhodesia/Zimbabwe, 1970s.

Floating Life (1996); Clara Law; Hong Kong, Australia, Germany, 1990s.

Gandhi (1982); Richard Attenborough; India and South Africa, 1893–1948.

The Garden of the Finzi-Continis/Il Giardino dei Finzi-Contini (1970); Vittorio De Sica; Italy, 1938–1943.

A Generation/Pokolenie (1954); Andrzej Wajda; Warsaw, Poland, 1942.

Germany, Pale Mother/Deutschland, bleiche Mutter (1980); Helma Sanders-Brahms; Germany, 1930s and 1940s.

Germinal (1993); Claude Berri; France, 1860s.

Girls in Uniform/Mädchen in Uniform (1931); Leontine Sagan; Prussia, Germany, 1913.

The Gleiwitz Case/Der fall Gleiwitz (1961); Gerhard Klein; Poland, 1939.

Goodbye, Children/Au revoir les enfants (1987); Louis Malle; France, 1944.

The Great White Man of Lambaréné/Le grand blanc de Lambaréné (1995); Bassek Ba Kobhio; Gabon, 1944–1965.

Heimat/Heimat: Eine deutsche Chronik (1984); Edgar Reitz; Germany, 1918–1982.

Hiroshima, My Love/Hiroshima, mon amour (1959); Alain Resnais; Japan, 1959.

How Tasty Was My Little Frenchman/Como era gostoso o meu francês (1971); Nelson Pereira dos Santos; Brazil, 16th century.

I, Pierre Rivière, Having Slaughtered My Mother, My Sister and My Brother .../Moi, Pierre Rivière, ayant égorgé ma mère, ma soeur et mon frère ... (1974); René Allio; France, 1835.

Identity Pieces/Pièces d'identités (1998); Mweze Ngangura; Belgium and Congo, contemporary.

Indochine (1992); Régis Wargnier; Indochina, 1930–1954.

The Inner Circle/Blizhniy krug (1991); Andrei Konchalovsky; Soviet Union, 1939–1953.

It Happened Here (1966); Kevin Brownlow and Andrew Mollo; England, 1944.

Ivan the Terrible, Part One/Ivan Groznyj I (1945); Sergei M. Eisenstein; Russia, 1547–1564.

Ivan the Terrible, Part Two/The Boyars' Plot/Ivan Groznyj II: Boyarsky zagovor (1958); Sergei M. Eisenstein and M. Filimonova; Russia, 1560s.

Jericho/Jericó (1991); Luis Alberto Lamata; Amazon region, 16th century.

Journey of Hope/Reise der Hoffnung (1990); Xavier Koller; Turkey and Switzerland, 1980s.

Journey to the Sun/Günese yolculuk (1999); Yesim Ustaoglu; Turkey, contemporary.

The Joyless Street/Die freudlose Gasse (1925); G.W. Pabst; Vienna, Austria, early 1920s.

Judgment at Nuremberg (1961); Stanley Kramer; West Germany, 1948.

Kameradschaft (1931); G.W. Pabst; German-French border, 1919.

Kedma (2002); Amos Gitai; Palestine, 1948.

Korczak (1990); Andrzej Wajda; Warsaw, Poland, 1930s and 1940s.

Kristin Lavransdatter (1995); Liv Ullmann; Norway, 14th century.

Lamerica (1994); Gianni Amelio; Albania, early 1990s.

Land and Freedom (1995); Ken Loach; Spain, 1930s.

Land in Anguish/Terra em transe (1967); Glauber Rocha; Brazil, 1500/1960s.

The Last Supper/La Última cena (1974); Tomás Gutiérrez Alea; Cuba, 18th century.

Lawrence of Arabia (1962); David Lean; Middle East, 1916–1918.

The Leopard/Il Gattopardo (1963); Luchino Visconti; Sicily, 1860–1862.

Libertarias/Freedomfighters (1996); Vicente Aranda; Spain, 1936–1939.

Lin Zexu (1959); Zheng Junli; China, 1838–1841.

Luther: Genius, Rebel, Liberator (2003); Eric Till; Germany, 1519–1525.

The Madness of King George (1994); Nicolas Hytner; Great Britain, 18th century.

A Man For All Seasons (1966); Fred Zinnemann; England, 16th century.

Man of Iron/Czlowiek z zelaza (1981); Andrzej Wajda; Poland, 1968, 1970, and 1980.

Man of Marble/Czlowiek z marmuru (1977); Andrzej Wajda; Poland, 1950s and 1970s.

Marianne and Juliane/Die bleierne Zeit (1981); Margarethe von Trotta; West Germany, 1970s.

La Marseillaise (1938); Jean Renoir; France, 1789–1792.

Mephisto (1981); István Szabó; Hamburg and Berlin, 1930s.

Moonlighting (1982); Jerzy Skolimowski; London, 1981.

Napoléon/Abel Gance's Napoléon/Napoléon vu par Abel Gance (1927); Abel Gance; France, 18th century.

The Nasty Girl/Das schreckliche Mädchen (1990); Michael Verhoeven; Germany, 1970s and 1980s.

The Navigator: A Medieval Odyssey (1988); Vincent Ward; England, 1348, and contemporary unspecified Western city.

The Night at Varennes/La nuit de Varennes (1982); Ettore Scola; France, 1791.

Night of the Shooting Stars/La notte di San Lorenzo (1982); Paolo Taviani and Vittorio Taviani; Italy, 1944.

October (Ten Days That Shook the World)/Oktyabr (1927); Grigori Aleksandrov and Sergei M. Eisenstein; Russia, 1917.

The Opium War/Yapian zhanzheng (1997); Xie Jin; China, 1839–1842.

The Organizer/I Compagni (1963); Mario Monicelli; Turin, Italy, late 19th century.

Orlando (1992); Sally Potter; England, Central Asia, Central Europe, 16th–20th centuries.

Pan Tadeusz/The Last Foray in Lithuania (1999); Andrzej Wajda; Lithuania, 1811–1812.

The Passion of Joan of Arc/La Passion de Jeanne d'Arc (1928); Carl Theodor Dreyer; France, 1431.

Paths of Glory (1957); Stanley Kubrick; France, WW1.

Pelle the Conqueror (1988); Bille August; Denmark, 1860s.

The Pianist (2002); Roman Polanski; Warsaw, Poland, 1939–1945.

The Private Life of Henry VIII (1933); Alexander Korda; England, 1530s and 1540s.

Promised Land/Ziemia obiecana (1974); Andrzej Wajda; Lodz, Poland, late 19th century.

Rasputin/Agony/Agoniya (1977); Elem Klimov; Russia, 1915–1916.

The Red and the White/Csillagosok, katonák (1967); Miklós Jancsó; Ukraine, 1919.

Red River Valley/Honghe gu (1996); Feng Xiaoning; Tibet, turn of the 20th century to 1904.

Repentance/Pokayaniye/Pokaianie (1986); Tengiz Abuladze; Soviet Union, 1930s.

The Return of Martin Guerre/Le retour de Martin Guerre (1982); Daniel Vigne; France, 1530s–1560s.

Ridicule (1996); Patrice Leconte; France, 1783.

The Rise of Louis XIV/La prise de pouvoir par Louis XIV (1966); Roberto Rossellini; France, 17th century.

Rosa Luxemburg (1986); Margarethe von Trotta; Poland and Germany, 1900–1919.

Rosenstrasse (2003); Margarethe von Trotta; Berlin, 1943 and contemporary New York.

The Round-Up/Szegénylegények (1965); Miklós Jancsó; Hungary, mid-19th century.

Russian Ark/Russkiy kovcheg (2002); Aleksandr Sokurov; St. Petersburg, Russia, 18th and 19th centuries.

Sarraounia (1986); Med Hondo; Niger region, West Africa, late 19th century.

Schindler's List (1993); Steven Spielberg; Poland and Czechoslovakia, 1939–1945

Seven Years in Tibet (1997); Jean-Jacques Annaud; Austria, India and Tibet, 1935–1959.

The Seventh Seal/Det sjunde inseglet (1957); Ingmar Bergman; Sweden, 14th century.

The Shop on Main Street/Obchod na korze (1965); Ján Kadár and Elmar Klos; Slovak Republic, 1941–1942.

The Sibiriade/Sibiriada (1979); Andrei Konchalovsky; Siberia, 1909 to the 1960s.

Soleil O (1970); Med Hondo; Africa and France, historical and contemporary.

Sorceress/Le Moine et la sorcière (1987); Suzanne Schiffman; France, 13th century.

St. Michael Had a Rooster/San Michele aveva un gallo (1971); Paolo and Vittorio Taviani; Italy, 1870.

Stalingrad (1993); Joseph Vilsmaier; Soviet Union, 1942–1943.

The Story of Women/Une affaire de Femmes (1988); Claude Chabrol; Vichy France, WWII.

The Sun-Seekers/Sonnensucher (1958/1972); Konrad Wolf; East Germany, 1950s.

Sunshine/A napfény íze (1999); István Szabó; Hungary, late 19th century to 1989.

Swing Kids (1993); Thomas Carter; Germany, 1930s.

Teutonic Knights/Knights of the Teutonic Order/Krzyzazy (1960); Aleksander Ford; Poland, 15th century.

Those Whom Death Refused/Mortu Nega (1988); Flora Gomes; Guinea-Bissau, 1973–1975.

Time Bandits (1981); Terry Gilliam; Napoleonic Italy, medieval England, ancient Greece, and others.

Tjoet Nja' Dhien (1988); Eros Djarot; Aceh, Sumatra, 1896–1905.

Transport from Paradise/Transport z ráje (1962); Zbynek Brynych; Czechoslovakia, 1944.

The Travelling Players/O Thiassos (1975); Theo Angelopoulos; Greece 1939–1952.

The Tree of Wooden Clogs/L'albero degli zoccoli (1978); Ermanno Olmi; Italy, early 20th century.

Trek of Life/Yol (1982); Şerif Gören; Turkey, 1980s.

Ulysses' Gaze/To Vlemma tou Odyssea (1995); Theo Angelopoulos; Balkans, 20th century.

Underground/Bila jednom jedna zemlja (1995); Emir Kusturica; Yugoslavia, World War II to 1990s.

Vatel (2000); Roland Joffé; France, 1671.

The Vikings (1958); Richard Fleischer; Northumbria, Great Britain, 9th century.

The Wannsee Conference/Die Wannseekonferenz (1984); Heinz Schirk; Germany, 1942.

Waterland (1992); Stephen Gyllenhaal; England, 1911–1940s and Pittsburgh, 1970s.

Welcome, Mr. Marshall!/¡Bienvenido, Mr. Marshall! (1953); Luis García Berlanga; Spain, post-WWII.

The White Rose/Die Weiße Rose (1982); Michael Verhoeven; Germany, WWII.

Winstanley (1975); Kevin Brownlow and Andrew Mollo; England, 1649–1650.

Zulu (1964); Cy Endfield; Southern Africa, 1879.

Latin America and the Caribbean

1492: Conquest of Paradise (1992); Ridley Scott; Spain and the Caribbean, 1492–1501.

Aguirre, the Wrath of God/Aguirre, der Zorn Göttes (1972); Werner Herzog; Amazon River, 1560–1561.

Alsino and the Condor/Alsino y el cóndor (1982); Miguel Littín; Nicaragua, late 1970s.

At Play in the Fields of the Lord (1991); Hector Babenco; Brazil, contemporary.

Barren Lives/Vidas secas (1963); Nelson Pereira dos Santos; Brazil, 1940s.

The Battle of Canudos/Guerra de Canudos (1997); Sergio Rezende; Brazil, 1890s.

Bitter Sea/Amargo mar (1984); Antonio Eguino; Bolivia, 1879.

Blood of the Condor/Yawar Mallku (1969); Jorge Sanjinés; Bolivia, 1960s.

Burn!/Queimada! (1969); Gillo Pontecorvo; fictional Caribbean island, mid-19th century.

Cabeza de Vaca (1991); Nicolás Echevarría; Colonial Mexico, 1520s and 1530s.

Camila (1995); María Luisa Bemberg; Argentina, 1840s.

Canoa (1976); Felipe Cazals; Mexico, 1968.

Chac the Rain God/Chac: Dios de la lluvia (1974); Rolando Klein; Mexico, unspecified/mythic.

The Courage of the People/The Night of San Juan/El coraje del pueblo/La Noche de San Juan (1971); Jorge Sanjinés; Bolivia, 1942–1967.

The First Charge of the Machete/La primera carga al machete (1969); Manuel Octavio Gómez; Cuba, 1868.

A Funny, Dirty Little War/No habrá más penas ni olvido (1983); Héctor Olivera; Argentina, 1970s.

Gaijín: A Brazilian Odyssey/Gaijín, Caminhos da Liberdade (1980); Tizuka Yamasaki; Japan and Brazil, early 20th century.

How Tasty Was My Little Frenchman/Como era gostoso o meu francês (1971); Nelson Pereira dos Santos; Brazil, 16th century.

I, The Worst of All/Yo, la peor de todas (1990); María Luisa Bemberg; Mexico, 17th century.

It's Raining on Santiago/Il pleut sur Santiago (1976); Helvio Soto; Chile 1970–1973.

Jericho/Jericó (1991); Luis Alberto Lamata; Amazon region, 16th century.

A King and His Movie/La película del Rey (1986); Carlos Sorin; Argentina, 1860s and 1980s.

Land in Anguish/Terra em transe (1967); Glauber Rocha; Brazil, 1500/1960s.

The Last Supper/La Última cena (1974); Tomás Gutiérrez Alea; Cuba, 18th century.

Letters from Marusia/Actas de Marusia (1975); Miguel Littín; Chile, 1907.

The Lion's Den/La boca del lobo (1988); Francisco J. Lombardi; Peru, 1980s.

Lucía (1969); Humberto Solás; Cuba 1895, 1933, 1960.

The Man By the Shore/L' Homme sur les quais (1993); Raoul Peck; Haiti, 1960s.

The Mission (1986); Roland Joffé; South America, 1750–1754.

The Night of the Pencils/La noche de los lápices (1986); Héctor Olivera; Argentina, 1976.

The Official Story/La historia oficial (1985); Luis Puenzo; Argentina, 1983.

The Principal Enemy/El enemigo principal (1972); Jorge Sanjinés; Peru, 1965.

The Promised Land/La tierra prometida (1973); Miguel Littín; Chile 1930–1932.

Quilombo (1984); Carlos Diegues; Palmares, Brazil, 1650–1695.

Rebellion in Patagonia/La Patagonia rebelde (1974); Héctor Olivera; Argentina, 1920s.

Red Dawn/Rojo amanecer (1989); Jorge Fons; Mexico City, 1968.

Song of Chile/Cantata de Chile (1976); Humberto Solás; Chile, 16th–20th centuries.

The Traitors/Los traidores (1972); Raymundo Gleyzer; Argentina, 1950s and 1970s.

The Uprising/La Insurrección (1980); Peter Lilienthal; Nicaragua, 1979.

Viva Zapata! (1952); Elia Kazan; Mexico, late 19th and early 20th centuries.

Middle East and North Africa

Adieu Bonaparte/Wadaan ya Bonaparte/Al-Wada' ya Bonaparte (1985); Youssef Chahine; Egypt, 1798–1799.

The Battle of Algiers/La bataille d'Alger (1966); Gillo Pontecorvo; Algeria, 1954–1957.

Berlin Jerusalem/Berlin-Yerushalaim (1989); Amos Gitai; Berlin and Palestine, 1904–1945.

Boycott/Baycot (1985); Mohsen Makhmalbaf; Iran, 1970s.

Chronicle of the Years of Embers/Chronique des années de braise/Waqaii Sanawat Al-Jamr (1975); Mohammed Lakhdar-Hamina; Algeria, 1939–1954.

Circle of Deceit/Die Fälschung (1981); Volker Schlöndorff; Lebanon, late 1970s.

The Dupes/al-Makhdu'un (1972); Tewfik Saleh; Iraq, 1950s.

Exodus (1960); Otto Preminger; Cyprus and Palestine, 1947–1948.

Gallipoli (1981); Peter Weir; Australia, Egypt and Dardanelles, Ottoman Empire, 1914–1915.

Hamsin/Eastern Wind (1982); Daniel Wachsmann; Israel, 1982.

Hill 24 Doesn't Answer/Giv'a 24 Eina Ona (1955); Thorold Dickinson; Palestine, 1947.

The House on Chelouche Street/Ha-Bayit Berechov Chelouche / Habayit B'Rechov Chelouche (1973); Moshé Mizrahi; Tel Aviv, 1946–1948.

Journey of Hope/Reise der Hoffnung (1990); Xavier Koller; Turkey and Switzerland, 1980s.

Journey to the Sun/Günese yolculuk (1999); Yesim Ustaoglu; Turkey, contemporary.

Kafr Kassem (1974); Borhane Alaouie; Israel, 1956.

Kedma (2002); Amos Gitai; Palestine, 1948.

Kippur (2000); Amos Gitai; Israel, 1973.

The Land/al-Ard (1969); Youssef Chahine; Egypt, 1933.

Lawrence of Arabia (1962); David Lean; Middle East, 1916–1918.

The Message: The Story of Islam/Al-Risala (1977); Moustapha Akkad; Mecca and Medina, 7th century.

Nasser 56/Nasser Sitawkhamseen (1996); Mohamed Fadel; Egypt, 1956.

The Night /al-Lail/al-Leil (1992); Mohamad Malas; Syria, 1930s and 1940s.

The Night of Counting the Years/The Mummy/El-mumia/Al-mummia (1969) Shadi Abdel Salam; Egypt, 1881.

Ramparts of Clay/Remparts d'argile (1971); Jean-Louis Bertucelli; Tunisia, 1962.

Saladin/Al-Nasir Salah al-Din (1963); Youssef Chahine; Palestine, 1187–1192.

The Sealed Soil/Khak-e Sar Behmorh (1977); Marva Nabili; Iran, 1970s.

Silences of the Palace/Saimt el qusur (1994); Moufida Tlatli; Tunisia, early 1950s.

The Sparrow/Al-Usfur (1972); Youssef Chahine; Egypt, 1967.

Trek of Life/Yol (1982); Şerif Gören; Turkey, 1980s.

Under the Domim Tree/Etz Hadomim Tafus (1994); Eli Cohen; Israel, 1953.

The Wooden Gun/Roveh Huliot (1979); Ilan Moshenson; Tel Aviv, 1950s.

Sub-Saharan and North Africa

Adanggaman (2000); Roger Gnoan M'Bala; West Africa, 17th century.

Adieu Bonaparte/Wadaan ya Bonaparte/Al-Wada' ya Bonaparte (1985); Youssef Chahine; Egypt, 1798–1799.

The Battle of Algiers/La bataille d'Alger (1966); Gillo Pontecorvo; Algeria, 1954–1957.

Black and White In Color/Noirs et blancs en couleur/La Victoire en chantant (1976); Jean-Jacques Annaud; fictional French African colony, World War I.

The Blue Eyes of Yonta/Udju azul di Yonta (1992); Flora Gomes; Guinea-Bissau, 1980s.

'Breaker' Morant (1979); Bruce Beresford; South Africa, 1901.

The Camp at Thiaroye/Camp de Thiaroye (1987); Ousmane Sembène and Thierno Faty Sow; Senegal, end of WWII.

Ceddo/The People (1977); Ousmane Sembène; West Africa, conflating the 17th–19th centuries.

Chronicle of the Years of Embers/Chronique des années de braise/Waqaii Sanawat Al-Jamr (1975); Mohammed Lakhdar-Hamina; Algeria, 1939–1954.

Cry Freedom (1987); Richard Attenborough; South Africa, 1970s.

A Dance for Heroes/Finzan (1990); Cheick Oumar Sissoko; Mali, contemporary.

A Dry White Season (1989); Euzhan Palcy; South Africa, 1976–1977.

Emitai/God of Thunder (1971); Ousmane Sembène; West Africa, early 1940s.

Flame (1996); Ingrid Sinclair; Rhodesia/Zimbabwe, 1970s.

God's Gift/Wend Kuuni (1982); Gaston Kaboré; Mossi village, Africa, mythic.

The Great White Man of Lambaréné/Le grand blanc de Lambaréné (1995); Bassek Ba Kobhio; Gabon, 1944–1965.

Harvest 3000 Years/Mirt sost shi amit (1976); Haile Gerima; Ethiopia, 1970s.

Hyenas/Hyènes (1992); Djibril Diop Mambety; Senegal, contemporary.

Identity Pieces/Pièces d'identités (1998); Mweze Ngangura; Belgium and Congo, contemporary.

Keïta! The Heritage of the Griot/Keita! L'héritage du griot (1994); Dani Kouyaté; Mali, mythic, 13th and 20th centuries.

Khartoum (1966); Basil Dearden and Eliot Elisofon; Sudan, late 19th century.

The Kitchen Toto (1987); Harry Hook; Kenya, 1950s.

The Land/al-Ard (1969); Youssef Chahine; Egypt, 1933.

Let There Be Peace/Daresalam (2000); Issa Serge Coelo; Chad, 1970s.

Lumumba (2000); Raoul Peck; Congo, 1959–1961.

The Making of the Mahatma (1996); Shyam Benegal; South Africa, 1893–1914.

Mapantsula (1988); Oliver Schmitz; South Africa, 1980s.

Nasser 56/Nasser Sitawkhamseen (1996); Mohamed Fadel; Egypt, 1956.

The Night of Counting the Years/The Mummy/El-mumia/Al-mummia (1969) Shadi Abdel Salam; Egypt, 1881.

Ramparts of Clay/Remparts d'argile (1971); Jean-Louis Bertucelli; Tunisia, 1962.

Saladin/Al-Nasir Salah al-Din (1963); Youssef Chahine; Palestine, 1187–1192.

Sambizanga (1972); Sarah Maldoror; Angola, early 1960s.

Sarraounia (1986); Med Hondo; Niger region, West Africa, late 19th century.

Silences of the Palace/Saimt el qusur (1994); Moufida Tlatli; Tunisia, early 1950s.

Soleil O (1970); Med Hondo; Africa and France, historical and contemporary.

Those Whom Death Refused/Mortu Nega (1988); Flora Gomes; Guinea-Bissau, 1973–1975.

Utopia/Saaraba (1988); Amadou Saalum Seck; Senegal, 1980s.

Yeelen/Brightness (1987); Souleymane Cissé; Mali, 13th century and mythic.

Zulu (1964); Cy Endfield; Southern Africa, 1879.

FILMS CROSS REFERENCED BY TIME PERIOD

Medieval (c. 600–1500)

1492: Conquest of Paradise (1992); Ridley Scott; Spain and the Caribbean, 1492–1501.

Alexander Nevsky/Aleksandr Nevsky (1938); Sergei M. Eisenstein and Dmitri Vasilyev; Russia, 13th century.

Braveheart (1995); Mel Gibson; Scotland, 1280–1314.

Fall of Otrar/Gibel Otrara (1990); Ardak Amirkulov; Central Asia, 13th century.

Gate of Hell/Jigoku mon (1953); Teinosuke Kinugasa; Japan, 12th century.

Kristin Lavransdatter (1995); Liv Ullmann; Norway, 14th century.

The Message: The Story of Islam/Al-Risala (1977); Moustapha Akkad; Mecca and Medina, 7th century.

The Navigator: A Medieval Odyssey (1988); Vincent Ward; England, 1348, and contemporary unspecified Western city.

The Passion of Joan of Arc/La Passion de Jeanne d'Arc (1928); Carl Theodor Dreyer; France, 1431.

Rashomon (1950); Akira Kurosawa; Japan, 12th century.

Saladin/Al-Nasir Salah al-Din (1963); Youssef Chahine; Palestine, 1187–1192.

Sansho the Bailiff/Sanshô dayû (1954); Kenji Mizoguchi; Japan, 11th century.

The Seventh Seal/Det sjunde inseglet (1957); Ingmar Bergman; Sweden, 14th century.

Sorceress/Le Moine et la sorcière (1987); Suzanne Schiffman; France, 13th century.

Spinning Wheel/Mulleya Mulleya (1984); Lee Doo-yong; Korea, 15th century.

Taira Clan Saga/Tales of the Taira Clan/Shin Heike monogatari (1955); Kenji Mizoguchi; Japan, 12th century.

Teutonic Knights/Knights of the Teutonic Order/Krzyżazy (1960); Aleksander Ford; Poland, 15th century.

The Vikings (1958); Richard Fleischer; Northumbria, Great Britain, 9th century.

Yeelen/Brightness (1987); Souleymane Cissé; Mali, 13[13] century and mythic.

Early Modern (c. 1500–1800)

1492: Conquest of Paradise (1992); Ridley Scott; Spain and the Caribbean, 1492–1501.

Adanggaman (2000); Roger Gnoan M'Bala; West Africa, 17th century.

Aguirre, the Wrath of God/Aguirre, der Zorn Göttes (1972); Werner Herzog; Amazon River, 1560–1561.

Anne of the Thousand Days (1969); Charles Jarrott; England, 1527–1536.

Black Robe (1991); Bruce Beresford; New France (Canada), 1634.

Cabeza de Vaca

Cromwell (1970); Ken Hughes; Great Britain, 1640–1653.

Danton (1983); Andrzej Wajda; France, 1793–1794.

Day of Wrath/Vredens Dag (1943); Carl Theodor Dreyer; Denmark, 1623.

Elizabeth (1998); Shekhar Kapur; England, 1558–c. 1563.

How Tasty Was My Little Frenchman/Como era gostoso o meu francês (1971); Nelson Pereira dos Santos; Brazil, 16th century.

I, Pierre Rivière, Having Slaughtered My Mother, My Sister and My Brother .../Moi, Pierre Rivière, ayant égorgé ma mère, ma soeur et mon frère ... (1974); René Allio; France, 1835.

I, The Worst of All/Yo, la peor de todas (1990); María Luisa Bemberg; Mexico, 17th century.

Ivan the Terrible, Part One

Ivan the Terrible, Part Two

Jericho/Jericó (1991); Luis Alberto Lamata; Amazon region, 16th century.

The Last Supper/La Última cena (1974); Tomás Gutiérrez Alea; Cuba, 18th century.

Life of Oharu/Saikaku Ichidai Onna (1952); Kenji Mizoguchi; Japan, 17th century.

Luther: Genius, Rebel, Liberator (2003); Eric Till; Germany, 1519–1525.

A Man For All Seasons (1966); Fred Zinnemann; England, 16th century.

La Marseillaise (1938); Jean Renoir; France, 1789–1792.

The Mission (1986); Roland Joffé; South America, 1750–1754.

Napoléon/Abel Gance's Napoléon/Napoléon vu par Abel Gance (1927); Abel Gance; France, 18th century.

The Night at Varennes/La nuit de Varennes (1982); Ettore Scola; France, 1791.

Orlando (1992); Sally Potter; England, Central Asia, Central Europe, 16th–20th centuries.

The Passion of Joan of Arc/La Passion de Jeanne d'Arc (1928); Carl Theodor Dreyer; France, 1431.

The Private Life of Henry VIII (1933); Alexander Korda; England, 1530s and 1540s.

Quilombo (1984); Carlos Diegues; Palmares, Brazil, 1650–1695.

Ran (1985); Akira Kurosawa; Japan, 16th century.

The Return of Martin Guerre/Le retour de Martin Guerre (1982); Daniel Vigne; France, 1530s–1560s.

Russian Ark

Vatel (2000); Roland Joffé; France, 1671.
Winstanley (1975); Kevin Brownlow and Andrew Mollo; England, 1649–1650.

Nineteenth Century

55 Days at Peking (1963); Nicholas Ray; China, 1900.
1900/Novecento (1976); Bernardo Bertolucci; Italy, 1900–1945.
The Battle of Canudos/Guerra de Canudos (1997); Sergio Rezende; Brazil, 1890s.
'Breaker' Morant (1979); Bruce Beresford; South Africa, 1901.
Bitter Sea/Amargo mar (1984); Antonio Eguino; Bolivia, 1879.
Burn!/¡Queimada! (1969); Gillo Pontecorvo; fictional Caribbean island, mid-19th century.
Camila (1995); María Luisa Bemberg; Argentina, 1840s.
The Captivating Star of Happiness/Zvezda plenitelnogo schastya (1975); Vladimir Motyl; Russia, 1820s.
Ceddo/The People (1977); Ousmane Sembène; West Africa, conflating the 17th–19th centuries.
The Chant of Jimmie Blacksmith (1978); Fred Schepisi; Australia, turn of the 20th century.
The Chess Players/Shatranj ke Khilari (1977); Satyajit Ray; India, 1850s.
Colonel Chabert/Le Colonel Chabert (1994); Yves Angelo; Battle of Eylau, 1807 and post-Napoleonic France.
Daens (1993); Stijn Coninx; Flanders, Belgium, 1890s–1907.
Effi Briest (1974); Rainer Werner Fassbinder; Germany, 19th century.
Eijanaika (1981); Shohei Imamura; Japan, 1860s.
The Emperor's New Clothes (2001); Alan Taylor; France, early 19th century.
The First Charge of the Machete/La primera carga al machete (1969); Manuel Octavio Gómez; Cuba, 1868.
Gandhi (1982); Richard Attenborough; India and South Africa, 1893–1948.
Germinal (1993); Claude Berri; France, 1860s.
I, Pierre Rivière, Having Slaughtered My Mother, My Sister and My Brother …/Moi, Pierre Rivière, ayant égorgé ma mère, ma soeur et mon frère … (1974); René Allio; France, 1835.
José Rizal (1998); Marilou Diaz-Abaya; Philippines, late 19th century.
Junoon (1978); Shyam Benegal; India, 1857–1858.
Khartoum (1966); Basil Dearden and Eliot Elisofon; Sudan, late 19th century.
A King and His Movie/La película del Rey (1986); Carlos Sorin; Argentina, 1860s and 1980s.
The Leopard/Il Gattopardo (1963); Luchino Visconti; Sicily, 1860–1862.
Lin Zexu (1959); Zheng Junli; China, 1838–1841.
Lucía (1969); Humberto Solás; Cuba 1895, 1933, 1960.
Max Havelaar (1976); Fons Rademakers; Indonesia, 19th century.
My Love Has Been Burning/Waga koi wa moenu (1949); Kenji Mizoguchi; Japan, 1880s.
The Night of Counting the Years/The Mummy/El-mumia/Al-mummia (1969) Shadi Abdel Salam; Egypt, 1881.
November 1828 (1979); Teguh Karya; Dutch colonial Java, 1828.
The Opium War/Yapian zhanzheng (1997); Xie Jin; China, 1839–1842.
The Organizer/I Compagni (1963); Mario Monicelli; Turin, Italy, late 19th century.
Orlando (1992); Sally Potter; England, Central Asia, Central Europe, 16th–20th centuries.
Pan Tadeusz/The Last Foray in Lithuania (1999); Andrzej Wajda; Lithuania, 1811–1812.
Pelle the Conqueror (1988); Bille August; Denmark, 1860s.
Promised Land/Ziemia obiecana (1974); Andrzej Wajda; Lodz, Poland, late 19th century.
Raden Ajeng Kartini/R. A. Kartini (1983); Sjuman Djaya; North Central Java, 1879–1904.
Red River Valley/Honghe gu (1996); Feng Xiaoning; Tibet, turn of the 20th century to 1904.

Rosa Luxemburg (1986); Margarethe von Trotta; Poland and Germany, 1900–1919.

The Round-Up/Szegénylegények (1965); Miklós Jancsó; Hungary, mid-19th century.

Russian Ark/Russkiy kovcheg (2002); Aleksandr Sokurov; St. Petersburg, Russia, 18th and 19th centuries.

Sarraounia (1986); Med Hondo; Niger region, West Africa, late 19th century.

Song of Chile/Cantata de Chile (1976); Humberto Solás; Chile, 16th–20th centuries.

St. Michael Had a Rooster/San Michele aveva un gallo (1971); Paolo and Vittorio Taviani; Italy, 1870.

Utu (1982); Geoff Murphy; New Zealand, 1870s.

Zulu (1964); Cy Endfield; Southern Africa, 1879.

Twentieth Century

55 Days at Peking (1963); Nicholas Ray; China, 1900.

1900/Novecento (1976); Bernardo Bertolucci; Italy, 1900–1945.

The Adalen Riots/Ådalen '31 (1969); Bo Widerberg; Sweden, 1931.

Alsino and the Condor/Alsino y el cóndor (1982); Miguel Littín; Nicaragua, late 1970s.

... And Give My Love to the Swallows/... a pozdravuji vlastovky (1972); Jaromil Jires; Czechoslovakia, World War II.

Ararat (2002); Atom Egoyan; Canada, present day, and Armenia, 1915–1918.

Ashes and Diamonds/Popiol i diament (1958); Andrzej Wajda; Poland, 1945.

At Play in the Fields of the Lord (1991); Hector Babenco; Brazil, contemporary.

Aya (1990); Solrun Hoaas; Australia, 1950s–1970s.

The Ball/Le bal (1982); Ettore Scola; France, 1930s–1980s.

Ballad of a Soldier/Ballada o soldate (1959); Grigori Chukhrai; Soviet Union, World War II.

Barren Lives/Vidas secas (1963); Nelson Pereira dos Santos; Brazil, 1940s.

The Battle of Algiers/La bataille d'Alger (1966); Gillo Pontecorvo; Algeria, 1954–1957.

The Battleship Potemkin/Bronenosets 'Potyomkin' (1925); Sergei M. Eisenstein; Russia, 1905.

Before the Rain/Pred dozhdot (1994); Milcho Manchevski; Macedonia and London, early 1990s.

Berlin Jerusalem/Berlin-Yerushalaim (1989); Amos Gitai; Berlin and Palestine, 1904–1945.

Bethune: The Making of a Hero/Dr. Bethune (1990); Phillip Borsos; Canada and China, 1920s and 1930s.

Beyond Rangoon (1995); John Boorman; Burma, 1988.

Black and White In Color/Noirs et blancs en couleur/La Victoire en chantant (1976); Jean-Jacques Annaud; fictional French African colony, World War I.

Black Cannon Incident/Heipao shijian (1986); Huang Jianxin; China, 1980s.

Black Rain/Kuroi Ame (1989); Shohei Imamura; Japan, 1945 and 1950.

Blood of the Condor/Yawar Mallku (1969); Jorge Sanjinés; Bolivia, 1960s.

Bloody Sunday (2002); Peter Greengrass; Northern Ireland, January 1972.

The Blue Eyes of Yonta/Udju azul di Yonta (1992); Flora Gomes; Guinea-Bissau, 1980s.

The Blue Kite/Lan feng zheng (1993); Tian Zhuangzhuang; China, 1953 to 1967.

The Boat/Das Boot (1981); Wolfgang Petersen; North Atlantic Ocean, 1942.

The Boat Is Full/Das Boot ist voll (1981); Markus Imhoof; Switzerland, WWII.

Boat People/Tou bun no hoi (1982); Ann Hui; South Vietnam, late 1970s.

Border Street/Ulica graniczna (1949); Aleksander Ford; Warsaw, Poland, 1939–1943.

Boycott/Baycot (1985); Mohsen Makhmalbaf; Iran, 1970s.

'Breaker' Morant (1979); Bruce Beresford; South Africa, 1901.

The Burmese Harp/Biruma no tategoto (1956); Kon Ichikawa; Burma, end of WWII.

The Camp at Thiaroye/Camp de Thiaroye (1987); Ousmane Sembène and Thierno Faty Sow; Senegal, end of WWII.

Canal/Kanal (1957); Andrzej Wajda; Poland, 1944.

Canoa (1976); Felipe Cazals; Mexico, 1968.

The Chant of Jimmie Blacksmith (1978); Fred Schepisi; Australia, turn of the 20th century.

The Chekist (1992); Alexandr Rogozhkin; Soviet Union, c. 1918–1922.

Chronicle of the Years of Embers/Chronique des années de braise/Waqaii Sanawat Al-Jamr (1975); Mohammed Lakhdar-Hamina; Algeria, 1939–1954.

Circle of Deceit/Die Fälschung (1981); Volker Schlöndorff; Lebanon, late 1970s.

City of Sadness/Beiqing chengshi (1989); Hou Hsiao-hsien; Taiwan, 1945–1949.

The Cloud-Capped Star/Meghe dhaka tara (1960); Ritwik Ghatak; Calcutta, late 1950s.

Come and See/Idi i smotri (1985); Elem Klimov; Byelorussia, WWII.

Le Coup de Grâce/Der Fangschuß (1976); Volker Schlöndorff; Latvia, 1919.

The Courage of the People/The Night of San Juan/El coraje del pueblo/La Noche de San Juan (1971); Jorge Sanjinés; Bolivia, 1942–1967.

Crows and Sparrows/Wuya yu maque (1949); Zheng Junli; Shanghai, China, 1948–1949.

Cry Freedom (1987); Richard Attenborough; South Africa, 1970s.

Daens (1993); Stijn Coninx; Flanders, Belgium, 1890s to 1907.

The Damned/La Caduta degli dei (1969); Luchino Visconti; Germany, 1933–1934.

A Dance for Heroes/Finzan (1990); Cheick Oumar Sissoko; Mali, contemporary.

Dersu Uzala (1975); Akira Kurosawa; Eastern Siberia, 1902–1910.

Diên Biên Phu (1992); Pierre Schoendoerffer; Vietnam, 1950s.

Distant Thunder/Ashani Sanket (1973); Satyajit Ray; Bengal, 1943.

A Dry White Season (1989); Euzhan Palcy; South Africa, 1976–1977.

Drylanders (1962); Don Haldane; Saskatchewan, Canada, 1907–1938.

The Dupes/al-Makhdu'un (1972); Tewfik Saleh; Iraq, 1950s.

Earth/Zemlya (1930); Alexander Dovzhenko; Ukraine, 1929.

Earth (1998); Deepa Mehta; Lahore, Punjab, 1947.

Emitai/God of Thunder (1971); Ousmane Sembène; West Africa, early 1940s.

Empire of the Sun (1987); Steven Spielberg; China, 1941–1945.

The End of St. Petersburg/Konets Sankt-Peterburga (1927); Vsevolod Pudovkin; Russia, WWI.

Enemy at the Gates (2001); Jean-Jacques Annaud; Soviet Union, 1942.

Europa, Europa/Hitlerjunge Salomon (1990); Agnieszka Holland; Germany, Soviet Union, and Poland, 1938–1945.

Exodus (1960); Otto Preminger; Cyprus and Palestine, 1947–1948.

The Family/La Famiglia (1987); Ettore Scola; Rome, Italy, 1906–1986.

Family/Jia (1957); Chen Xihe and Ye Ming; China, 1916–1920.

Farewell My Concubine/Ba wang bie ji (1993); Chen Kaige; China, 1920s–1970s.

Fever/Goraczka (1981); Agnieszka Holland; Poland, 1905.

Fires on the Plain/Nobi (1959); Kon Ichikawa; Philippines, 1945.

Flame (1996); Ingrid Sinclair; Rhodesia/Zimbabwe, 1970s.

Floating Life (1996); Clara Law; Hong Kong, Australia, Germany, 1990s.

A Funny, Dirty Little War/No habrá más penas ni olvido (1983); Héctor Olivera; Argentina, 1970s.

Gaijín: A Brazilian Odyssey/Gaijín, Caminhos da Liberdade (1980); Tizuka Yamasaki; Japan and Brazil, early 20th century.

Gallipoli (1981); Peter Weir; Australia, Egypt and Dardanelles, Ottoman Empire, 1914–1915.

Gandhi (1982); Richard Attenborough; India and South Africa, 1893–1948.

The Garden of the Finzi-Continis/Il Giardino dei Finzi-Contini (1970); Vittorio De Sica; Italy, 1938–1943.

A Generation/Pokolenie (1954); Andrzej Wajda; Warsaw, Poland, 1942.

Germany, Pale Mother/Deutschland, bleiche Mutter (1980); Helma Sanders-Brahms; Germany, 1930s and 1940s.

Girls in Uniform/Mädchen in Uniform (1931); Leontine Sagan; Prussia, Germany, 1913.

The Gleiwitz Case/Der fall Gleiwitz (1961); Gerhard Klein; Poland, 1939.

Gone, Gone Forever Gone/Gate, gate paragate (1996); Hô Quang Minh; Vietnam, 1940s–1980s.

Good Men, Good Women/Haonan haonu (1995); Hou Hsiao-hsien; Taiwan and China, 1940s and 1990s.

Goodbye, Children/Au revoir les enfants (1987); Louis Malle; France, 1944.

The Great White Man of Lambaréné/Le grand blanc de Lambaréné (1995); Bassek Ba Kobhio; Gabon, 1944–1965.

Hamsin/Eastern Wind (1982); Daniel Wachsmann; Israel, 1982.

Harvest 3000 Years/Mirt sost shi amit (1976); Haile Gerima; Ethiopia, 1970s.

Heimat/Heimat: Eine deutsche Chronik (1984); Edgar Reitz; Germany, 1918–1982.

Hill 24 Doesn't Answer/Giv'a 24 Eina Ona (1955); Thorold Dickinson; Palestine, 1947.

Hiroshima, My Love/Hiroshima, mon amour (1959); Alain Resnais; Japan, 1959.

The Home and the World/Ghare-Baire (1984); Satyajit Ray; Bengal, 1907–1908.

Hot Winds/Garam Hava/Garm Hawa (1973); M.S. Sathyu; India, late 1940s.

The House on Chelouche Street/Ha-Bayit Berechov Chelouche / Habayit B'Rechov Chelouche (1973); Moshé Mizrahi; Tel Aviv, 1946–1948.

The Human Condition: No Greater Love/Ningen no joken I (1958); Masaki Kobayashi; Manchuria, 1943.

The Human Condition: Road to Eternity/Ningen No Joken II (1959); Masaki Kobayashi; Manchuria, 1944–1945.

The Human Condition: A Soldier's Prayer/Ningen No Joken III (1961); Masaki Kobayashi; Siberia and Manchuria, 1945.

Hyenas/Hyènes (1992); Djibril Diop Mambety; Senegal, contemporary.

Identity Pieces/Pièces d'identités (1998); Mweze Ngangura; Belgium and Congo, contemporary.

In the Heat of the Sun/Yangguang canlan de rizi (1994); Jiang Wen; China, 1970s.

Indochine (1992); Régis Wargnier; Indochina, 1930–1954.

The Inner Circle/Blizhniy krug (1991); Andrei Konchalovsky; Soviet Union, 1939–1953.

It Happened Here (1966); Kevin Brownlow and Andrew Mollo; England, 1944.

It's Raining on Santiago/Il pleut sur Santiago (1976); Helvio Soto; Chile 1970–1973.

Journey of Hope/Reise der Hoffnung (1990); Xavier Koller; Turkey and Switzerland, 1980s.

Journey to the Sun/Günese yolculuk (1999); Yesim Ustaoglu; Turkey, contemporary.

The Joyless Street/Die freudlose Gasse (1925); G.W. Pabst; Vienna, Austria, early 1920s.

Judgment at Nuremberg (1961); Stanley Kramer; West Germany, 1948.

Kadarwati/The Five Faces of Kadarwati/Kadarwati, wanita dengan lima nama (1983); Sophan Sophiaan; Java and Singapore, 1942–1945.

Kafr Kassem (1974); Borhane Alaouie; Israel, 1956.

Kameradschaft (1931); G.W. Pabst; German–French border, 1919.

Kedma (2002); Amos Gitai; Palestine, 1948.

Keïta! The Heritage of the Griot/Keita! L'héritage du griot (1994); Dani Kouyaté; Mali, mythic, 13th and 20th centuries.

The Killing Fields (1984); Roland Joffé; Cambodia and New York, 1970s.

A King and His Movie/La película del Rey (1986); Carlos Sorin; Argentina, 1860s and 1980s.

King of the Children/Haizi wang (1987); Chen Kaige; China, 1970s.

Kippur (2000); Amos Gitai; Israel, 1973.

The Kitchen Toto (1987); Harry Hook; Kenya, 1950s.

Korczak (1990); Andrzej Wajda; Warsaw, Poland, 1930s and 1940s.

Kundun (1997); Martin Scorsese; Tibet, 1930s–1950s.

Lamerica (1994); Gianni Amelio; Albania, early 1990s.

The Land/al-Ard (1969); Youssef Chahine; Egypt, 1933.

Land and Freedom (1995); Ken Loach; Spain, 1930s.

Land in Anguish/Terra em transe (1967); Glauber Rocha; Brazil, 1500/1960s.

The Last Emperor (1987); Bernardo Bertolucci; China, 1908–1959.

Lawrence of Arabia (1962); David Lean; Middle East, 1916–1918.

Let There Be Peace/Daresalam (2000); Issa Serge Coelo; Chad, 1970s.

Letters from Marusia/Actas de Marusia (1975); Miguel Littín; Chile, 1907.

Libertarias/Freedomfighters (1996); Vicente Aranda; Spain, 1936–1939.

The Lion's Den/La boca del lobo (1988); Francisco J. Lombardi; Peru, 1980s.

Lucía (1969); Humberto Solás; Cuba 1895, 1933, 1960.

Lumumba (2000); Raoul Peck; Congo, 1959–1961.

MacArthur's Children/Setouchi shonen yakyudan (1984); Masahiro Shinoda; Japan, 1945.

The Making of the Mahatma (1996); Shyam Benegal; South Africa, 1893–1914.

The Makioka Sisters/Sasame Yuki (1983); Kon Ichikawa; Japan, 1930s.

The Man By the Shore/L' Homme sur les quais (1993); Raoul Peck; Haiti, 1960s.

Man of Iron/Czlowiek z zelaza (1981); Andrzej Wajda; Poland, 1968, 1970, and 1980.

Man of Marble/Czlowiek z marmuru (1977); Andrzej Wajda; Poland, 1950s and 1970s.

Mapantsula (1988); Oliver Schmitz; South Africa, 1980s.

Margaret's Museum (1995); Mort Ransen; Canada, late 1940s.

Marianne and Juliane/Die bleierne Zeit (1981); Margarethe von Trotta; West Germany, 1970s.

May & August/Wuyue Bayue (2002); Raymond To Kwok-Wai; China, 1937.

Mephisto (1981); István Szabó; Hamburg and Berlin, 1930s.

Mishima: A Life in Four Chapters (1985); Paul Schraeder; Japan, 1920s–1970.

Moonlighting (1982); Jerzy Skolimowski; London, 1981.

The Music Room/Jalsaghar (1958); Satyajit Ray; Bengal, 1920s.

Nasser 56/Nasser Sitawkhamseen (1996); Mohamed Fadel; Egypt, 1956.

The Nasty Girl/Das schreckliche Mädchen (1990); Michael Verhoeven; Germany, 1970s and 1980s.

The Navigator: A Medieval Odyssey (1988); Vincent Ward; England, 1348, and contemporary unspecified Western city.

Newsfront (1978); Phillip Noyce; Australia, 1940s and 1950s.

The Night/al-Lail/al-Leil (1992); Mohamad Malas; Syria, 1930s and 1940s.

Night and Fog in Japan/Nihon no yoru to kiri (1960); Nagisa Oshima; Japan, 1950s and 1960s.

The Night of the Pencils/La noche de los lápices (1986); Héctor Olivera; Argentina, 1976.

Night of the Shooting Stars/La notte di San Lorenzo (1982); Paolo Taviani and Vittorio Taviani; Italy, 1944.

October (Ten Days That Shook the World)/Oktyabr (1927); Grigori Aleksandrov and Sergei M. Eisenstein; Russia, 1917.

The Official Story/La historia oficial (1985); Luis Puenzo; Argentina, 1983.

Les Ordres (1974); Michel Brault; Quebec, Canada, 1970.

Orlando (1992); Sally Potter; England, Central Asia, Central Europe, 16th–20th centuries.

Paths of Glory (1957); Stanley Kubrick; France, WW1.

Perfumed Nightmare/Mababangong bangungot (1977); Kidlat Tahimik; Philippines, 1970s.

The Pianist (2002); Roman Polanski; Warsaw, Poland, 1939–1945.

Pioneers of Freedom/Para Perintis Kemerdekaan (1980); Asrul Sani; West Sumatra, Indonesia, 1920s.

The Principal Enemy/El enemigo principal (1972); Jorge Sanjinés; Peru, 1965.

The Promised Land/La tierra prometida (1973); Miguel Littín; Chile 1930–1932.

The Puppetmaster/Hsimeng rensheng (1993); Hou Hsiao-hsien; Taiwan, 1909–1945.

Raden Ajeng Kartini/R. A. Kartini (1983); Sjuman Djaya; North Central Java, 1879–1904.

Ramparts of Clay/Remparts d'argile (1971); Jean-Louis Bertucelli; Tunisia, 1962.

Rasputin/Agony/Agoniya (1977); Elem Klimov; Russia, 1915–1916.

Rebellion in Patagonia/La Patagonia rebelde (1974); Héctor Olivera; Argentina, 1920s.

Record of a Tenement Gentleman/Nagaya shinshiroku (1947); Yasujiro Ozu; Tokyo, post-World War II.

The Red and the White/Csillagosok, katonák (1967); Miklós Jancsó; Ukraine, 1919.

Red River Valley/Honghe gu (1996); Feng Xiaoning; Tibet, turn of the 20th century to 1904.

Red Dawn/Rojo amanecer (1989); Jorge Fons; Mexico City, 1968.

Repentance/Pokayaniye/Pokaianie (1986); Tengiz Abuladze; Soviet Union, 1930s.

A River Called Titas/Titash ekti nadir naam (1973); Ritwik Ghatak; East Bengal, 1930s.

Rosa Luxemburg (1986); Margarethe von Trotta; Poland and Germany, 1900–1919.

Rosenstrasse (2003); Margarethe von Trotta; Berlin, 1943 and contemporary New York.

Sambizanga (1972); Sarah Maldoror; Angola, early 1960s.

Schindler's List (1993); Steven Spielberg; Poland and Czechoslovakia, 1939–1945.

The Sealed Soil/Khak-e Sar Behmorh (1977); Marva Nabili; Iran, 1970s.

Seven Years in Tibet (1997); Jean-Jacques Annaud; Austria, India and Tibet, 1935–1959.

The Shop on Main Street/Obchod na korze (1965); Ján Kadár and Elmar Klos; Slovak Republic, 1941–1942.

The Sibiriade/Sibiriada (1979); Andrei Konchalovsky; Siberia, 1909 to the 1960s.

Silences of the Palace/Saimt el qusur (1994); Moufida Tlatli; Tunisia, early 1950s.

A Single Spark/Jeon tae-il (1996); Park Kwang-su; South Korea, 1960s and 1970s.

Soleil O (1970); Med Hondo; Africa and France, historical and contemporary.

Song of Chile/Cantata de Chile (1976); Humberto Solás; Chile, 16th–20th centuries.

The Sparrow/Al-Usfur (1972); Youssef Chahine; Egypt, 1967.

Spices/Mirch Masala (1985); Ketan Mehta; India, 1940s.

Stalingrad (1993); Joseph Vilsmaier; Soviet Union, 1942–1943.

The Story of Qiu Ju/Qiu Ju daguansi (1992); Zhang Yimou; China, 1980s.

The Story of Women/Une affaire de Femmes (1988); Claude Chabrol; Vichy France, WWII.

The Sun-Seekers/Sonnensucher (1958/1972); Konrad Wolf; East Germany, 1950s.

Sunshine/A napfény íze (1999); István Szabó; Hungary, late 19th century to 1989.

Swing Kids (1993); Thomas Carter; Germany, 1930s.

The Terrorist (1998); Santosh Sivan; India, 1990s.

Those Whom Death Refused/Mortu Nega (1988); Flora Gomes; Guinea-Bissau, 1973–1975.

A Time to Live and a Time to Die/Tongnian wangshi (1985); Hou Hsiao-hsien; Taiwan, 1940s and 1950s.

Tjoet Nja' Dhien (1988); Eros Djarot; Aceh, Sumatra, 1896–1905.

The Traitors/Los traidores (1972); Raymundo Gleyzer; Argentina, 1950s and 1970s.

Transport from Paradise/Transport z ráje (1962); Zbynek Brynych; Czechoslovakia, 1944.

The Travelling Players/O Thiassos (1975); Theo Angelopoulos; Greece 1939–1952.

The Tree of Wooden Clogs/L'albero degli zoccoli (1978); Ermanno Olmi; Italy, early 20th century.

Trek of Life/Yol (1982); Şerif Gören; Turkey, 1980s.

Ulysses' Gaze/To Vlemma tou Odyssea (1995); Theo Angelopoulos; Balkans, 20th century.

Under the Domim Tree/Etz Hadomim Tafus (1994); Eli Cohen; Israel, 1953.

Underground/Bila jednom jedna zemlja (1995); Emir Kusturica; Yugoslavia, World War II to 1990s.

The Uprising/La Insurrección (1980); Peter Lilienthal; Nicaragua, 1979.

Utopia/Saaraba (1988); Amadou Saalum Seck; Senegal, 1980s.

Viva Zapata! (1952); Elia Kazan; Mexico, late 19th and early 20th centuries.

The Wannsee Conference/Die Wannseekonferenz (1984); Heinz Schirk; Germany, 1942.

Waterland (1992); Stephen Gyllenhaal; England, 1911–1940s, and Pittsburgh, 1970s.

Welcome to Canada (1989); John M. Smith; Newfoundland, Canada, 1986.

Welcome, Mr. Marshall!/¡Bienvenido, Mr. Marshall! (1953); Luis García Berlanga; Spain, post-WWII.

The White Rose/Die Weiße Rose (1982); Michael Verhoeven; Germany, WWII.

The Wooden Gun/Roveh Huliot (1979); Ilan Moshenson; Tel Aviv, 1950s.

The Year of Living Dangerously (1982); Peter Weir; Indonesia, 1965.

Yellow Earth/Huang tudi (1984); Chen Kaige; China, 1939.

Mythic and Futuristic

Atanarjuat: The Fast Runner (2001); Zacharias Kunuk; (Canadian) Arctic, unspecified legendary times.

Chac the Rain God/Chac: Dios de la lluvia (1974); Rolando Klein; Mexico, unspecified/mythic.

God's Gift/Wend Kuuni (1982); Gaston Kaboré; Mossi village, Africa, mythic.

Keïta! The Heritage of the Griot/Keita! L'héritage du griot (1994); Dani Kouyaté; Mali, mythic, 13th and 20th centuries.

The Navigator: A Medieval Odyssey (1988); Vincent Ward; England, 1348, and contemporary unspecified Western city.

Orlando (1992); Sally Potter; England, Central Asia, Central Europe, 16th–20th centuries.

Time Bandits (1981); Terry Gilliam; Napoleonic Italy, medieval England, ancient Greece and others.

Yeelen/Brightness (1987); Souleymane Cissé; Mali, 13th century and mythic.

NOTE

1. See Peter N. Stearns, "Periodization in World History: Identifying the Big Changes," *The History Teacher* 20 (August 1987): 561–74, 579–80; Jerry H. Bentley, "Cross-Cultural Interaction and Periodization in World History," *American Historical Review* 101 (June 1996): 749–56; William A. Green, "Periodizing World History," *History and Theory* 34 (May 1995): 99–107, 109–11; Lawrence Besserman, ed., *The Challenge of Periodization: Old Paradigms and New Perspectives* (London: Routledge, 1996); and S. Patra, "The Un-Continent of Asia, *HIMAL South Asian* 16 (January 2003): www.himalmag.com/2003/january/asia_special_1.htm (accessed May 30, 2006).

Where to Find Feature Films

A NOTE ON HISTORICAL FILMS AND THE ADVENT OF THE DVD

The development of DVD production and consumption has encouraged a fairly rapid increase in the availability of film titles for home video audiences. Because digital versatile disks are able to contain more data than a VHS tape the provision of "special features" along with the feature film itself has become common practice in DVD production. There are benefits derived from these additional materials, but they should not be overstated.[1]

The 2001 release of Sir Richard Attenborough's 1982 biopic *Gandhi* on DVD was occasioned by marketing hyperbole common to the business of selling old movies to new (or revisiting) audiences. The DVD was promoted as veritably stuffed with new material that would justify its cost and warrant a second look at *Gandhi*. Viewers could enjoy a "theatrical trailer," "animated menus," multilingual subtitles, and "scene selections with motion images." A more theater-like experience was promised, the gift of "digitally remastered and anamorphic video." While the production of a "making of" documentary was ignored in the old pre-DVD era of Attenborough's production, buyers could nevertheless sneak a peek behind the screen by enjoying Ben Kingsley "talk about Gandhi" and staring at still images of "production notes" and a "making-of photo montage."

Savvy DVD connoisseurs in the twenty-first century would find the new *Gandhi*'s embellishments as thin as they are. Another category of "extras," however, might intrigue a historian: those inducements that provide viewers with historical "background," not to the film's production, but to its historical subject. In the case of *Gandhi*, a flick of the DVD controller would take them to "Original Newsreel Footage" (for example "Gandhi goes to England"), "The Words of Mahatma Gandhi," and a "Web Link to the Official Mahatma Gandhi Website." These extras, by association with the feature film presentation, have the potential to reinforce, justifiably or not, the credibility of the history presented in the film itself, and one should approach them warily as evidence of the historical film's veracity.

DVD editions of historical films sometimes include very substantial commentary by experts, an example being the audio commentary track by David Bordwell on Criterion's *Alexander Nevsky*. Kino's DVD version of Amos Gitai's *Kedma*, on the other hand, provides the promisingly titled "The History behind *Kedma*," but delivers only a still-text description of Palestine's history from 1917 to 1948; while fairly detailed, it associates "history" with a basic chronology of events.

RENTAL, PURCHASE, AND VIEWING OPTIONS FOR HISTORICAL FILMS

There are several options available for the rental, purchase, or viewing of historical feature films. Use of a feature film in a classroom is often defined as a form of "public performance" of that work; be sure to check with your institution about public performance rights, as these are not always attached to the film bought or rented. Such rights are not required if you are acquiring or borrowing a film for personal use, such as research. It's also very important when renting and purchasing home videos of foreign origin to determine if English subtitling is provided (should you require it), and if the format of the DVD or VHS is suitable for North American media players.

Rental sources for historical feature films:

1. Local home video stores sometimes have outstanding VHS and DVD collections of classic films, foreign films, and art films.
2. Internet-based DVD rental services such as Netflix, Zip, or Videomatica—to name a few—offer a subscription-based DVD mail-rental service. The service allows you to access titles that might not be available locally.
3. Public and institutional Libraries (such as found at Universities and Colleges) in North America are very important repositories of hard-to-find and out-of-print films, as well as more recent films. Some of these libraries have reciprocal borrowing agreements, allowing you to use your own university's interlibrary loan service to access the film. Many libraries—but not all—for which you have no borrowing rights will allow you viewing privileges on site, where you may view the film in facilities equipped with television screens and DVD, VHS, and VCD players.

Purchase of films is often desirable, or sometimes the last resort if you cannot access the film through any rental service or institutional library. There are many home video distributors, subdistributors, and resellers based in the United States. The following highly selective list includes some foreign-based distributors to whom you might resort for titles that have no current U.S. distributor.

SOME HOME VIDEO DISTRIBUTORS, SUBDISTRIBUTORS, AND RESELLERS

Anchor Bay Entertainment, 1699 Stutz Drive, Troy, MI 48084, 248-816-0909, www.anchorbayentertainment.com.

Arab Film Distribution, 206-322-0882, www.arabfilm.com.

Belle & Blade War Video, 124 Penn Ave., Dover, NJ 07801, 973-328-8488, www.belleandblade.com.

Between Three Worlds Video, Monash Asia Institute, Monash University, Victoria 3800, Australia, 61-3-9905-4991, www.arts.monash.edu.au/mai/films/contacts.html (Indonesian and Thai film).

British Film Institute, www.bfi.org.uk/.

Buena Vista Home Entertainment, 500 S. Buena Vista St., Burbank, CA 91521, 818-560-1000, www.bventertainment.go.com.

California Newsreel, 500 Third Street, Suite 505, San Francisco, CA 94107, 415-284-7800, www.newsreel.org (African film).

The Cinema Guild, 130 Madison Avenue, New York, NY 10016-7038, 800-723-5522, www.cinemaguild.com.

Columbia/TriStar Home Video, 10202 West Washington Boulevard, Culver City, CA 90232-3195, 310-202-3788, www.sonypictures.com.

Criterion Collection, Image Entertainment, 20525 Nordhoff St. Suite 200, Chatsworth, CA 91311, www.criterionco.com

DEFA Film Library, University of Massachusetts Amherst, 504 Herter Hall, 161 Presidents Drive, Amherst, MA 01003, 413-545-6681, www.umass.edu/defa (East German film).

Ergo Media/Jewish Home Video, PO Box 2037, Teaneck, NJ 07666-1437, 877-539-4748, www.jewishvideo.com.

Eros International, 550 County Avenue, Secaucus, NJ 07094, 201-558-9001, www.erosentertainment.com (Indian film).

Facets Multimedia, 1517 W. Fullerton Ave., Chicago, IL 60614, 773-281-9075, www.facets.org.

First Run Features, The Film Center Building, 630 Ninth Avenue, Suite 1213, New York, NY 10036, 212-243-0600, www.firstrunfeatures.com.

Fox Lorber (see Wellspring Media).

Hen's Tooth Video, www.henstoothvideo.com.

Home Vision Entertainment (see Image Entertainment).

Image Entertainment, 20525 Nordhoff St. Suite 200, Chatsworth, CA 91311, www.image-entertainment.com.

Kino International and Kino on Video, 333 West 39th Street, New York, NY 10018, 800-562-3330, www.kino.com.

Latin American Video Archives, 124 Washington Place, New York, NY 10014, 212-243-4804, www.latinamericanvideo.org.

MGM Home Entertainment, 10250 Constellation Blvd, Los Angeles, CA 90067, 310-449-3000, www.mgm.com.

Milestone Films, P.O. Box 128, Harrington Park, NJ 07640-0128, 800-603-1104, www.milestonefilms.com.

Miramax Films, 8439 Sunset Blvd., West Hollywood, CA 90069, 323-822-4100, www.miramax.com.

Mypheduh Films, PO Box 10035, Washington, DC 20018-0035, 1-800-524-3895, www.sankofa.com (African and World film).

Mystic Fire Video, PO Box 2330, Montauk, NY 11954, 1-800-292-9001, www.mysticfire.com.

The National Center for Jewish Film, Brandeis University, Lown 102, MS053, Waltham, MA 02454P, 781-899-7044, www.brandeis.edu/jewishfilm/ncjf.htm.

New Line Home Video, 116 North Robertson Blvd, Los Angeles, CA 90048, 310-854-5811, www.newline.com.

New Yorker Films, 16 West 61st Street, New York, NY 10023, 212-645-4600, www.newyorkerfilms.com.

Oxxo Films, 16130 Ventura Blvd #640, Encino, CA 91436, 800-995-6996, www.oxxofilms.com (Mexican and Spanish-language film).

Paramount Home Entertainment, 5555 Melrose Avenue, Hollywood, CA 90038-3197, 323-956-5000, www.paramount.com.

Polart Distribution, 5700 Sarah Ave, Sarasota, FL 34233-3446, 800-278-9393, www.polart.com (Polish film).

Ronin Films, PO Box 1005, Civic Square, Canberra ACT 2608, Australia, 02-6248-0851, www.roninfilms.com.au (Australian and New Zealand film).

Sisu Home Entertainment, 340 W. 39th Street, 6th Floor, New York, NY 10018, 212-947-7888, www.sisuent.com (Israeli and Jewish film).

Sony Pictures Home Entertainment, 10202 West Washington Blvd., Suite 3900 Culver City, CA 90232-3195, www.sonyclassics.com.

Tai Seng Entertainment, 170 S. Spruce Ave. Suite 200, South San Francisco, CA 94080, 800-888-3836, www.taiseng.com (Asian film).

Twentieth Century Fox, 10201 West Pico Blvd., Los Angeles, CA 90035, 310-369-1000, www.fox.com.

Universal Home Entertainment, 100 Universal City Plaza, Universal City, CA 91608, 818-777-1000, www.universalstudios.com.

Warner Home Video, 3400 Riverside Drive, Burbank, CA 91522-0001, 818-954-6000, www.warnerbros.com.

Wellspring Media (formerly Fox Lorber), 2230 Broadway, Santa Monica, CA 90404, 310-453-1222, www.wellspring.com/movies.

Zeitgeist Films, 247 Centre St., New York, NY 10013, 212-274-1989, www.zeitgeistfilms.com.

NOTE

1. For discussion of the DVD format and other technological changes affecting the cinema, see: Gary Crowdus, "Providing a Film Archive for the Home Viewer: An Interview with Peter Becker of the Criterion Collection," *Cineaste* 25, 1 (December 1999): 47–50; Anne Friedberg, "The End of Cinema: Multimedia and Technological Change," In *Reinventing Film Studies*, edited by Christine Gledhill and Linda Williams (London: Arnold, 2000): 438–52; Kay Hoffmann, "Celluloid Goes Digital: Historical-Critical Editions of Films on DVD and the Internet: Proceedings of the First International Trier Conference on Film and New Media, October 2002 (Review)," *The Moving Image* 4, 1 (Spring 2004): 161–64; and Deborah Parker and Mark Parker, "Directors and DVD Commentary: The Specifics of Intention," *The Journal of Aesthetics and Art Criticism* 62, 1 (2004): 13–22.

Further Reading

Historical Films; Teaching with Films; World History; and Ancient, Classical, and Biblical History in Films

Abrash, Barbara, and Daniel J. Walkowitz. "Sub/Versions of History: A Meditation on Film and Historical Narrative." *History Workshop Journal* 38(1) (1994): 203–14.

Babington, Bruce, and Peter William Evans. *Biblical Epics: Sacred Narration in the Hollywood Cinema.* Manchester: Manchester University Press, 1993.

Bann, Stephen. *The Clothing of Clio.* Cambridge: Cambridge University Press, 1984.

———. "The Odd Man Out: Historical Narrative and the Cinematic Image." In *The Inventions of History: Essays on the Representation of the Past,* 171–99. Manchester: Manchester University Press, 1999.

Barta, Tony, ed. *Screening the Past: Film and the Representation of History.* Westport, CT: Praeger, 1998.

Bartholeynes, Gil, and Isabella Palin. "Representation of the Past in Films: Between Historicity and Authenticity." *Diogenes* 48(1) (2000): 31–47.

Bentley, Jerry H. *Old World Encounters: Cross-Cultural Contacts and Exchanges in Pre-Modern Times.* New York: Oxford University Press, 1993.

———. *Shapes of World History in Twentieth-Century Scholarship.* Washington, DC: American Historical Association, 1995.

Burke, Peter. *Eyewitnessing: The Uses of Images as Historical Evidence.* Ithaca, NY: Cornell University Press, 2001.

Carnes, Mark C., ed. *Past Imperfect: History According to the Movies.* New York: Henry Holt, 1995.

Carson, Diane, and Lester D. Friedman, eds. *Shared Differences: Multicultural Media and Practical Pedagogy.* Urbana, IL: University of Illinois Press, 1995.

Crofts, Stephen. "Not a Window on the Past: How Films and Television Construct History." *Film & History: An Interdisciplinary Journal of Film and Television Studies* 17(4) (1987): 90–95.

Confino, Alon. "Collective Memory and Cultural History: Problems of Method." *American Historical Review* 102 (1997): 1386–403.

Cortes, Carlos, and Tom Thompson. "Feature Films and the Teaching of World History." *Social Studies Review* 29(2) (Winter 1990): 46–53.

Dalle Vacche, Angela. *Cinema and Painting: How Art Is Used in Film.* Austin, TX: University of Texas Press, 1996.

Davis, Natalie Zemon. "'Any Resemblance to Persons Living or Dead': Film and the Challenge of Authenticity." *The Yale Review* 76(4) (1987): 457–82.

———. "Movie or Monograph? A Historian/Filmmaker's Perspective." *The Public Historian* 25(3) (Summer 2003): 45–48.

Dunn, Ross E., ed. *The New World History: A Teacher's Companion.* Boston, MA: Bedford, 2000.

Edgerton, Gary R., Michael T. Marsden, and John G. Nachbar, eds. *In the Eye of the Beholder: Critical Perspectives in Popular Film and Television.* Bowling Green, OH: Bowling Green State University Popular Press, 1997.

Elliott, Kamilla. *Rethinking the Novel/Film Debate.* Cambridge: Cambridge University Press, 2003.

Ferro, Marc. *Cinema and History.* Translated by Naomi Greene. Detroit, MI: Wayne State University Press, 1988.

———. "The Fiction Film and Historical Analysis." In *The Historian and Film*, edited by Paul Smith, 80–94. Cambridge: Cambridge University Press, 1976.

Foucault, Michel. "Film and Popular Memory." In *Foucault Live (Interviews, 1966–84)*, edited by Sylvère Lotringer, 89–106. New York: Semiotext(e), 1989.

Ginsberg, Terri. "Towards a Critical Pedagogy of Holocaust and Film." *The Review of Education, Pedagogy, and Cultural Studies* 26(1) (January–March 2004): 47–59.

Gorbman, Claudia. *Unheard Melodies: Narrative Film Music.* London: British Film Institute, 1987.

Grindon, Leger. "Drama and Spectacle as Historical Explanation in the Historical Fiction Film." *Film & History* 17(4) (1987): 74–80.

———. *Shadows on the Past: Studies in the Historical Fiction Film.* Philadelphia, PA: Temple University Press, 1994.

Gwynn, Terence, and Ian Willis. "The Role of Feature Films in the Teaching of History." *Teaching History: A Journal of Methods* 3 (1974): 204–8.

Harper, Sue. *Picturing the Past: The Rise and Fall of the British Costume Film.* London: British Film Institute, 1994.

Herlihy, David. "Am I a Camera? Other Reflections on Films and History." *American Historical Review* 93(5) (December 1988): 1186–92.

Herman, Gerald H., and Wendy S. Wilson. *World History on the Screen: Film and Video Resources.* Portland, ME: Walch, 1990.

Hesling, Willem. "The Past as Story: The Narrative Structure of Historical Films." *European Journal of Cultural Studies* 4(2) (2001): 189–205.

Kaes, Anton. "History and Film: Public Memory in the Age of Electronic Dissemination." *History and Memory* 2(1) (1990): 111–29.

Kozloff, Sarah. *Invisible Storytellers: Voice-over Narration in American Fiction Film.* Berkeley, CA: University of California Press, 1988.

———. *Overhearing Film Dialogue.* Berkeley, CA: University of California Press, 2000.

Landy, Marcia. *Cinematic Uses of the Past.* Minneapolis, MN: University of Minnesota Press, 1996.

———, ed. *The Historical Film: History and Memory in Media.* New Brunswick, NJ: Rutgers University Press, 2001.

Lee, Patricia-Ann. "Teaching Film and Television as Interpreters of History." In *Image as Artifact: The Historical Analysis of Film and Television*, edited by John E. O'Connor, 96–107. Malabar, FL: Robert E. Krieger, 1990.

Lipkin, Steven N. "Dramatic Evidence: Docudrama and Historical Representation." In *Real Emotional Logic: Film and Television Docudrama as Persuasive Practice*, edited by Steven N. Lipkin, 32–46. Carbondale, IL: Southern Illinois University Press, 2002.

McAlister, Melani. *Epic Encounters: Culture, Media, and U.S. Interests in the Middle East, 1945–2000*. Berkeley, CA: University of California Press, 2001.

Maeder, Edward, ed. *Hollywood and History: Costume Design in Film*. New York: Thames and Hudson, 1987.

Manning, Patrick. *Navigating World History: Historians Create a Global Past*. New York: Palgrave Macmillan, 2003.

Naremore, James, ed. *Film Adaptation*. New Brunswick, NJ: Rutgers University Press, 2000.

Nowell-Smith, Geoffrey, ed. *The Oxford History of World Cinema*. London: Oxford University Press, 1998.

O'Connor, John E., ed. *Image as Artifact: The Historical Analysis of Film and Television*. Malabar, FL: Robert E. Krieger, 1990.

Perlmutter, David D. "Visual Historical Methods: Problems, Prospects, Applications." *Historical Methods* 27(4) (1994): 167–84.

Peterson, Arthur. "History at the Cinema: A Guide for the Movie-Going History Student." *The History Teacher* 7(1) (November 1973): 79–88.

Rosenstone, Robert A. "History in Images/History in Words: Reflections on the Possibility of Really Putting History onto Film." *American Historical Review* 93(5) (December 1988): 1173–85.

———. "The Historical Film: Looking at the Past in a Postliterate Age." In *Visions of the Past: The Challenge of Film to Our Idea of History*, 45–79. Cambridge, MA: Harvard University Press, 1995.

———. "Like Writing History with Lightning: Historical Film/Historical Truth." *Contention* 2 (1993): 191–204.

———. "The Reel Joan of Arc: Reflections on the Theory and Practice of the Historical Film." *The Public Historian* 25(3) (Summer 2003): 61–77.

———, ed. *Revisioning History: Film and the Construction of a New Past*. Princeton, NJ: Princeton University Press, 1995.

Salmi, Hannu. "Film as Historical Narrative." *Film-Historia* 5(1) (1995): 45–54.

Seixas, Peter. "Confronting the Moral Frames of Popular Film: Young People Respond to Historical Revisionism." *American Journal of Education* 102(3) (May 1994): 261–85.

Sklar, Robert. *A World History of Film*. New York: Harry N. Abrams, 2002.

Smith, Gary A. *Epic Films: Casts, Credits, and Commentary on over 250 Historical Spectacle Movies*. Jefferson, NC: McFarland, 1991.

Smith, Greg M. *Film Structure and the Emotion System*. Cambridge, UK: Cambridge University Press, 2003.

Sobchack, Vivian. "The Insistent Fringe: Moving Images and Historical Consciousness." *History and Theory* 36(4) (December 1997): 4–20.

———, ed. *The Persistence of History: Cinema, Television, and the Modern Event*. New York: Routledge, 1996.

Solomon, Jon. *The Ancient World in the Cinema*. Rev. and expanded ed. New Haven, CT: Yale University Press, 2001.

Sorlin, Pierre. *The Film in History: Restaging the Past*. Totowa, New Jersey: Barnes and Noble, 1980.

———. "Historical Films as Tools for Historians." In *Image as Artifact: The Historical Analysis of Film and Television*, edited by John E. O'Connor, 42–68. Malabar, FL: Robert E. Krieger, 1990.

Staiger, Janet. "Securing the Fictional Narrative as a Tale of the Historical Real." *South Atlantic Quarterly* 88 (1989): 393–412.

Stevens, Donald Fithian. "Never Read History Again? The Possibilities and Perils of Cinema as Historical Depiction." In *Based on a True Story: Latin American History at the Movies,* edited by Donald Fithian Stevens, 1–11. Wilmington, DE: SR Books, 1997.

Tashiro, C.S. *Pretty Pictures: Production Design and the History Film.* Austin, TX: University of Texas Press, 1998.

Weinstein, Paul B. "Movies as the Gateway to History: The History and Film Project." *The History Teacher* 35(1) (November 2001): 27–48.

White, Hayden. "Historiography and Historiophoty." *American Historical Review* 93(5) (December 1988): 1193–99.

Wilton, Shirley. "Class Struggles: Teaching History in the Postmodern Age." *The History Teacher* 33(1) (1999): 25–32.

Wright, Melanie Jane. *Moses in America: The Cultural Uses of Biblical Narrative.* New York: Oxford University Press, 2003.

Wyke, Maria. "Projecting Ancient Rome." In *The Historical Film: History and Memory in Media,* edited by Marcia Landy, 125–42. Piscataway, NJ: Rutgers University Press, 2001.

———. *Projecting the Past: Ancient Rome, Cinema, and History.* New York: Routledge, 1997.

———. "Make Like Nero! The Appeal of a Cinematic Emperor." In *Reflections of Nero: Culture, History, and Representation,* edited by Jaś Elsner and Jamie Masters, 11–28. Chapel Hill, NC: University of North Carolina Press.

Index of Entries